Nurturing Faith Commentary, Year A, Volume 1
Lectionary Resources for Preaching and Teaching: Advent, Christmas, Epiphany

Nurturing Faith Commentary, Year A, Volume 2
Lectionary Resources for Preaching and Teaching: Lent, Easter, Pentecost

Nurturing Faith Commentary, Year A, Volume 3
Lectionary Resources for Preaching and Teaching: Season after Pentecost, Proper 1–14

Nurturing Faith Commentary, Year A, Volume 4
Lectionary Resources for Preaching and Teaching: Season after Pentecost, Proper 15–29

*

Nurturing Faith Commentary, Year B, Volume 1
Lectionary Resources for Preaching and Teaching: Advent, Christmas, Epiphany

Nurturing Faith Commentary, Year B, Volume 2
Lectionary Resources for Preaching and Teaching: Lent, Easter, Pentecost

Nurturing Faith Commentary, Year B, Volume 3
Lectionary Resources for Preaching and Teaching: Season after Pentecost, Proper 1–14

Nurturing Faith Commentary, Year B, Volume 4
Lectionary Resources for Preaching and Teaching: Season after Pentecost, Proper 15–29

*

Nurturing Faith Commentary, Year C, Volume 1
Lectionary Resources for Preaching and Teaching: Advent, Christmas, Epiphany

Nurturing Faith Commentary, Year C, Volume 2
Lectionary Resources for Preaching and Teaching: Lent, Easter, Pentecost

Nurturing Faith Commentary, Year C, Volume 3
Lectionary Resources for Preaching and Teaching: Season after Pentecost, Proper 1–14

Nurturing Faith Commentary, Year C, Volume 4
Lectionary Resources for Preaching and Teaching: Season after Pentecost, Proper 15–29

Nurturing Faith Commentary

Year A, Volume 1

Lectionary Resources for Preaching and Teaching:
Advent, Christmas, Epiphany

TONY W. CARTLEDGE

Nurturing Faith Commentary is sponsored
by a generous gift from Bob and Pat Barker.

Contents

Publisher's Preface

More than a decade in the making, *Nurturing Faith Commentary* is unique in its intent and content. Anyone seeking to teach, preach, and/or learn from a broad swath of carefully explored biblical texts will find this to be a reliable, helpful, and treasured resource.

Tony Cartledge brings the mind of a scholar, the heart of a pastor, and the writing skills of an experienced author to this extensive yet accessible multi-volume resource. Rooted in a trusted weekly Bible study, lessons are provided for every possible Sunday of the Christian Year.

Following scripture texts as found in the three-year cycle designated by the Revised Common Lectionary, these lessons are both scholarly and applicable.

The purpose of these Bible studies goes beyond gaining knowledge — although the insights are plentiful — to discovering the inspiration and fresh possibilities for living out biblical truth in one's daily experiences and spheres of influence.

The many years of excellent work in which Tony poured himself into writing thoughtful, weekly Bible studies now form the basis of these volumes. These lessons reflect his wisdom, interpretive skills, diligence, and humility that never prescribe how others are to think and believe.

"Nurturing Faith" is more than just the overall title of this multivolume resource. Learning is seen as the road to redemption and transformation by an individual encountering not just facts, but a living God.

Each week, Tony's lessons have impacted individuals and classes of all shapes and sizes in seeking to learn and apply biblical truths. Having these volumes easily at hand will provide access to a multitude of ideas, insights, and illustrations for those heeding the call to equip disciples to more faithfully follow in the ways of Jesus.

A unique mark of these lessons is the way readers and listeners are treated respectfully and intelligently regardless of their backgrounds. The lessons are never dumbed down to the point of ignoring known scholarly findings.

Yet the purpose is not to impress, but to communicate. Though a Bible scholar and teacher of note, Tony seeks to convey biblical insights effectively rather than using language exclusive to the scholarly community.

When it comes to sharing helpful insights from biblical scholarship with his readers, Tony — intentionally using double negatives for effect — has often said: "I'll never not tell you something I know if it's relevant."

This honest and appreciated approach contrasts with a long history of Bible study curriculum providers that "hand-cuff" writers and therefore "mind-cuff" learners with narrow doctrinal and marketing parameters.

In contrast, *Nurturing Faith Commentary* has no such restrictions — allowing for the freedom of both writer and readers to question, pray, seek, disagree, or apply whatever arises from the exploration of these ancient texts.

The Nurturing Faith approach to Bible study does have a lens, however. It is based on the belief that Jesus is God's fullest revelation, the Living Word through whom all else is filtered in a search for truth.

These insightful and inspiring lessons are a gift — coming from the sharp mind and generous spirit of a minister-scholar who helps us dig more deeply into the rich soil of truth formed by the many layers of experiences, reflections, and stories compiled in what we know and value as the Bible. Dig in!

John D. Pierce
Executive Editor/Publisher
Good Faith Media

Introduction

The 12 volumes of *Nurturing Faith Commentary* are the product of a committed desire to provide quality Bible study for Christians who come to the scripture with open minds and a desire to go beneath a surface reading. Our goal has been to provide pastors, teachers, and other Bible students with both academic and pastoral insights in approachable language.

The project began in early 2011, when John Pierce, editor of what is now *Nurturing Faith Journal*, envisioned the idea of including a weekly Bible study in the print version of the journal, along with additional resources provided online. The studies were to be based on texts from the Revised Common Lectionary and use the New Revised Standard Version as the primary text. Use of the lectionary had become increasingly common in worship among progressive Baptists, who had been our primary audience, but resources for Bible study were lacking.

With many years of experience as a pastor, academician, professor, writer, and editor, I was asked to take on the challenge of writing these studies. With some trepidation, I accepted, and the first studies appeared in the July 2011 issue of *Baptists Today*. The studies have continued now for more than a decade, even as the newspaper-style *Baptists Today* morphed into the magazine format of *Nurturing Faith Journal and Bible Studies*.

For those who subscribe to the journal, additional resources are available online, including detailed insights through "Digging Deeper," helps for troublesome issues through "The Hardest Question," a weekly video in which I offer a summary of the lesson, plus additional teaching resources for youth and adults prepared by other writers. In this resource, Digging Deeper and The Hardest Question are incorporated into print.*

As years of publication and lectionary cycles piled up, we thought it fruitful to update and compile these lessons in a convenient format for teachers, preachers, or others who rely on helpful Bible studies, especially when lectionary based. That, plus the addition of many new commentaries for texts not previously covered, is now coming to fruition in a 12-volume set of Bible studies, with four volumes for each of the three lectionary years.

The project is a massive undertaking, and we are grateful to all who have contributed time, energy, and finances to the project.

---

* All photos used in Digging Deeper and The Hardest Question, unless otherwise indicated, are by Tony Cartledge.

Using This Resource

The Revised Common Lectionary (RCL), devised by a consortium of Protestant and Catholic representatives on the Consultation of Common Texts, was published in 1992. Since then, it has become a standard resource for both Roman Catholics and mainline Protestants.

The lectionary contains hundreds of texts chosen to reflect a progressive study of primary texts in the Bible, along with texts representative of the church year. It follows a three-year cycle known as "Year A," "Year B," and "Year C," then repeats the cycle, using the same texts. Year A relies mainly on Matthew for the gospel readings, while Year B focuses on Mark, and Year C draws mainly from Luke. Selections from the gospel of John are scattered through the three years.

Most days on the lectionary calendar include four readings. These typically follow a pattern of one reading from the Old Testament narratives, prophets, or wisdom; one text from Psalms; one text from the New Testament gospels; and one text from the epistles. Exceptions are many, especially during the Season after Pentecost, when most Sundays include two additional readings as options.

The RCL includes texts for both Sunday worship and other special days. *Nurturing Faith Commentary* focuses on texts for Sundays rather than every "feast day" on the church calendar, many of which are not observed through active services, especially in Protestant churches. We do include texts chosen for New Year's Day, Epiphany, and All Saints' Day, however, because sometimes they fall on Sunday.

A small handful of optional texts from the Apocrypha or "Deuterocanonicals," which are regarded as scripture by Roman Catholics, appear in the lectionary. Given that I write as a Protestant and our audience is mainly Protestant, apocryphal texts are not included in this resource.

The studies in these volumes are not dated, because we want them to be useful in any calendar year, and no year contains all the potential Sundays. Persons who use the text for preaching and teaching may easily consult online and print resources for the specific dates associated with each lectionary Sunday. (Vanderbilt University's library provides an ideal resource at https://lectionary.library.vanderbilt.edu.)

The RCL sometimes uses the same texts on multiple Sundays. When those occur, the study for that text will be printed only once per volume, with appropriate notes to indicate where it may be found if it is indicated on multiple Sundays.

Lectionary texts follow the church year rather than the calendar year, beginning with Advent, the four Sundays prior to Christmas day. Three optional sets of texts are provided for use on Christmas Eve or Christmas Day. These are sometimes referred to as "Christmas 1, 2, and 3," or as "Proper 1, 2, and 3" for Christmas. The first three potential Sundays after Trinity Sunday are also called "Proper 1, 2, and 3," so in this resource we will use the terms "Christmas 1, 2, and 3."

For the sake of completeness, we include studies for all three Christmas options in Volume 1. Many churches hold Christmas Eve services, and Christmas Day sometimes falls on Sunday.

One or two Sundays may follow Christmas, depending on the number of Sundays between Christmas Day and Epiphany. Texts for the second Sunday after Christmas are rarely used and always the same. Studies on those texts are also provided in Volume 1. The texts are sometimes similar to texts for New Year's Day.

Epiphany is celebrated with special texts on January 6, which commonly occurs during the week, but studies on these texts are also included in this resource because Epiphany sometimes occurs on a Sunday. Ministers also sometimes choose to use texts for Epiphany on the Sunday nearest January 6.

The season of Epiphany may include from four to nine Sundays before concluding with Transfiguration Sunday. The number of weeks depends on the date of Easter, which moves about on the calendar, likewise affecting the dates of Ash Wednesday and the beginning of Lent. The last few weeks of Epiphany aren't used in each cycle, but they are included for the sake of those years that do have them. Their location is in Volume 3 of each year, as will be explained below.

Lent always includes six Sundays, concluding with Palm Sunday, which can be celebrated with texts focusing on Jesus' entry to Jerusalem, or on the following passion. Both are provided.

The Season of Easter has seven Sundays leading up to the day of Pentecost, 50 days after Easter.

The first Sunday after Pentecost is always Trinity Sunday. Depending on the calendar, from 23 to 29 Sundays follow Pentecost, ending on the last Sunday before Advent. These are called "Proper" Sundays. The RCL handles the dilemma of differing calendars by starting at the end with Proper 29 as the Sunday before Advent, then working backward. In this system, the texts for Proper 7 through Proper 29 appear in each year's cycle. Texts for Proper Sundays 1–6 are not always used, but are provided for those calendar years in which they appear.

Since Epiphany 6–9 and Proper 1–4 are the least likely to occur, they share the same texts: Epiphany 6 = Proper 1, Epiphany 7 = Proper 2, Epiphany 8 = Proper 3, and Epiphany 9 = Proper 4. Studies for these Sundays are included in Volume 3 for each year, which begins the Season after Pentecost, with their location noted in Volume 1, which contains lessons for the Season of Epiphany.

The number of "Sundays after Pentecost" for a given "Proper" Sunday is different from year to year, so in this resource they will be designated by the "Proper" number, which can be coordinated with each year's number of "Sundays after Pentecost," which will vary.

Texts, especially from the psalms, are often short and designed more for liturgical reading than for individual study. Even so, all texts receive full treatment in Bible study form.

Readers familiar with the RCL know that texts are often chopped and spliced for liturgical reading, which isn't always ideal for a connected Bible study. In many of those cases, the Bible study in these volumes will expand the RCL selection to provide greater context and continuity. Texts listed in the Table of Contents, with each lesson/commentary, and in the index, are based on the actual text examined, which may be longer than the RCL text, but not shorter.

The basic outline of the series is as follows, for each of the three cycles:

Volume 1 – Advent through Epiphany
Volume 2 – Lent through Pentecost
Volume 3 – Season after Pentecost (Propers 1–14)
Volume 4 – Season after Pentecost (Propers 15–29)

Abbreviations

BCE	Before the Common Era
cf.	confer
ch., chs.	chapter, chapters
cp.	compare
CE	Common Era
CEB	Common English Bible
CSB	Christian Standard Bible
e.g.	for example
et. al.	and others
etc.	and others
f., ff.	the following verse, verses
HCSB	Holman Christian Standard Bible
KJV	King James Version of the Bible
LXX	Septuagint
MT	Masoretic Text
NASB95	New American Standard Bible, 1995 edition
NASB20	New American Standard Bible, 2020 edition
NET	New English Translation of the Bible
NET2	New English Translation, 2nd edition
NIV11	New International Version, 2011 edition
NJPS	New Jewish Publication Society
NRSV	New Revised Standard Version of the Bible
RCL	Revised Common Lectionary
v., vv.	verse, verses

First Sunday of Advent
First Reading
Isaiah 2:1-5

When Soldiers Plow

He shall judge between the nations, and shall arbitrate for many peoples; they shall beat their swords into plowshares, and their spears into pruning hooks; nation shall not lift up sword against nation, neither shall they learn war any more. (Isa. 2:4)

Of all human aspirations, is there anything more basic, or more powerful, than hope? It is hope that leads us to work for a better world, to seek love and community, to keep plodding away though life's prospects seem bleak. Even when faith stumbles, hope soldiers on.

We hope for security, for peace, for justice, for love. We want our lives to *mean* something beyond daily existence.

On close inspection, all such hopes are related. Our basic desire for survival requires sustenance and security and the ability to earn a living. These require a setting in which principles of peace and justice are known and practiced. When these things are in place, we have the luxury of hoping for meaningful relationships in which we can love and be loved. We can hope for opportunities to serve others and know that we have a purpose in life.

Today's lesson marks the beginning of the Advent season, which typically begins with a hopeful theme. Though Advent is often celebrated with gospel texts, it is also traditional to study passages from the book of Isaiah that New Testament writers related to the coming messiah. **[Isaiah of Jerusalem]**

Wherever we find ourselves along the spectrum of hopefulness, from struggling for survival to yearning for meaningful purpose, the prophet Isaiah has a word for us. Today's text offers an image so inspiring and iconic that the prophet Micah also used it to encourage the people who were on the verge of giving up hope (Mic. 4:1-4).

It is the image of a promised day when Jerusalem would be established as "the Mountain of Yahweh" and people from around the globe would travel there to learn what it means to live in justice and peace, what it means

---

Isaiah of Jerusalem: Isaiah of Jerusalem, who many scholars believe was largely responsible for much of the first 33 chapters of the book that bears his name, lived an active prophetic life in and around Jerusalem during much of the third quarter of the eighth century, BCE. The long and prosperous reign of King Uzziah came to an end just as Isaiah received his prophetic call, if we are to read Isaiah 6 as the prophet's initial call.

Uzziah, according to 2 Chron. 26:1-23, had modernized the army and conquered the Philistines, Arabians, and Ammonites. With control over the major trade routes allowing the collection of tariffs from traveling merchants, he was able to expand Israel's manufacturing and agricultural economy.

The country's prosperity had a downside. Wealthy landowners began to buy up more and more property, often leaving the poor without a home and forcing them to work as indentured servants. Both Isaiah and the prophet Micah, his contemporary, would have much to say about the poor ethics of his countrymen.

---

to build a place where combat weapons could be melted down and re-forged as farming tools because war has become a thing of the past.

Can you imagine such a world?

Would it be worth our efforts to make it happen?

A promised day
(vv. 1-3)

Isaiah of Jerusalem lived and worked during the last half of the eighth century BCE. Judah had enjoyed a period of relative prosperity under the long rule of Uzziah, but days of peace and plenty had led to a false sense of security. Some

> **Trouble on every side:** Isaiah would have lived through several periods of political crisis that influenced his prophesies. During the Syro-Ephraimitic Crisis of 734–732 BCE, Syria (also known as Aram) and Israel (the northern kingdom, also known as Ephraim) pressured Judah's King Jotham to join a rebellion against the Assyrians. When Jotham refused, the two nations invaded Judah. Troops from Edom and Philistia took advantage and sent their own raiding parties. Jotham died and was succeeded by his son Ahaz, who called on the Assyrian king Tiglath-Pileser III for assistance. The Assyrian army halted the enemies' advance, but the situation was little improved, for Ahaz was forced to pay tribute to the Assyrians and reportedly bowed before their gods.
>
> Twenty years later (715–711 BCE), leaders of the city-state of Ashdod, just south of Judah, tried to persuade both Egypt and Judah to join in a rebellion against Assyria. Isaiah urged King Hezekiah not to get involved, insisting that security could be found in Yahweh alone, but Hezekiah ignored the prophet and joined the rebellion. The Assyrians quashed it, bringing greater hardship to Judah.
>
> Hezekiah later chose to withhold tribute on his own (705–701 BCE), leading to an invasion by Assyrian forces that destroyed many Judahite cities and put Jerusalem under siege, but stopped short of taking the city.
>
> The revolts led to great political instability and increasing oppression by the Assyrians, who conquered the northern kingdom of Israel in 722 BCE and persisted as a constant threat to Jerusalem.

people believed that keeping up the temple rituals was all that was needed to fulfill their part of the covenant. They expected a "day of the Lord" to come as a time of glory for Israel, and seemed confident that God would never allow Jerusalem, the home of the temple, to be captured.

From about 735 BCE, however, a series of serious conflicts with surrounding nations deeply threatened national security. Syria and Israel tried to force Judah into an alliance against Assyria, and attacked the country when King Ahaz refused. Hezekiah later joined an alliance with Ashdod and Egypt against Assyria, with disastrous consequences. Political instability was rife, and economic disparity was on every hand. [**Trouble on every side**]

We cannot be sure if today's text was first spoken during the spiritually corrupt days of King Uzziah or during the troubled days of later years, under Ahaz or Hezekiah. Whatever the setting, Isaiah held hopes for a better future despite the odds, and that hope found its voice in this prophecy of a coming day when not just Judah, but every nation would turn to God.

"In days to come the mountain of the LORD's house shall be established as the highest of the mountains," Isaiah wrote, "and shall be raised above the hills; all the nations shall stream to it" (v. 2). The "mountain of the LORD" is an obvious reference to the temple mount in Jerusalem. Isaiah envisioned a day when it would become more than a spiritual height for Israel, a day when the mountain would rise to a preeminence above all others and become a landmark to which all peoples would come.

The important thing is not the height of the mountain but the presence of God, which Isaiah saw as being so tangible that all would know it as the Mountain of Yahweh, and people from every nation would "stream to it" for a global gathering in which "he may teach us his ways, and that we may walk in his paths."

Jerusalem, in Isaiah's vision, would become the center of learning for those who wanted to know God and know God's way: "For out of Zion shall go forth instruction, and the word of the LORD from Jerusalem" (v. 3a).

Note, however, that the future Jerusalem would be more than a learning center for scholars seeking an understanding of the ways of God and humankind. The promised instruction, "That he may teach us his ways," would be followed by action: "that we may walk in his paths" (v. 3b).

Knowing God's way is laudable, but it means nothing if we do not also follow God's teaching. Isaiah saw the future Jerusalem as a place of both education and inspiration.

An age of peace
(v. 4)

Isaiah reveled in the thought of people coming to Jerusalem not only to learn of God's ways, but also to seek God's guidance to settle grievances: "He shall judge between the nations, and shall arbitrate for many peoples." The result is expressed in the classic image of a happily shocking scene: "they shall beat their swords into plowshares, and their spears into pruning hooks; nation shall not lift up sword against nation, neither shall they learn war anymore" (v. 4).

Images of peace: One of the more iconic images of unlikely peace in our world is Evgeniy Vuchetich's sculpture *Let Us Beat Our Swords Into Plowshares*, which Russia gave to the U.S. in 1959, at the height of the Cold War. It is located on the grounds of the United Nations in New York City. Photo courtesy of Wikimedia Commons

Can you imagine the appeal of such a hope? Isaiah lived in a day when the deadliest weapon was a sword or spear, while we live in a world where a single automatic rifle can kill scores of people, powerful bombs can kill hundreds, and nuclear weapons can kill millions.

When we consider the intractable political issues that continue to plague Isaiah's former home in the Middle East, the prospect of peace in our own day still seems beyond any hope short of divine intervention.

In recent memory, civil war in Syria and the attempt of ISIS to establish an Islamic caliphate through terror and violence caused more than a hundred thousand deaths and sent even greater numbers fleeing to refugee camps. When one terrorist group is repressed, others arise.

In the State of Israel, settlers backed by the Israeli government and Orthodox immigrants from America push deeper and deeper into Palestinian territory, illegally occupying their land while creating tensions and hardship for millions.

Those countries are not alone. In Afghanistan and Pakistan, Iraq and Iran, Sudan and Somalia, political peace seems far away. Dictatorships, cabals, and poverty in Central and South America have led to thousands of victims who suffer mightily as they seek safety and survival for their children, only to be blocked at the U.S border.

We know how issues underlying political unrest or drug-related crime in other parts of the world may also haunt and threaten our own peaceful existence. Global terrorists seek to harm all they consider to be enemies, and international versions of the Mafia can strike anywhere.

Can you imagine anything more desirable than a day when all nations will live at peace, when our technology can be turned from cruise missiles and nuclear warheads to more effective and environmentally responsible methods of agriculture and industry?

Isaiah saw just such a day, and the power of the image is unabated. [**Images of peace**]

A present challenge
(v. 5)

Some scholars believe v. 5 should be seen as the beginning of the next oracle, but one can make a good case that it serves as an appropriate conclusion of 2:1-4: the vision of future peace concludes with a call for present action. The covenant people of Israel already knew what God expected of them, but they lacked the will to act on it.

In v. 3, Isaiah had spoken of a day when all would seek to learn God's ways and "walk in his paths," but Isaiah saw no need for his compatriots to wait for that future day. Thus, he pleaded: "O house of Jacob, come, let us walk in the light of the LORD!"

Isaiah's great hopes did not call for the people of Israel to sit back on their haunches and just wait for God to make their lives better. The vision of a day when all would live according to God's teaching calls for God's people to work toward that day even now. It calls for us to make the effort needed to communicate with others to work out our differences and seek justice without resorting to violence.

It is when we learn to walk in God's ways, then put on our shoes and get on with it, that God's word to the world takes shape. When we trust God to teach us about justice and commit to walking in the ways of peace, then we can divert our budget resources from guns to gardens; we can shift our focus from feuding to friendship; from war efforts to food production. When we walk in God's ways and put feet to our hopes, we may discover that they're more likely to come true. Guns can't turn themselves into garden tools: they need help.

The Hardest Question
Which came first: Isa. 2:2-4 or Mic. 4:1-4?

Compare the following two texts, from the NRSV:

In days to come the mountain of the LORD's house shall be established as the highest of the mountains, and shall be raised above the hills; all the nations shall stream to it.

Many peoples shall come and say, "Come, let us go up to the mountain of the LORD, to the house of the God of Jacob; that he may teach us his ways and that we may walk in his paths." For out of Zion shall go forth instruction, and the word of the Lord from Jerusalem.

He shall judge between the nations, and shall arbitrate for many peoples; they shall beat their swords into plowshares, and their spears into pruning hooks; nation shall not lift up sword against nation, neither shall they learn war any more. (Isa. 2:2-4)

In days to come the mountain of the LORD's house shall be established as the highest of the mountains, and shall be raised up above the hills.

Peoples shall stream to it, and many nations shall come and say: "Come, let us go up to the mountain of the LORD, to the house of the God of Jacob; that he may teach us his ways and that we may walk in his paths." For out of Zion shall go forth instruction, and the word of the LORD from Jerusalem.

He shall judge between many peoples, and shall arbitrate between strong nations far away; they shall beat their swords into plowshares, and their spears into pruning hooks; nation shall not lift up sword against nation, neither shall they learn war any more. (Mic. 4:1-3)

The texts have slight differences, but are clearly variations on the same oracle. Did Micah copy Isaiah, did Isaiah copy Micah, did they both borrow the oracle from an earlier tradition, or was the vision from a later period, but inserted into both books?

The priority of both Micah and Isaiah has been argued, though the case for Isaiah's oracle being original is stronger because it fits better into his larger scheme and themes. Even so, the arguments for Isaiah's authorship are not wholly convincing.

Many scholars are inclined to believe that the inspiring vision of Jerusalem as the "Mountain of Yahweh" to which all nations would stream derived from a previously known liturgical oracle or "Song of Zion." In this view, both Isaiah and Micah would have made use of the popular image to encourage the people of Jerusalem and challenge them to live in God's way.

Yet, a growing number of other scholars believe the oracle originated at a later time, perhaps near the end of the exile or shortly thereafter, and that later editors inserted it into the works attributed both to Isaiah and Micah.

Note how the two books use the oracle in different ways. Isaiah used it as a challenge, laying out a beautiful image and then calling upon the "house of Jacob" to walk in God's ways so they can make such an image a reality, with the end being that all nations come to Jerusalem to learn from Yahweh.

Micah, on the other hand, envisioned a time of universal peace in which each family could rest beneath its grape arbor or fig tree and the people of Israel would "walk in the name of the LORD our God," even as other nations followed their own gods (Mic. 4:4-5).

First Sunday of Advent

Second Reading
Psalm 122

Can Jerusalem Find Peace?

Pray for the peace of Jerusalem: May they prosper who love you. (Ps. 122:6)

If it were in your power to bring peace to any one city in the world, what city would it be? One might think of American cities torn by racial strife, European cities stricken by terrorist attacks, or Middle Eastern and South Asian cities that are ravaged by war. Any of those cities would welcome the sense of safety and hopeful optimism that comes with peace.

Of all the world's cities, however, none is more crucial to world peace than the city of Jerusalem. Modern visitors to the Old City of Jerusalem find it divided into Jewish, Christian, Muslim, and Armenian quarters. The Old City is only a small part of Jerusalem, however. The more significant divide is between West Jerusalem, controlled by the Israeli government, and East Jerusalem, historically populated by Palestinians.

Since 1949, Israelis have occupied East Jerusalem, ignoring earlier peace agreements while building Jewish settlements on Palestinian land, erecting "separation barriers," and forcefully annexing portions of East Jerusalem. This has contributed greatly to ongoing strife, not only in Israel and the West Bank, but also throughout the world: anger over perceived wrongs against Palestinians fuels much of the rage behind jihadists who bring terror to other cities.

If we should pray for the peace of any city in this hopeful Advent season, we should pray for the peace of Jerusalem.

A happy pilgrim
(vv. 1-2)

Psalm 122 is one of 15 "Songs of Ascents," which are generally associated with pilgrims from the surrounding countryside who would travel to Jerusalem for one of the annual festivals. [**Songs of Ascent**] Persons living at

Songs of Ascent: Fifteen of the psalms (120–134), located together are known as the "Songs of Ascent." Scholars have advanced a variety of conjectures about what the title means, but none have been conclusive.

Some scholars believe the songs would have been sung by priests as they climbed stairs toward the temple or altar, but most think of them as pilgrim songs typically chanted by those who came to Jerusalem during the three annual feasts, or at other times. Since Jerusalem is on a high hill, one cannot enter the city without ascending from one of the surrounding valleys.

In addition to being physically elevated, Jerusalem was the religious, political, and economic heart of the nation, so in biblical language, one always "went up" to it.

Perhaps we can imagine a group of suffering pilgrims making their way to Jerusalem, intending to bring their case before God and plead for vindication. Like slaves who sing haunting but hopeful spirituals as they work, pilgrims may have sung these songs as they climbed into the city where God was thought to dwell.

The ancient steps in the picture above, from the Second Temple period, were uncovered below the southern wall of the Temple Mount in Jerusalem. From here, first-century pilgrims ascended to one of several gates that led to stairways accessing the temple courts.

some distance could visit Jerusalem only rarely, and each pilgrimage was a special occasion to be marked by singing and celebration.

The first verse of Psalm 122 has long been a favorite memory verse used in Sunday School or children's sermons: "I was glad when they said to me, 'Let us go to the house of the LORD!'"

Modern readers typically associate the verse with church attendance, but the original context pictures a time when town or village leaders would have organized periodic trips to Jerusalem, recruiting pilgrims like a modern minister organizing a trip to the Holy Land. Making a pilgrimage to Jerusalem involved long journeys by foot or donkey, camping out along the way. It could be a dangerous undertaking, best done in groups for protection against bandits who preyed on lone travelers.

One such pilgrim, traveling in the company of others, is the likely author of this psalm. He speaks as an individual (vv. 1, 8-9), but also references "our feet" (v. 2) and addresses his companions (v. 6). He was glad to be invited to join the communal pilgrimage, and even happier to find himself "standing within your gates, O Jerusalem" (v. 2). [**Not David**]

Not David: The superscription to Psalm 122 identifies it as "A Song of Ascents. Of David." This is one of 73 psalms bearing the ascription "*ledawîd*," and many readers assume this means that David was the author. The preposition *le* can mean "to" or "for" or "of," however, so psalms labeled *ledawîd* could have been dedicated to David just as easily as written by David.

David could not have written Psalm 122, for it depicts a time when Jerusalem was fully built and the temple was functioning: the psalm begins "I was glad when they said to me, 'Let us go to the house of the LORD!'" Although David erected a tent to house the Ark of the Covenant, the temple was built well after David's death, by his son Solomon.

The psalmist speaks of David in the third person, and does so from the perspective of one who lived generations later. The psalm celebrates David's contributions to Jerusalem and could easily have been dedicated to him, but David almost certainly could not have been the author.

A mighty city
(vv. 3-5)

The psalmist, standing inside the city's impressive gates, gives voice to unadulterated joy, reciting three reasons to love Jerusalem. First, it is structurally impressive: "built as a city that is bound firmly together" (v. 3). The psalm likely dates to a period in the seventh or eighth centuries, when Jerusalem's strong walls had been expanded and fortified by defensive towers at crucial points. The city had become prosperous as the center of government and faith, culture and commerce; the economic engine of the surrounding area.

If the psalmist had hailed from a village or small town, the city would have seemed even more splendid, a breathtaking amalgam of broad avenues, monumental buildings, and crowded markets. Sensing a connection between the majestic city and its powerful God, the author would have resonated with the poet behind Ps. 48:12-14: "Walk about Zion, go all around it, count its towers, consider well its ramparts; go through its citadels, that you may tell the next generation that this is God, our God forever and ever. He will be our guide forever."

Secondly, the psalmist – so glad to be in Jerusalem – celebrated its role as the one location to which all "the tribes go up, the tribes of the LORD, as was decreed for Israel, to give thanks to the name of the LORD" (v. 4). The expression "tribes of Yahweh" (*shivte-yah*) is striking. The tribes of Israel are mentioned often in the Hebrew Bible, but this is the only place where "tribes of Yahweh" is used.

Early in Israel's history, the Israelites offered worship and sacrifice in a variety of places. After the temple was built in Jerusalem, however, Hebrew theologians came to believe that the people should bring their sacrifices, celebrate their festivals, and offer their worship in Jerusalem alone. This elevated the status of Jerusalem even more, making it a pilgrimage site that all faithful Hebrews should visit as often as possible, especially during one or more of the three annual festivals. [**Festivals**]

Within its walls, Solomon's temple was an impressive sight, built of skillfully cut stones and columns, gilded with gold at strategic points and gleaming in the sun atop the temple mount. Public worship took place in

Festivals: The three major festivals in Judaism were Passover, Shavuot, and Sukkot.

Passover celebrated the Hebrews' exodus from Egypt and specifically the night when the angel of death "passed over" the homes of Hebrews who had marked their doorframes with blood from a sacrificial lamb. It also marked the beginning of a new planting season after the winter rains.

Shavuot (pronounced "sha-voo-OTE"), also known as the Feast of Weeks, occurred seven weeks (a "week" of weeks) after Passover, at the time of the late spring harvest.

Sukkot ("soo-KOTE"), better known as the Feast of Booths, recalled God's provision as Israel wandered in the wilderness after leaving Egypt. It occurred during the fall harvest season, before the winter rains began. It began five days after Yom Kippur, the Day of Atonement.

courtyards surrounding the temple, for only priests could enter the sanctuary itself.

Jerusalem was not only an architectural marvel and host to the sacred temple; it was also the seat of justice for the Hebrews: "there the thrones for judgment were set up, the thrones of the house of David" (v. 5). The use of the plural for "thrones" refers to the respective thrones used by David, Solomon, and their descendants.

David was known for administering justice (2 Sam. 8:15), including a case related to his son Absalom (2 Samuel 14). Absalom, in turn, planned a coup and campaigned against his father, falsely accusing him of failing to render justice (2 Sam. 15:1-6). Solomon was famed for his wisdom pronounced in judgment (1 Kgs. 3:16-28).

Prophets such as Isaiah grew livid when they perceived that justice was not done (Isa. 1:21-26, 10:1-2, among others). Isaiah spoke hopefully of a future ruler who would "not judge by what his eyes see, or decide by what his ears hear; but with righteousness he shall judge the poor, and decide with equity for the meek of the earth" (Isa. 11:3b-4, see also Isa. 16:5).

Those who love a righteous God, by definition, also love justice. It's no surprise that the psalmist celebrated Jerusalem as the center of both spiritual worship and the place where justice could be dispensed.

A prayer for peace
(vv. 6-9)

Upon entering a home or city, Middle Easterners typically offered greetings of peace. Before David became king, while appealing to a landowner named Nabal for aid, he instructed his messengers to greet him by saying "Peace be to you, and peace be to your house, and peace be to all that you have" (1 Sam. 25:6). Many years later, as Jesus sent his disciples on mission, he instructed them to find lodging with locally worthy folk. "As you enter the house," he said, "greet it. If the house is worthy, let your peace come upon it; but if it is not worthy, let your peace return to you" (Matt. 10:12-13).

Filled with love for Jerusalem, the psalmist calls his companions to "Pray for the peace of Jerusalem: 'May they prosper who love you. Peace be within your walls, and security within your towers'" (vv. 6-7). The plea, in essence, is a prayer for the city to live out the meaning of its name: in Hebrew, *yerushalayim* means something akin to "foundation of peace." The last part of the word is from *shalôm*, which means "peace," "health," or "wholeness."

Having invited others to pray, the psalmist adds his own entreaty and promise. While some interpreters believe he was fulfilling a promise to pray in behalf of friends and neighbors who could not make the journey, it is probable that his purpose was much broader: "For the sake of my relatives and friends I will say, 'Peace be within you.' For the sake of the house of the LORD our God, I will seek your good" (vv. 8-9).

The NRSV gives a wider nuance to the phrase "relatives and friends," which literally means "brothers and neighbors." This is appropriate, for the psalmist recognized the importance of Jerusalem to the entire community of faith – not just to his relatives and friends back home, but to all who looked toward "the house of the LORD our God."

The psalmist understood that when Jerusalem experienced peace, the entire country was likely to enjoy security and rest. When the rulers practiced justice and the people sought righteousness, peace would not only prevail in Jerusalem, but also pervade the towns and villages of the nation. To pray for the peace of Jerusalem was to pray for the welfare of all, but the psalmist promised to do more than pray: "I will seek your good," he pledged.

Though much has changed since these words were written more than 2500 years ago, the central truth has not changed: indeed, it has broadened. To pray for the peace of Jerusalem – and to work for it – is not just a wish for the welfare of Israel, but a prayer for the world.

The Hardest Question
When was Jerusalem set as the only valid place for Hebrew worship and sacrifice?

Early in Israel's history, even after entering the "promised land" of Canaan, the Hebrews offered worship and sacrifice in a variety of places: sanctuaries were located at Shiloh and Nob (1 Sam. 1:3, 21), and sacrifices were offered at places such as Mount Ebal (Josh. 8:30-33), Gilgal (Josh. 5:10, 1 Sam. 10:8), Beth Shemesh (1 Sam. 6:13-15), and Mizpah (1 Sam. 7:1-6).

Such worship occurred, chronologically, long after the events described in Deuteronomy, where Moses reportedly insisted that when the people come into the land, they should worship and seek serious judicial decisions at a single central location, in "the place that the LORD your God will choose" (Deut. 12:5, 11, 18; 14:25; 16:6, 7, 11; 17:8; 26:2), an obvious euphemism for Jerusalem.

While Deuteronomy purports to be a collection of sermons or instructions from Moses prior to the people's entry into Canaan, the book was largely composed by someone writing in Moses' name in the late seventh century, when a "book of the law" was found during temple renovations authorized by young king Josiah, sometime around 625 BCE (2 Kings 22). This "book of the law," likely a form of the book of Deuteronomy, appears to have become the impetus for a series of reforms instituted by Josiah, including the destruction of all other altars and an insistence that worship take place only in Jerusalem.

The book of Deuteronomy provided the theological base for the composition of what is called the "Deuteronomistic History," consisting of Joshua–2 Kings (with the exception of Ruth). The language is very similar, and the narrative books of the Deuteronomistic History illustrate the blessing/cursing theology of the book of Deuteronomy. Those books, sometimes called "the former prophets," were drawn from a variety of existing sources and traditions, and composed during the exile (roughly 587–538 BCE) with the purpose of providing a theological explanation for Israel's defeat at the hands of the Babylonians: as Moses predicted in Deuteronomy, a lack of obedience would result in judgment. The books end during the exile with the hopeful note that the deposed king Jehoiachin had been released from prison and was allowed to eat at the table with the Babylonian king (2 Kgs. 25:25-30).

While earlier traditions about Moses' teaching surely existed, Deuteronomy was shaped to reflect the late-blooming belief that worship should take place only in Jerusalem, under a centralized authority. The authors recognized that Jerusalem became Israel's capital and worship center long after Moses' death, however, so they could not name Jerusalem as the central place of worship. Instead, they had Moses speak of it as "the place that the LORD your God will choose."

First Sunday of Advent

Third Reading
Romans 13:8-14*

Lawful Love

Owe no one anything, except to love one another; for the one who loves another has fulfilled the law. (Rom. 13:8)

Are you a rule-follower? Many people find comfort in having an external list of guidelines, knowing what the rules are, and then following them. Others prefer to work from an internal system of values from which they develop their own behavioral decisions.

The Apostle Paul had strong feelings about rules, and we read about his thoughts in today's text. Note that the lectionary text includes only vv. 11-14, but we will begin at v. 8.

Boiling it down
(13:8-10)

In Paul's day, Rabbinic Judaism had sought to "build a hedge about the law" by expanding Old Testament teachings to develop a system of 613 specific commandments. The Babylonian Talmud says "There is full agreement that these 613 *mitzvot* can be broken down into 248 positive *mitzvot* [one for each bone and organ of the male body] and 365 negative *mitzvot* [one for each day of the solar year]" (*Makkot* 23b-24a, accessible at jewishvirtuallibrary. org/jsource/Judaism/mitzvoth.html).

Some devout persons, such as the Pharisees, sought to live in accordance with every religious prescription, no matter how onerous. Other Jews were less inclined toward a legalistic faith, but still familiar with the complex expectations of the rabbis.

As Paul wrote to the Christians in Rome, he knew that some were former Jews who had come – as he had – from a background of prescribed behaviors that promoted religious and ethnic conformity. [**Conformity**] In contrast, believers

---

> **Conformity:** The strict codes of Rabbinic Judaism served a purpose beyond a desire to be legalistic. During the hard centuries after the surviving Israelites returned from exile in Babylon, the people existed as a sub-province of Persia, in a small area surrounding Jerusalem that was known as Yehud.
>
> After the exile, the Hebrews had no real national identity and could have gone the way of other conquered peoples who simply assimilated into other cultures. To prevent this, religious and political leaders such as Ezra and Nehemiah sparked the development of what we now know as Judaism: the people could no longer express their identity as a political entity, but they could establish a religious and ethnic identity through adherence to a code of beliefs and behaviors that would make them distinct from other peoples.
>
> Though Christians may look askance at what appears to be a burdensome and legalistic system of laws, the Jews' devotion to maintaining their religious/ethnic identity is precisely what has enabled them to survive as a people through many centuries and multiple efforts to eradicate them. Thus, while the powerful Babylonians and Philistines exist only as dusty memories, the Jews have survived all odds, and remain a distinct presence in the world.

---

from a Gentile background may have been unfamiliar with guidelines as basic as the Ten Commandments.

In his letter to the church at Rome, Paul sought to help both Jewish and Gentile Christians understand what kind of behaviors and attitudes are most pleasing to God, without getting them caught up in a list of legalistic rules. In ch. 12, he had encouraged readers to be transformed by the power of God's Spirit, becoming new people in Christ and loving one another with genuine love. Chapter 13 began with a

---

This text also appears as a reading for Proper 18 in Year A.

reminder that believers, like all people, have obligations that include the payment of taxes and other debts.

Beginning with 13:8, Paul tackled the issue of rule keeping by reducing the commandments to a single law, speaking of it as one obligation that persists: the debt of love.

In doing so, Paul ran through a quick synopsis of four of the Ten Commandments (v. 9) – all negatively worded directives that have to do with attitudes or actions toward other people. Believers should avoid adultery, theft, murder, and covetousness – four examples of selfish actions that could bring harm to others. Paul told his readers that all of those "thou shalt nots" could be summed up in the single positive command found in Lev. 19:18: "Love your neighbor as yourself."

Paul was not the first or only New Testament thinker to summarize the law in terms of love. Paul rarely quoted Jesus, and the gospel of John was written long after Paul's letter to the Romans, but he may have been familiar with the teaching attributed to Jesus in John 13:34, where he described the law of love as a new approach: "I give you a new commandment, that you love one another. Just as I have loved you, you also should love one another."

Paul was particularly interested in maintaining the Old Testament connection, however. In an earlier letter to the Galatians, he had used the same argument found in Romans 13: "For the whole law is summed up in a single commandment, 'You shall love your neighbor as yourself'" (Gal. 5:14, citing Lev. 19:18).

Similarly, the author of James spoke of the same command as the law of the kingdom: "You do well if you really fulfill the royal law according to the scripture, 'You shall love your neighbor as yourself'" (Jas. 2:8).

In v. 10, Paul argued that a life of love fulfills the law because "love does no wrong to a neighbor." On the surface, this suggests a rather anemic view of love, an approach that avoids harm but doesn't necessarily help, either.

It is unlikely, however, that Paul would think of love in such shallow terms. In these verses, he consistently used the word *agape*, a rich term adopted by the early church to describe Christ-like, self-giving love. In other places (such as 1 Corinthians 13), Paul emphasized the active nature of such love.

Indifference: The late Jewish author, Holocaust survivor, and Pulitzer Prize winner Elie Wiesel often spoke of the dangers of indifference. In a speech at the White House in 1999, Wiesel said: "Indifference, after all, is more dangerous than anger and hatred. Anger can at times be creative. One writes a great poem, a great symphony, one does something special for the sake of humanity because one is angry at the injustice that one witnesses. But indifference is never creative. Even hatred at times may elicit a response. You fight it. You denounce it. You disarm it. Indifference elicits no response. Indifference is not a response." (The full speech may be found at http://www.historyplace.com/speeches/wiesel.htm.)

Thus, we cannot mistake a life of non-involvement or indifference for love just because those attitudes do not cause direct harm to others.

Love may be many things, but it can never be indifferent. **[Indifference]**

True love cares, acts, and gives – even when it hurts. This theme is not unique to religious thought: admiration of sacrificial love is a common theme in literature, such as Oscar Wilde's tale of "The Happy Prince" or Shel Silverstein's *The Giving Tree*.

Living it out
(13:11-14)

Paul followed his exhortation to love with a strong note of eschatological urgency. Like other early Christian leaders from Jesus (Matt. 10:23; Mark 9:1, 14:62) to James (Jas. 5:8) and Peter (1 Pet. 4:17), Paul believed the end of the age was near (see also 1 Thess. 4:17, 1 Cor. 15:51, Phil. 4:7). He and others seemed to take it for granted that Christ would soon return.

Paul offered no rationale for his expectation of imminent judgment, but wrote as if the belief was widespread: "Besides this, you know what time it is … For salvation is nearer to us now than when we became believers … the night is far gone, the day is near." With judgment day approaching, Paul insisted, believers should "wake from sleep" and rise up to "lay aside the works of darkness and put on the armor of light" (excerpts from 12:11-12).

Waking from sleep suggests shaking off one's spiritual lethargy and devoting one's energy to a life of renewed commitment to Christ. Similar uses of the metaphor can be found in Mark 13:35-36, 1 Thess. 5:6, and Rev. 3:1-3.

Paul often employed the image of changing clothes. In addition to this passage (vv. 12-14), he spoke of both "putting on" and "taking off" in Eph. 4:22, 25 and Col. 3:8, 12 and employed the metaphor of "putting on" alone in 1 Thess. 5:8 and Eph. 6:11-17.

The metaphor of changing clothes suggests that believers are first to put aside their sinful "works of darkness," just as they would remove worn or dirty clothes. In v. 13, Paul spelled out the sort of dark behaviors he had in mind: "reveling and drunkenness," "debauchery and licentiousness," "quarreling and jealousy" – all harmful actions that roughly parallel the earlier-mentioned commandments not to commit adultery, covet, steal, or murder (v. 9).

Having removed their sinful/soiled garments, the newly awakened were then to adorn themselves with the "armor of light" (v. 12), an alternate way of saying "put on the Lord Jesus Christ" (v. 14).

For Paul, putting on the "armor of light" enabled one to "live honorably during the day" – that is, to walk unashamed in the daylight, knowing that one's behavior is worthy of respect rather than reproach.

Likewise, those who "put on the Lord Jesus Christ" would be so focused on following Jesus that they "make no provision for the flesh, to gratify its desires." This does not suggest that Christ-followers do not have human needs – that they do not get hungry or cold or sleepy. Rather, Paul used "the flesh" and its "desires" to refer to the same kind of sinful and self-directed behaviors described above.

Paul's point is not that believers should forgo all human comfort or ignore physical needs, quit their jobs and camp out on a hill while awaiting the Second Coming. Rather, he wanted Christians to live with a conscious and constant awareness that Christ could return at any moment. Those who keep Christ's return in mind are less likely to lose themselves in selfish or harmful behaviors, and more likely to give themselves in loving service to others. Motivated by eschatological awareness and clothed with Christ, believers have no need for a list of commandments, but fulfill the law by living in love.

The Hardest Question
Is love really enough?

In today's text, and also in Gal. 5:14, Paul summarized the entire law into the single command to love others as we love ourselves. Such an approach has great appeal, but is it enough? Can love alone provide an adequate guide to behavior?

Let's drop back for a moment to Jesus' thought. As mentioned earlier, Jesus spoke of giving his disciples a new commandment – presumably in place of the old ones – that they love one another as he had loved them (John 13:34). We also have instances from the synoptic gospels in which Jesus asserted or agreed that the greatest commands are to love God with all one's being, and to love others as oneself (Mark 12:29-31, Matt. 22:36-40, Luke 10:25-28). So, in Jesus' teaching, loving God and loving others are the heart and soul of obedience: "On these two commandments hang all the law and the prophets" (Matt. 22:40).

This suggests a belief that one who makes decisions based on love for God and love for neighbor will consequently fulfill both the moral prescriptions of the law and the ethical directives of the prophets.

Paul's teaching in Rom. 13:8-10 speaks only of the love for one's neighbor, but the sample commandments he gave in v. 9 relate to all others. When we broaden the text to include vv. 11-14, we find that Paul also emphasized the importance of putting aside selfish desires and "putting on the Lord Jesus Christ," another way of saying that one's primary allegiance and love should be directed toward God.

One who truly loves God will choose behaviors that he or she believes will bring joy to God. One who truly loves others will act in ways that are helpful rather than hurtful, thus keeping the commandments.

The rule of love would not have been considered sufficient by Jewish believers who held to the 613 *mitzvot*, because many of those laws are ritual prescriptions specific to Judaism. Eating shrimp or combining cotton and wool in a garment neither show nor deny love: their purpose is to preserve an identity by relating to God in a certain way. Both Jesus and Paul appear to suggest that such prescriptions are not required of Christians.

Others will find fault with the rule of love because it is by nature subjective: it allows for differing views without painting all questions in black and white. In Rom. 12:2, Paul had urged believers to surrender fully to Christ so they could "be transformed by the renewing of your minds, so that you may discern what is the will of God—what is good and acceptable and perfect." But human minds, no matter how transformed, may still see things differently.

Some Christians, for example, believe that love compels the church to offer full acceptance to persons whose gender identity or orientation differs from traditional heterosexual norms. Others, who also claim to be motivated by love, oppose the affirmation of anyone who does not fit within a much narrower view.

When both Jesus and Paul agree that love is a sufficient guideline for behavior, it's hard to argue with them. When it comes to interpreting just what love demands, however, believers won't always see eye to eye. Let us hope that those who disagree can do so in love.

First Sunday of Advent

Fourth Reading
Matthew 24:36-44

Watch Out!

But about that day and hour no one knows, neither the angels of heaven, nor the Son, but only the Father. (Matt. 24:36)

I once had a friend who occasionally made his farewell by saying "Watch yourself!" His intention was not that I spend the remainder of the day in front of a mirror, but that I take care of myself by being watchful and staying out of harm's way.

On more than one occasion, Jesus admonished his disciples to be watchful – not just for trouble, but for good. Indeed, Jesus bade them be constantly watchful for what many would consider the greatest good: his own return in glory. Since Jesus had not yet left his disciples, they found it hard to understand these words when they were spoken. Only later did they come to appreciate their significance and see to it that they were recorded in those early documents that came to be incorporated into the New Testament.

Matthew's gospel records a series of three warnings about watchfulness, each employing a word picture to stress the seriousness of the situation.

Be alert!
(v. 36)

The context of this call to alertness is the aptly named "Little Apocalypse," a series of teachings about the end of the age and the return of Christ (Matthew 24, Mark 13, Luke 21). Many first-century Jews saw little evidence of God's favor in the political reality of their situation in life. Yet, the Hebrew scriptures insisted that one day God would step in and vindicate his people, defeating all evil and making things right. **[Apocalyptic]**

Apocalyptic literature found in the Old Testament suggested that God's historic intervention would be accompanied by heavenly signs and cosmic upheaval. Jesus alludes to these and adds other predictions in Matt.

> **Apocalyptic:** The early church remembered Jesus' talk of a second coming and preserved it in the apocalyptic style of writing that grew out of Israel's greatest times of stress and persecution. Texts including Isaiah 24–27, Daniel 7–12, Ezekiel 38–39, and Zechariah 9–14 make much use of metaphor as a kind of code, offering hope to insiders that present oppressors will be brought down by the mighty power of God. The enemy's defeat was often described in terms of cataclysmic changes in the cosmos.
>
> We find the same kind of language in the book of Revelation, and also in what is often called the "Little Apocalypse," which appears with variations in all three synoptic gospels (Mark 13, Matthew 24, Luke 21).

24:3-35, closing with a positive claim that his words are true and lasting: "Heaven and earth will pass away, but my words will not pass away" (v. 35).

What follows this bold assertion seems almost a contradiction: after pointing to several "signs of the times" that would foreshadow the end as certainly as emerging fig leaves indicate the coming of summer, Jesus forcefully averred that no one would know when the day is coming (v. 36). This is the basic point of the entire teaching in vv. 36-44, illustrated in three different ways: no one knows when the end will come.

Noah and his neighbors
(vv. 37-39)

The first warning (vv. 37-39) draws on the familiar story of Noah. According to the narrative recorded in Genesis 6–9, only Noah was perceptive or attentive enough to prepare for a watery cataclysm. Others went about their life as usual: eating and drinking, getting married, going to work, raising crops and rearing children.

Popular imagination and countless children's books have portrayed Noah's neighbors as proud and foolish people who periodically stopped by to ridicule Noah for building an ark in the desert, but the account itself suggests nothing of the sort. Jesus says only that they "knew nothing" until the rain started falling, and by that time it was too late to learn, because Noah and his family were already sealed in the ark.

Just so, Jesus warned, when the Son of Man returns to claim his own, most people will be going about their daily business with no thought of eternity crashing into their lives. When that day comes, it will be too late for repentance and the future will hold little more hope than it did for Noah's neighbors.

Luke's version of this discourse includes an additional reference to Lot, warning readers against turning back from the proper path as Lot's wife was reputed to have done (Luke 17:31; cf. Gen. 19:24-28).

Two, and one
(vv. 40-42)

The story of Noah pointed to a time when only a tiny fraction of the world's population found redemption because of their faith and faithfulness. Jesus' second illustration imagines a scene in which one out of two are taken up to be with Christ at his return.

This use of numbers, as in the previous illustration, is not intended to predict the percentage of the population whom Christ will claim. Rather, it is an effective way of bringing the reality of the moment home.

Imagine that two men are working together in a field, or two women are kneeling side by side pounding grain into flour. Suddenly one is taken up to be with Christ, while the other is left to ponder his or her past failure and present inability to follow.

Jesus' conclusion is that all should "Keep awake, for you do not know on what day your Lord is coming" (v. 42). The verb suggests far more than the opposite of sleep, implying a constant alertness or watchfulness.

Jesus, the thief?
(vv. 43-44)

Jesus added a third picture that took an entirely different tack. Everyone understands that thieves can be a threat.

So, most people take precautions by locking their doors. In our day, many take the additional step of installing security cameras so they can keep watch even when away from home.

In a world where someone couldn't just call the police, if by chance a family suspected that a robber would target their home on a certain night, they would remain awake and be on the lookout, rather than merely going to sleep as if there was no present danger. Unfortunately, thieves rarely give notice of their pernicious plans.

Neither would Jesus announce the timing of his return to intervene in our history, intrude into our world, and invade our daily (or nightly) existence. New Testament authors believed he will come to receive those who have trusted him, and to judge those who have not. He will not, however, telegraph his coming so that all may repent at the last moment. He will come as a thief in the night, when we least expect it.

With these words, Jesus has given fair warning. Those who are wise will be alert for his arrival. "Therefore you also must be ready, for the Son of Man is coming at an unexpected hour" (v. 44). **[Paradox]**

Luke's gospel also contains the warning about being prepared for a thief in the night, but there (Luke 12:39-40) it is connected to a parable concerning the danger of piling up personal possessions rather than giving sacrificially, as Jesus taught.

Paul uses a similar metaphor in 1 Thess. 5:2-4. There, however, the "Day of the Lord" is a surprise only for the unbeliever, for the believer expects it and is prepared (cp. also 2 Pet. 3:10).

The metaphor of Jesus as a thief is implied in these texts, but unmistakably stated in the book of Revelation. As John the Elder described his vision of what is to come, he quoted Jesus as speaking to the church at Sardis. "If you will not awake, I will come like a thief, and you will not know at what hour I will come upon you" (Rev. 3:3).

In the frightening prediction of the "seven bowls of wrath," there is a parenthetical observation: "Lo, I am coming like a thief! Blessed is he who is awake, keeping his garments that he may not go naked and be seen exposed!" (Rev. 16:15).

> **Paradox:** Jesus' teaching is paradoxical in that he tells the disciples to be watchful and look for signs while also insisting that they cannot know when the *Parousia* will take place. Just before today's assigned text, Matthew related an analogy of a fig tree that produces fruit in season, with Jesus saying: "From the fig tree learn its lesson: as soon as its branch becomes tender and puts forth its leaves, you know that summer is near. So also, when you see all these things, you know that he is near, at the very gates. Truly I tell you, this generation will not pass away until all these things have taken place. Heaven and earth will pass away, but my words will not pass away."
>
> It also seems paradoxical that Jesus seems to be predicting that his return would take place before the present generation died out. That did not occur, leaving interpreters to scramble for meaning. Perhaps Jesus used the expression simply to emphasize the importance of being watchful in the moment. Another option is to regard "this generation" as a broad reference to the "generation" or age of the church.

The Hardest Question
How do the four gospels relate to each other?

We have noted above that some form of the "Little Apocalypse" is found in Matthew, Mark, and Luke, but with variations. A careful reading shows that they often tell the stories of Jesus in very different ways. Why?

The gospels of Matthew, Mark, and Luke are quite similar at so many points that they are called the "synoptic gospels" ("synoptic" comes from a Greek word that means "seen together"). The Fourth Gospel was written later and is obviously quite different from the first three.

A few scholars have argued that Matthew was written first, and that Mark and Luke abbreviated what was found there. Most scholars, however, agree that Mark, the shortest of the gospels, was written first: when Matthew and Luke include stories that follow the same order, it is those sections that they have in common with Mark.

A tradition holds that the gospel of Mark reflects the memories of the Apostle Peter, with whom Mark worked, and some Latin-influenced words may suggest a setting in Rome. Many scholars believe Mark may have been written before the destruction of Jerusalem in 70 CE.

The gospel of Matthew appears to have been written in the last third of the first century, probably by a later disciple writing in Matthew's name. The writer of Matthew puts extra emphasis on the Jews, in addition to the fulfillment of Old Testament prophecies.

Luke is the author of both Luke and Acts. He was a Gentile who described himself as a physician who had come to know Christ and sought to gain as much information as he could before writing his books, which were addressed to "Theophilus," meaning "lover of God." His gospel was written about the same time as Matthew.

Both Matthew and Luke appear to have made use of Mark's gospel as an outline, though they depart from it at various points. They include much of Mark's material in their books, often in a slightly abbreviated form, or shaped to emphasize their personal interests. Some scholars believe Matthew was writing mainly to a Jewish audience, while Luke wrote with attention to other Gentiles. Luke's gospel also gives extra attention to the role of women and to the sick and poor.

Matthew and Luke also have in common a number of Jesus' teachings that are not in Mark. This material is often attributed to an otherwise unknown collection of Jesus' "sayings" that scholars call "Q" (from *Quelle*, a German word meaning "source").

In addition, both Matthew and Luke incorporate unique materials not included elsewhere, notably their separate narratives about the birth and infancy of Jesus: Matthew has more to say about Joseph's place in the story, while Luke focuses more on Mary. Both Matthew and Luke sometimes mix and match their various materials in different ways.

Thus, Matthew is thought to consist mainly of material from Mark, Q, and Matthew's distinctive source, while Luke consists of material from Mark, Q, and Luke's separate source. Each author shaped the stories to his own audience and interests.

We don't need timelines, but wakefulness is always appropriate.

Second Sunday of Advent
First Reading
Isaiah 11:1-10

When Stumps Sprout

The wolf shall live with the lamb, the leopard shall lie down with the kid, the calf and the lion and the fatling together, and a little child shall lead them. (Isa. 11:6)

Do you ever worry about wild animals? When hiking in Glacier National Park, or in other places where bears are known to roam, hikers are encouraged to carry an air horn and bear spray (a sizable can of pepper spray), and to talk loudly so bears or other large predators will stay in hiding.

Isaiah of Jerusalem lived in a time when wolves, leopards, and lions were endemic to Israel and a constant threat to livestock. When the prophet imagined a time of God-sent peace, it surprisingly included animal amity. Wolves and lambs and leopards and kids and lions and calves could take a nap together, and even a little child could shepherd them safely.

Do you remember the first time you saw a depiction of the idyllic scenes of Isa. 11:6-9? Whether it was in the pages of a children's book or one of Edward Hicks' folksy 19th-century paintings, the image has an enduring appeal. We love the thought of a world where lions and tigers and bears can play with lambs and bunnies and children. [*The Peaceable Kingdom*]

The second Sunday of Advent traditionally centers on the theme of peace, and one could hardly find a better text than Isa. 11:1-10 to celebrate the hope of a peaceable kingdom.

A wise counselor
(vv. 1-3a)

Another text in Isaiah, 2:1-5, envisions the hope of a world in which war would be a thing of the past and combat weapons would be turned into farming tools.

Today's text brings yet another image of peace, this one led by a righteous ruler who establishes an Eden-like world in which predators and prey live in perfect harmony.

Both texts imply that God's people should not just wish for such things: they should also work for them.

The Peaceable Kingdom: Edward Hicks (1780–1849) was a Quaker minister and folk artist who traveled Pennsylvania as a preacher and supplemented his income with ornamental painting, including tavern signs. After coming under fire from some Quaker brethren who thought his ornamental work violated their plain customs, he tried farming but nearly went bankrupt.

Hicks later took up painting again, but typically added a religious dimension to his work. In keeping with the Friends' peace-loving heritage, he created at least 61 versions of a scene called *The Peaceable Kingdom*. Typically, he portrays animals living in harmony with children on the right, while William Penn negotiates a peace treaty with Native Americans on the left.

Photo courtesty of Wikimedia Commons

Isaiah 11 is part of a larger unit that begins with 9:1-7, which speaks of the birth of a righteous king, predicts judgment on Israel and Judah for their prideful lack of justice (9:8–10:4), and declares that the Assyrians who oppress them will be brought low (10:5-19, 28-34) as God preserves a remnant of the scattered Hebrews (10:20-27).

In 11:1-9, the text returns to the theme of a righteous ruler who would establish a blissful age and bring all nations to God (11:10-16).

Isaiah, who often employed metaphors, described the coming king as a shoot sprouting from the stump of Jesse (v. 1), the father of David and thus an ancestor of the Davidic line of kings. The tree of David's line had diminished considerably, but it would not die. The Hebrews believed that God had promised to David an eternal kingdom (see 2 Samuel 7), and Isaiah saw a day when a new and righteous king would rise as a green sprout from an old stump, a fresh branch from the roots of David's line. [**Shoot and branch**]

Isaiah describes the new ruler with three pairs of laudable attributes, all related to wisdom (vv. 2-3, cp. to Prov. 8:12-15). The coming king's admirable virtues would have their source in "the Spirit of the LORD" that "will rest on him," bringing "the spirit of wisdom and understanding, the spirit of counsel and might, the spirit of knowledge and the fear of the LORD."

"Wisdom and understanding" suggest that the ruler would not only possess a great depth of knowledge, but also would know how to use it properly.

"Counsel and might" (reminiscent of Isa. 9:6) portray the ruler as one who is not only strong, but who also uses his power in appropriate ways. The same Hebrew phrase also appears in Isa. 36:5, but on the taunting lips of the Assyrian envoy Rabshakeh, who says "Do you think that mere words are strategy and power for war?"

"Knowledge and the fear of the LORD" are paired as a reminder that information is most valuable when used in service to God and God's people. "The fear of the LORD is the beginning of wisdom" was the mantra of Israel's wisdom teachers (Ps. 111:10, Prov. 9:10).

The coming king, Isaiah said, would find joy in that very thing: "His delight shall be in the fear of the LORD" (v. 3a)

A righteous judge
(vv. 3b-5)

Ancient Near Eastern rulers, even those from Assyria and Babylon, prided themselves on ruling with justice, though their concept of fairness often differed from biblical ideals. Isaiah declared that the coming ruler, wise in the ways of God and of the world, would govern with divine justice. Like God, he would not base his judgments on people's outward appearance or on their testimony, but on something deeper.

The passage recalls 1 Sam. 16:7, where Samuel was about to anoint Jesse's oldest son Eliab as Israel's next king before Yahweh said, "Do not look on his appearance or on the height of his stature, because I have rejected him; for the LORD does not see as mortals see; they look on the outward appearance, but the LORD looks on the heart." Only David, the eighth and youngest son of Jesse, was chosen as a man "after God's own heart."

Isaiah, like his contemporary Micah, had a special concern for poor people who were exploited by their wealthy neighbors. A cozy legal system requiring just two witnesses to appear before village elders made it relatively easy for a large estate owner to accuse a poor neighbor on false charges, hire a couple of lying witnesses, and take the poor person's land. The elders who passed judgment were also men of means.

Earlier, Isaiah had pronounced woe upon those "who join house to house, who add field to field" to build large estates (Isa. 5:8). In contrast, the coming king would judge the poor rightly "and decide with equity for the meek of the earth" (v. 4a).

The second half of v. 4 sounds surprisingly violent to modern ears, but "he shall strike the earth with the rod of

---

Shoot and branch: Isaiah is not the only prophet to speak of a coming king as a shoot or branch from the stump of Jesse. Writing much later, Jeremiah saw past the coming exile to a day of hope when God would raise up "a righteous branch" from the house of David (Jer. 23:5-6).

Following the exile, Zechariah used the same metaphor to express hope that Zerubbabel, a descendant of David and a grandson of Jehoiachin, was the chosen "Branch" who would rebuild the temple and the nation (3:8, 6:12).

> **Belt, or underwear?** The Hebrew word *ezôr* refers to an article of clothing wrapped around the waist. Depending on the context, it could refer to a belt of skin or cloth that is wrapped and tied about the waist, or it could refer to an undergarment wound about the waist and probably between the legs.
>
> A note on this verse from the NET Bible acknowledges that the meaning is uncertain in Isa. 11:5, and suggests "If a belt worn outside the robe is in view, then the point might be that justice/integrity will be readily visible or that these qualities will give support to his rule. If an undergarment is in view, then the idea might be that these characteristics support his rule or that they are basic to everything else."

his mouth" probably refers to the king's spoken decrees demanding justice for the poor, not to a shout-induced earthquake. The reference to his "breath" killing the wicked is in parallel with the preceding line, and its main intention is not murder, but to indicate that the coming king would overcome wickedness, wearing righteousness and faithfulness as a doubled belt (v. 5). [**Belt, or underwear?**]

A promise of peace
(vv. 6-10)

As the coming ruler's power and sense of justice would bring an end to greedy humans preying on one another, Isaiah declared, such justice would extend even to the animal kingdom, bringing all creatures great and small into a time of harmony echoing themes of creation, when all animals (including humans) were to eat only green plants (Gen. 1:30).

Isaiah's image plays on the imagination like tuned wind chimes in a gentle breeze. A wolf lives side by side with a lamb. A leopard stretches out beside a resting baby goat. A cow and a lion munch on grass while a child watches over the odd but amazing flock and a baby plays safely with snakes.

Would you ever, in your wildest imagination, have come up with an image like that? It seems completely antithetical to the world as we know it, a world of predators and prey, eaters and the eaten. [**Two animals, or three?**]

What remains is for us to ask whether Isaiah believed the world would ever truly become a happy paradise where humans and animals roam freely and none are afraid, or whether he was using the animals as metaphors for something else.

Some commentators have suggested that the various predators symbolized aggressive countries that would lay down their arms and live together in peace with their weaker neighbors. Others believe Isaiah's main intent was to forecast an image of what a wonderful world it could be if a leader emerged to inspire such a peaceable kingdom.

Finding a clear answer to this question is not nearly so important as catching the sublime emotional feel of Isaiah's imagery, and considering what steps we might take toward creating a world where violence and destruction give way to a land infused with "the knowledge of the LORD" (v. 9).

Some believers take this text so seriously that they choose not only to live at peace with other people, but also to tread so lightly upon the earth that they subsist happily on fruits, grains, and vegetables, and do not contribute to the death of animals.

Most readers are unlikely to go that far, but perhaps Isaiah's vision can inspire us to seek justice and better lives even for animals, working toward that peaceable kingdom ruled by the promised shoot from the stump of Jesse (v. 10).

Isaiah did not live to see such a king arise, nor did any of his spiritual descendants who added to his book over the next 200 years. No ruler has yet to touch the ideals displayed by the "signal to the peoples" that Isaiah envisioned – but believers who read this text through the lens of the New Testament believe that the shoot from Jesse's stump has emerged – and been cut down – and has risen again.

Jesus came as precisely the kind of leader that Isaiah imagined, proclaiming the inbreaking of the Kingdom of God. Those around him could not understand the importance of the kingdom, which has yet to reach its fullness. We may long with the writer of Revelation for a new

> **Two animals, or three?** In v. 7, the NRSV has "the cow and the lion and the fatling together," a rather literal reading of the text. Since the other animals are all in pairs, some ancient sources read the word "fatling" as "grazed" or "grew fat" (1QIsa^a, one of the Dead Sea Scrolls, has this reading). The NET chooses this option, rendering it as "an ox and a young lion will graze together."

heaven and earth, but we remain responsible for working toward that kingdom in our own time.

With church attendance in decline across the country, we may sometimes feel that the church has also been reduced to a stump, but there is still life in it as we trust in God's Spirit for the wisdom, compassion, and courage needed to bring kingdom growth through justice and equity for all.

That would be glorious indeed.

The Hardest Question
Is Isaiah 11 a prophecy of the Messiah?

Today's text, along with Isaiah 7 and 9, and also the "servant songs" in Isaiah 42:1-4, 49:1-6, 50:4-9, and 52:13–53:12, are often cited as passages that predict the coming of a messiah to deliver Israel and lead it into a golden age.

The Hebrew word *meshiach*, which we transliterate as "messiah," literally means "anointed one." It appears 39 times in the Old Testament, most commonly with reference to kings or priests who were anointed with oil when they took office. In 1 Sam. 24:6, David refers to Saul as "the LORD's anointed," and in 2 Sam. 19:21, Abishai refers to David with the same expression. Leviticus 4 and following chapters speak of the "anointed priests" while describing their duties. Psalm 105:15 refers to the people of Israel as God's "anointed ones," as does Hab. 13:3.

While several Old Testament passages speak of a coming deliverer and future king, they never use the word "messiah" to describe him. The closest thing to it is found in Isaiah, but there it speaks of the Persian king Cyrus, described as the one God had anointed to defeat the Babylonians, setting the stage for the Hebrews to be freed from captivity (Isa. 45:1).

After the return, the prophets Haggai and Zechariah had brief hopes that the appointed governor Zerubbabel, a descendant of David, might prove to be the "righteous branch" of which Isaiah had spoken, but they do not call him a messiah.

In her commentary on Isaiah 1–39, Patricia Tull notes that there was little evidence of interest in a return to the monarchy during the Second Temple period. The Hasmonean family under Judas Maccabeus wrested control from the Seleucid kings and established a short-lived Jewish kingdom in the second century BCE, but the deliverers became oppressive in their own way, leading to an emergence of hope for a better kind of king.

At this point, Tull adds, Isaiah 11 began to be quoted in various Jewish writings, including the Sybilline Oracles, the Psalms of Solomon, and various documents at Qumran, where the Dead Sea Scrolls were found.

By the first century, the use of the term "messiah" to describe the hoped-for ruler became common, occurring in the apocryphal book of 2 Esdras (7:28, 12:32) and appearing frequently in the gospels, where it is uniformly used as a title for Jesus.

Some scholars see Isaiah 11 in the background of John the baptizer's declaration that "the ax is lying at the root of the tree" (Matt. 3:10, Luke 3:9). In this view, the image of an ax felling a tree could have been drawn from Isa. 10:33-34, and the Spirit's descent upon the newly baptized Jesus could have reflected the Spirit of the LORD resting on the shoot of Jesse from Isa. 11:2.

The book of Isaiah does not refer to the predicted "shoot of Jesse" as a "messiah" in so many words, but it does express hope that a descendant of David would one day arise to lead Israel. In later centuries, New Testament writers interpreted prophecies of Isaiah and others as predictions of anticipating a messiah. In this sense, looking through the lens of the New Testament, we can describe them as "messianic" prophecies.

Second Sunday of Advent

Second Reading
Psalm 72:1-19*

Praying for Justice

May he judge your people with righteousness, and your poor with justice. (Ps. 72:2)

Why would the same Psalm be read for Advent and Epiphany? The psalm probably originated as a prayer used in the coronation of a new king, expressing hope that the king would rule with justice and righteousness.

From the perspective of Advent, hopes for Israel's ancient kings are used to reflect on Christ as the one ruler whose personal character and concern for justice were impeccable.

The perspective of Epiphany is similar, expressing belief that the hopes of the psalmist had become embodied in Christ and the inbreaking of the kingdom of God, the divine realm of Christ's rule that exists even now and offers a spiritual glimmer of a "new heaven and a new earth" to come, a kingdom in which God is king and justice reigns.

For the purposes of Bible study, it works better to consider the entire psalm rather than select verses chosen for a liturgical reading, so we will consider all of vv. 1-19. The psalm appears to have 20 verses, but v. 20 is an editorial note that "The prayers of David son of Jesse are ended."

A prayer for a just king
(v. 1-4)

As noted above, Psalm 72 appears to have been used as a coronation prayer for a king in ancient Israel or Judah, a typical king who was willing to "go out before us and fight our battles" (1 Sam. 8:20), and who would rule with justice.

For that author, the best way to intercede for his country and people was to pray for a just, powerful, and

> **The king as judge:** The classic example of the king as judge is the story of two prostitutes who brought their case to King Solomon after one of them accidentally smothered her baby while sleeping, and claimed that the other woman's child was her own. Solomon famously declared that the living child should be sliced in half and divided between them, revealing the true mother when she cried out against the idea (1 Kgs. 3:16-28).

long-lived king. The superscription of Psalm 72 reflects a tradition that this psalm was written for Solomon's coronation, but the psalm itself is written so it could be used for any king. The psalmist prays that God will inspire divine righteousness in "a king's son" – more literally, "a son of a king."

The first verse of the psalm sets the stage for all that follows: "Give the king your justice, O God, and your righteousness to a king's son." The Hebrew word order puts special emphasis on these desired qualities. Literally, it reads "O God, your justice to the king give; your righteousness to a king's son." The psalmist prays for the king to have nothing less than God's own perfect justice and righteousness to guide him throughout his reign. [The king as judge]

The word for "justice" is *mishpat*, which has to do with making right and fair decisions, especially in legal matters. The king in Israel was the arbiter of last resort, so the psalmist prays that the king would make decisions as God would make them.

"Righteousness" translates the important term *tsedaqâ*, which refers to right doing in every sense: spiri-

---

tual, social, and moral – right doing that grows from a right relationship with God and others.

Justice comes when right judgments (v. 2) are rendered for all people, including the poor. Disadvantaged people are often lost or underserved in a system run by the powerful. The true measure of a king, then, is whether he does right by the neediest of his subjects. The psalmist prays for such justice to pervade the land until the very mountains resound with wholeness and well-being (*shalôm*), as the hills are awash with righteousness (v. 3).

Other nations might oppress the poor, but Israel was to be different. The Torah included specific laws and warnings designed to protect the poor from usurious interest and the loss of their ancestral land (see, for example, Deuteronomy 15). Indeed, God's intent was to bless faithful Israel to the extent that none would be poor.

The nation's history was far short of sterling, however. Wealthy but unscrupulous people ignored the law or sought loopholes allowing them to take advantage of those who were less fortunate. Prophets such as Isaiah lambasted those who amassed large holdings by squeezing out the poor (Isa. 5:1-10).

The word for "poor" in v. 2 is *'ōnî*. It describes one who not only lacks material things, but also is "bowed down" by the circumstances of life. The verbal form could be used to describe intentional affliction or rape, as in Amnon's abuse of his sister Tamar in 2 Sam. 13:14 – a reminder that unjust economic systems may actively hold others down, making it very difficult for even hardworking people to escape poverty.

Americans should be quite familiar with the scenario, as our economic system is stacked to favor the rich – in particular the ultrarich – while the poor struggle to make ends meet at poverty-level, minimum-wage jobs and can only dream of ever owning a home.

We note that the psalmist speaks of *your* poor, as God's poor. Though God of all, Yahweh displayed a consistent and special concern for those who lacked the necessities of life (Deut. 10:17-19; Ps. 9:12, 34:6). God's concern for the poor is at the heart of the movement we know as liberation theology.

As a rule, most wealthy people are far more interested in increasing their riches than in helping the poor improve their standard of living. The psalmist knew that if the king

---

Same old, same old: Political leaders often campaign on the promise of a commitment to care for the poor. It's no secret, however, that political systems tend to be dominated by those who have the most money, promoting policies that favor the wealthy rather than using resources to lift up the poor.

People who live under a ruling monarchy have no input into who their next leader will be. Americans have never had any liking for a king, but we do have leaders who exercise political power. While the psalmist could only pray for a just ruler, we have the opportunity and obligation to vote for leaders who are concerned with promoting justice for all.

What qualities should we look for in our leaders as we not only pray for them, but also vote?

---

did not proactively advocate for the poor and weak, the *status quo* would prevail. A good king would seek justice for all persons by stepping in to help those who could not defend themselves against greedy lenders and corrupt officials (v. 4). In doing so, he would champion the cause of God's special people. [**Same old, same old**]

A prayer for an enduring kingdom
(vv. 5-17)

Any king who could rule with such careful probity and concern for all people would certainly be a boon to his nation, beloved by his people. The only way to make his reign better would be to make it longer. Thus, the psalmist launches into a rhapsodic plea that the just king and his dynasty might last forever.

"May he live while the sun endures, and as long as the moon, throughout all generations," the psalmist prayed (v. 5). Ancient life was filled with many uncertainties, but there were two things that did not vary. The sun rose every morning to blanket the earth with its faithful, warming light. And, the moon moved so resolutely through its phases that the ancient Hebrew calendar was based on the lunar cycle.

The psalmist knew that a consistent, dependable, and trustworthy leader would be most likely to bring peace to the people.

As the sun and moon resided in the heavens, so did the rain, occasionally pouring itself onto the earth in a watery barrage of blessing. The psalmist prayed for the king's rule to be not only long, but also as welcome as the annual rains (v. 6).

Most of the annual rainfall in Israel occurs during the winter months, framed by less certain "early rains" in the fall and "latter rains" in the spring. The authors of scripture often employed the motif of early and late rains as signs of God's special beneficence to Israel (Deut. 11:14, Jer. 5:24, Joel 2:23), for they allowed the planting of additional crops.

Thus, the author prays for a just king who would be as consistent as the solar system and as invigorating as welcome rain. "Rain that falls on the mown grass" may be an intentional reference to the latter rains, which came after the harvest – after the fields had been cut. Or, the skillful poet may have intended to touch the hearer's (and reader's) senses by calling to mind the lush smell of spring rain on fields newly mown.

The king could not bring rain, but he could foster an atmosphere in which righteousness and peace might flourish throughout the kingdom (v. 7a). What more could one ask than for such leadership to last as long as the moon marks the passing of time (v. 7b)?

Verses 8-17 continue and expand the theme with prayers that the king's dominion would extend from sea to sea, conquering enemies and setting an example for all nations (vv. 8-11).

Power alone does not make a great king, however: the ideal leader is one who "delivers the needy when they call, the poor and those who have no helper." Such a king "has pity on the weak and the needy" and saves their lives, for "precious is their blood in his sight" (vv. 12-14). A truly good leader has concern for all people.

In vv. 15-17, the psalmist returns to the hope for a long-lived king who would rule over a fertile and blessed land. No earthly king could live forever, but one could pray that his legacy would continue: "May his name endure forever, his fame continue as long as the sun."

Beyond dominion and long life, the psalmist prayed for a king so just that all nations could benefit from his leadership – a hope that echoes God's promise to Abraham (Gen. 12:3).

A blessing for the true King
(vv. 18-19)

The final two verses of the psalm were probably a later addition. While the main body of the psalm is a carefully

> **A fitting doxology:** The last two verses of Psalm 72 may have been added as a conclusion, not only for the psalm, but also to serve as an appropriate benediction marking the conclusion of "Book II" of Psalms (42–72). This section is often called the "Elohistic Psalter" because God is frequently (though not exclusively) called "Elohim" in these chapters. "Book II" may have originally circulated as an independent collection, later integrated into the main body of the psalms. Just as Psalm 150 serves as a benediction for the entire compilation, so these two verses bring the Elohistic Psalter to a fitting close. And, they are not entirely unrelated to the psalm in which they appear. They declare that Yahweh alone is Israel's true king, the only one whose glory can fill the earth and outlive the sun.

shaped prayer for the new king, these verses are a doxology to Yahweh, Israel's God, "who alone does wondrous things" (v. 18). The poet praises God's glorious name, and prays for the glory of God's presence to pervade all the earth. The Hebrew word *amen* (repeated for emphasis) means something akin to "so let it be." [**A fitting doxology**]

The psalmist's heartfelt prayer for justice has never been fulfilled by a king on a throne or any other national leader. Only in Jesus do we find a righteous ruler whose compassion extends to all people and whose reign will outlast even the sun and the moon.

The Hardest Question
Why are there so many psalms about kings?

Given the image of Christ as king, it is not surprising that the psalm texts for both the second Sunday of Advent (Year A) and Epiphany (every year) derive from one of the "Royal Psalms," and is designed as a prayer for a just king.

At least 11 psalms may be classified as Royal Psalms related to the rule of David and his dynasty in Jerusalem (2, 18, 20, 21, 45, 72, 89, 101, 110, 132, 144). Some writers also refer to Psalms 93–99 as Royal Psalms, but they are different in that they focus on praising God as king.

Psalm 72 was probably composed for use in coronation festivities when a new king ascended the throne. An old tradition, reflected in the superscription, suggests that the king was Solomon, perhaps because of the psalm's emphasis on wise justice. Some traditions even hold that the prayer was written by David for Solomon.

But why do we have so many psalms about kings? The northern kingdom of Israel was destroyed by the Assyrians around 722 BCE, and there were no more kings. The southern kingdom of Judah was defeated by the Babylonians in 587 BCE, bringing kingship to an end in Jerusalem. After the exile, Hebrews were allowed to return to Jerusalem, but ruled by a Persian-appointed governor, not a king.

Still, psalms about kingship and prayers for a just king remained popular long after Israel and Judah had a king, or any immediate hope for one. Indeed, the Royal Psalms not only persist, but some of them also occupy strategic places in the psalter. The second psalm in the collection, following the introductory wisdom psalm, celebrates the king's enthronement. Psalm 72 concludes "Book 2" of the five collections making up the psalms with a prayer for a king who embodies justice. Similarly, Psalm 89, which laments the loss of the monarchy, closes "Book 3" (the five divisions are 1–41, 42–72, 73–89, 90–106, and 107–150). The last of the Royal Psalms, Psalm 144, seems to transfer the responsibilities of the king to the people.

Thus, while the Royal Psalms recall Israel's kings with fondness, the kings were representatives of the people, and all were called to bring God's will to bear on earth through lives characterized by justice, righteousness, and the state of peace and prosperity embodied in the word *shalom*.

These qualities, of course, are at the heart of Psalm 72, which recognizes that true justice, righteousness, and peaceful prosperity can only occur when the poor are empowered and included as equal citizens. The prophets consistently criticized both kings and people for falling short of God's ideal, but the lasting hope for a just, righteous, and prosperous society remained.

Considering these things reminds Christians that we serve the eternal King, who desires that we be the very agents of divine love and justice. Repeatedly, Jesus showed compassion for the poorest and neediest of the land and also instructed his followers to do the same.

If we would desire a just, righteous, and peacefully prosperous nation, we must go beyond praying for and voting for good leaders: the work of justice belongs to all of us.

Third Reading
Romans 15:1-13

Can't We All Get Along?

Welcome one another, therefore, just as Christ has welcomed you, for the glory of God. (Rom. 15:7)

On March 3, 1991, a Los Angeles man named Rodney King was stopped by police officers for speeding and driving while intoxicated. When King, who was Black, initially resisted arrest, he was beaten without mercy. The incident might have gone unreported if a man on a nearby balcony had not filmed the encounter and sent the footage to a local news station. Public anger erupted, resulting in riots that resulted in 63 deaths; more than 2,000 injuries; 7,000 fires; and damage to 3,100 businesses.

Distraught by the aftermath, King sought to quell the riots by appearing on television. As part of his appeal, he said "I just want to say – you know – can we get along? Can we, can we get along?" The words became a legacy to his efforts, usually paraphrased as "Can we all just get along?"

The Apostle Paul did not try to face down massive riots, but he also dealt with high emotions in a church that was struggling. As he came to the end of his letter to the Romans, he encouraged believers not only to get along, but also to fully accept each other and to reach beyond themselves to welcome others.

The lectionary text for the day is Rom. 15:4-13, but the pericope begins with v. 1, as will we.

The example of Jesus
(vv. 1-6)

In ch. 15, Paul continues an appeal for unity that began in the previous chapter, which discussed the matter of different eating habits. Some people ate only vegetables, perhaps thinking that all available meat had been offered to an idol before being sold in the market. Perhaps they looked down on meat-eaters as idol worshipers. On the other hand, carnivores may have considered the vegetarians to be too persnickety.

Paul charges them not to judge one another's eating habits (14:1-4) or observation of particular days (14:5-6). We don't live or die to ourselves, but to the Lord, he said (14:7-9). Therefore, we should avoid judging each other and should respect others' scruples, even if we regard them as a sign of weakness. Otherwise, we might become a stumbling block to their faith (14:10-23).

Paul summarizes his argument in 15:1-2: those who are strong in the faith should put up with the failings of the weak rather than to please themselves alone. We do this for the sake of our neighbors, in order to build them up. The word translated "put up with" (*bastazo*) can mean "carry," "endure," or "tolerate." The word for "build up" could refer to physically building something, but in relationships it suggests the idea of "edifying" others or helping them to grow in faith. It is the same term found in 1 Cor. 10:23-24, where Paul argues that all things are lawful, but not all things are edifying, so each Christian should seek what is best for her neighbor.

The idea of allowing the weakest member of the church to set the menu for church suppers is not an appealing notion. Doesn't that mean that we are reducing ourselves to the lowest common denominator? Paul knew this idea would not be popular, so he appealed to the example of Christ, just as he did in Phil. 2:4ff. He reminds his readers that "Christ did not please himself; but, as it is written, 'The insults of those who insult you have fallen on me'" (v. 3). The Lord of all took our human weakness upon himself – accepting the jeers of the most unholy rabble – and he did it for our sake.

Paul's argument seems to be, "If Christ could give up his divine prerogatives and suffer death for our sakes, can we not give up our choice of food for the sake of a weaker brother?" The strong bear the burden for the weak (cf. Gal. 6:2). We remain free, but are urged to limit our freedom voluntarily.

The Old Testament quotation in v. 3 comes from Ps. 69:9, and Paul uses it to call upon the authority of the scriptures along with the example of Christ, whom he saw reflected in the quotation. Such scriptures were written to instruct followers' lives, he said (v. 4).

Utilizing a nice literary touch, Paul turns to a prayer that plays on the words found in his Old Testament quotation, then reprises the example of Christ. Paul had reminded his readers that those who are *steadfast* in trusting the scriptures would find in them *encouragement* and hope (v. 4). Now, he offers a benedictory wish that "the God of *steadfastness* and *encouragement*" would empower them to live in harmony with one another according to the example of Christ (v. 5).

The goal is unity, for which God gives us hope. So, Paul's prayer concludes with a reminder that those who live in harmony "may with one voice glorify the God and Father of our Lord Jesus Christ" (v. 6). We may be diverse in our cultural backgrounds, our theological interpretations, and our progress in Christian growth, but even so we may offer praise to God with one voice.

The Russian author Leo Tolstoy was not only one of the world's greatest novelists, but also a fascinating moral thinker. After writing his two greatest novels, *War and Peace* and *Anna Karanina*, he committed his life to Christ – or at least, to his own understanding of who Christ was and what he taught. The church of his day rejected Tolstoy, but he remained deeply committed to his views, refused to accept any further payment for his writings, and sought to live as simply as possible.

Tolstoy told a story about meeting a Russian beggar who was seeking money during a famine. He took the beggar by the hand and said, "Don't be angry with me, Brother. I have nothing to give." The beggar stood a little taller and replied, "But you *have* given me something; you called me brother, and that is a greater gift than money" (James E. Hightower, *Illustrating Paul's Letter to the Romans* [Baptist Sunday School Board, 1984], 110). To

follow Christ's example is to love one another by offering the gift of acceptance.

The rewards of inclusivity
(vv. 7-13)

Believers should be welcoming people, Paul believed, challenging the Romans to "Welcome one another, therefore, just as Christ has welcomed you, for the glory of God" (v. 7). The word translated "welcome" (*proslambánō*) can mean to "take in" or "add to," and in that sense to accept or welcome others, to take them into our lives.

Christ set the example of reaching out to all people, Paul said. He came as "a servant of the circumcised" to "confirm the promises given to the patriarchs," but also in order that the Gentiles might glorify God for his mercy" (v. 8). The awkwardness of the phrasing in this verse may be Paul's way of saying that Christ came first for the Jews, then for the Gentiles.

To support his position – to assure his readers that he isn't just making things up as he goes along – Paul goes on to quote four additional Old Testament passages in vv. 9-12, all of which point to the praise of God for the influx of Gentiles into the church. It is inevitable that the addition of new people from different cultures makes the challenge of unity more difficult – something that many of us have experienced in congregational life – but the blessing of God depends on it.

We all want to be loved, don't we? But we also want to be accepted fully, as who we are, and the two don't always meet. For two people to have a successful marriage, they must learn to accept each other as they are, with all of their cultural shaping and childhood baggage, growing and supporting each other in positive ways. For a church to reflect the example of Christ, we must open our arms and hearts to each other regardless of skin color, economic status, or gender identity. In these days, some might think it even more impressive if Democrats and Republicans could embrace for the common good rather than being slavishly devoted to ideological agendas.

We need to accept each other for who we are, not for what we have achieved or where we have come from, or even where we hope to go.

Perhaps we should search for another word. It's too easy for us to say that we accept people without it

> **Accepting acceptance:** Accepting others begins with accepting ourselves, something Fred Rogers of *Mister Rogers' Neighborhood* understood well.
>
> In *Wisdom from the World According to Mister Rogers: Important Things to Remember*, he wrote: "Deep within us—no matter who we are—there lives a feeling of wanting to be lovable, of wanting to be the kind of person that others like to be with. And the greatest thing we can do is to let people know they are loved and are capable of loving" (Peter Pauper Press, 2006, 29).
>
> Love and acceptance work both ways. When we know what it is like to be fully accepted—to be *seen* and still loved—we can learn to accept others, too.

meaning anything. It's not enough to say "I'm ok, you're ok … whatever." We want more than that: we want to be *wanted*. We want others to care that we exist, to be glad that we are around. That's what true welcome and acceptance means, that we want other people in our lives and in our churches – and that we accept that we are wanted, too. That's how we glorify God. [**Accepting acceptance**]

Paul had no doubt that the effort we put into achieving harmony will be worthwhile. Having counseled unity, he closes with a prayer for the church that returns to the theme of hope he had first broached in v. 4: "May the God of hope fill you with all joy and peace in believing, so that you may abound in hope by the power of the Holy Spirit." (v. 13). Through the Spirit, those who work together in harmony may experience not only saving belief but also joy, peace, and hope. Could there be a better wish for the season of Advent?

The Hardest Question
Why are Paul's quotations often different from the Old Testament we read?

Readers who check the references may note that Paul's Old Testament quotations support his belief that Christ came to all people, including the Gentiles.

In v. 9, he says "As it is written, 'Therefore I will confess you among the Gentiles, and sing praises to your name,'" a quotation from Ps. 18:49, where the NRSV has "For this I will extol you, O Lord, among the nations, and sing praise to your name."

Verse 10 declares "Rejoice, O Gentiles, with his people," a loose reference to Deut. 32:43, part of a lengthy poem that appeals, "Praise, O heavens, his people, worship him, all you gods!"

Paul then turns to a very similar line from Ps. 117:1. His version is "Praise the Lord, all you Gentiles, and let all the peoples praise him." Translating from the Hebrew, NRSV has "Praise the Lord, all you nations! Extol him, all you peoples!"

Finally, Paul cites Isa. 11:10, which he renders as "The root of Jesse shall come, the one who rises to rule the Gentiles; in him the Gentiles shall hope." The Hebrew version, according to the NRSV, has "On that day the root of Jesse shall stand as a signal to the peoples; the nations shall inquire of him, and his dwelling shall be glorious."

Paul's renderings are often different because he sometimes paraphrases, but mainly because he nearly always quotes from the Septuagint, the early Greek translation of the Old Testament. The LXX was translated from Hebrew texts extant in Egypt during the second and third centuries BCE, probably carried there by refugees from Israel when Babylon conquered Judah. Jeremiah, among others, went to Egypt.

The commonly accepted Hebrew text (the Masoretic text) was based on scrolls that had been preserved among the exiles in Babylon, which they brought back with them to Jerusalem and considered to be more valid.

During the 200–300 years that elapsed from the time of the exile to the time of translation into the Greek version, the scrolls would have been copied many times and perhaps incorporated different traditions. The LXX text of 1–2 Samuel, for example, is about one-seventh longer than the Hebrew version.

It may seem strange that Paul preferred the LXX, for we may assume that, as a former rabbi, he would have been able to read Hebrew scrolls. Whether he lacked access to those scrolls, or leaned to the LXX because Greek was the common language spoken in his mission churches, we can't be sure.

Second Sunday of Advent
Fourth Reading
Matthew 3:1-12

Starving for Hope

Repent, for the kingdom of heaven has come near. (Matt. 3:2)

What does it take to get your attention during worship? Imagine that one Sunday morning, as the choir concluded the anthem, a bushy-haired wild man dressed in a burlap bag should come dancing down the aisle shouting "Good news! *Repent!* Good news! *Repent!* Good news! *Repent!*"

He would get your attention. He might even get attention from the police if an overzealous member should dial 911. It's unlikely that anyone would sleep through *that* service.

No one went to sleep when John the Baptist preached either, and he did not have to invade the quiet synagogues of Judah to get an audience. John went out into the wilderness near the Jordan River, started shouting, and people came out in droves to hear him.

Why?

John the prophet
(vv. 1-5)

Jesus' cousin was no ordinary character. He would probably have attracted an audience no matter what he said, for it was evident to any good Hebrew that he looked like a reincarnation of Elijah the prophet, and they had been hoping for Elijah's return.

Many Jewish people of Jesus' day were anxiously awaiting a messiah to come and rescue them from Roman domination. They wanted God to put the promise back in the Promised Land. Rabbis reminded them that the great prophet Isaiah had spoken of a messenger who would appear in the wilderness to prepare the way for the Lord's coming (Isa. 40:3).

More to the point, one of the last prophets of the Old Testament period had predicted that just before the Messiah came to usher in the world-changing "Day of the Lord," Elijah the prophet would reappear on the earth to get people ready. A tradition recorded in 2 Kings 2 held that Elijah did not die a normal death, but had been transported from the earth by a whirlwind.

Five hundred years later, the prophet Malachi was inspired by a vision and made a promise: "See, I will send you the prophet Elijah before that great and dreadful day of the LORD comes. He will turn the hearts of the fathers to their children, and the hearts of the children to their fathers; or else I will come and strike the land with a curse" (Mal. 4:5-6).

It's not surprising, then, that people with eschatological hopes were looking for the return of Elijah, who was described as a man who had lived in the wilderness, eating what the land provided and wearing nothing more than a piece of rough cloth woven from animal hair about his waist, cinched up with a piece of leather (2 Kgs. 1:8).

Elijah's appearance had been so distinctive that no one who had seen him would fail to recognize him again. A story in 2 Kings says that King Ahaziah of Israel once fell through the lattice of his upstairs porch in Samaria and injured himself. He sent messengers to inquire of the god Baal-Zebub in his behalf, but Elijah intercepted the messengers. He said, "Go tell that worthless king: 'Is there no god in Israel, so that you have to consult Baal-Zebub? You're a dead man.'"

When Ahaziah heard this, he asked the messenger, "What did this man look like who told you this?" The messenger replied, "All he had on was a waistcloth

John and Elijah: In early Christian tradition, John the Baptizer was seen as the fulfillment of the promise that Elijah would return: in the prediction of John's birth, the angel Gabriel reportedly told his father Zechariah that "he will go on before the Lord, in the spirit and power of Elijah, to turn the hearts of the fathers to their children and the disobedient to the wisdom of the righteous—to make ready a people prepared for the Lord" (Luke 1:17). Note the similarity of language to Malachi's prophecy.

In the gospel of John, when the Baptizer was asked by a group of priests and Levites if he was indeed Elijah, he denied it, speaking of himself rather as the fulfillment of Isaiah's prediction of one "crying in the wilderness" (John 1:19-23).

Matthew's gospel, however, has Jesus affirm that John was the fulfillment of the promise of Elijah: "The disciples asked him, 'Why then do the teachers of the law say that Elijah must come first?' Jesus replied, 'To be sure, Elijah comes and will restore all things. But I tell you, Elijah has already come, and they did not recognize him, but have done to him everything they wished. In the same way the Son of Man is going to suffer at their hands.' Then the disciples understood that he was talking to them about John the Baptist" (17:10-13).

These passages do not necessarily imply that John was literally a reincarnated version of Elijah. As one who came in the spirit and character of Elijah, John fulfilled the prediction that "Elijah" would come and call the people of Israel to repentance. Jesus' remarks also indicate that, just as John was rejected in his role as Elijah, so Jesus would be rejected as the Messiah.

Jewish tradition still awaits a messiah, and thus still awaits the return of Elijah. To remember this, observant families always set a place for Elijah at their Passover table.

made from hair and leather belt to hold it up." The king said, "That's Elijah!" (2 Kgs. 1:1-8, my translation).

Nine hundred years later, John showed up looking like Elijah. He dressed in camel's hair, dwelt in the desert, and offended just about everyone he met. He lived off the land, getting his protein from dried locusts and his carbohydrates from wild honey (v. 4). When people looked at him, they thought "That's Elijah!" [**John and Elijah**]

John the preacher
(vv. 2, 7-12)

John not only *looked* like Elijah; he *sounded* like him. Elijah had called for the leaders of Israel to repent of their idolatry and return to the Lord before it was too late. When John started preaching to anyone in shouting distance, this was his message: "Repent! For the kingdom of heaven is near" (v. 2).

The word "repent," in biblical language, means to turn around. It means to change our minds and change our ways. It means to turn away from selfishness and idolatry so we can turn toward God and experience forgiveness and right living. We demonstrate the reality of repentance through the positive changes in the way we live and relate to others. Jesus reflected the same thought in his challenge for potential followers to "bring forth fruit worthy of repentance" (v. 8, cp. Matt. 7:16, 20).

John's fervent message was fueled by his belief that the kingdom of heaven had come near, that God was close by

and doing something new. When the gospel writers talked about the "kingdom of heaven" or the "kingdom of God," they were referring to the rule or reign of God. They were certain that God rules whether we like it or not, whether we believe it or not. They also believed people can choose whether to live obediently and trustfully as God's subjects.

John's preaching took on a special urgency because he believed the Messiah was coming and would soon be revealed. "I baptize you with water for repentance," he said, "but one who is more powerful than I is coming after me; I am not worthy to carry his sandals. He will baptize you with the Holy Spirit and fire" (v. 11). [**Spirit and fire**]

Through Jesus, God was about to show the world just what the kingdom was all about – what it truly meant to know God and to be known, to love God and to experience

Spirit and fire: While Matt. 3:11 and Luke 3:16 have John say that the Messiah would baptize with the Spirit and with fire, parallel passages in Mark 1:8 and Acts 1:5, 11:16 omit the word "fire."

Why?

Mark's account was primarily focused on Jesus rather than John, and so omits John's fiery warnings about judgment. Luke includes John's reference to fire along with the Spirit in his gospel, but when writing Acts 1:5 and 11:16, Luke may have wanted to separate the two so he could focus on the symbolic "tongues of fire" that accompanied the inrushing of the Spirit, rather than the aspect of judgment more basic to John's message in Luke 3:16-17.

God's love. The coming of Christ would also set in motion a process of judgment. To those who accepted him, Jesus would become a stepping-stone to the kingdom. To those who rejected him, Jesus would become a stumbling block they couldn't get past.

Unlike much of today's feel-good preaching, John's sermons majored on judgment, with language that was as shocking and colorful as his appearance. He used strong words and striking images to declare the coming danger, directing his harshest criticism toward those who considered themselves to be the most religious. John called the Pharisees and Sadducees a "brood of vipers" and urged them to repent. He warned of approaching destruction if they did not produce some proof of repentance (vv. 7-12).

We can't help but note John's graphic imagery: he pictured the most "righteous" people around as a den of snakes, squirming away from imminent danger. He spoke of God raising up faithful children from river rocks. He conjured the image of a whistling ax slicing into the roots of impressive but unfruitful trees, clearing them out so truly repentant persons might take their place. He called to mind a farmer's winnowing fork throwing threshed grain into the air to separate it from useless chaff.

Why would people from Hebron to Nazareth come trotting out into the desert to hear a sermon like that? Because they were curious? Because they were afraid? Or because they knew it was time for a change?

The ax and the winnowing fork were images of change, of clearing out the old and bringing in the new. They also pointed to both danger and hope. While they threatened destruction to those who rejected the message, they also promised the possibility of grace and a future to those who were ready for it.

John called for people to repent, and that's essentially what "repent" means: to change, to turn away from the crooked road that leads to destruction, and to turn toward the path of life.

Some people don't like change. Herod Antipas didn't like change, and his wife Herodias liked it even less, and so they took John's head off and served it up on a platter (Matthew 14). They were happy with the *status quo*. They did not want anyone threatening their security or their self-image. But multitudes of others came out to hear

John preach because they were looking for change, and John dared to speak of what change requires.

Many people resist change. The prospect of changing jobs, houses, schools, or churches can cause all sorts of alarms to go off in our heads. And the hardest change to make is precisely the one that takes place right there – in our heads. The hardest change to make is a change in our self-image, a change in the way we think, a change in our personal behavior, a change in our lifestyle. Any good psychologist will affirm that change is hard.

People cannot begin to change unless they first believe in the possibility of change. This was John's message. Everything about John, from his strange appearance to his shocking sermons, was different. That difference in John symbolized the truth that we can also be different.

John the Baptizer
(v. 6)

John had a very special way of demonstrating that change to people: he baptized them. John's baptism was no quiet ceremony in an elevated sanctum where quiet organ music played in the background. It had little resemblance to the carefully orchestrated lustrations by which Jewish proselytes or Essene devotees baptized themselves.

This was something radical, something with an edge. This was Weird John standing waist-deep in the Jordan River, taking repentant sinners by the scruff of the neck and dousing them in the muddy water as an unforgettable reminder that, through repentance, their lives had changed forever.

Could our lives benefit from some changes? What changes do we need most?

The Hardest Question
Why did John baptize?

Why did John practice baptism as a sign of repentance? Many scholars presume that John became an adherent of baptism from his conjectured association with the Essenes, a strict sect within Judaism. Some Essenes lived in wilderness areas such as the desert village of Qumran, while others lived in towns but made periodic retreats to the desert. They taught the importance of regular confession and frequent ablutions to ensure ritual purity.

These ceremonies may have been based on the purification rituals of Leviticus 15, or on Old Testament references to washing as a symbol of confession and forgiveness (see Ps. 51:7, Isa. 1:16, Jer. 4:14). Both John and the Essenes emphasized, however, that washing in water was ineffective apart from true repentance.

Those who came to John for baptism were more likely to have been familiar with Jewish practices that involved ritual immersion in special pools as a means of restoring ritual purity. How would these relate to John's baptism?

We note, first, that neither Luke nor the other gospels describe the precise way that John performed baptisms. The Greek word *baptizō* means "to immerse" or "to dip," and the reference to Jesus "coming up out of the water" after his baptism (Mark 1:10) is often taken to suggest baptism by immersion. The phrase could have meant nothing more than walking up to the riverbank from the water, but Paul's later references to baptism as a symbol of death and burial (Rom. 6:1-3) suggest that early believers were immersed completely in water.

This would have been in keeping with first-century Jewish practices relative to maintaining ritual purity. One means that archaeologists have of distinguishing predominantly Jewish villages from Gentile neighborhoods is the presence of ritual pools called *miqvōt* (the singular form is *miqveh*). These pools were dug into the ground, with steps for entry and exit, and coated with plaster to keep the water from seeping out.

Water in the pools had to be "natural," taken from a spring or collected from rainwater. An ideal pool would be fed by a spring and fitted with an overflow, so the water was moving and stayed fresh.

Any number of ordinary things could make a person ritually unclean: entering a Gentile's home, touching something dead, having a menstrual period, engaging in intercourse, and a variety of other ordinary occurrences. To participate in Sabbath observances, enter the temple,

or be fully accepted in the community, one could regain ritual purity through immersion in a *miqveh*, river, or lake, and then waiting for sundown.

While this seems similar in some ways to John's baptism, Richard B. Vinson points to three important differences:

1. In Jewish practice, the ritual was a private act: one submerged himself or herself in water, then waited for sundown to be considered ritually pure. With John's baptism, John administered the baptism in broad daylight as a public declaration of repentance.
2. Jewish immersions were repeated events, practiced whenever one became ritually unclean. John's baptism, however, was presumably a one-time event: people traveled to meet John as if on a pilgrimage, expressed repentance, and were baptized.
3. Jewish baptism dealt mainly with ritual impurities but not with inward sin, which could only be atoned through sacrifices at the temple. "But John claimed that his baptism not only cleansed, but atoned; that is, it not only took away ritual impurities, but also the effects of sin."

(*The Gospel of Luke*, Smyth & Helwys Bible Commentary [Smyth & Helwys, 2008], 89-90)

Thus, while Jewish ablutions were periodic acts designed to restore ritual purity and ensure participation in the religious community, John's baptism symbolized a change of life in which one repented of sin, received forgiveness, and demonstrated internal transformation by bearing the "fruits of repentance."

In our day, adult church members sometimes express a desire to be re-baptized, especially when they come back to the church after a period away. Sometimes they explain that they did not understand what they were doing when they were baptized as children. Do you think John would grant their request?

Third Sunday of Advent

First Reading
Isaiah 35*

When Sorrow Flees

The wilderness and the dry land shall be glad, the desert shall rejoice and blossom … (Isa. 35:1a)

When moments of joy come into your life, how do you express them? Do you dance? Laugh? Sing? Do you clap your hands or pump your fists like a basketball player who has hit the winning shot in overtime, or a golfer who sinks a long putt?

Joy finds expression in many ways, from quiet smiles to exuberant activity. Today's text speaks of euphoric joy that calls for a jubilant response to God's delivering power.

Many churches celebrate Advent through a progression of themes from hope to peace to joy and love. The third Sunday of Advent is sometimes called "Gaudete Sunday" because *gaudete*, Latin for "rejoice," is the first word in the Roman Catholic mass for the day.

Today's text is just that, a call to rejoice, directed to a bedraggled people who were clinging to their last shreds of hope. Despite their woeful situation, it promised a day when the desert would bloom and the lame would dance.

Isaiah 35 should be read with an awareness of the previous chapter, with ch. 34 being the yin to ch. 35's yang. Isaiah 34 is a dark picture of desolation for Edom,

Israel's unfriendly southern neighbor, preceding a bright image of redemption for Israel.

Israel's tradition held that the Israelites and Edomites were descended from the twin brothers Jacob and Esau, and the prophets often referenced that tradition in discussing the fates of Israel and Edom (see also Ezekiel 35–36 and Malachi 1). [**The text in context**]

A desert that blooms
(vv. 1-2)

When things are going so badly that life could hardly get worse, it may seem that the only hope is for a wholesale change. Sometimes that leads to social or political revolution within a country. When the oppressor is a foreign power with a clearly superior military advantage, however, revolution is risky.

King Hezekiah of Judah learned that lesson when he revolted against Assyria's King Sennacherib (c. 705–701 BCE), who ravaged the land and besieged Jerusalem. King Jehoiakim learned it when he rebelled against the

---

The text in context: Isaiah 35 can be seen as part of a larger section (chs. 13–35) that deals with Yahweh's judgment on the nations, and a smaller unit (chs. 28–35) focused around six combination woe-and-salvation oracles related to Judah's proud and misguided leaders, the sinful people of Israel, and the oppressive Assyrians.

Chapters 34–35 function as a unit in which ch. 34 could portray God's victory over the nations that oppress Israel (symbolized by Edom), while ch. 35 describes a new future for Zion that is similar, though not identical, to the peaceable kingdom of ch. 11.

Though earlier parts of the section focus on the Assyrians, Judah's eighth-century nemesis, ch. 34's obvious antipathy toward Edom fits better in the context of exile, after the Edomites aided the Babylonians in sacking Jerusalem.

Thus, while some commentators argue that chs. 34–35 should be read in relation to Hezekiah's revolt (705–701 BCE), most critical scholars believe they derive from the exilic period and serve as an introduction to what is often called "Second Isaiah" (chs. 40–65), with chs. 36–39 (a large narrative block taken almost verbatim from 2 Kgs. 18:13–20:19) having been inserted at some point.

A portion of this text, Isaiah 35:4-7a, also appears as a reading for Proper 18 in Year B.

Babylonians in 601 BCE and died when Nebuchadnezzar conquered Jerusalem three years later. Babylonian domination grew over the next few years, with waves of Hebrew captives being taken into exile until King Nebuchadnezzar's forces leveled the city of Jerusalem and destroyed the temple in 587, carrying even more into exile.

That dark period of ethnic homelessness may be reflected in the background of today's text, with the Edomites – some of whom reportedly aided the Babylonians in destroying Jerusalem – serving as an emblem for all of Israel's enemies.

Isaiah 34 depicts a slaughter of "all the nations" outside of Israel, with special attention given to Edom. The chapter is filled with imagery of desiccation, an unfolding picture of Edom's fields and flora becoming parched as water sources dry up and once-fertile land enters a period of empty desolation.

Chapter 35 portrays a beautifully opposite future for Israel, promising life instead of death. Note the contrasts: in Edom, streams would turn to pitch (34:9), while in Israel, fresh streams would appear in the desert (35:6). Only thorns and thistles would grow in Edom (34:13a),

while Israel would see reeds and rushes sprout beside pools of water (35:7). Edom would become a haunt of jackals and demons (34:13b-14), while Israel would become lush and free of predators (35:9). No one could pass through Edom (34:10), but a "highway of holiness" would bring the ransomed home to Israel (35:10).

"The desert shall rejoice and blossom," Isaiah said, "like the crocus it shall blossom abundantly, and rejoice with joy and singing" (vv. 1b-2a). Crocuses are prolific bloomers that can thrive in habitats from meadowlands to tundra and even desert lands.

In 33:9, the prophet claimed that the typically fertile areas of Lebanon, Sharon, Bashan, and Carmel had withered away. Now he names Lebanon, Carmel, and Sharon as prime examples of the land's revitalization due to the presence and activity of God. Isaiah declared that in the "glory" of Lebanon and the "majesty" of Carmel, "they shall see the glory of the LORD, the majesty of our God" (v. 2).

Carmel, often referred to as "Mount Carmel," is not a single peak but a long ridge near the Mediterranean coast, just north of the fertile plain known as Sharon, which extends inland from Mount Carmel in the north to Joppa

The difference water makes: Jericho, often billed as the world's oldest continuing city, sits in the middle of a dry and barren wilderness, but the presence of a single strong spring makes it a fruitful oasis that can support many people. The picture above, taken from atop the *tel* of ancient Jericho with the Dead Sea and the barren mountains of Moab appearing faintly in the background, shows the difference that one strong spring can make. The source of the spring is at the base of the *tel*, just below the field of view in the photo.

(now the southern part of Tel Aviv-Jaffo) in the south. Parts of the plain are naturally fertile, though much of it is sandy and suitable mainly for pastureland (1 Chron. 27:29). Isaiah saw it as a place of great beauty (35:2, 65:10).

The power of water in a dry land is obvious to anyone who has ever flown over the southwestern U.S., where giant green circles of farmland or lush fairways of golf courses sit amid a barren landscape.

Ancient travelers in Israel's environs would have seen the wonder of places such as Jericho, where a single spring can turn desert land into an oasis. [**The difference water makes**]

Sufferers who rejoice
(vv. 3-7)

In vv. 3-6a, Isaiah's imagery shifts from a transformed landscape to people who need a similar transformation. With striking imperative verbs, he offered encouragement to his hearers and challenged them to pass on their hopeful confidence to others. The redeemed should actively "strengthen the weak hands and make firm the feeble knees," inspiring others to be strong and not fear (vv. 3-4a).

The prophet went on to call forth an image of God deleting what is evil and opening the door to a new world in which the blind and weak would leap for joy at God's salvation, introducing an era in which those who once faced physical limitations would dance with joy in praise to God: "Tell those who panic, be strong! Do not fear! Look, your God comes to avenge! With divine retribution he comes to deliver you" (vv. 4b-6a, NET).

With vv. 6b-7, Isaiah returned to his overriding image of a land that is not just renewed to its former state, but more verdant than ever before. "Waters shall break forth in the wilderness," he said, "and streams in the desert" (v. 6b).

The "burning sand" of v. 7 may describe a desert mirage in which shimmering heat waves create the image of water. In God's new day, visions of desert lakes would become real, and the former wilderness haunts of wild jackals would give way to land so saturated that it supported tall grass, reeds, and rushes.

The NRSV's use of the word "swamp" is an unfortunate translation, obscuring the positive image with one that most readers would find unappealing, as we think of a swamp as an unpleasant place crawling with alligators, snakes, and dangerous insects. There is no word for "swamp" in the text,

which says that the former lairs or "resting places" of jackals will sprout lush plants that normally grow only in water-fed wetlands, usually near riverbanks.

A highway to Zion
(vv. 8-10)

Isaiah's paean to God's restoration of Israel concludes by describing a highway for redeemed pilgrims to use as they return through the transformed desert on their way to Jerusalem. While we may call our roads expressways or parkways, this road would be called "the Holy Way," a limited-access road where the toll would be paid by divine grace and only the righteous could pass.

Those who would follow the holy highway, furthermore, would be perfectly safe. Only the righteous would be there, and none of them would need to fear lions or other predators that could make travel by foot a dangerous enterprise. The wild beasts who had previously terrorized the way might be symbolic of the Edomites, who had formerly controlled the southern highway leading from the Negev to Jerusalem. [**Righteous fools**]

Isaiah envisioned a day when "the ransomed of the LORD" would return to Zion amid songs of everlasting joy. Just as desolation would depart from the land and

---

Righteous fools? Interestingly enough, v. 8 says "no traveler, not even fools, shall go astray" before insisting that the road would harbor no dangers, for only "the redeemed shall walk there" (v. 9).

This translation, from the NRSV, offers the appealing notion that God cares for those who are intellectually challenged, who could be counted among the righteous. The HCSB takes a similar approach, rendering the phrase "Even the fool will not go astray."

A problem with this translation is that the various Hebrew words typically translated as "fool" nearly always describe one who is morally corrupt rather than mentally deficient. Thus, instead of saying that even mentally handicapped persons cannot wander off the path, an optional reading is that morally corrupt people cannot stray onto it. This reading is followed by the NET ("fools will not stray into it") and the NIV ("wicked fools shall not go about on it").

Whether the Holy Way is safe *for* the mentally challenged or safe *from* the foolishly corrupt, the point is the same: it is a secure path where pilgrims can rest easy while journeying toward their spiritual home.

the wicked would be barred from the Holy Way, he said, "sorrow and sighing shall flee away" (v. 10, cp. 65:19). The scene echoes Isa. 25:8, a promise that God will wipe away all tears, an image that reappears much later in Rev. 7:17 and 21:4.

This image of a secure freeway by which pilgrims could joyfully sing their way toward Jerusalem was so appealing that the same promise appears again in Isa. 51:11.

The question we must ask about this text is whether the prophet spoke in metaphoric hyperbole – wildly exaggerating the change in fortunes of the exiles as they returned to Jerusalem – or whether he was thinking eschatologically, as in the hopeful prophecies of 2:1-5 and 11:1-10.

If we assume an exilic setting, it's likely that the prophet had in mind the exiles' return to Jerusalem along a highway not unlike that spoken of in Isa. 62:10, and that he used the metaphor of a transformed landscape as a hopeful image of a better future. Many Hebrews did return from exile to Jerusalem, but it was not through a transformed desert bordered by flowers and fruit. The return to the ruined city was characterized more by trouble than by everlasting joy. The ultimate fulfillment of Isaiah's prophecy is yet to come.

What are modern readers to make of this prophetic and poetic call for praise to God?

We don't have to be captive in a foreign land to feel restricted or in bondage to circumstances that can make life burdensome or hard. We don't have to live in a desert to experience such spiritual desiccation that we wonder if we'll ever sense God's presence again.

None of us have been threatened by Edomites, but many continue to be oppressed by those whose racist, homophobic, self-serving, and outright boorish behavior puts them at odds with God, even though some of them claim their attitudes are biblical.

Are these situations likely to change? Not without the kind of intervention that could only be divine. Still, whether we look toward the return of Christ or a new life in heaven, Isaiah points to a day when joy abounds and all "sorrow and sighing shall flee away."

And what makes that hope possible? The coming of Jesus. Remembering that is what Advent is all about.

The Hardest Question
Where do chs. 34–35 of Isaiah belong?

A major question relative to these two chapters has to do with the time frame to which they belong. Should they be read in the context of Hezekiah's revolt in the last years of the eighth century BCE, or in the context of the exile and return, more than 150 years later?

Gary V. Smith, writing in the conservative New American Commentary, argues that chs. 30–33 and 36–39 relate to Hezekiah's troubles in 705–701 BCE, which he sees as the likely setting for the eschatological prophesies of chs. 34–35. He acknowledges, however, that neither chapter contains any internal historical information, and they could have been composed at any time of national crisis (*Isaiah 1-39*, the New American Commentary [B&H Publishing, 2007], 467-69).

Some scholars believe chs. 34–35 should be seen as beginning the second part of the Isaiah corpus (chs. 40–66). Isaiah 40–55 is typically seen as having been written by a later prophet who spoke in the spirit of Isaiah to the people who lived in exile during the mid-sixth century BCE, and chs. 56–66 appear to have been written in the context of the exiles' return to Jerusalem and the surrounding area.

Writing in the old Broadman Bible Commentary, Page H. Kelley argued that chs. 34–35 fit best with the latter part of the book, noting that "affinity in vocabulary, literary form, and theological content between the two sections is unmistakable, although it is difficult to explain how they became separated." Kelley lists specific parallels between chs. 34–35 and 40–66 (*Proverbs-Isaiah*, The Broadman Bible Commentary [Broadman Press, 1971], 286, 288-89).

Other writers think of the text as a redactional bridge between the work of Isaiah of Jerusalem and Isaiah of the exile. Patricia Tull notes a similar attitude toward Edom in the exilic books of Ezekiel (chs. 35–36) and Obadiah, and speaks of chs. 34–35 as a "hinge passage" between the two main sections of Isaiah (*Isaiah 1–39*, Smyth & Helwys Bible Commentary [Smyth & Helwys, 2010], 503).

A common suggestion is that chs. 34–35 were separated from chs. 40–66 when an editor inserted the supplementary history of chs. 36–39, which was lifted directly from 2 Kgs. 18:13–20:19 and tweaked to emphasize Isaiah's role. One of the Dead Sea Scrolls, known as IQIsᵃ, has three blank lines after ch. 33, suggesting that there was a time when ch. 34 was understood as beginning a new section of the work.

While multi-volume commentaries on Isaiah typically deal with chs. 1–39 and chs. 40–66, John D.W. Watts' two-volume Word Biblical Commentary consists of *Isaiah 1–33* (1985) and *Isaiah 34–66* (1987), indicating his belief that chs. 34–35 belong with the latter section.

Readers who attribute the whole of Isaiah to a single author would not be troubled by these issues, but those who acknowledge that the book speaks to three widely divergent time periods will have more concern for the setting.

If we regard the text's current position between chs. 30–33 and 36–39 as the primary clue, we would read it as having been written during the stressful time of Hezekiah's revolt following the death of the Assyrian king Sargon II in 705 BCE and the ascendancy of his son Sennacherib, whose power was yet unproven. During this time, Hezekiah had high but unfounded hopes that Egypt would come to his aid. A major problem with reading chs. 34–35 in this context is their primary emphasis on Edom

as an arch enemy at a time Edom was not a major player on the international scene.

If we regard the material from 2 Kgs. 18:13–20:19 in Isaiah 36–39 as an obvious insertion and couple the text with chs. 40–66, the presence of Edom is more understandable. The books of Kings and Chronicles do not mention Edom in their accounts of Judah's defeat by the Babylonians, but Obadiah's taunt songs against Edom assert that the Edomites allied with the Babylonians, joining in the sacking of Jerusalem and preventing survivors from escaping (Obad. 10-14). Obadiah specifically referred to Edom as "Esau" (vv. 6, 18-19, 21) and decried Edom's "slaughter and violence done to your brother Jacob" (v. 10).

The prophet Malachi echoed a similar refrain, contending that God loved Israel but hated Esau/Edom (Mal. 1:1-5). Even though Edom had long ceased to exist as a national power, the Edomites lived on in Israel's memory as back-stabbing brothers and despised rivals, an effective figure for evil nations and a perfect foil for the prophets' insistence that God would judge the wicked (symbolized by Edom/Esau) and save the righteous remnant of Israel/Jacob.

Third Sunday of Advent

Second Reading
Psalm 146*

A Hallelujah Chorus

I will praise the LORD as long as I live; I will sing praises to my God all my life long. (Ps. 146:2)

It's not uncommon, especially in the comics, to see a depiction of someone who has sought out a guru living on a mountaintop in hopes of finding the meaning of life. A quick Google search turns up a page full of them.

Imagine the guru responding: "The meaning of life? Gee, that's kind of a toughie … ," or "I don't know: the computers are down." A more flippant guru might answer: "The meaning of life? You do the Hokey Pokey and you turn yourself around: that's what it's all about."

One of my favorite cartoons has the guru saying "If I knew the meaning of life, do you think I'd be sitting here on top of a mountain?"

What *does* it take to live a meaningful and happy life? The author of Psalm 146 believed he knew the answer.

An invitation to praise
(vv. 1-2)

Psalm 146 is the prayer of an individual who has experienced divine aid and who desires to give public testimony of God's help through corporate worship. We don't know what his or her problems had been, and that's good: the generic nature of the psalm allows us to incorporate it more easily in our own praise and worship on troubled days. [Hallelujah psalms]

The poet's praise is unadulterated. In the first two verses, he skillfully uses repetition to intensify words of adulation. He begins by calling the congregation to praise the Lord, then immediately calls himself to offer praise: "Praise the LORD! Praise the LORD, O my soul!" (v. 1).

"O my soul" translates the Hebrew word *nafshî*, from the noun *nefesh*. The Hebrews did not share the Greek concept of a soul that was separate from the body. The concept of a *nefesh* refers to one's innermost being or truest self. So, the psalmist challenges himself to offer praise from the deepest part of who he is.

The psalmist then moves to a declaration that he will not only praise God *with* all his life, but also *for* all his life: "I will praise the LORD as long as I live; I will sing praises to my God all my life long" (v. 2).

Having used the same word for "praise" (*halal*) in the first three lines of his invitation, the psalmist switches in the last line to a special word for singing praise (*zamar*). "I will sing praises to my God all my life long," he says – literally, "in all of my continuing." The psalmist's personal praise serves as a public challenge for the worshiping congregation to join him in song.

The psalmist's invitation to praise prompts us to recall the many things for which we can give praise to God – and it also reminds us how our own testimonies of praise may encourage others to trust in God and to sing hallelujahs of their own.

> **Hallelujah psalms:** The last five songs of the psalter, including today's text, are all hymns of praise, and they all share the same beginning and ending: the Hebrew word *halelu-yah*. The compound word is straightforward, meaning "Praise Yah!" ("Yah" was a common abbreviation for "Yahweh"). So, whenever we say "Hallelujah!" we are not only speaking Hebrew, but also using the personal name God revealed to Israel.

This joyful text also appears as a reading for Proper Sundays 18, 26, and 27 of Year B, and for Proper 5 and 21 in Year C.

An invitation to trust
(vv. 3-4)

Why should we worship God? The psalmist argues that we turn to God because there is no other source of sure and lasting help – especially in other humans, even royal ones. A few "royal psalms" offer both praise and prayer for the king, but the poet advises against putting too much trust in royalty or in other mortal beings, "in whom there is no help" (v. 3). Humans may have great plans and good intentions, but they all have at least one failing in common: they die (v. 4).

Given the reference to "princes," we wonder if the psalmist was writing in the aftermath of a popular king's death. Many were doubtless dejected, for example, when young King Josiah, who had followed the teachings of Deuteronomy to institute many cultic reforms, was killed in an unwise conflict with Pharaoh Neco of Egypt. Prophets and others had hoped Josiah's reforms would lead to a national revival and encourage God to keep the nation safe despite the growing power of Babylon. With Josiah's death, hope faded.

The observation that everyone dies (v. 4) may provide a clue to the psalmist's personal experience. Perhaps someone he loved or leaned on for support had died, and he had known the feeling of abandonment that comes when that happens. Grief-stricken persons often have a vague sense of anger at their loved ones for dying and leaving them. Human relationships can be wonderful and supportive, and none of us could enjoy life without them. But human support is always limited by human finitude. Those who are wise also rely on the one source of help whose being has no bounds.

Jeremiah knew this truth. He declared that those who trust in mortals alone would be like lonely shrubs in the desert, experiencing the curse of dry hearts and empty lives. On the other hand, he believed that people who put their ultimate trust in God would be like trees in the fruitful community of an eternal oasis (Jer. 17:5-8).

Most of us have experienced something like that. Maybe someone we loved and depended on has died. Or maybe someone just left us, essentially becoming dead to us. We've known what it is like to love someone and to lose them. We've learned that we need the support of one who will never leave us or forsake us, even by death, and we can rejoice that God is present and willing to supply that need.

A celebration of deliverance
(vv. 5-9)

In vv. 5-9, the worshiper shows the contrast between finite humans and the infinite God. Those who put their trust in God experience happiness, he says: "Happy are those whose help is the God of Jacob, whose help is in the LORD their God" (v. 5). [**Happiness**]

And why does the psalmist believe Yahweh is so trustworthy as to bring happiness? Because it is God who created the great triad of heaven, earth, and sea – and all that lives within them (v. 6). If God is the author of life, then God can be trusted to keep faith with those who live.

Yahweh's credibility is seen not only in God's *creation*, but also in God's *relations* with humankind. In vv. 7-9, the poet reminds his hearers of God's continual kindness toward his people. Yahweh gives justice to the oppressed and food to the hungry, sets prisoners free, and gives sight to the blind. The LORD lifts up those who are bowed down by the burdens of life. Yahweh cares for those who cannot help themselves. In ancient society, the most helpless people were those who had no family to support them: immigrants, orphans, and widows. God has the power to bless the way of the righteous and to ruin the plans of the wicked.

The themes mentioned here are echoed in Isa. 61:1, often interpreted as a description of the coming messiah: "The Spirit of the Lord God is upon me, because the Lord has anointed me; he has sent me to bring good news to the oppressed, to bind up the brokenhearted, to proclaim liberty to the captives and release to the prisoners ..."

Happiness: The word translated as "happy" in v. 5 is *'ashrê*, a plural construct form that is usually translated "happiness" or "blessedness." It comes from a root that means "to go straight," or "to advance." Those who put their hope in Yahweh do not wander about in a morass of uncertainty, but go forward in joyful trust.

We find a similar situation in Jesus' "Beatitudes" of Matthew 5. Though most translations have "Blessed" are the poor in spirit ... blessed are those who mourn ...," etc., the word translated as "blessed" is *makarios*, which could also mean "happy," as rendered in the Good News translation.

Jesus, apparently familiar with this text, took it as his own mission statement in his first sermon at the Capernaum synagogue (Luke 4:18).

A problem with reading and interpreting vv. 7-9 is the reality that many people remain oppressed, needy, blind, or imprisoned, while wicked people may prosper and not face ruin.

The psalm is no promise that everyone who looks to God will be delivered from trouble and restored to freedom, health, or financial security – or that every evildoer will get a comeuppance in this world.

Still, for persons who find themselves downtrodden or in need, the psalm offers hope for the ongoing presence and comfort of God. In addition, the psalm is a reminder that those who worship God and understand God's call to love their neighbors may become the instrument of God's care to those in need.

A doxology for eternity
(v. 10)

The poet has offered praise to Yahweh as the only one who gives lasting help, as Israel's true and eternal king. While earthly rulers are temporary, "the LORD will reign forever" over countless generations of his people (v. 10).

Hebrews living during the Old Testament period did not have the same concept of eternal life in heaven that became popular by New Testament times. For them, "forever" implied an unending presence of God's special people on earth.

The psalmist concludes in the same way he began, "*halelu-yah* – Praise the LORD!" We can imagine that the congregation might have joined him in this final "Hallelujah!"

The depth of feeling in this psalm suggests that the psalmist had personal experience with the hard side of life. He knew what it was like to be pressed down by trials and abandoned by those who had promised help. Yet, the testimony of this psalm is that he found God to be present in the darkness, perhaps even in the valley of the shadow of death.

His words continue to offer comfort to the hurting, assurance that Yahweh is personally concerned – *especially* concerned – for those who suffer, and that even in our suffering we can praise God as we discover that praise itself brings strength and courage to face another day.

The Hardest Question
Does the Bible promise deliverance from every trial?

A primary problem in interpreting texts such as the one for today, whether in the psalms, the prophets, or the words of Christ, is that their apparently confident claims don't always come true. Many people remain poor and oppressed throughout their lives. There are widows, orphans, and homeless persons who never rise above poverty level. Sometimes justice is not done. People who trust in God don't always experience happiness.

Is the promise of God's help nothing but smoke, or do we fail to understand how the promise is to be understood?

The ancient Hebrews expected a messiah to set all things right, but Jesus' agenda did not include healing for every sick person or earthly wealth for all who were poor. Jesus himself acknowledged that the poor would always be among us (Matt. 26:11). Human society on its own will never overcome its proclivity for social injustice. Thus, we must look for God's help in an *internal* sense, and an *eternal* one. Those who are poor – those who trust in God, at least – may be assured that their place in eternity will be much kinder than their fate on earth. Jesus pointed this out in the parable of the rich man and Lazarus (Luke 16:19-31).

But is there hope for this life, for light in the present darkness? Yes, of course. The presence of God can bring inner serenity even in the bleakest of human circumstances. Those who trust in God may find spiritual strength to endure the most difficult days. In fact, many people have discovered that it is in those places – when life has dealt its harshest cards – that God's presence seems most real.

I still remember, as a teenager, hearing a guest speaker say, "I didn't realize that God was all I needed until God was all I had." Many of us have learned to resonate with that. As long as things are going well, we think of ourselves as self-sufficient, and give little attention to God. But, in times of trauma or tragedy or deep disappointment, we, like the psalmist, are more likely to turn to God. In doing so, we may have experienced the kind of blessing in disguise that led Jesus to say: "Blessed are you who are poor … who hunger now … who weep" (Luke 6:20-21).

Outward circumstances may argue otherwise, but those who put their trust in God may experience genuine blessings both internal and eternal.

Third Sunday of Advent

Second Reading
Luke 1:39-55*

Fetal Attraction

When Elizabeth heard Mary's greeting, the child leaped in her womb. (Luke 1:41a)

It's hard to imagine – even to begin to imagine – what it must have been like when two of the world's most unlikely pregnant women first embraced each other in a familial reunion. The most obviously expectant one was Elizabeth, who had long been childless and was getting on in years (Luke 1:7), but who had surprisingly conceived after her dumbstruck husband Zechariah had been visited by the angel Gabriel (1:8-20).

Hurrying to meet Elizabeth was her niece Mary, barely more than a child, who had become pregnant in even more miraculous fashion. Gabriel had visited her, too, declaring that she had been chosen to bear a son who would be called the Son of God – while she remained a virgin (1:26-35). The boy was to be named Jesus (*yeshua*), which means something akin to "Yahweh saves."

The angel had told Elizabeth's husband that their son, to be named John, would become a great man for God, in the spirit and power of Elijah (1:14-17). He later told the skeptical Mary about Elizabeth's pregnancy as a way of encouraging her to believe, because "nothing will be impossible for God" (1:36-37).

Just try, then, to imagine the joyous reunion of two women at such different stages of life, but both carrying miracle babies.

A joyful journey
(vv. 39-40)

To understand the absolute joy experienced by the two women – and the impact their children could have – we must remember that for several hundred years, messianic expectations had been growing among the Hebrews. As a subservient people ruled by outsiders, many Jews longed for the birth of a messiah who would deliver Israel from the Romans and set up a new order with Israel in a favored position.

Neither Mary nor Elizabeth yet understood that Jesus was to be a radically different kind of messiah than expected in popular thought, but their spiritual insight was clear enough to perceive that God was about to use their sons to shake up the world.

Luke gives the impression that Mary went to visit Elizabeth very soon after her encounter with the angel Gabriel, possibly before she experienced any signs of her own pregnancy. The angel had told her about Elizabeth's gravid state as a sign to strengthen Mary's faith. No doubt filled with questions and perhaps anxious for confirmation of the sign, Mary went to visit Elizabeth. Luke tells us, in fact, that she set out "in haste" (v. 39). **[Traveling with Mary]**

On foot or by donkey, a journey of that length over rocky roads would require at least three or four days. It is possible that Mary journeyed in company with a trade caravan or a group of pilgrims to Jerusalem for part of the journey, but when she arrived at Elizabeth's home, she was alone. Works of art often portray Elizabeth running out to meet Mary, but Luke insists that Mary first entered Elizabeth's house, which becomes the setting of their encounter (v. 40).

---

*Luke 1:46b-55 is an alternate reading to Psalm 146 for the third Sunday of Advent in Year A, and is also read on the third and fourth Sundays of Advent in Year B. Luke 1:39-45 is used for the fourth Sunday of Advent in Year C.

Traveling with Mary: Mary's journey to visit Elizabeth leads us to ask a variety of questions. Was her visit motivated by a desire to see that Elizabeth really was pregnant, as a way of confirming news given to her by the angel? Was it an effort to get away from Joseph for a while, so she wouldn't have to explain her pregnancy? Or was it, as some argue, a journey of pure joy, an opportunity for happy sharing between two unlikely mothers-to-be?

It was not typical for a woman to travel alone for long distances, adding to the extraordinary nature of the story. Mary's hometown of Nazareth was located about 20 miles west of the southern end of the Sea of Galilee. It was more than 60 miles north of Jerusalem, near the northern boundary of "the hill country" of Judea, where Elizabeth and Zechariah lived in an unnamed town. Thus, Mary would probably have traveled 70 miles or more. In first-century Jewish culture, young women were typically betrothed in their early teens. Mary's probable youth adds to the surprising nature of the journey.

Luke tells the story by using a quick series of active verbs: Mary "set out," "went with haste," "entered the house," and "greeted Elizabeth." Notice how this also moves the narrative from the more general to the more specific in a spatial sense: Mary went to the hill country, to a village of Judea, to the house, then to Elizabeth (Alan Culpepper, "The Gospel of Luke," *The New Interpreter's Bible IX: Luke, John* [Abingdon Press, 1995], 54).

A prophetic greeting
(vv. 41-45)

Elizabeth appeared to have been startled by Mary's happy greeting. When we are surprised in a good way, we may sense that our heart jumps within us, or we may think our stomach is doing flips. When Elizabeth heard Mary's joyful voice, Luke says, her unborn child "leaped in her womb." Simultaneously (and more significantly), Elizabeth was "filled with the Holy Spirit," who inspired the content of her breathless response to Mary's arrival. The inrushing of the Holy Spirit upon Elizabeth (and apparently her unborn but active infant) fulfills the angel's earlier prophecy that John would be filled with the Holy Spirit "even before his birth" (Luke 1:15).

The text describes Elizabeth and Mary as relatives, but it does not specify their relationship: we know only that Elizabeth is considerably older, perhaps an aunt. Bound by both blood and the common experience of miraculous pregnancies, Mary and Elizabeth also shared the bond of the Holy Spirit's presence within them.

Keep in mind that Mary had come "in haste" after Gabriel's annunciation of Jesus, so the story implies that her pregnancy had just begun. Yet Elizabeth (and apparently the fetal John) perceived that Mary was with child. The reader assumes that the Holy Spirit inspired this perception, in addition to Elizabeth's address to Mary as "the mother of my Lord." There is no indication that the women had communicated previously or that an angelic messenger had prepared Elizabeth for Mary's arrival.

The pronouncements of Elizabeth in vv. 41-45 could be understood as a prophetic oracle, either a longer oracle in four parts, or a series of briefer oracles. Some writers speak of this as the "Song of Elizabeth," and it has some poetic qualities, but these are better explained by its oracular nature.

Elizabeth first spoke to the blessedness of Mary and the child she bore (v. 42). This blessing upon Mary has been understood in Catholic tradition to convey semi-divine status upon Mary, but it simply means "blessed." The Greek word is *'eulogēménē*, the root of our word "eulogy." Elizabeth's "eulogy" was pronounced near the beginning of a life, however, not at the end.

The older woman's words did not impute a state of blessedness to Mary, but they recognized that God had already blessed her. The wording of Elizabeth's joyous proclamation is similar to those pronounced on Jael (Judg. 5:24), and Judith (Jdt. 13:18; Judith is an apocryphal book not found in most Protestant Bibles). In his commentary, Alan Culpepper notes the irony involved: Jael and Judith were praised for their heroism in wielding a weapon, while Mary would experience a stab of pain to her own heart (v. 35; Culpepper, 55).

Elizabeth's second speech asked why "the mother of my Lord" should come to her. Note Luke's emphasis on Elizabeth's humility. "Why has this happened to me?" implies something like "How could this happen to one so unworthy?" (v. 43). Elizabeth had been inspired to know that Mary bore the Messiah – whom she describes as "my Lord" – but she was not jealous. Rather, she was overwhelmed with gratitude that Mary would deign to come and visit her.

Elizabeth's third assertion affirms the connection between Mary's voice and the intrauterine activity of the unborn John, as she insisted that the infant was wiggling for joy to be so close to the newly conceived Jesus (v. 44). Joy is a common theme in the text, as it is for the third Sunday in Advent.

Finally, Elizabeth pronounced a beatitude on Mary (using *makarios*, the same word translated as "blessed" or "happy" in the more famous "Beatitudes" of Matt. 5:1-12). Elizabeth praised Mary's faith in believing the angel's promise.

A special song
(vv. 46-55)

Mary's response to Elizabeth came in the form of a hymn. [**Spontaneous hymns?**] The likelihood of Mary erupting in spontaneous song may seem unlikely to us, but that is the way Luke has fashioned the story, inserting a song of praise that had been attributed to Mary.

The poem falls naturally into two sections, with the first focusing on what God had done for Mary (vv. 46-50) and the second celebrating what God had done for all people (vv. 51-55; see Richard B. Vinson, *Luke*, Smyth & Helwys Bible Commentary [Smyth & Helwys, 2008], 42-43).

The hymn itself is an impressive piece of work. If we are to imagine it really did originate in response to Elizabeth, we would wonder if Mary had rehearsed the song in her mind on the long trip down, or whether the song was inspired by the same Holy Spirit who had moved Elizabeth to perceive Mary's own pregnancy. Parts of the song

---

Birthing lessons? The comment in v. 56 that Mary remained with Elizabeth for about three months (after first learning of her pregnancy when she was in the sixth month) suggests that she may have stayed long enough to see the birth of John.

As a young woman, Mary probably knew little about such things. She had much to learn, but since she was committed to fulfilling God's call, we assume that she took every opportunity to prepare herself for the task.

What do we believe is God's call to us, and what are we doing to prepare for it?

---

are very similar to the Song of Hannah in 1 Sam. 2:1-10. Both songs praise God as one who remembers the faithful, topples the proud, and reverses the fortunes of the poor.

Scholars have often noted that Hannah's song might have been more appropriate for Elizabeth, since those two women conceived long after everyone had assumed that they were barren. Some ancient versions attribute the song to Elizabeth, but the strongest traditions assign it to Mary. [**Birthing lessons**]

The key theme of Mary's song is praise. It lauds God's power, holiness, and mercy toward the faithful (vv. 47-50). It celebrates God's justice and concern for the poor, expressed in the "reversal of fortunes" theme that echoes Hannah's song (vv. 51-53). God could be trusted as reliable and faithful in dealing with Israel, even as God's promises had proven true for Mary and Elizabeth. Following a pattern that grammarians sometimes call the "prophetic perfect," Luke has Mary speak of things yet to come but in the past tense, as if they had already happened. In doing so, the song expresses confidence that God's promises would be fulfilled.

What promises do we associate with God's work in Christ? Do we feel as confident as Mary did?

The Hardest Question
Is Mary's song good news for us?

The hardest question about today's text may not be one of interpretation, but of challenge. Take a close look at Mary's song, which came to be known in church tradition as the "Magnificat" (from the Latin word for "magnify" in the phrase "my soul magnifies the Lord," v. 41).

Spontaneous hymns? Did Mary really respond to Elizabeth's oracular greeting with a song, as in a musical stage production where characters periodically interrupt the dialogue by bursting into song? Does that sound like real life?

Much of Mary's song (in addition to Elizabeth's references to "my Lord") has the ring of Christian confession. It includes snatches of a variety of Old Testament texts from the Septuagint (Greek) translation. Scholars commonly suggest that traditions regarding the meeting of Mary and Elizabeth grew over time and may have been incorporated into the worship of the early church as a hymn.

We typically read (or sing) it joyfully as a proclamation of good news, but should we?

Mary, like Hannah before her, predicts a reversal of fortunes between those who are poor, lowly, and oppressed, and those who are proud, powerful, and rich. Take a second look at vv. 51-53: "He has shown strength with his arm; he has scattered the proud in the thoughts of their hearts. He has brought down the powerful from their thrones, and lifted up the lowly; he has filled the hungry with good things, and sent the rich away empty."

Where do we find ourselves in that double portrait? Are we following in the steps of John's and Jesus' pattern of ministry among the poor and disadvantaged, or are we focused on maintaining or improving our social and financial status?

Richard B. Vinson posed an insightful question: "Luke's Gospel, Mary's God, and Mary's son will not prove easy for me or my readers, or else we are not paying attention. This year Americans gave less to the poor than the year before; in fact, we Americans spent more on dog food, or chewing gum, or many other single convenience items, than we gave to the poor. We must face the truth: we are the bad guys in this story we're reading. If God chooses the poor, we are doomed. If God scatters the rich, the proud, and the powerful, we will be dust in the wind" (*Luke*, Smyth & Helwys Bible Commentary [Smyth & Helwys, 2008], 45).

Does this change our reading of Mary's happy hymn? Does it suggest potential changes or challenges for our lives?

Third Reading
James 5:7-20

While You're Waiting …

Be patient, therefore, beloved, until the coming of the Lord. The farmer waits for the precious crop from the earth, being patient with it until it receives the early and the late rains. (Jas. 5:7)

Are you a patient person? Are you always changing lanes while driving, or looking for the shortest checkout line at the grocery store? Do you get ill if someone shows up late for an appointment?

How we handle minor things may be indicative of how we handle larger issues, such as being patient through the years necessary to finish college, to advance in our occupation, or to see a desired relationship develop. Times of illness, misfortune, or disappointment may call for patience rather than a hurried response. **[The text]**

One thing we don't mind waiting for is death: we'd like to wait as long as possible before graduating from this life. We should note, then, that when James encouraged his readers to be patient, what they were waiting for was a departure from this world.

Many early believers fully expected Christ to return within their generation. Based on things Jesus had said, James, Paul, and other disciples promoted the belief. Especially, those who were poor and suffering longed for the coming return of Christ as a day of vindication and restoration. In our text for today, James has words of encouragement for life in the meantime. **[Anticipation]**

Whether we think much about it or not, all of us are in some way waiting for the end of our life. The road we are

The text: The lectionary reading for the day covers only vv. 7-10, a brief call to patience in the midst of a hodgepodge of seemingly random observations and instructions. The brief reading does well for a liturgical reading, and we will focus on those verses, but also continue through the remainder of the chapter.

Anticipation: Early believers had reason to think that Jesus would return in their lifetimes. Matthew, Mark, and Luke all contain a version of what we call the "Little Apocalypse," in which Jesus reportedly talked about the end times and the final judgment. The three evangelists often recorded things differently, but they all held that Jesus concluded the discourse by saying, "I tell you the truth, this generation will certainly not pass away until all these things have happened" (Matt. 24:34, Mark 13:30, Luke 21:32).

We know that things did not turn out as they expected. Christ did not return in glory to bring history to a close in that first century, nor has he done so since. Though many people have sought to "interpret the signs" and predict the time of Jesus' return, the most certain thing Jesus said about his second coming was that we will be surprised, that the day of the Lord would come like a thief in the night (Matt. 24:43; cf. 1 Thess. 5:2).

traveling will have an end, and we all have to decide what we will do with the life that remains to us between now and then. In our text, James offers advice for what to do while we are waiting. In short, he encourages believers to be patient in our attitudes (vv. 7-12), to be faithful in prayer (vv. 13-18), and to be concerned about others (vv. 19-20).

Enduring patience
(vv. 7-12)

After an opening screed against those who pile up riches by oppressing the poor (vv. 1-6), James encouraged his audience – which must have included some of those downtrodden folk – to "Be patient, therefore, beloved, until the coming of the Lord. The farmer waits for the precious crop from the earth, being patient with it until

> **The patience of Job?** Anyone who reads the book of Job will see that he ran out of patience after ch. 2, and immediately set about complaining about his condition and wishing that he could die (ch. 3). We can speak of Job's endurance through trials and his determination to get answers from God, but Job wasn't always patient.

it receives the early and the late rains. You also must be patient. Strengthen your hearts, for the coming of the Lord is near" (vv. 7-9).

James wanted his readers to find hope in the Lord's coming, but he didn't want them to be so consumed with future hopes that they failed to deal with the present. So, he told them to be patient.

He illustrated the need for patience in three ways. Farmers know they can't expect immediate yields from their planting, but patiently await the harvest (vv. 8-9). Prophets suffered in God's behalf, but demonstrated patience and trust in God's ultimate justification (v. 10). Finally, righteous Job suffered more than anyone, but he endured with patience and experienced God's compassion (v. 11).

When we get impatient, we tend to take out our frustrations on others. Perhaps that is why James warned his readers not to "grumble against one another," since Christ's return would be a day of judgment (v. 9).

The patience James promoted is not just a passive "waiting" for the inevitable, but an active confrontation with the struggles of daily life. His words challenge us to sow the seed of faithfulness, as farmers sow their crops; to proclaim the message of God in the face of adversity, as the prophets did; to struggle with the meaning of suffering and work to overcome it, as Job did. The attitude that endures and experiences the blessing of God is not "wimpy waiting," but persistent patience. [**The patience of Job?**]

Since we often show our impatience in hurtful or thoughtless words, James warned against careless speech, thoughtless grumbling, or relying on oaths (v. 12).

Faithful prayer
(vv. 13-18)

Patient people are also called to be faithful people through all the ups and downs of life, especially in prayer.

James first addressed those who were facing difficulties: "Are any among you suffering? They should pray"

(v. 13a). When difficult times come and we have done all we can do to resolve them, we can cry, complain, or call attention to ourselves with a big pity party. Or, we can pray.

James did not endorse a particular type of prayer. He did not say to pray that the suffering will be over, or to pray for acceptance in the face of suffering, or to pray for those who have caused the suffering. The important thing is not *what* we pray, but *that* we pray. In hard times, the presence of God is especially needful, and we seek God's presence through prayer.

Prayer is also appropriate in times of joy, as the many prayers of praise in the book of Psalms attest. James asked, "Are any cheerful? They should sing songs of praise" (v. 13b). Sorrow may quickly drive us to our knees, but when things are going well, prayer may be the last thing that comes to mind.

Earlier, James reminded his readers that every good thing and every generous gift comes from God (1:17). We know the importance of expressing gratitude in response to the generosity of others. We don't send "thank you" cards to God, however: we pray. How often does that happen?

But there are also times of sickness. James' readers lived in a time when good medicine was virtually nonexistent. While folk medicine could be effective for some ills, sickness was often more serious. People routinely sought relief by using magical charms or special oils. James urged his readers to put their trust in God rather than in superstition.

What follows can be difficult to interpret, for James appears to have promised blanket healing: "Are any among you sick? They should call for the elders of the church and have them pray over them, anointing them with oil in the name of the Lord. The prayer of faith will save the sick, and the Lord will raise them up; and anyone who has committed sins will be forgiven" (vv. 14-15).

We know, however, that prayer doesn't always result in physical healing. Many people, even devout people, suffer loss or die despite the most earnest of prayers being offered in their behalf.

Was James wrong, or do we fail to understand him? If James meant to say that the prayer of faith will always save the sick, and yet our prayers don't bring healing, does that mean we have not prayed with sufficient faith? Well-

> **Deep healing:** One could argue that the greatest kind of healing we can experience is the healing of our wounded spirits. God may not always heal our broken bodies, but God can be trusted to heal the broken souls of those who seek divine grace. We recall the assurance found in 1 John: "If we confess our sins, he who is faithful and just will forgive us our sins and cleanse us from all unrighteousness" (1:9).

meaning people sometimes suggest that, but for persons who have already suffered a great loss, the last thing they need is for someone to shame them for a supposed failure of faith.

Perhaps a solution may be found in a closer look at James' terminology. Notice what he says: the prayer of faith "will save the sick, and they will be raised up" (v. 15). This is the vocabulary of eternal salvation and the promise of resurrection at the last day, which is the context of James' larger discussion. It may be that James was not promising a guarantee of physical healing after all, but the assurance of eternal life for those who give themselves into God's care. Note that James concluded the statement with a promise that "anyone who has committed sins will be forgiven." Salvation is the most potent healing of all.

That reminds us of another occasion that calls for prayer: when we have sinned. James' assurance that prayer would lead to forgiveness assumes that the person being prayed for is praying, too. Indeed, he went on to say: "Therefore confess your sins to one another, and pray for one another, so that you may be healed" (v. 16a). **[Deep healing]**

James insisted that "the prayer of the righteous is powerful and effective" (v. 16b). Some people interpret this scripture to mean prayer can get us anything, but we must not overlook the word "righteous." The prayers of the *righteous* are powerful and effective. To be righteous is to seek the will of God. Earlier, James had noted that the elders should anoint persons "in the name of the Lord" (v. 14).

The true prayer of faith is always offered in the context of God's will (cf. 4:15), not our own. James closed the section by calling on the prophet Elijah as an illustration and inspiration. Elijah once prayed that it would not rain, and there was no rain for three and a half years — until Elijah changed his prayer and asked for the drought to be broken (vv. 17-18, cf. 1 Kings 17–18). The reader should remember, however, that Elijah was acting on God's instructions, not his own initiative (1 Kgs. 18:1).

James warned against presumption several times throughout his letter, and he would not have had Christians presume that they could tell God what to do or whom to heal. If we cannot make assumptions about our own life (4:13-15), we can hardly presume to know God's will for others. Still, it is always appropriate to pray for one another. In doing so, we assist each other in our spiritual growth and sense of "connectedness" with God, so that we experience forgiveness. In the mutual confession of sins and in the shared prayers of the church, there is great power indeed.

Loving concern
(vv. 19-20)

James closed his letter by reminding believers not only to be patient and prayerful, but also to care about others. He showed particular concern for those who grew tired of waiting for Christ's return and left the church. He urged believers to care enough about their wandering brothers and sisters to go after them, knowing that "whoever brings back a sinner from wandering will save the sinner's soul from death and will cover a multitude of sin" (vv. 19-20).

We must be careful not to wrongly interpret this as a promise that the one who reclaims a wandering brother or sister obtains a reward of bonus forgiveness points, for example, a bounty paid to cowboys who retrieve lost cattle. It is the errant one who finds renewed forgiveness upon their return and thus is saved from spiritual death. In a sense, this is what James was attempting to do with his entire letter. He saw churches wandering away from their faithfulness to God, and sought by his advice to lead them toward repentance and restoration, to forgiveness and faith.

With this, James comes to the end of his plain-spoken letter to the churches, in which he has encouraged them to get serious about their faith, because following Jesus is serious business.

That thought may lead us to wonder how serious we are about this faith we claim.

The Hardest Question
Who wrote the book of James?

We cannot be dogmatic about the author of this letter, except to say that his mother didn't call him James. His name was really Jacob, a good Hebrew name. Though the Greek form *Iakobos* mirrors the Hebrew, it is always translated into English as "James."

Several men named James appear in the New Testament. A traditional view is that the book was written by James, the younger half-brother of Jesus, who was recognized as the leader of the church in Jerusalem. It is possible that it could have been written by another church leader with the same name, or by someone else who attributed the letter to a more famous person – a common practice during the first century.

The book itself is in the form of a sermonic letter with occasional asides that sound more like wisdom literature. The letter is addressed "to the twelve tribes in the Dispersion" (v. 1). "Dispersion" reflects a technical term (*diaspora*) used to describe those Jews who had been scattered throughout the world during Israel's stormy history. Thus, it is generally thought that the letter was intended as a message to Jewish Christians, many of whom were forced to leave Jerusalem because of persecution. The audience, then, was predominantly Jewish by heritage, probably including few Gentiles. The letter is strongly flavored by Jewish traditions.

If James the brother of Jesus was the author, the date of writing would be no later than the early 60s CE. The Jewish historian Josephus (*Antiquities* XX, ix, 197-203) says that James was stoned to death in the year 62.

In the book of Acts, James, the brother of John, is pictured as a leader of the early church and one who took a mediating position between the Jewish Christians who thought all believers should work to follow the Jewish law (sometimes called "Judaizers"), and those who agreed with Paul that faith was pre-eminent. These themes of faith and works are central in the book of James, because faith, rightly understood, is active. Faith works.

Third Sunday of Advent

Fourth Reading
Matthew 11:2-11

The Real McCoy

When John heard in prison what the Messiah was doing, he sent word by his disciples and said to him,
"Are you the one who is to come, or are we to wait for another?" (Matt. 11:2-3)

Did you ever think you had someone figured out, only to be surprised when they went off on an entirely different tack than you ever expected? Perhaps you've made a new friend at some point, enjoying the many things you had in common. Later, though, you learn things about your friend that are surprising or puzzling. You wonder whether you have been deceived, or if you simply misunderstood – or if you still don't fully understand where they're coming from. Such was the case with John the Baptist and Jesus. [**A new section**]

When John baptized his cousin, he felt led of God to declare that Jesus was "the coming one," the Messiah of God who had been at the heart of Jewish hopes for many years. John expressed this confidence in terms of common messianic expectations that Jesus would bring judgment to the wicked and vindication to the righteous.

"The axe is laid to the root of the trees," he had said, so that all who failed to bear good fruit would be cut down and thrown into the fire (Matt. 3:10). "His winnowing fork is in his hand," John went on, so he could gather in the harvest of good seed while separating the chaff (Matt. 3:12).

John's own testimony suggests that he, like Jesus' own disciples and many others of his day, expected Jesus to position himself as a powerful messiah who would dispense

with the Romans, judge the wicked, and make all things right with the world. Instead, Jesus went around healing people and preaching a gospel that called for repentance but majored on love. In Matthew 5–10, the gospel writer portrays Jesus as a conundrum within his world. No one knew just what to make of him.

A question and an answer
(vv. 2-6)

For this reason, perhaps, Matthew chose to include a question from John the Baptist. Jesus' response speaks to the issue of his identity and his unexpected behavior, pointing to often-overlooked prophecies that spoke of a messiah who was more servant than soldier.

Matthew had reported in 4:12 that John had been imprisoned, though he does not relate the story of John's arrest until ch. 14. There we learn that John had been jailed after daring to publicly castigate Herod Antipas, who ruled over Judea and Samaria, for his immoral lifestyle. [**The Herod brothers**]

The story has all the makings of a soap opera. Herod's brother Philip, who ruled the outlying territories of Iturea and Trachonitis, had married a woman named Herodias, who reportedly lusted for power. Though Philip may have been the most able ruler of the three brothers, he seemed content to rule his quiet provinces. This did not satisfy Herodias, who violated Jewish custom by taking the initiative to divorce Philip, and then marrying his more ambitious brother Antipas. Ultimately, her prodding led Antipas to pressure Rome for the title of king. The gambit

---

A new section: Matt. 11:1 marks a new section in Matthew's gospel. We know this, in part, because of a structural cue. Matthew's structure includes five major sections of Jesus' teachings, each section ending with the phrase "When Jesus had finished … " That phrase is found here, as in 7:28, 13:53, 19:1, and 26:1.

The Herod brothers: "Herod" was a family name shared by Herod Antipas and his two brothers, Phillip and Archelaus. Their father, commonly known as Herod the Great, had ruled as king over all of Palestine, but upon his death the Romans divided the territory between the brothers. Archelaus was given control of the southern territories of Judea, Samaria, and Idumea. He was such a poor and cruel ruler that his territory was later made into a procuratorship and given over to Pontius Pilate. Antipas was given charge of Galilee (an area west of the Sea of Galilee) and Perea (a larger southern territory east of the Jordan River). Their brother Phillip was entrusted with the northern border territories of Iturea and Tracheonitis, also east of the Jordan.

backfired: Antipas was deposed in 39 CE, after which he and Herodias were banished to Gaul.

Matthew's account says that Herod had John arrested after he criticized their ill-conceived marriage, and Herodias later demanded John's head, though Antipas himself appeared less than excited about the execution (Matt. 14:1-12). Josephus, a Jewish historian of the first century, suggested that John's arrest resulted from the paranoid Antipas' fear of John's popularity.

Antipas had tried to silence John by holding him in a rustic wilderness fortress at Machaerus, east of the Dead Sea and as far from everyone else as he could get him. Despite the remote location of his prison, John heard rumors of Jesus' activities from disciples who came to bring provisions and comfort. John expressed confusion about what he heard, sending messengers to ask Jesus if he had been mistaken about his identity.

We note that John never suggested any doubt of Jesus' integrity, for he addressed the question directly to him and anticipated a truthful answer: "Are you the one who is to come, or are we to wait for another?" (v. 3). The word translated "another" means "another of a different kind," suggesting that Jesus' ministry was not what John had expected. Had John been mistaken about who the Messiah was, or what kind of Messiah he was to be? [Luke's version]

Jesus did not answer the question directly, but responded by pointing to "what you hear and see," events that Matthew had recorded in chs. 5–7 (Jesus' teachings) and chs. 8–9 (Jesus' miracles). Jesus' words and his works had fulfilled popular messianic prophecies such as

Isa. 29:18-19, 35:5-6, and 61:1-2. Blind people were gaining sight, lame people were walking, and the poor were hearing good news of the kingdom. Jesus' added comment that lepers were being healed and the dead raised goes beyond even the prophetic hopes (vv. 4-5). Jesus left it to John to connect the dots and conclude that he had no need to look for another: the object of prophetic hopes had arrived.

John's problem was not with Jesus or his actions, but with his perception of Jesus' mission. Jesus had fulfilled many prophecies, but not in the way people expected. In his response, Jesus pronounced a blessing to those who took no offense but accepted him as the kind of messiah he intended to be (v. 6). John was not offended so much as confused: he had failed to understand how the various prophecies complemented each other. [Beatitudes]

While Jesus included the various miracles he had done as witness of his work, at the forefront was his proclamation of hope and joy to the poor and downtrodden. Eduard Schweizer noted that miracles were indeed signs of authority, but for Jesus, "miracles were not the point; what is most important in his ministry is what is least pretentious – his message of love and hope" (*The Good News According to Matthew* [John Knox Press, 1975], 256).

Luke's version: The gospel of Luke includes a parallel account of John's question and Jesus' response (Luke 7:18-23). It is slightly longer, because Matthew tends to abbreviate, while Luke includes a fuller account, with added detail about John's interaction with his disciples and their conversation with Jesus (vv. 18-20), and an editorial note before Jesus' response: "Jesus had just then cured many people of diseases, plagues, and evil spirits, and had given sight to many who were blind" (v. 21).

This gives added emphasis to Jesus' response to the messengers: "Go and tell John what you have seen and heard: the blind receive their sight, the lame walk, the lepers are cleansed, the deaf hear, the dead are raised, the poor have good news brought to them. And blessed is anyone who takes no offense at me" (vv. 22-23).

This is one of many parallel texts found in Matthew and Luke, but not in Mark. They are thought to derive from an early collection of Jesus' sayings that was known to Matthew and Luke, but not to Mark. Scholars refer to this source as "Q," from the German word *Quelle*, meaning "source."

> **Beatitudes:** Jesus' comment in Matt. 11:6, "Blessed is anyone who takes no offense in me," takes the same form as the beatitudes that open the Sermon on the Mount in 5:3-11. Note that it also follows Jesus' reprise of his ministries to the blind, the lame, the lepers, the deaf, and even the dead – all examples of how "the poor have good news brought to them" in deed and in word. The poor, then and now, can be thought of as both poor in possessions and poor in spirit. It does not bother or offend them that Jesus has not set up an earthly kingdom or eliminated the wicked: they accept Jesus for who he is and rejoice in the blessings he has brought to them.

A word of praise
(vv. 7-11)

The dialogue between John and Jesus, carried on by messengers, would have been a public matter. Not wanting those who had overheard to have an incorrect perception of John, Jesus turned to the surrounding crowds and addressed the identity and role of the baptizer.

Prophets, by definition, thrive on certainty and the belief that they have been privy to God's inner council. Some, perhaps, may have thought that John's evident confusion about Jesus' actions meant the once-stalwart prophet had become weak and wavering. Lest they lose respect for John, Jesus made it clear that John was not like the windblown reeds that lined the Jordan River where John baptized. Nor was he some wimpy royal courtesan lounging in silk pajamas, such as those who populated the Herod brothers' palaces (vv. 7-8).

The stern and ascetic John was no softy. Clad in his trademark camel hair cloth and leather belt, he was nothing less than a prophet, Jesus insisted, and deserving of respect. Indeed, John was more than a prophet (v. 9): he was the culminating representative of all prophets who had come before. John did not just predict the Messiah; he had introduced him.

It was impressive enough that Jesus called John a prophet, for many Jews believed that the age of prophecy had come to an end. Popular expectation, however, looked for a return of prophecy as a prelude to the Messiah's advent. Some traditions such as Mal. 3:1 anticipated that a special messenger would come to announce the

Messiah's arrival: Malachi named the coming prophet as none other than the great Elijah himself (4:5-6).

Jesus endorsed John's identity as that very person. He quoted Malachi's prophecy (v. 10), and he insisted that "among those born of women no one has arisen greater than John the Baptist" (v. 11a). As the late Malcolm Tolbert once put it, "In terms of his character, his commitment to God, and the courage of his ministry, no greater man than John had ever been born" (*Good News from Matthew* [Broadman Press, 1975], 101).

Yet, there was a paradox in John's identity. Though he was the greatest of all men, Jesus said, "yet the least in the kingdom of heaven is greater than he" (v. 11b). What did Jesus mean?

Some scholars argue that Jesus' reference to the "least in the kingdom" referred to himself and thus a claim to being greater than John, but there is little to commend this view. It is more likely that Jesus' statement should be understood not in the context of John's personal character, but of his position at the juncture of two ages. The old age of the law was passing, and with Jesus the new age of the kingdom was beginning. John, though greater than all who represented the old age, would be martyred before Jesus fulfilled his kingdom-inducing ministry.

John was the forerunner of the kingdom, which so exceeded the old age that even the greatest of its heroes would be considered less blessed than the least of those in the new kingdom: all who choose to become Christ's disciples enter a different plane of relationship with God. This is our great opportunity, marked this Advent season by the constant reminder of Christ's arrival in our world. It's an opportunity we don't want to miss.

The Hardest Question
Why was John confused about Jesus as the Messiah?

Donald Hagner, in the Word Biblical Commentary, notes that John's puzzlement is understandable: while John had expected Jesus as Messiah to separate the wheat from the chaff and judge the wicked (3:12), he himself was being held captive by the wicked Herod Antipas, who above all deserved judgment. While Jesus proclaimed liberty to the captives among the sick and afflicted (Isa. 42:7, 61:1),

John remained a captive in Herod's imposing fortress at Machaerus, in a wilderness area east of the Dead Sea.

John had heard of Jesus' mighty works, but they were not what he had expected, causing him to doubt his earlier sense of certainty that Jesus was the long-awaited "coming one." Thus, he wondered if "another one" was yet to come.

Hagner makes a significant observation for modern believers who can learn from John's confusion:

> There is an important lesson to be learned here for those inclined to a triumphalism of an over-realized eschatology. Without question the kingdom brought by Jesus involves the experience of wonderful things, even if one does not experience the more spectacular miracles mentioned in v. 5. Nevertheless, for all the joy and fulfillment available to the recipients of the kingdom in the present, there is at the same time the undeniable reality of the continued experience of the effects of evil in this world. When confronted by the latter, it is possible for Christians to "take offense" at Jesus and the nature of the salvation he has brought. If Jesus has brought the kingdom and if Christians have begun to experience eschatological blessings through the ministry of the Holy Spirit, it is perhaps natural to expect and want the eschaton now. But that is precisely what Jesus does not offer. And thus in the present the disciple of Jesus must be prepared for something less – indeed, for the reality of suffering and death – while even confessing the messianic identity and authority of Jesus (cf. Acts 7:55-56), thereby expressing faith in the good news he has announced. John the Baptist was the first person who had to learn this paradox, and since John, the paradox of existence in an era of fulfillment that is nevertheless short of the consummation has had to be learned by the apostles, by the members of Matthew's church, and by each Christian of every generation. (*Matthew 1–13*, vol. 33A, Word Biblical Commentary [Zondervan, 1993], 301-302)

Like John, we may think the coming of Jesus and the inbreaking of the Spirit should bring us a trouble-free life, or the answer to every prayer. John had hoped the Messiah would introduce a new age for the righteous and execute judgment on the wicked at the beginning of his ministry. Sometimes we may wish for the same, but this story is a reminder that such things will take place in God's time, not ours.

Fourth Sunday of Advent
First Reading
Isaiah 7:10-17

A Sign, and a Son

Therefore the Lord himself will give you a sign. Look, the young woman is with child and shall bear a son, and shall name him Immanuel. (Isa. 7:14)

Many seminary students struggle when their advanced studies introduce them to new ideas that challenge the embedded theology they acquired from years of Sunday School or sermons in particularly conservative churches.

Readers of this resource may also feel stretched occasionally, for it doesn't hide or gloss over the same insights from academic study that students learn in a good divinity school.

Today's text could be one of those tension points, because it involves a very familiar passage that our Christian tradition reads in a particular way, but rarely with an appreciation for its background and original intention.

Many people may have heard Isa. 7:14 only in the context of Christmas and remember it mainly from the King James translation: "Behold, a virgin shall conceive, and bear a son, and shall call his name Immanuel." We are thus inclined to think of it as a prophecy of Jesus' birth from the beginning. A closer look at the verse in its context will show that to be incorrect, but without necessarily negating the way New Testament writers interpreted it. **[Celebrating Advent]**

Let's find out what was really going on in Isa. 7:10-17.

A doubtful king
(vv. 10-13)

We need first to consider how the text fits into its literary and historical setting. For once, the historical situation is unambiguous: we find Isaiah confronting King Ahaz, who came to the throne at age 20 and inherited a foreign policy crisis that was not of his own making.

> **Celebrating Advent:** Advent texts for Year A contain four consecutive lessons from the book of Isaiah. The idyllic forecast of Isa. 2:1-5 supports the theme of hope, traditionally celebrated on the first Sunday of Advent. The "peaceable kingdom" described in Isa. 11:1-10 fits well with the second Sunday's emphasis on peace, and the happy image of streams in the desert from Isa. 35:1-10 augments the theme of joy typical of the third Sunday.
>
> The fourth Sunday of Advent upholds the theme of love as expressed in the salvation God has made possible for all persons, and today's text deals with the theme of divine salvation, albeit not in the way many Christians imagine.

Around 735 BCE, the Assyrian king Tiglath-Pileser III (745–727) was pushing westward, which caused King Rezin of Aram (Syria) and King Pekah of Israel to form a defensive alliance. The two kings pressured Judah to join the coalition, but King Jotham refused shortly before his death, and his young successor Ahaz followed suit. Syria and Israel invaded Judah, attempting to depose Ahaz. **[Serious actions]**

At some point in the conflict, Isaiah approached King Ahaz and told him not to fear the two northern kings, whom he dismissed as the smoking remains of burned-out torches (Isa. 7:1-7). Isaiah predicted that their coalition would not last (7:8) and insisted that Ahaz – known for having turned to foreign gods – needed to trust in Yahweh alone: "If you do not stand firm in faith," Isaiah declared, "you shall not stand at all" (7:9). In Hebrew, the phrase contains a strong wordplay: "if you do not *ta'aminu*, you will not *te'amenu*."

Sometime later, Isaiah approached Ahaz again, possibly in the palace. Speaking for Yahweh and seeking to bolster

> **Serious actions:** The kings of Syria and Israel wanted to depose Ahaz and replace him with a more cooperative person called only "the son of Tabeel," a derisive term that may indicate "a nobody." As Syria and Israel attacked, the outnumbered Ahaz was in desperate straits, and this may have been the occasion when he reportedly sacrificed his own son in the worship of foreign gods by making him "pass through the fire" (2 Kgs. 16:3-4, 2 Chron. 28:3-4).
>
> The account in 2 Chronicles claims that Judah suffered significant losses: though the numbers are certainly exaggerated, 2 Chron. 28:5-8 says that 120,000 men of Judah were killed in one day, along with a son of the king and two high palace officials, and that 200,000 people were taken captive.

> **Testing God:** As a rule, the Bible discourages testing God: Deut. 6:16 says "Do not put the LORD to the test, as you tested him at Massah," though in context that could mean something similar to "do not try God's patience."
>
> Gideon famously put out a fleece on two occasions, asking God for a sign. Though he did so with fear and trembling, Gideon was not criticized for his actions and God responded positively, according to Judg. 6:36-40. God, however, then tested Gideon by shrinking his army, perhaps in response to Gideon's effrontery.
>
> In the present text, God offered the sign (see also 1 Sam. 10:7-9, 2:34), so there would have been no presumption on Ahaz's part in stating what sign of divine favor he wished to see.

the king's confidence, he challenged Ahaz to ask for a sign that God would deliver. He could ask for anything: the sign could be "as deep as Sheol or high as heaven" (v. 11).

Ahaz, whether pretending piety or simply unwilling, declared "I will not ask, and I will not put the LORD to the test" (v. 12). This prompted Isaiah to charge him with wearying God through his obstinance and refusal to trust in Yahweh. It was he who was being tested, and he was failing badly (vv. 13). **[Testing God]**

A shift to plural verbs alerts the reader that others were present, probably including members of the royal family. It also reminds us that the story is not about Ahaz alone, but involves the future of David's royal line.

A promised sign
(v. 14)

We now come to the familiar part of the passage: "Therefore the LORD himself will give you a sign," Isaiah said. "Look, the young woman is with child and shall bear a son, and shall name him Immanuel."

Several matters deserve comment. First, Isaiah declared that God would give Ahaz a sign whether he wanted it or not. The sign would involve a young woman who would bear a child. Here we run into several issues related to translation. The word translated by the NRSV as "young woman" means exactly that: the word 'almah comes from a root that means "ripe" and refers generically to a young woman who has achieved puberty: the masculine form of the word ('elem) was used for a young man.

Young women were often married shortly after reaching puberty during that period, so an 'almah may or may

not have been a virgin. Isaiah could easily have used the word betulah, a specific word for "virgin," but chose the less specific word to indicate a stage of physical maturity rather than sexual experience.

It is likely that the woman Isaiah had in mind was not only married, but also present and pregnant. The direct article is attached to the word "'almah, so it should be translated as "the young woman" (NRSV) or even "this young woman" (NET).

The familiar KJV's reference to "a virgin," then, mistranslates the Hebrew text on two points, ignoring the direct article and using the more specific word "virgin" when the text did not demand it.

The state of the young woman's pregnancy depends on another iffy translation: the Hebrew word rendered as "will conceive" in the Greek Septuagint (or LXX, followed by the Latin Vulgate and the KJV) is not a future tense verb meaning "will conceive," but an adjective that means "pregnant." Thus, the NRSV renders it properly as "the young woman is with child."

The young woman is not identified. Scholars have speculated that she may have been one of the king's wives, or Isaiah's wife, or an unknown member of the royal court. **[Who was she?]**

Translation difficulties continue with the woman's naming of her child. The NRSV translates the text as a third person verb ("and shall name him …"), but the form of the verb used could also be translated in the second person, as if Isaiah looked at the woman – or at the king – and said, "you shall call his name Immanuel."

Who was she? Who is the young woman who is either pregnant or about to become so? Isaiah spoke as if she was present, and one has the impression that he might have pointed as he spoke. Speculation generally focuses on two options: the young woman was one of King Ahaz's wives or consorts; or she was Isaiah's wife, whom he referred to as "the prophetess" (8:3).

Both arguments have pros and cons. The king had reportedly sacrificed one son and lost another in the Syro-Ephraimitic conflict. The "house of David" to which Isaiah referred, reflecting God's promise in 2 Samuel 7 that a descendant of David would always sit upon the throne, could have been imperiled.

A Jewish tradition holds that the child Isaiah had in mind was Hezekiah, the son of Ahaz's wife Abiah. This is hard to reconcile with the account of Hezekiah's accession to the throne in 2 Kgs. 18:1-2, which would suggest that he may have been about nine years old during the Syro-Ephraimitic crisis. The chronology of such accounts is often questionable, however.

The view that Isaiah spoke of his own wife and a son that would soon be born is supported by the idea that Isaiah would have known if his wife was pregnant and he could have influenced what the child was named – in addition to his diet, described later. A problem with this view is the following account in which Isaiah reports getting his wife pregnant with a son, but Yahweh instructed him to name the child Maher-shalal-hash-baz, not Immanuel.

The lack of any specific identifiers – which would have been easy to include – suggests that the unidentified young woman was neither the king's nor the prophet's wife, but someone who would have been known to them both.

"Immanuel" is composed of words that are written separately in the Hebrew: *immanu 'el*, meaning "with us, God," or "God [is] with us."

Now we get to the real significance of the sign: it was to show Ahaz that God was present with the people of Judah, including him. The assuring words appear again in 8:8 and 8:10 in the context of an oracle describing Assyria's coming devastation, serving as a reminder that even in the most difficult of times, God would be present.

One purpose of the sign may have been to remind Ahaz that despite the hard days and continuing threats, a young woman would have the courage and faith to name her child "God is with us." Perhaps Isaiah hoped that the powerful but fearful Ahaz would take a lesson from a vulnerable young woman who showed firm faith under trying circumstances.

Deliverance … and judgment
(vv. 15-17)

Isaiah continued to explain the sign in v. 15, which is also difficult to interpret, but seems to be a promise that before the soon-arriving child reached the age of knowing good from bad, the lands of Syria and Israel would be desolate and the threat they posed to Judah would be over.

"He shall eat curds and honey by the time he knows how to refuse the evil and choose the good" is subject to varying interpretations. This appears to suggest moral agency, what we sometimes call "the age of accountability." Since the verse is in the context of eating, however, it is possible that it refers only to the child's ability to tell good food from something spoiled – something that could have occurred within 2-3 years, rather than 8-10. This would have made Isaiah's promise that the land of his two neighboring adversaries would be deserted a more immediate prospect.

A diet of "curds and honey" has a positive sound, but Isaiah used it to reflect a time of deprivation when Israel's inhabitants would be forced from their cities and farms, returning to a nomadic lifestyle that depended heavily on milk products supplemented by honey or other foods that could be gathered from the scrubby land. [**Good times or hard?**]

Good times or hard? Does Isaiah consider a diet of curds and honey a sign of luxury, or deprivation? On the one hand, the protein of curds and the sweetness of honey sounds attractive, assuming one has developed a taste for clotted milk – but in a land with no refrigeration, one would learn to enjoy milk products in a variety of ways. As the Israelites left Egypt and made their way toward the Promised Land, one of the most glowing reports was that it was a land of milk and honey (Exod. 3:8, 17; 13:5; 33:3; Lev. 20:24; and many others).

It is more likely, however, that Isaiah sees curdled milk and honey as a deprivation diet, the kind of foods one would have to rely on if relegated to a nomadic life in the wilderness with only goats for company. In the following oracle, clearly connected to this one, Isaiah predicted that God would send the king of Assyria, like a hired barber, to shave the people of Judah to the nub so that only a few cows and sheep would be left to them, and "everyone that is left in the land shall eat curds and honey" (7:21-22) – clearly a negative implication.

The bottom line of the sign was that within a few years – by the time the boy about to be born could tell good from bad – the threat would be gone: "the land before whose two kings you are in dread will be deserted" (v. 16).

The oracle of salvation quickly switched to judgment, however. Rather than trusting Yahweh to take care of Syria and Israel, Ahaz appealed to the Assyrian king for help, sending lavish gifts – including gold vessels from the temple – and asking him to attack Judah's northern enemies (2 Kgs. 16:7-9).

Tiglath-Pileser III took the bait and attacked Syria, but Ahaz soon discovered that he had escaped two cats only to encounter a lion. Judah became a vassal to the Assyrians, forced to pay a heavy annual tribute. Isaiah saw the Assyrian domination as divine discipline, predicting that Yahweh would "bring on you and your ancestral house such days as have not come since the day that Ephraim departed from Judah – the king of Assyria" (v. 17).

What can a modern reader do with this ancient text? It is not enough for us to hear it only as a happy promise ultimately fulfilled in the virgin birth of Jesus, for that was not its purpose, though New Testament writers saw a deeper meaning in it.

The text reminds us of several things. Sin has consequences. Bad things happen. Hard times, whether we've brought them on ourselves or not, can be expected. That's not the end of the story, however. Even in trials, we can trust and believe that God is with us.

In this sense, Matthew's use of the text at a time when Israel longed for deliverance is appropriate. New Testament writers including Matthew typically quoted from the Septuagint, which translated "young woman" as "virgin." Matthew called on Isaiah's encounter with Ahaz not only to bolster the account of Jesus' virgin birth, but also to remind believers that in Christ we find the ultimate sign of Immanuel, the promise that God is with us, not just at Christmas, but through all the times and circumstances of our lives.

The Hardest Question
How did "young woman" become "virgin"?

Christians and non-Christians alike are familiar with Christmas liturgies, music, and scripture quotations that reflect the King James translation of Isa. 7:14: "Behold, a virgin shall conceive, and bear a son, and shall call his name Immanuel."

But why did the KJV translate it this way, and why did Matthew use the Greek word for "virgin" when he quoted the passage in Matt. 1:23, the context in which we most commonly hear these words?

To answer that question, we look at an early Greek translation of the Hebrew scriptures known as "the Septuagint." Probably around the mid-third century BCE, when few people spoke Hebrew and Greek had become a standard language (as English is today), a group of Hebrew scholars traveled to Alexandria, Egypt, to translate the Torah, or first five books of the Hebrew Bible. Over time, the remainder of the LXX was translated.

A tradition preserved in the second century BCE "Letter of Aristeas" asserts that the high priest in Jerusalem sent 72 scholars (six from each tribe) to Alexandria, where they finished the translation in 72 days. This led, according to Aristeas, to great rejoicing, an official acceptance of the translation, and the pronouncing of curses on anyone who should change it. The details of the letter are no doubt exaggerated, but there is probably a kernel of truth behind it.

Later, the translation came to be known as the "Septuagint," from the Latin term *septuagina*, meaning "seventy" (rounded off from 72). It became customary to represent this with the Roman numerals LXX.

The translation of the LXX is uneven: sometimes it is close to literal, and at other times quite loose. The Hebrew scrolls preserved in Alexandria also appear to have developed some differences from the text preserved in Babylon.

For unknown reasons, the scholars who produced the LXX chose to translate the Hebrew term *'almah* (young woman) with the Greek word *parthenos*, which refers specifically to a virgin. The LXX was not the only early Greek translation, and some of the others more accurately used the word *neanis*, which means "young woman," but the most popular version had the reading *parthenos*. Most New Testament quotations of the Old Testament are not drawn from the Hebrew, but from the LXX – and then often quite loosely.

A prominent scholar named Jerome was commissioned in 382 CE by Pope Damasus to produce a Latin translation of the Bible. That translation, known as the

Vulgate, became the authoritative version used by the church for more than a thousand years. In line with the New Testament tradition, Jerome followed the LXX rather than the Hebrew text when translating Isa. 7:14, using the expression *virgo concipiet* – "a virgin will conceive" rather than the Hebrew "the young woman is pregnant."

When King James of England ordered scholars to produce an official English translation for the Anglican church in the early 17ᵗʰ century, they followed the Vulgate closely, even though they had access to Hebrew manuscripts. Thus, the KJV's "virgin" follows the Latin and Greek mistranslations of a word that, in Hebrew, simply means "young woman."

When the early church considered the belief that Mary (though unmarried) conceived a child by the Holy Spirit, some recalled this text from Isaiah and interpreted it as a messianic prophecy not fulfilled until Mary's conception of Jesus (Matt. 1:23), even though Isaiah was talking about a child to be born within a year of his prophecy (around 735 BCE), to be named Immanuel, and to serve as a sign to King Ahaz. In the case of Jesus, the gospels insist that a divine messenger instructed Mary and Joseph to name the child Jesus (from a Hebrew and Aramaic word meaning "salvation"), not Immanuel (Matt. 1:21, Luke 1:31).

In the first century, a method of interpretation had become popular by which people searched through the Old Testament scriptures and freely took passages out of context, arguing that God had imbued them with a secret meaning to be revealed later. Modern scholars would hold that searching for hidden meanings in isolated texts lacks exegetical rigor (to put it mildly), but the practice was widely accepted during the New Testament period – and remains popular among less responsible proof-texting preachers today.

One might argue that God intentionally endowed Isaiah's prophecy with a secondary significance that required a mistranslation into Greek for it to be revealed, but it's more likely that the LXX reference to a "virgin" conception is coincidental. Fortunately, believing that Jesus was born of a virgin does not depend on finding an ancient prophecy that reportedly points to it: the angelic birth announcements recorded in Matthew and Luke, along with Mary's personal experience, provide quite sufficient evidence to support the belief.

Fourth Sunday of Advent

Second Reading
Psalm 80*

Restore Us, Lord

Restore us, O God; let your face shine, that we may be saved. (Ps. 80:3)

The years of 2020 and 2021 will be remembered by many people as years of lament. The persistent COVID-19 pandemic triggered economic upheaval, made travel difficult, and isolated families. Political polarities mounted in the tension between those who were more concerned with public health and those more focused on getting back to a "normal" life.

With the nation already under stress, extrajudicial police killings involving Black victims sparked a season of protests for racial justice that occasionally turned into riots, and the transition between presidents was marked by a violent insurrection at the U.S. Capitol.

As ministers and others sought to deal with their own grief and offer comfort to others, the perfect storm of misery drove many to the psalms of lament to join the poets of Israel in crying "How long?"

Israel's hymnbook contained many laments, including Psalm 80. We can't be sure what particular situation led to this mournful prayer, but it clearly emerged from a perspective of deep loss and frustration on a national level. **[What was the trouble?]** The psalmist wrote in behalf of a people who had fallen far from their ideals and were in danger of losing their identity.

Psalm 80 is preceded by a complex superscription that probably has to do with the song's tune. It appears to instruct the leader to use a tune that includes the word *shoshannîm*, which means "lilies," though some commentators have speculated that the term could also refer to an otherwise unknown stringed instrument.

> **What was the trouble?** Scholars have put forward many ideas about the situation in history that led to this plaintive psalm. Some suggest it was written in the northern kingdom of Israel, around 722 B.C., when the Assyrians were ravaging the land. The "Joseph" tribes of Ephraim and Manasseh are mentioned, along with Benjamin – and they were all northern tribes. In support of this view, the Septuagint (an early Greek translation) adds "concerning the Assyrians" to the superscription.
>
> Others think the psalm may have come from a troublesome time in the southern kingdom, from the years in exile, or even from the early post-exilic period. Though the author in those settings would have been from Judah, references to tribes from the defunct northern kingdom could have expressed a wish for the remaining Hebrews to be reunited.

The psalm is also identified as an *eduth*, belonging to a collection attributed to Asaph. *Eduth* can be translated as "covenant" (NRSV) or "testimony" (HCSB), but many interpreters believe it should be read in conjunction with *shoshannîm*. Thus, the NIV has "According to [the tune of] 'The Lilies of the Covenant.'" The uncertainty of translation leads some versions to simply transliterate the Hebrew words either singly (NAS95) or in combination (KJV, NET).

Restore us, O God …
vv. 1-3)

Psalm 80 is a prime example of a communal lament in which a leader either sang in behalf of the community or led the congregation in a plaintive prayer to God. Laments

---

*This text of lament and hope also appears as a reading for the first Sunday of Advent in Year B. Other selections from Psalm 80 appear in the lections for Proper 22 in Year A (80:7-15), and both the fourth Sunday of Advent (80:1-7) and Proper 15 in Year C (80:1-2, 8-19). Partial readings do well as lections, but for Bible study it is best to consider all of Psalm 80.

All together now: The thrice-repeated chorus (vv. 3, 7, 19) is identical except for the divine names used in the address. Verse 3 addresses "God" (*elohîm*), v. 7 appeals to "God of Hosts" (*elohîm s^ebaōt*), and v. 19 calls out to "Yahweh God of Hosts" (usually translated LORD God of Hosts," *Yahweh elohîm s^ebaōt*). In deference to English style, most translations begin the address with the exclamation "O," but there is no equivalent in the Hebrew.

"Restore us" translates the *hiphil* stem of the verb *shub*, which means "to turn," "to return," or by extension, "to repent." While the psalmist may simply be asking God to return Israel to an earlier situation of peace and security, the prayer has overtones of asking God to "turn us around" or "cause us to repent," which the poet believed would lead to the same result, that "we shall be saved."

typically contain an address to God, a complaint about the present plight, a plea for help, and often an expression of trust.

A threefold plea for Yahweh to save (vv. 3, 7, 19) divides the psalm into an invocation and appeal (vv. 1-3), a complaint (vv. 4-7), and a melancholy entreaty comparing Israel to a ruined vine and asking God to restore it, concluding with a vow (vv. 8-19). [**All together now**]

The psalmist plaintively addresses God as "Shepherd of Israel," "you who lead Joseph like a flock," and "you who are enthroned upon the cherubim" (v. 1). These epithets recall the tradition of God visibly leading Israel through the wilderness after the Exodus from Egypt.

The psalmist pleads for the exalted God who had led Israel in the past to "shine forth" before Ephraim, Benjamin, and Manasseh, to "stir up" divine power, and to come with salvation (vv. 1-2).

Benjamin was remembered as a full brother of Joseph, whose two sons were Ephraim and Manasseh. Their grandfather Jacob claimed that he had adopted the two as his own sons. In blessing them, Jacob claimed that God had been his shepherd his entire life (Gen. 48:15).

The familiar notion of God as a guiding shepherd was also present in the Exodus account (Exod. 15:13), in the prophets (Ezek. 34:11-16, 31), and in other psalms (Psalm 23, 100:3).

The image of God as being enthroned between or above the cherubim is drawn from the description of the sacred Ark of the Covenant, topped by two golden cherubim, as a locus for God's special presence (Exod. 25:19-22, Num. 7:89, 1 Sam. 4:4, 2 Sam. 6:2).

In the Exodus narratives, the Ark of the Covenant was carried at the head of the procession as the Israelites traveled from Sinai to the land of promise, following God's symbolic presence in a cloud by day and a pillar of fire by night (Exod. 13:21-22, Num. 14:14, Neh. 9:12). And, according to Num. 2:17-24, the first three tribes in line were Ephraim, Benjamin, and Manasseh, in the same order as Ps. 80:2. It is as if the psalmist is praying for God to come again and lead the tribes through their present trial. [**Recalling the Exodus**]

Ephraim and Manasseh were also the largest tribes in the northern kingdom of Israel. This may suggest that the psalm has its roots in a time of crisis in the northern kingdom, which was conquered by Assyria in 722 BCE.

The psalmist's imaginative prayer asked God to "shine forth" and come to save Israel. The plea is repeated three times: "Restore us, O God; let your face shine, that we may be saved" (v. 3, see also vv. 7 and 20).

Hebrew tradition held that God's face glowed with glory, so much that ordinary humans could not bear a direct view and live. Moses' face was said to have shone after being in God's presence, as if reflecting the divine glory or radiating sacred energy he may have absorbed (Exod. 34:29).

The familiar Aaronic blessing of Num. 6:24-26 prays, "The LORD bless you and keep you; the LORD make his face to shine upon you, and be gracious to you; the LORD lift up his countenance upon you, and give you peace."

Calling upon God to "shine forth" was a poetic way of asking God to show favor toward Israel and come with saving power. A similar sentiment is echoed in a popular

Recalling the Exodus: Marvin Tate, writing in the Word Bible Commentary, notes that four imperative verbs are used in the psalmist's petitions of vv. 2-3: Give ear, shine forth, rouse, and come. Tate notes: "The parallel with the deliverance from Egypt is striking. In the call of Moses, Yahweh says, 'I have seen, I have heard, I am concerned, so I have come to lead' (Exod. 3:7–8)" (*Psalms 51–100*, vol. 20, Word Biblical Commentary [Zondervan, 1990], 313).

praise song by Graham Kendrick. "Shine, Jesus, Shine" (1988) prays for Christ to "fill this land with the Father's glory," bringing a Christian slant to the ancient prayer.

Let your face shine upon us …
(vv. 4-6)

Why would this request be appropriate? Because the people seemed convinced that God was furious with them and no longer listened to their prayers. God's face, rather than beaming with beneficence, was wreathed in the smoke of smoldering anger (v. 4).

The people had been praying, the psalmist implies, but God had responded with fumes rather than favor. How long (literally, "until when?") would God allow this state of affairs to continue?

The psalmist laments that God had not only *allowed* their troubles to occur, but had *actively caused* them, giving the people "the bread of tears" to eat and buckets of tears to drink (v. 5). [**Torrents of tears**]

"You have made us a source of contention to our neighbors," the psalmist cried, "and our enemies mock us" (v. 6).

The belief that God would bless or curse the people in keeping with their behavior lies behind the Deuteronomistic premise that God used foreign nations as divine agents to punish the Hebrews when they chose to reject God's leadership and follow other gods.

The books of Job and Ecclesiastes questioned the adequacy of such a *quid pro quo* theology, and the New Testament introduced a new covenant in which salvation comes by grace. Even so, the notion that "you get what you deserve" remains a popular belief.

In the psalmist's mind, good or bad fortune was always divinely determined. We may not hold to the same theology, but we may still be tempted to blame our troubles on God rather than accepting responsibility for

our own actions. As a result, we sometimes think of God more as a cosmic repairman we call on to fix things rather than a loving shepherd we follow every day.

Restore this vine
(vv. 7-16)

A second plea for God to "restore us" is followed by an extended metaphor in which the psalmist pictures God as a planter who took a grape vine from Egypt, cleared out the promised land, and transplanted it in a new home (vv. 8-9). The verdant vine then spread from the mountains of the southern Negev to the cedars of Lebanon, from the Mediterranean Sea to the Euphrates River – borders reportedly promised in Deut. 11:22-25 and approximately realized under David's rule (vv. 10-11).

But that was in the past. The psalmist mourns that God had broken down the protective walls of the vineyard, allowing anyone to pick its fruit and wild animals to ravage it (vv. 12-13, cf. Isa. 5:1-7). He cries for the community as the personified vine, pleading for God to have pity on it as "the stock that your right hand planted" (v. 15), but which had been cut and burned (v. 16).

The psalm would be particularly appropriate if expressed near the time when the Assyrian armies devastated the area, scattering the population of the northern kingdom while subjugating Judah as a vassal forced to pay tribute.

The request of favor for "the one at your right hand" (v. 17) parallels "the stock that your right hand planted" in v. 15. The straightforward allusion is to Israel, the vine that God had initially blessed and later cursed.

Our national grief is not the same. We are in no immediate danger of being conquered by a foreign foe – but we have felt what it is like to be weakened by internal division, torn by persistent injustice, and threatened by a deadly virus.

How long, O Lord?

That we may be saved
(vv. 17-19)

How might the psalmist persuade God to show favor on the desolate nation? In times of extremity, ancient peoples often resorted to making vows to the gods, and the

---

Torrents of tears: The term "bowlful" (NRSV) as a measure of tears to be drunk translates the word *shalish*, which means "a third." Here it refers to a third of a larger measure, just as we think of a "quart" as a fourth of a gallon. Unfortunately, the text doesn't say which larger measure the psalmist has in mind, but the clear implication is that Israel drank tears in quantity. Whether we think of kegs, steins, jugs, or buckets, the image is clear.

Hebrews were no exception. Such "vows" had the form of conditional promises that asked God for a favor and promised something in return.

Thus, the prayer for the hand of God's blessing in v. 17 is followed by the promise "then we will never turn back from you" (v. 18a). The vow is then repeated, but in different words: "give us life, and we will call on your name" (v. 18b).

The closing verse repeats the refrain found in vv. 3 and 7, asking God to come with shining face to deliver the people from their trouble.

Does this psalm reflect the way we sometimes pray? Have we ever prayed: "Oh God, if you will get me out of this mess, I promise to straighten up" – or "I promise to get back in church," or "I'll do whatever you want me to do"?

It's not that easy, is it? We cannot blame God for national unrest provoked by centuries of systemic racism, decades of growing wealth disparity, and the failure of political leaders to work for the good of all people. Nor can we blame God for the coronavirus in all its variants.

But we can take the psalmist's prayer to heart. We can grieve over what we have lost and what we have become. We can pray for God to turn our hearts from selfish goals to mutual care and a more just society. We can ask God to show us the world through Jesus' eyes by listening to our neighbors, even those who don't live in our neighborhoods, and by rebuilding community one relationship at a time.

Perhaps God is asking us, "How long?"

The Hardest Question
What's wrong – or right – with this prayer?

Psalm 80 is clearly a part of scripture. Two things should give us pause. First, the prayer approaches God as one whose primary business is bailing us out. We all are created in the image of God, who gives us both the right and the responsibility to make personal decisions for good or evil. There are times when trouble comes calling with no invitation, but often the trouble we experience is of our own making.

The Old Testament narratives repeatedly recount how Israel was prone to rebellion against God, falling into idolatry, and generally turning their backs on the way God had taught them to live. When they got in trouble, however, they had tended to start acting religious. There was something wrong with that then, and there's something wrong with that now.

Second, the prayer tries to swing a deal with God. The prayer concludes with a promise that, if God will only save Israel, *then* they will be faithful and worship God as they should. Because humans are prone to making deals, we assume that God is, too, but God does not need a promised payoff in order to hear and respond to our prayers.

Positively, the prayer does acknowledge that in some matters, only God can help, and in those times, it is appropriate to seek God's aid. God promises to love us and care for us and be present with us. God does not, however, promise to make life easy for us, or to always say "yes" when we ask for something.

It is true that sometimes, when we pray, it seems that God is silent. God may seem silent because we don't know how to listen, or don't take the time. God may seem silent because the answer to our prayer is not "yes," and that's the only answer we are listening for. Sometimes, however, the heavens seem quiet because God *is* silent (cp. 1 Kgs. 19:11-12). Sometimes silence is the most powerful way of speaking. Sometimes God's apparent absence may be what it takes to make us hungrier for God's presence. And sometimes, the answer we need is "no," for which we may later be grateful.

There may be other areas that we don't understand and maybe in this life we never will. Some things we won't understand until we get a chance to stand face to face and ask God ourselves. In the meantime, we live by trust and faith that God does hear our prayer, and that God's presence is sure even when divine intervention is not.

Fourth Sunday of Advent
Third Reading
Romans 1:1-17

The Power of God

… and was declared to be Son of God with power according to the spirit of holiness by resurrection from the dead, Jesus Christ our Lord … (Rom. 1:4)

How long has it been since you have written a letter, even in the form of an email? We learn in school how to address letters, and what sort of salutation to use depending on whether it's a personal or a business letter.

Paul's letter to the Romans was very personal, but he also meant business – and his salutation was like a message in itself.

The lectionary uses Paul's impressive prescript to the Romans for this week's third reading, and we'll examine it. But, for the sake of a fuller treatment, we'll take a look at the entire chapter. [**When was Romans written?**]

A lengthy salutation
(vv. 1-7)

Romans contains the longest salutation of Paul's letters, emphasizing the degree to which he was sold out to Christ. Many people lack purpose in life: Paul was not among them: he couldn't get through the first sentence without launching into a synopsis of the gospel, much of which sounds like an early creedal statement.

Paul said he was called to be an apostle, "set apart for the gospel of God" (v. 1), a gospel "promised beforehand through his prophets in the holy scriptures" (v. 2). Like others in the early church, he interpreted many Old Testament texts as prophesies of Jesus, believing that they contained deeper meanings than the prophet's original intent.

Paul likewise affirmed a belief that Jesus "was descended from David according to the flesh" (v. 3). Writing long after Paul, both Matthew and Luke compiled elaborate genealogies for Jesus, though in different ways. [**Jesus' genealogies**] Whatever tradition Paul knew, he was satisfied that Jesus was descended from David in a physical sense, and equally confident that Jesus had been "declared to be Son of God with power according to the spirit of holiness by resurrection from the dead" (v. 4). In other words, Christ's divine sonship had been revealed through the power of the Spirit at work in Jesus' life, and

---

When was Romans written? Paul's authentic authorship of Romans is rarely questioned. According to Rom. 16:22, he did not write it in his own hand, but dictated the letter to a scribe whose name was Tertius.

Most scholars agree that Romans was written during Paul's third missionary journey, either from Ephesus, where he spent three years, or from Corinth, where he spent three months prior to taking an offering to Jerusalem (Acts 20:3-6; 2 Cor. 13:1, 10).

Some suggest Corinth as the most likely place, since Paul makes a point of commending Phoebe, from the nearby seaport town of Cenchrea (Rom. 16:1-2), and who may have delivered the letter.

Having established churches throughout the Eastern Mediterranean area, Paul longed to preach in more "pioneer territory." After delivering an offering collected for the poor in Jerusalem, he planned to carry the gospel to Spain, with a stopover in Rome as he traveled. The letter was probably written around 54–57 CE, though it is more likely near the end of the period. In a sense, Paul was introducing himself and his understanding of the gospel to the Romans, because he hoped they would support his goal of ultimately preaching in Spain.

Jesus' genealogies: Both Matthew (1:1-17) and Luke (3:23-38) appear to trace Jesus' line through Joseph, but they follow different lines after David and arrive at a different father for Joseph (Heli in Luke, Jacob in Matthew). Several explanations have been proposed for the discrepancy.

Both genealogies are designed with a point in view, with Matthew's three sets of 14 generations emphasizing Jesus' Jewish heritage and Luke's going back to Adam to support his more universal concern. Some scholars have suggested that Heli might have been Mary's father, with Joseph named as a son because he took legal responsibility for Jesus, and because genealogies routinely named a sequence of fathers. In this case, Luke's genealogy would have been tracing Mary's line, adding Joseph at the end as Jesus' legal father, though he may have been Heli's son-in-law. This would be appropriate, since he approached the story from Mary's point of view, while Matthew gave more attention to Joseph.

through his mind-bending resurrection from the dead. Many Jews had longed for a messiah who would be a "son of David," but they had not expected him to be the "Son of God."

Through Christ, Paul said, he had received the grace that brought him to salvation, as well as the calling to "apostleship" for the purpose of spreading the gospel "to bring about the obedience of faith among all the Gentiles for the sake of his name" (v. 5). Paul's goal of reaching "all the Gentiles" included his readers in Rome, who were not only "called to belong to Jesus Christ" (v. 6), but also "to be saints" (v. 7).

Being "saints" does not imply moral perfection. Like the Hebrew concept of holiness, it denotes a state of being set apart. Paul considered all believers to be "set apart" from their old lives and called to live for Christ wherever they were.

Though Paul was writing to first-century Christians in Rome, his words continue speaking when we read them, for we have the same calling – to be "saints" who let Christ guide our lives in ways that reflect a "Jesus worldview" and draw others to follow Christ.

Following his lengthy digression from the traditional salutation, Paul came back to it with the conclusion of v. 7: "Grace to you and peace from God our Father and the Lord Jesus Christ."

A thankful prayer
(vv. 8-15)

Paul introduced the remainder of his letter by explaining his desire to visit the Roman church and share with them, that both he and they might be mutually encouraged (vv. 8-15).

Paul typically began his letters with a prayer for the recipients. Only in his frustrated letter to the Galatians did Paul fail to begin in this way.

In Romans, the prayer of thanks serves a dual purpose: to express gratitude to God for the Romans, and also to encourage them in their faith. Paul was moved by the courageous faith of the Christians in Rome, as they often suffered persecution from without and division from within, and assured them of his constant prayers for them (vv. 8-9).

Though Paul had heard of the Romans and their struggles, he had not yet visited them in person, but prayed that he might soon do so and "share with you some spiritual gift to strengthen you" (vv. 10-11). This was not a one-way enterprise, as if Paul could bring a trunk filled with spiritual gifts and pass them out. He wanted to use his gifts in preaching the gospel and helping the Roman church to grow, but also hoped "that we may be mutually encouraged by each other's faith, both yours and mine" (v. 12).

Paul may have been in Ephesus when writing these lines, or possibly Corinth, preparing for his final trip to Jerusalem. He had no idea that when he eventually arrived in Rome, it would be as a prisoner (Acts 19:21, 23:11, 28:11-16).

Paul's agricultural metaphor of wanting to visit Rome so he could "reap some harvest among you as I have among the rest of the Gentiles" (v. 13) may sound arrogant to modern ears, but it was a colorful way of saying how committed he was to preaching the gospel and seeing others come to know Christ.

Paul was not suggesting that the gospel enterprise depended on him, but he felt an obligation to spread the gospel to everyone. He expressed his sense of owing his best efforts as a debt: "I am a debtor both to Greeks and to barbarians, both to the wise and to the foolish – hence my eagerness to proclaim the gospel to you also who are in Rome" (vv. 14-15). A clearer translation would be "I am obligated ... ," as in NIV11.

A firm declaration
(vv. 16-17)

From there Paul pressed forward in declaring his eagerness to preach the gospel message: "For I am not ashamed of the gospel; it is the power of God for salvation to everyone who has faith, to the Jew first and also to the Greek. For in it the righteousness of God is revealed through faith for faith; as it is written, 'The one who is righteous will live by faith.'"

In saying he was "not ashamed" of the gospel, Paul used a rhetorical figure of speech to emphasize his commitment to the gospel, using a negative expression to stress a positive reality. We do the same: to stress how clean something is, we say it is "spotless." A perfect diamond is "flawless." A gentle person "doesn't have a mean bone in his body." To say "I am not ashamed of the gospel" was an emphatic way of saying "I'm proud of the gospel."

Christians in Rome lived in a world that considered the gospel to be foolish. Excavations on Palatine Hill in Rome uncovered a bit of first-century graffiti, a crude drawing of a man kneeling before a man on a cross with the head of a donkey. An inscription said, "Alex the Jew worships his god." Facing such ridicule, some early Christians may have kept their faith quiet, but not Paul. He was jeered for his faith, jailed for his faith, beaten for his faith, and run out of town for his faith, but through it all he continued to say, "I am not ashamed of the gospel." [**Foolishness**]

Foolishness: The graffito referenced in the lesson can be found here, both as a line drawing (http://upload.wikimedia.org/wikipedia/commons/a/a9/AlexGraffito.svg) and from the original (http://en.wikipedia.org/wiki/File:Alexorig.jpg). The date is uncertain, with estimates ranging from the first to the third centuries CE.

Modern believers may struggle with how open to be about our faith. If we pause to say grace in a restaurant or keep a Bible on our desk, would it be seen as a positive witness, or do we fear that others would think we are being "holier than thou"? We don't want to be ashamed of our faith, but we may worry that others will think we are flaunting our faith. Authenticity is the key.

Paul's impetus for sharing the gospel was clear: "it is the power of God for salvation to everyone who has faith" (v. 16b). Paul was like a research scientist who has just discovered a cure for cancer and cannot keep the good news to herself. She will burst if she does not let everyone know about the life-saving potential of the discovery.

There is power in the gospel. The word Paul uses is *dunamis*, the root of our words "dynamic" and "dynamite." The gospel has the power to shake us loose from sin-hardened ways, to change our lives, and to bring us into relationship with the Lord of the universe. We call that "salvation," and it is available to everyone who believes, and that is good news. It is not something to be ashamed of, but excited about.

The salvation we experience is the result of the righteousness of God that is granted to us. In Hebrew thought, righteousness was not so much a moral quality as a legal standing. We know that none of us can attain moral perfection or righteous standing on the basis of our own merits. Paul's great discovery was that God through Christ is willing to impute his own righteous standing to those who believe.

Some interpreters suggest that the phrase often translated as "from faith to faith" may mean something akin to "from the faith of the Old Testament to faith in Christ," "from the preacher's faith to the hearer's faith," "faith from first to last," or other options. The meaning is not necessarily self-evident, because the referents of "faith" are not clear. Charles Talbert has suggested that Paul intended to say the gospel arises from/out of God's or Jesus' faithfulness, *for* the faith of humans (*Romans*, Smyth & Helwys Bible Commentary [Smyth & Helwys, 2002], 41).

Paul's quotation of Hab. 2:4b in v. 17 has also been translated and interpreted in different ways. The familiar KJV says "The just shall live by faith," while NRSV has "The one who is righteous will live by faith" and NET translates "The righteous by faith will live." The point is that whatever righteousness we possess comes through faith in Christ, which calls us to live out our calling.

Paul's affirmation of Christ as both the Son of God and a descendant of David makes this text particularly appropriate for the Advent season. His prayer challenges us to ask in what ways our faith in Christ gives us hope and finds expression in our lives through every season of the year.

The Hardest Question
What does "the righteousness of God" mean?

Paul spoke of "the righteousness of God" being "revealed through faith for faith." What did he mean by that? Here is what Martin Luther, whose writings would spark the Protestant Reformation, thought of it:

In his life as a Roman Catholic, Luther was an Augustinian monk who taught biblical theology at the University of Wittenburg. In August of 1513, he began a series of lectures on the book of Psalms. Luther had been struggling, finding his embedded understanding of faith to be frustrating and empty. In his own words, he was engaged in an agonizing search "to find a gracious God."

Luther was enamored with the psalmist's prayer "in thy righteousness deliver me!" (Ps. 31:1), but he could not understand it. Luther had always thought of God's righteousness as the righteous judgment of sinners, so he tended to think of "condemnation" rather than "deliverance." Luther was so plagued by feelings of guilt that he would often fast, spend hours in prayer, and even afflict himself physically in a futile effort to find atonement. It was said that he went to confession so often that other monks would hide when they saw him coming.

Ultimately, Luther began to study Paul's claim in Rom. 1:17 that "the righteousness of God is revealed through faith for faith; as it is written, 'He who through faith is righteous shall live.'" Later, Luther wrote this description of what happened:

Night and day I pondered until ... I grasped the truth that the righteousness of God is that righteousness whereby, through grace and sheer mercy, he justifies us by faith. Thereupon I felt reborn and to have gone through open doors into paradise. The whole of scripture took on new meaning, and whereas before "the righteousness of God" had filled me with hate, now it became to me inexpressibly sweet in greater love. This passage of Paul became to me a gateway into heaven.

(drawn from F.F. Bruce, *Romans*, 2nd ed. [Intervarsity Press, 1985], 56-57; and James E. Hightower, Jr., *Illustrating Paul's Letter to the Romans* [Baptist Sunday School Board, 1984], 13-15)

Fourth Sunday of Advent
Fourth Reading
Matthew 1:18-25

The Invisible Man

Joseph, son of David, do not be afraid to take Mary as your wife, for the child conceived in her is from the Holy Spirit. She will bear a son, and you are to name him Jesus, for he will save his people from their sins. (Matt. 1:20b-21)

Today's text is a story we have heard many times over, but without getting to know the main character very well. Joseph is the quintessential background player. He's the guy leading the donkey on Christmas cards, or the tall kid in the striped bathrobe who gets no lines in the Christmas pageant.

Is there more we can learn about this man who played such an important role in Jesus' early life, but who disappeared from the story before Jesus preached his first sermon?

Joseph's dilemma
(vv. 18-19)

Blended families are far more common now than in the first century. Statistics show that in America, about 40 percent of children are born to women who aren't married, a trend that has held steady for more than a decade. Children may grow up with multiple father figures, or no father in sight.

Life was different in the first century, at least within Jewish culture, where marriage was the norm, divorce was rare, and single mothers were usually widows. This is not to suggest that the situation was ideal: marriages were typically arranged by parents, and children were often married by their mid-teens. In our time, when adolescence sometimes stretches into the late 20s, this may sound strange – but that was the world into which Jesus was born.

Stories in both Matthew and Luke insist that God brought about Mary's miraculous pregnancy while she remained a virgin. Joseph, then, was not Jesus' biological father – but he was his legal father.

This is why, perhaps, Matthew traces Jesus' bloodline through Joseph, even though Jesus would not have been genetically related. The genealogy found in Matt. 1:1-17 is clearly stylized and somewhat artificial. It begins with Abraham and goes forward to Jesus, marking 14 generations from Abraham to David, 14 more from David to the exile, and another 14 from the exile to the birth of Jesus. On close examination, the numbers don't all add up and several kings known to be in the line are omitted, but Matthew's purpose is clear. **[Matthew and Luke]**

While following the tradition of citing male ancestors, Matthew's genealogy notably mentions four women in addition to Mary, all of whom might be considered outside the norm. The first is Tamar, a Canaanite widow who tricked her father-in-law, Judah, into getting her pregnant after he refused to allow his youngest son to marry her in keeping with the Levirate custom (Genesis 38). Rahab, of Jericho, was widely considered to have been

---

Matthew and Luke: Matthew's genealogy, along with its internal inconsistencies, is also notably different from the one in Luke 3:23-38. While Matthew begins with Abraham and goes forward to Jesus, Luke begins with Jesus and goes backward to Adam, largely following a different line of ancestry. The differences begin with Joseph's father, whom Luke names as Heli, rather than Jacob, as in Matthew.

A traditional proposal for explaining the differences is to suggest that Heli was Mary's father, so that Luke's genealogy follows Mary's ancestral line. This is in keeping with the greater emphasis Luke's nativity story places on Mary. According to the argument, Joseph was named rather than Mary because genealogies typically list only males. Joseph could be included, proponents say, because he was the son-in-law of Mary's father.

a prostitute before casting her lot with the Israelites (Josh. 2:1-21). Ruth was a non-Israelite native of Moab (Ruth 1:4) and an ancestor of Jesus, despite the rule that Moabites were not allowed in "the assembly of the Lord" (Deut. 23:3). David's wife Bathsheba may not have been a native Hebrew: she was originally married to a soldier known as Uriah the Hittite before David committed adultery with her and orchestrated Uriah's death (2 Samuel 11).

It is hard to imagine a less likely set of ancestors for the Messiah: perhaps Matthew's intent is to remind skeptical readers that God works in mysterious ways and is not bound by human conventions or expectations. Mary's pregnancy might have seemed scandalous to many, and the presence of these women in Jesus' line might show that God had long been willing to work outside of typical norms. Another possibility is that Matthew was preparing his audience to understand that Jesus came to save both Jews and Gentiles: several of Jesus' ancestors were not born Jewish.

Matthew's intent was to identify Jesus as both a son of Abraham and "son of David" (1:1), a title that Matthew frequently used. God had promised David that his descendants would rule after him, according to 2 Sam. 7:12. After the kingdom of Judah was destroyed and Davidic scions no longer ruled in Jerusalem, the Jews began to interpret the passage as a prophecy of a Davidic descendant who would arise as a Messiah and set up a new kingdom.

But let's return our attention to Joseph, the honest carpenter who was engaged to Mary when "she was found to be with child from the Holy Spirit" (v. 18). Can you imagine how Joseph must have felt when Mary broke the news to him? Joseph did not have two millennia of Christian tradition to dull his senses to the shocking news that his betrothed wife-to-be was pregnant. Did he take the news calmly, or go to his shop and start breaking things? We may guess that Mary told him about her earlier encounter with an angel and the promise that she would conceive a child by the Holy Spirit, but would Joseph have believed such a story?

Maybe not. But still, "being a righteous man and unwilling to expose her to public disgrace," Joseph resolved to end their marriage quietly (v. 19). Early Jewish writings suggest that parents often arranged marriages while their children were still in their early to mid-teens. A ceremony before witnesses marked the betrothal as a binding agreement, with the wedding usually occurring about a year later.

During the betrothal period, the two were expected to get to know each other, but not allowed to have sexual relations. Even though a wedding had not taken place, the terminology of "husband" and "wife" could be used, as in v. 19. To break the engagement, one had to initiate formal divorce proceedings. Though Joseph planned to keep the divorce low-key, his desire to terminate the relationship suggests that he was not fully on board with Mary's explanation of the pregnancy. Would you have been?

The angel's revelation
(vv. 20-21)

Amid Joseph's questioning turmoil, "an angel of the Lord" appeared to him in a dream, saying "Joseph, son of David, do not be afraid to take Mary as your wife, for the child conceived in her is from the Holy Spirit" (v. 20).

We note with some surprise that the angel addressed Joseph as "son of David," the only time in Matthew's gospel where that refers to anyone other than Jesus. This continues to serve Matthew's purpose of identifying Jesus as a descendant of David.

The angel's speech drips with theological significance. It affirms that Jesus' conception is "from the Holy Spirit." Unlike Greek, Roman, or ancient Near Eastern myths in which lustful gods have sexual relations with human women or men, Matthew's account emphasizes God's creative power to generate a new life within Mary by spiritual means. [**Passive activity**]

Expectant couples in our day typically look forward to the first sonogram, hoping to learn the gender of their child months before its actual birth. Joseph did not gain that information from a gynecologist, but from the angel, who said "she will bear a son." More significant than gender, however, was the name to be given: "you are to name him Jesus, for he will save his people from their sins" (v. 21).

> **Passive activity:** In v. 20, the phrase "the child conceived in her" (more literally, "what is conceived in her"), translates a passive participle. This emphasizes the passive cooperation of Mary and Joseph, while it is God who plays the active role.

The English name "Jesus" transliterates the Greek *Iēsous*, which is derived from the Hebrew name *Yehōshua* or the Aramaic *Yeshua*, typically translated as "Joshua." In the ancient world, names often indicated parental hopes for the character and destiny of the child. The Hebrew version of Jesus' name means "Yahweh is salvation."

The Jews of Jesus' day had long expected a messianic son of David to arise and deliver them from the power of the Romans, restoring Israel to its former glory as an independent nation. The angel's words, then, would have come as a surprise: the Messiah's purpose would be to "save his people from their sins" – not from Roman rule, but from their own human failures.

When Jesus began his ministry, he demonstrated such miraculous powers that many people believed he could have led Israel to a military victory, and activists were deeply disappointed to learn that Jesus was more concerned with sin than with soldiers. Yet, his mission to save people from their sins was far more profound and far-reaching than any military victory. While "his people" may initially lead us to think of the Jews only, and Jesus spoke of his ministry as beginning with the Jews, the gospel makes it clear that Jesus came for all nations (Matt. 28:19).

Matthew's explanation
(vv. 22-25)

The angel's speech concludes with v. 21, so we understand vv. 22-25 as Matthew's own commentary: he believed Jesus' birth fulfilled the prophecy of Isa. 7:14, which he

> **Isaiah's prediction:** Isaiah reinforced his prediction of a son named "Immanuel" with further references in Isa. 8:8-10 and surrounding passages that speak of a golden age in which the wicked would be judged and the righteous would rule.

quotes from the Septuagint, an early Greek translation of the Hebrew Scriptures.

The text he quotes comes from a particular historical context around 735 BCE. King Ahaz of Judah, who had come to the throne at age 20, was being pressured to join an alliance with Syria and Egypt in an effort to hold off military advances of the Assyrian king Tiglath-Pileser. Isaiah cautioned Ahaz to stay out of the coalition and trust Yahweh to defend the nation.

As a sign of God's faithfulness, Isaiah announced: "Look, the young woman is with child and shall bear a son, and shall name him Immanuel." The obvious purpose of the sign was to assure Ahaz of God's present power by predicting that a young woman – probably Ahaz's wife or possibly Isaiah's – would give birth to a son and call him "Immanuel," a Hebrew phrase meaning "God with us."
[Isaiah's prediction]

Isaiah described the mother-to-be as an *'almah*, a Hebrew word used to describe a young woman of marriageable age. The word does not necessarily imply virginity, but the Septuagint translators used the Greek word *parthenos*, which specifically means "virgin."

> **Perpetual virginity?** Verse 25 notes that Joseph did not have sexual relations with Mary "until she had borne a son." This clearly implies that he did have relations with her afterward, and the New Testament speaks several times of Jesus having brothers and sisters. Mark 6:3 names James, Joses, Judas, and Simon as brothers, along with unnamed sisters. Luke speaks of Jesus' mother and brothers wanting to see him (Luke 8:19-21). John says that Jesus "went down to Capernaum with his mother, his brothers, and his disciples" after turning water to wine at Cana (John 2:12). In Acts 1:14, we read that "Mary the mother of Jesus, as well as his brothers," were among those who constantly devoted themselves to prayer after Jesus' resurrection.
>
> Some early Christians with great adoration for Mary as the mother of Jesus could not imagine her having sex or birthing other children, however. Within the Catholic tradition, a belief developed that Mary herself had been conceived by the Holy Spirit (the so-called "immaculate conception"), and that she remained a perpetual virgin. According to this view, Mary never had sex, even with Joseph, and thus Jesus' siblings mentioned in the New Testament were not Mary's biological children. Some scholars propose that they were cousins, the children of Mary's sister, while others speculate that they were children of Joseph by a former marriage. The latter proposal conjectures that Joseph was an older widower, with children, when he and Mary were married. Since Joseph is not mentioned after Luke 2:41-52, when Jesus' parents took him to the temple at age 12, it is often assumed that he died before Jesus began his public ministry, explaining his absence from those stories. While adherents of Mary's perpetual virginity cite this in support of their theory, it remains speculation. Few people lived into old age during the first century.

The child Isaiah mentioned would have been born shortly afterward, but later Jewish interpreters began to read this verse as a messianic prediction of a child who would bring God's delivering power to bear in Israel's behalf. The translation "virgin" rather than "young woman" added to the belief that the coming child would be born under miraculous circumstances.

Joseph was sufficiently impressed by the dream to do as the angel had instructed. He did not divorce Mary, but went through with the formal marriage ceremony, taking her as his wife (v. 24). Even though they lived together, Matthew is careful to point out that they had no sexual relations until after Mary had given birth to a son, whom they obediently named Jesus (v. 25). [**Perpetual virginity?**]

In this Advent season, we find ourselves caught between remembrances of Jesus' long expected birth and ministry on the one hand, and our own hopeful anticipation of Christ's return on the other. It took serious faith for Joseph to believe Mary's story, even when supported by an angel who visited his dreams. It can also be hard for us to trust in Christ's promised future, and to respond with obedience in the meantime. What helps to keep faith alive?

We could profit from remembering that Joseph, who lived mainly in the background, was a crucial member of the Christmas cast: his obedience protected Mary's reputation and gave Jesus a stable home. May we express gratitude to Joseph, the invisible but essential man.

The Hardest Question
Why did Joseph want to divorce Mary?

On the one hand, the answer seems obvious: we might assume that Joseph didn't believe Mary's story about being pregnant by the Holy Spirit. If he assumed that she had committed adultery, it's understandable that he might want to terminate the betrothal before the marriage officially began.

The story is not so simple, however. Though some rabbis were rather lenient, others insisted that the only acceptable ground for divorce was adultery, and the official penalty for adultery was death by stoning (Deut. 22:20-21, 23-24). We cannot be sure how regularly the penalty was enforced during the New Testament era, but John 8:3-11 recounts how Jesus prevented the stoning of a woman caught in adultery.

Joseph did not want the pregnant Mary to be publicly shamed as an adulteress, so his plan was to "dismiss her quietly," which would probably involve a behind-the-scenes divorce before two witnesses, after which Mary could move to another town where she would not be well known.

But what can we say about Joseph's personal feelings? Donald Hagner notes three possible ways to interpret the description of Joseph's motivation in v. 19, based on different understandings of the prepositions used.

One option is to see tension in the text, so that one could translate "*although* being righteous" (and thus beholden to the law concerning adultery), he was "*yet* not willing to make an example of her." This implies that Joseph's "righteousness" had to do with his desire to obey the law, in contrast with his personal wishes, which may have been to stay with Mary.

Another option sees greater harmony between the clauses, so that the second would read "and *therefore* not willing to make an example of her." This view assumes that Joseph may have believed Mary was guilty, but still cared for her and wanted to protect her from undue embarrassment or harm.

A third option is to assume that Joseph believed Mary's story that her pregnancy was of divine origin, and was so overcome with awe that he felt unworthy to go through with the marriage with one who had been so touched by God. This is unlikely, since vv. 20-21 appear designed to convince Joseph, who had already decided to divorce Mary, that her pregnancy was due to the Holy Spirit.

The first option appears most in line with Matthew's purpose, accounting for Joseph's compulsion to remain "righteous" while also showing benevolence to Mary. (For more, see Donald A. Hagner, *Matthew 1–13*, vol. 33A, Word Biblical Commentary [Zondervan, 1993].)

Christmas 1*

First Reading
Isaiah 9:1-7

A Son Is Born

For a child has been born for us, a son given to us; authority rests upon his shoulders; and he is named Wonderful Counselor, Mighty God, Everlasting Father, Prince of Peace. (Isa. 9:6)

Where did you first hear Christmas celebrated with the words "for unto us a child is born, unto us a child is given … and his name shall be called Wonderful, Counselor, the Mighty God, the Everlasting Father, the Prince of Peace" (KJV)?

It may have been in the stirring strains of Handel's *Messiah*, or in a 1960s-era cantata such as John W. Peterson's *Night of Miracles*, or it might simply have been in a sermon.

However we may have heard them, the words have become a part of our Christmas celebrations, as ingrained as the sheep and the manger and the baby Jesus. We hear them as an integral part of the Christmas story, a prophetic prediction of the coming Christ.

The words are so familiar that it may be hard to hear that the prophet who wrote them almost certainly had nothing of the sort in mind: Isaiah would be amazed to learn what his oracle of inspiration came to mean in the context of the church.

In today's lesson we'll explore what Isaiah, not Handel, had in mind when he envisioned a world of hope wrapped up in the swaddling clothes of a child.

A troubled time
(v. 1)

The lectionary text begins with the prophetic oracle in v. 2, but we cannot begin to grasp Isaiah's message without some understanding of the historical context. We get a glimpse of that in 9:1, which follows directly on the final verse of the previous chapter (8:22). Indeed, in the Hebrew text, 9:1 is numbered as the last verse in the previous chapter.

The political setting of Isaiah 7–11 appears to reflect the aftermath of a devastating invasion by the Assyrians, probably around 733 BCE. [**A troubled time**] It speaks of "distress and darkness, the gloom of anguish," and the threat of "thick darkness" (8:22). These images carry over into 9:1, which predicts better days to come: "But there will be no gloom for those who were in anguish" was spoken to the northern tribal lands of Zebulun and Naphtali, which had been the first to be overrun by the Assyrian forces and thus "brought into contempt."

Isaiah sees light ahead, a "latter time" when God "will make glorious the way of the sea, the land beyond the Jordan, Galilee of the nations." These three descriptors may be alternate names given to those regions by the Assyrians. Isaiah speaks of a day when the pervasive darkness and gloom will give way to light and hope.

A vision of hope
(vv. 2-5)

The poetic oracle of vv. 2-7 has been described in ways ranging from a psalm of thanksgiving to an accession hymn to a royal birth announcement. However we might classify the text, it clearly offers a hopeful outlook to Isaiah's audience.

Readers may note an underlying tension in the text, for the verbs in vv. 2-6 are mostly perfect tenses and would typically be translated as past tense. This is sometimes

---

A troubled time: The social and political setting of Isa. 9:2-7 reflects a very troubled time in the history of Judah and Israel. Isaiah prophesied during the last half of the eighth century, BCE, at a time when the United Kingdom of David and Solomon had been divided for 200 years. The first half of the eighth century had been a relatively stable and prosperous time for both the northern kingdom (Israel) and the southern kingdom (Judah), but things began to erode with the rise of the Neo-Assyrian king Tiglath-Pileser III (745–727), referred to in the Bible as "Pul." A powerful ruler, he quickly conquered Babylonia to the south and Urartu to the north. He then moved against Syria, Tyre, Israel, and Judah, no later than 738.

King Menahem (752–742) of Israel paid heavy tribute to Assyria (2 Kgs. 15:19-20), as did his son Pekahiah (742–740). This was not a popular course, however, and Pekahiah was soon assassinated and replaced by Pekah (740–732), who made an alliance with Rezin, the king of Syria, to oppose the Assyrians. This is often referred to as the "Syro-Ephraimitic Coalition."

Pekah and Rezin tried to draw Judah into the anti-Assyrian alliance, but Jotham (750–732), the king, refused. Israel and Syria then invaded Judah (2 Kgs. 15:37), and about the same time Jotham died. He was succeeded by his 20-year-old son Ahaz, whom Pekah and Rezin sought to depose. Isaiah counseled Ahaz to trust in God, assuring him that God would deal with Pekah and Rezin (7:2-9). Ahaz did not listen, however, and appealed to the Assyrian king Tiglath-Pileser to protect him against his northern neighbors (2 Kgs. 16:7-9).

Isaiah predicted that the coalition would fall and that Judah would come under increasing Assyrian domination. His predictions were correct: within a few years the northern kingdom of Israel was conquered and many residents were carried into captivity by Tiglath-Pileser's successors, Shalmaneser V (727–722) and Sargon II (722–705). Judah retained its national identity, but effectively became a vassal of Assyria (2 Kgs. 16:10-18), forced to pay tribute to avoid an outright invasion.

---

called the "prophetic perfect," in which someone spoke of something yet to come, but thought to be so certain that it could be said to have happened already. The verbal forms shift to imperfect in v. 7, often translated as future. The mixture of past and future tense verbs adds a natural tension to the reading as we try to puzzle out the prophet's meaning.

Verse 2 picks up on the contrast between darkness and light from v. 1, declaring that "the people who walked in darkness have seen a great light; those who lived in a land of deep darkness – on them light has shined" (NRSV).

In a fashion typical of Hebrew poetry, the second line advances and intensifies the thought of the first: "darkness" becomes "deep darkness" (*tsalmawet* – the same word sometimes translated as "shadow of death" in Ps. 23:4). But, the people "have seen a great light" because "light has shined on them." As the opposite of darkness, light promises the hope of salvation.

With v. 3, the prophet shifts from a third person observation to a second person address, praising God for having "multiplied the nation" and "increased its joy." [**"Not," or "his"?**] The word translated as "multiplied" doesn't necessarily refer to a growing population; it could also mean "you have made the nation great" or "you have enlarged the nation," which may catch the meaning better.

Whether the growth is in people or in power, the result is rejoicing. Isaiah sees a nation walking out of darkness, into the light, celebrating newfound strength and

confidence. Two metaphors call up joyful images: successful farmers beaming at the sight of a banner harvest, and victorious soldiers dividing the booty taken from their vanquished enemies (v. 3b).

The military metaphor morphs into reality with v. 4, as the prophet proclaims freedom from Israel's foes, whose "yoke," "bar," and "rod" – all symbols of oppression – have been (or will be) broken in a victory as unexpected as Gideon's unlikely triumph over the Midianites (Judges 6–7). In the heady aftermath of the promised victory, Isaiah predicts celebratory bonfires built of bloody clothes and battle boots (v. 5) – but such happy times were not yet.

How could the prophet's suffering hearers believe that such things would happen? What sign of hope might mark a turning point in the fortunes of Israel and Judah?

"Not," or "his"? In v. 3, the preserved Hebrew text literally reads "You enlarge the nation, you do not increase the joy," but such a reading is an internal contradiction. There is obviously a problem with the text here, and fortunately, it is easy to solve. The word translated as "not" (*l'o*) is pronounced exactly as the word meaning "its" (*lô*). At some point, a scribe misspelled the word when copying the text. The Masoretes responsible for preserving the text recognized the problem long ago. Rather than changing the text, however, they inserted the correct spelling in brackets beside the incorrect version, indicating that readers should choose the alternate version.

A child of promise
(vv. 6-7)

As he did in 7:10-17, Isaiah finds hope in the birth of a child. Indeed, he speaks as if the child has already been born: "For a child has been born for us, a son given to us . . ." (v. 6). Did Isaiah have in mind the child predicted in 7:14, or possibly Hezekiah, the son of Ahaz who would later become one of Judah's most fondly remembered kings? Of all kings who ruled over Judah and Israel, only Hezekiah and the later king Josiah received unqualified praise from the author of 1–2 Kings.

Whether or not Isaiah was thinking of Hezekiah, there is no question that he had in mind a descendant of David who would lead with authority and preside over an era of unprecedented glory for the nation.

Even so, how do we reconcile the thought of an earthly ruler with the expansive titles he attributed to the coming king? [**How many titles?**]

"Wonderful Counselor" is straightforward, as it implies something akin to "Extraordinary Strategist" or "Wise Advisor," a valuable leader in wartime.

But what are we to make of the name "Mighty God"? Although kings in Egypt and Mesopotamia sometimes claimed to be gods, this was not the case in Israel. Biblical coronation hymns suggest, however, a tradition that God "adopted" each king upon his coronation (see Ps. 2:7).

How many titles? The various names given to the coming king have occasioned much discussion. Does the collection of impressive words indicate four titles? Five? More?

The words typically translated as "wonderful," "counselor," "mighty," and "God" are written separately, while the two words translated as "everlasting father" are written together in Hebrew, and the two words for "Prince of Peace" are connected in the text with a hyphen.

One might suggest, then, that there are six titles: "Wonderful," "Counselor," "Mighty One," "God," "Everlasting Father," and "Prince of Peace."

It seems best, however, to follow the lead of the last two titles and interpret the list as four epithets made of paired words, whether they are written together or not. Thus, "Wonderful Counselor," "Mighty God," "Everlasting Father," and "Prince of Peace" would be honorifics used to describe the coming king.

A forever father?: How do we understand the title "Everlasting Father"? Contemporary Christians often refer to God as "Father," perhaps following the pattern set by Jesus, but it was unusual for God to be called "Father" in the Old Testament. There are a few instances in which God is described as a father (Deut. 32:6; 2 Sam. 7:14; Jer. 3:4, 19; Isa. 63:16; Mal. 2:10), but combination terms such as "Everlasting Father" are otherwise unknown.

Kings were even less likely to be called "father" among the Hebrews (1 Sam. 24:11 is a rare exception), but the term was not inappropriate for a good and compassionate leader.

Likewise, individuals are not thought of as being "everlasting" in Hebrew thought, but God's promise to David in 2 Samuel 7 was said to ensure a kingdom that would last forever (2 Sam. 7:13, 16). Perhaps, then, we are to think of the coming king as one who would perpetuate the everlasting dynasty promised to David.

Many Hebrew names include God (*'el*) or Yahweh (usually *-iah*) as an integral element. For example, "Isaiah" means "Salvation of Yahweh," "Elijah" means "my God is Yahweh," and Hezekiah means something similar to "Strengthened by Yahweh."

The title "Mighty God" (*'el gibbôr*) is spelled as two words, however, and the same term is used in 10:21 with clear reference to God. This suggests that the king in question, at the very least, bears a close relationship with God.

The title "Everlasting Father" offers a conundrum for interpretation. [**A forever father?**] It might be intended to express hope that the coming king, who would be in the Davidic line, would represent the everlasting dynasty promised to David in 2 Samuel 7.

Like "Wonderful Counselor," the term "Prince of Peace" raises few questions. People naturally idolized a king who brought peace and security for his subjects.

With v. 7, the prophet clearly turns to the future. He sees the coming king's authority and rule of peace growing endlessly, a tangible fulfillment of the promise that David's descendants would rule over an everlasting kingdom.

The new king would bring more than security, however: he would rule with the ideals of justice and righteousness "from this time onward and forevermore."

Such promises sound too good to be true, don't they? Isaiah knew that his hearers would be skeptical, too. Thus, he concludes with the assurance that "The zeal of the LORD of hosts will do this."

A puzzle for interpreters

How do we interpret this text? We can see how it functioned as a promise of hope for troubled Judahites in the eighth century BCE, but we are much more likely to remember it from quotations in the New Testament. Isaiah almost certainly hoped that Hezekiah would fulfill his rosy predictions, but when that did not happen, later believers transposed his prophetic oracle to a future messiah. The gospel writers believed the birth of Christ finally fulfilled the promise of a child who would live into the names "Wonderful Counselor, Mighty God, Everlasting Father, Prince of Peace" (9:6), one who would establish a just and peaceful dominion without end (9:7).

This text challenges us to do more than celebrate the birth of Jesus, however. Instead of simply spiritualizing Isaiah's message, we should remember that the people of our world also face days of darkness and gloom. Many people long for light and security, justice and righteousness that are not only a future hope, but also a present reality.

As children of God and followers of the Prince of Peace, believers are called to devote our best efforts toward bringing peace and justice – security and equality – to the world in which we live.

As we recall Isaiah's promise that "the zeal of the LORD of hosts will do this," let us remember that we are counted among the hosts of those whom God has called to live as model citizens of the Kingdom, working for peace and justice throughout the earth.

The Hardest Question
Did Isaiah predict the coming of Christ?

When Isaiah spoke the hopeful words of Isa. 9:2-7, did he have in mind an earthly king who would bring a quick end to the Assyrian threat, or did his vision intentionally look beyond to a messianic ruler who would usher in the eschatological end of the age?

The truth is, no one can look into a long-dead prophet's mind and know for sure what he intended. We are confident, however, that the Hebrew prophets generally addressed their message to people in their own time and context, so it is most likely that Isaiah was expressing high hopes that Hezekiah and his rule would become the embodied fulfillment of God's promise to David.

Some interpreters believe that Isaiah was looking further into the future, thinking of a messiah with divine attributes. The written preaching of Isaiah of Jerusalem, however, never uses the term "messiah," a Hebrew word that literally means "anointed." Second Isaiah, the prophet of the exile, spoke once of "God's anointed" deliverer (45:1) – but with specific reference to Cyrus, the Persian ruler who conquered Babylon and granted Hebrew exiles the right to return home. Third Isaiah, who spoke both comforting and challenging words many years later, during the postexilic period, did use the term, declaring that "The Spirit of the LORD is upon me, because the LORD has anointed me …" (61:1), a text that Jesus later cited as a sort of mission statement.

Looking back from our perspective, we know that neither Hezekiah nor any other Hebrew ruler ever achieved anything approaching the illustrious predictions of Isa. 9:2-7. As time went on, the Jewish people recognized that the promise to David seemed unfulfilled, so their hopes began to focus on a future day when a divinely anointed messiah would rise to introduce a new age of salvation and hope for Israel. This messianic hope developed mainly in the late postexilic period, however, long after Isaiah of Jerusalem's time.

Today we are likely to view Isaiah's oracle through the lens of the New Testament, seeing Jesus as the only one worthy of being called Wonderful Counselor, Mighty God, Everlasting Father, and Prince of Peace. We see Christ as the one who inaugurated the eternal Kingdom of God into human history and the one who will bring about its ultimate, eternal fulfillment. What Isaiah saw taking place through military victory and strong rule on earth, we see in spiritual terms that equate salvation with eternal life in a heavenly kingdom.

So, it is likely that Isaiah truly hoped that Hezekiah would prove to be the Davidic ruler of his dreams, but when that did not happen, later generations sought the fulfillment of his promise through a delivering messiah who was yet to come. Many Jewish people still await the Messiah's arrival, but those who follow Jesus call him "Christ" – the Greek term for "anointed" – believing him to be the promised prince of Isaiah's announcement.

Second Reading
Psalm 96*

Be Honored, Lord

Sing to the LORD, bless his name; tell of his salvation from day to day. (Ps. 96:2)

Have you ever noticed how the music we listened to as teenagers imprints itself as the playlist of our lives? Though some of us enjoy discovering new artists and new music, others figure there's no point in learning to appreciate Maroon 5 when we can still listen to the Beatles, or in cultivating a taste for rap or reggae when we're perfectly happy with rhythm & blues or rock & roll.

But sometimes a new song catches our ear, and we can't help humming the tune, even if we don't know who's singing it.

When the songwriter-theologian who penned Psalm 96 composed a new song, he had high hopes that it would catch on, and it did, for it remains popular at least 2,500 years after its debut.

Christians most commonly hear it read in services during the Christmas season, and for good reason: the psalm looks joyfully to the day when the God who reigns over all will come to set things right.

Sing, earth!
(vv. 1-6)

The psalm falls into three hymnic verses, each beginning with a call to praise God, followed by the reasons why praise is due. [**How many verses?**]

The first verse begins with a repetitive call to "sing to the LORD a new song; sing to the LORD all the earth. Sing to the LORD, bless his name" (vv. 1-2a).

The purpose of singing to the LORD was threefold: to "bless his name," to "tell of his salvation," and to "declare his glory among the nations, his marvelous works among

> **How many verses?** While I have followed some scholars in perceiving three primary sections in Psalm 96 (vv. 1-6, 7-10, 11-13), others divide it into two (vv. 1-6, 7-13), and still others break it into four parts (vv. 1-3, 4-6, 7-10, 11-13). The important thing is to note that the psalm contains both calls to rejoice and reasons for the rejoicing.

all the peoples" (v. 3). These include some powerful words: the term translated as "glory" is *chabôd*, a noun derived from a verb that means "to be heavy" or "to be honored." The noun form was commonly used to speak of the heavyweight glory or honor that was due to God.

The expression "marvelous works" (NRSV) or "amazing deeds" (NET) is a passive participle of a verb meaning "to be wonderful." Terms such as "works" and "deeds" are not in the text, but often added for clarity: a literal translation might be "tell all the peoples about his being wonderful," or "about his awesomeness."

The choral testimony was not only powerful, but also designed to be persistent, offered "from day to day." It's easier to sing praise on some days than on others, but many people find that the very act of singing praise – especially in the company of fellow believers – can lift their spirits in a significant and lasting way.

One reason worship in predominantly Black churches may last two hours or more, and feature joyful songs with victorious themes, is that people who have felt oppressed and downtrodden can find in such worship the strength and encouragement to help them face another week.

Singing praise is good for the soul, but not its primary purpose. We tell of God's greatness because God is worthy

---

*Psalm 96 also appears as a reading for Proper 24 in Year A and Proper 4 in Year C.

And the stars also: Yahweh is to be feared above all gods, the psalmist said, "For all the gods of the peoples are idols, but the LORD made the heavens." Mesopotamian gods such as Shamash and Sîn and Ishtar were identified with heavenly bodies such as the sun, moon, and planet Venus, but it was Yahweh who made the heavens and all that is in them.

Biblical writers intentionally avoided similar connections. For example, the opening chapter of Genesis does not mention the sun or moon by name, lest they be thought of as gods. Rather, the author wrote that God created the "greater light to rule the day," and "the lesser light to rule the night." As if it was an afterthought, he added "and the stars."

The word choice is emphatic, insisting that the sun, moon, and stars were creations of the creator God, not divine beings in themselves.

of our acclaim, as we learn in vv. 4-6, which begin: "Great is the LORD, and greatly to be praised."

Why should we do this? Because Yahweh is "to be revered above all gods."

"The gods of the peoples are idols," the psalmist said – mere constructs of stone or wood or bronze combined with the human imagination. While popular gods were human projections of themselves, "the LORD made the heavens" (v. 5).

The psalmist insisted that gods such as Baal and Asherah, Dagon and Mot could be powerful in imagination but were impotent in reality. They might be thought of as the gods of rain and fertility and grain and death, but Yahweh reigned above all. "Honor and majesty are before him; strength and beauty are in his sanctuary" (v. 6). [**And the stars also**]

This is one of the reasons church architects – especially those who designed the great cathedrals – have sought to create a large space that exhibits both beauty and grandeur while making the worshiper feel small before the greatness of God.

Praise, people!
(vv. 7-10)

The second verse of the hymn switches the active verb from "sing" to "ascribe," again repeating it three times: "Ascribe to the LORD, O families of the peoples, ascribe to the LORD glory and strength. Ascribe to the LORD the glory due his name" (vv. 7-8a).

The word "ascribe" – used three times in vv. 7-8 – is not common in English, but preferred by most translations (NRSV, NET, NIV11, HCSB, NASB95, ESV). It translates a word more commonly rendered as "give," as in the KJV, but the context suggests a spoken component. Verbs such as "attribute" or "credit" could catch the sense, but are no less unwieldy than "ascribe."

The psalmist is calling for a vocal offering of praise in addition to the material offerings (*minhâ*) to be brought into the place of worship. The reference to physical offerings of grain or flour, wine or money was a reminder that our worship also includes costly elements as tangible demonstrations of our faith and gratitude.

The word for "worship" in v. 9 literally means "to bow down" or "to prostrate oneself." Some mainline churches have "kneeling benches" attached to the back of the pews, but many modern worshipers would never think of kneeling as a part of public worship, much less stretching out on the floor. [**Prostration**]

The psalmist calls us to bow before Yahweh "in holy splendor," which may relate to the impressive sanctuary, the attire of the worshipers, or an awareness of worship's sacred nature.

The second half for v. 9 seems to echo the abject humility of the call to "bow before the LORD" in the first half. Most modern versions have "tremble before him, all the earth." The word translated as "tremble" means "to whirl," "to dance," or "to writhe." It could be used of joyful dance, of writhing in pain, or of anxious waiting. While "tremble" is a reasonable reading, it's possible that the psalmist had in mind a joyful dance, for he is singing a joyful song and calling others to join the celebration.

Prostration: The psalmist's call for worshipers to bow down or prostrate themselves before Yahweh may seem alien to most Christians, but would resonate clearly with those who practice Islam. Mosques typically feature carpet with a distinct pattern but no pews: worshipers stand or kneel on designated lines for much of the service, occasionally prostrating themselves during prayer. Those who pray at home or in other places at designated times of prayer also roll out a mat and kneel or prostrate themselves to show humility as they pray.

And what was there to celebrate? "Say among the nations, 'The LORD is king! The world is firmly established; it shall never be moved. He will judge the peoples with equity'" (v. 10).

The message is not for Israel alone, but for all the nations – indeed, for "all the earth," as in v. 9 and in the following verses. And the message is that "The LORD is king!" *God reigns.*

What was the central message of Jesus when he went about preaching? "The kingdom of God is at hand" (Mark 1:15). Jesus constantly taught of God's rule or reign, and his teachings were peppered with references to what the kingdom of God is like, or what it means to live in God's kingdom.

The psalmist did not know the extent of God's gracious love that we have come to know in Jesus, but he fully believed that God ruled over the earth and was coming to "judge the peoples with equity."

The root meaning of the word translated "equity" is "evenness." In an ethical sense, it refers to fairness: God will judge all people fairly and justly. In a world marred by injustice where the level of privilege often depends on the color of one's skin, the affirmation that God judges all people with equity is welcome news.

Rejoice, all!
(vv. 11-13)

When God rules, humans are not the only ones to rejoice: the psalmist imagined all of creation expressing euphoric glee to be part of God's universal kingdom. He called for the heavens to be glad and the earth to rejoice as the sea shouted along with all creatures within it. "Let the field exult," he sang, "and everything in it," while "the trees of the forest sing for joy" (vv. 11-12). [**The eco-psalmist**]

Anticipation that God "is coming to judge the earth" leads the planet itself to rejoice. That thought resonates even more clearly in our day, when humans have brought so much damage to the environment. Again the psalm emphasizes that, unlike humans who are subject to error or partiality, God "will judge the world with righteousness, and the peoples with his truth" (v. 13).

We may find it difficult to think of judgment as a time for rejoicing, for we typically picture judgment as a guilty defendant standing to be condemned and sentenced.

> **The eco-psalmist:** Long before modern ecologists began to emphasize the interdependence of the natural environment, the psalmist understood that all things are connected. He could not have described the importance of the ozone layer in the upper atmosphere, the dangers of acidification of the oceans, or the perils of pollution on land and streams, but he understood that everything from the skies to the seas and from fields to forests was part of God's good creation.

For the psalmist, however, God's coming judgment would restore proper order and put all things right.

We know that many things are out of order in our world; many things are not right. There is endemic injustice in an economic system that allows a small fraction of people to control most of the world's wealth, for example.

In America, rampant injustice has long marked our penal system, which locks up more of its population than any other country, and where people of color are far more likely to be convicted of crimes and to have longer sentences than whites.

Disparities in convictions and sentencing are due not only to racial bias, but also to wealth disparities: those who can afford high-priced lawyers are much more likely to walk free than those who rely on public defenders.

We could name other areas of injustice based on gender or gender preference. Ethnicity, age, social status, and other factors often leave people on the outside looking in.

Sadly, many of us fail to recognize the privilege we have, or to appreciate the obstacles that others face.

When Jesus came to proclaim the kingdom of God, he equated it to doing justice: "The Spirit of the Lord is upon me," Jesus said, "because he has anointed me to bring good news to the poor. He has sent me to proclaim release to the captives and recovery of sight to the blind, to let the oppressed go free" (Luke 4:18).

Jesus' teaching focused on ways in which those who live under God's reign and live with a Christ-like point of view are called to be people of justice who do the Lord's work of setting things right in a world gone wrong.

This raises a question for each of us: "What have I done this week to make this world a more just and equitable place?" Or perhaps, more importantly, "What will I do *next* week?"

The Hardest Question
What does it mean to "Worship the LORD in holy splendor"?

In v. 9, the psalmist calls for people to "Worship the LORD in holy splendor." Knowing how to interpret this verse is difficult because the Hebrew expression is rarely used.

One view is that it might refer to the "holy splendor" of the sanctuary, or with reference to God, imaginatively clothed in majestic holiness. The NIV11 and HCSB both have "Worship the LORD in the splendor of his holiness." The KJV takes a similar approach, calling people to "worship the LORD in the beauty of holiness."

The NRSV seems to connect the phrase to the worshiper, but without much clarity: "Worship the LORD in holy splendor." Is it God's holy splendor, or a characteristic of the worshipers?

The word rendered as "splendor" occurs only five times in the Hebrew Bible, once as "the glory of a king (Prov. 14:28) and elsewhere in the context of worship (1 Chron. 16:29; 2 Chron. 20:21; Ps. 29:2, 96:9). In most cases, it seems to describe impressive clothing such as that worn by a king, the priests, or the temple singers. Thus, the NET and NASB95 indicate that those who praise God are to "worship the LORD in holy attire."

If this is the correct interpretation, it does not suggest that a person cannot worship in jeans and a T-shirt, but it does imply a certain formality to worship, one reason why many people like to dress in their "Sunday best" as a means of showing respect to God.

However we interpret it, the phrase indicates that worshipers, like God, should be characterized by a spirit of holiness – which is a splendid thing.

Christmas 1

Third Reading
Titus 2:11-14

Salvation Matters

For the grace of God has appeared, bringing salvation to all, training us to renounce impiety and worldly passions, and in the present age to live lives that are self-controlled, upright, and godly ... (Titus 2:11-12)

The celebration of Christmas focuses on the belief that Christ came into the world to make possible our salvation from sin and initiation into a new and more hopeful life. This text from Titus insists that experiencing salvation should do more than put our names on a church roll: it should lead to a noticeable difference in our lives. The author was not alone in affirming that our faith should be reflected in our behavior, but this brief text is particularly emphatic.

Grace at work
(v. 11)

The short epistle, which claims to be from Paul, portrays Titus as a gifted minister and faithful companion whom Paul had appointed to lead the churches in Crete and to teach them with authority. [**Who wrote the epistle to Titus?**]

Lectionary readings from Titus appear only during the Christmas season, when they are sure to be overshadowed by more impressive, inspiring, or familiar passages. That may be for good reason: the letter has a grumpy tone that is high on instruction but short on inspiration. The letter counsels women to submit to their husbands (2:5) and slaves to be submissive to their masters, never stealing or talking back to them (2:9). People of all ages are warned to be temperate and self-controlled (2:2, 5, 6). Do we really want to read this letter?

It can be hard to get past the cultural conditioning of the author's advice, but it is important to remember that he wrote as a child of his time, immersed in a culture in which slavery and female submission were part of the air that people breathed.

Who wrote the epistle to Titus? Titus was frequently cited as a companion of Paul. He joined Paul on an important visit to Jerusalem (Gal. 2:1-3), and on two occasions Paul sent Titus to the church in Corinth bearing letters or seeking to strengthen Paul's relation to the church (2 Cor. 7:6-7, 13-14; 8:6, 16-17). The letter of Titus asserts that he had been with Paul on the island of Crete, and that Paul had put him in charge of new churches there.

Even so, scholars often question whether Paul was the author of 1–2 Timothy and Titus, known as the "Pastoral Epistles." The vocabulary and style of the letters are quite different from letters more commonly attributed to Paul, and they lack some of themes that Paul usually emphasized.

It is possible that Paul is the author, but some scholars argue it is more likely that a close disciple of Paul wrote the letters in his name. Fortunately, understanding the letter's message is not dependent on a clear identification of the author.

If we can lower our contemporary cultural hackles, we may find some solid encouragement for our own culturally conditioned lives.

Today's brief text follows a reference to "the doctrine of God our Savior" and precedes a charge for Titus to faithfully teach what he has learned. Though it serves mainly as a transition, the short text is packed with significance.

"For the grace of God has appeared, bringing salvation to all" is a proper text for the Christmas season, a reminder that in Jesus God's grace became manifest in the flesh for the eternal purpose of bringing redemption into the world. The word translated as "has appeared" comes from *'epiphaínō*, the root of our word "epiphany."

The pastoral epistles used the term to describe both the incarnation of Jesus (2 Tim. 1:10, Titus 3:4) and his anticipated second coming (1 Tim. 6:14; 2 Tim. 4:1, 8). We now use it to name the season of Epiphany, which focuses on the appearance or revelation of Christ in the world.

The author reminds Titus that the life-changing grace that appeared in Christ is not just for "the elect" or any other limited group, but "to all."

Both Titus and the members of the churches he led had experienced the freedom of spirit associated with salvation, but there is more to salvation than forgiveness of sin. Our new relationship with God calls us to a new kind of life.

Salvation at work
(v. 12)

We don't normally think of grace as a teacher, but the word "grace" in v. 11 remains the subject of the sentence that continues in v. 12: "training us to renounce impiety and worldly passions, and in the present age to live lives that are self-controlled, upright, and godly."

The verb rendered "training" comes from *paideúō*, and is closely related to the word for child, *paidíon*. Its basic meaning is "to train children," which leads to an additional sense of "to chastise" or admonish another in hopes of shaping their character in positive ways. When any of us come to Christ, we come as spiritual children.

Thinking on a more adult level, however, as a personal trainer or lifestyle coach might work with us to overcome harmful habits, improve our diets, and increase our fitness, so the reality of grace motivates us toward healthier living, both spiritually and otherwise.

That begins with "renouncing impiety and worldly passions." The word for "impiety" is often translated as "ungodliness" (NIV11) or "godless ways" (NET), that is, attitudes and behaviors that are shaped by culture and not by Christ.

"Worldly passions" are not limited to the carnal vices of lust, greed, and gluttony, but can also include our desires for power and control, the aspiration to manage our own lives without concern for others or for God.

Grace leading to salvation takes us out of that sphere, the writer insisted, turning us in the opposite direction so we may be "self-controlled, upright, and godly." As noted

> **Positive and negative:** Verse 11's counsel to avoid ungodliness and to be godly uses two forms related to the same verb (*sébomai*) that relates to expressing one's allegiance to a particular deity. The noun form with the negative prefix *'a* (*'asébeian*) means "ungodliness," not following the deity's ways. An adverbial form with the positive prefix *eu* (*'eusébōs*) means "godly."

earlier, self-control is a prime virtue for the writer, as it was in the teachings of philosophers who often counseled self-control, temperance, or discretion — all potential translations of the Greek word *sōphrónōs*.

Grace likewise calls us to be upright, from a word that emphasizes acting with justice. Avoiding ungodliness, we are to be godly, patterning our living after God's teaching as revealed in Christ. These are not ideal hopes for a future time, but a challenge for now, for the lives we live "in the present age." [**Positive and negative**]

Hope at work
(vv. 13-14)

Though we read this text while celebrating Christ's first advent, the writer of Titus was also looking toward a second advent, and he was encouraging his readers to do the same. The call to practice godly living "in the present age" takes place "while we wait for the blessed hope and the manifestation of the glory of our great God and Savior, Jesus Christ" (v. 13).

Like other believers of his time, the author of Titus held to the "blessed hope" that Christ would return in glory, and soon. In doing so, he identified Jesus Christ not only as Savior, but also as God. In the Greek construction, "God and Savior," both words point to the same person: Jesus Christ. This is among the clearest affirmations of the deity of Christ to be found in the New Testament.

The writer seems amazed in pondering the idea that Jesus, being one with God, would have suffered the indignities of incarnation and crucifixion. He does not want the magnitude of this act to be lost on readers, but insists that it should be transformative. "He it is who gave himself for us that he might redeem us from all iniquity and purify for himself a people of his own who are zealous for good deeds" (v. 14).

Our redemption and cleansing from sin are not for our sake alone, but also for God's sake. God has made us "for himself a people of his own." This recalls Exod. 19:5-6, where God instructed Moses to charge the Israelites: "if you obey my voice and keep my covenant, you shall be my treasured possession out of all the peoples. Indeed, the whole earth is mine, but you shall be for me a priestly kingdom and a holy nation."

The Hebrew Bible consistently lambasts Israel for its failure to live up to that calling, and Christian believers find it no less challenging to live fully before God as "a people of his own," especially people "who are zealous for good deeds."

The author of Titus calls believers to be passionate when it comes to serving Christ. Though self-controlled with respect to worldly desires, we are to be "zealous" for good works. Though drawn directly from the Greek *zēlōtēs*, from which we get the English word "zealot," the challenge is not that we become religious fanatics who spend our lives preaching on street corners, but that we be eager to do what is right, to practice justice, to be generous with our time and our resources in seeking to live as Christ would have us to.

Reading this text during the Christmas season, we know how easy it is for both children and adults to be filled with excitement about colorful decorations, time with family, abundant food, and gifts under the tree. The author calls us to have the same zeal for living out our faith.

While some people today believe that "living for Jesus" means adhering to a so-called "biblical worldview" drawn mainly from proof-texted social norms in line with past tradition, we are challenged to live with a Jesus-focused worldview, seeking to see our own worlds as Jesus would see, and to do as Jesus would do.

Or, as the author would put it, our challenge is to let the grace of Christ be not only our savior, but also our trainer in living godly lives. That, he believed, was what Jesus' coming was all about.

The Hardest Question
What does the author mean by "worldly passions"?

The word translated as "worldly" is *kosmikos*, the adjectival form of *kosmos*, from which we get "cosmos," "cosmic," and other words related to the universe in general.

Kosmos could mean "universe," but it typically meant "world," and in common use, *kosmikos* referred to the material world and had no particularly spiritual connotations, but early Christians came to use the word in a largely pejorative way, associating "worldly" things with human systems or practices or passions that served human needs without reference to God – or in opposition to God.

The Fourth Gospel, for example, has Jesus say: "I have given them your word, and the world has hated them because they do not belong to the world, just as I do not belong to the world. I am not asking you to take them out of the world, but I ask you to protect them from the evil one. They do not belong to the world, just as I do not belong to the world" (John 17:14-16). Here, the world is not just a physical place, but human ways of doing things apart from God.

Paul spoke of living in the world as living in opposition to God. "We have received not the spirit of the world," he wrote to the Corinthians, "but the Spirit that is from God" (1 Cor. 2:12). One should put the world behind, he believed. To the Galatians, he said "May I never boast of anything except the cross of my Lord Jesus Christ, by which the world has been crucified to me and I to the world" (Gal. 6:14).

Paul wanted others to move beyond the world, too, exhorting the church at Colossae with a sharp question: "If with Christ you died to the elemental spirits of the universe (*kosmos*), why do you live as if you still belonged to the world (*kosmos*)?" (Col. 2:20).

The author of 1 John saw the world as an entity opposed to God, and he advised readers to seek a more spiritual focus: "Do not love the world or the things in the world. The love of the Father is not in those who love the world; for all that is in the world – the desire of the flesh, the desire of the eyes, the pride in riches – comes not from the Father but from the world. And the world and its desire are passing away, but those who do the will of God live forever" (1 John 2:15-17).

The Johannine author's elaboration of "the world" as "the desire of the flesh, the desire of the eyes, the pride in riches" may help us to interpret Titus' warning against "worldly desires."

Christmas 1

Fourth Reading
Luke 2:1-20*

A Different Angle

… to you is born this day in the city of David a Savior, who is the Messiah, the Lord. (Luke 2:11)

The Christmas story is so familiar that a routine commentary might put many people to sleep. We could talk about the problems of the date or the anomaly of Quirinius, but that wouldn't keep most people interested long. We could discuss theological implications of the Christmas story, but those are also familiar. As a change of pace, consider this imaginative retelling of Luke 2:1-20 from the perspective of the stable hand at the Bethlehem inn. Perhaps the change in viewpoint can provide useful background color while helping us to appreciate the story in new ways. Just imagine that the speaker has come to visit your church and to tell his story.

Bethlehem

Well, this place looks nothin' like Bethlehem. I see there's lots of room in *this* inn.

You don't look much like Bethlehem people, either; you all look too … *clean*. Bethlehem ain't much of a town, but there's a few folks that'll stop here. We're about six miles or so south of Jerusalem, on the main road from Hebron and the Negev. Sometimes traveling merchants coming from Egypt or Arabia will stop here to rest up at the inn before they head to the bazaars in Jerusalem early the next morning.

That's where I came in. No, I wasn't the innkeeper. His name was Lumas, and he ran the only caravansary in town, out by the road. Called it "Caravan 6." I don't know why. He always kept a big oil lamp burnin' out by the road so you wouldn't miss it at night.

It wasn't really much of an inn, at least not the way you would think of it. There was an archway that led into a big open courtyard with a well in it, and that was surrounded by rooms that were mostly mud brick stalls on stone foundations with a thatched roof over the top. It was a dry place to unroll your sleeping blankets, and that's all most folks expected. You could boil your own mush over the community campfire or pay a little extra and Lumas' wife would bring you some mutton stew. There was a privy out back, and you could tie your animals right out in the courtyard where you could keep an eye on them.

So, I'm the guy who looked after the camels and the donkeys, not to mention the sheep and goats Lumas kept penned up out back. I'd bring hay up from the shed just down the hill so the animals could eat, and then I had to shovel up what the hay turned into. You'd be surprised how much manure a few camels and a dozen donkeys can produce. Lumas might let folks keep their animals in the courtyard, but he didn't want the place to smell like a stable, so I scooped their poop and covered the wet spots with fresh hay.

That's why nobody remembers my real name anymore. It's hard to shovel manure all day without pickin' up a certain *cachet*, so I got the nickname "Domen," which is just one of the many Hebrew words we have for "manure."

There's a big compost pile out back, behind the hay shed and the stable where Lumas keeps his own animals. When I shovel up the dirty hay and the manure, we mix it all together and let it work magic over the winter. Next spring we'll spread it on the fields for fertilizer. We've always been into what you call recycling.

A similar form of this text (Luke 2:1-7, 8-20) is used for Christmas 2. A study of Luke 2:1-20 is provided here to serve both options.

The Census

But you're not interested in all that stuff, are you? *You want to know about that baby.* Everybody does.

Well, the baby got here in the usual way, though not without a whole lot of commotion and hand-wringing and hurry-upping. And it never would have happened here at all if it hadn't been for that strange Roman census. Normally they just count people where they live, but this year, the muckety-mucks got a wild idea that everybody should go back to their ever-so-many great-grandaddy's hometown so they could count noses and charge more taxes. [**Census**]

What that meant is that poor little Bethlehem was swamped, because everybody knows that the great king David came from Bethlehem, and he had lots of wives and many children, and his son Solomon had even more wives and more children than I can count, and every one of their descendants can count back to David, and all of them are proud of their pedigree. Now, Bethlehem was just a hamlet when David was born, and it was still a small town when I was around, so there is no way on God's green earth that you could fit all of David's descendants in the place.

Not that people didn't try: Bethlehem started filling up long before the appointed day, and everybody who was even remotely kin to somebody local just moved right in and imposed themselves on the kinfolks' hospitality. People were camping out beside the road, and of course, Lumas' Caravan 6 and Travel Supply Emporium was overflowing. He went up on his rates and double-booked the rooms

and still had more business than he could handle – and I had more manure than I could shovel. All in all, it was a mess, I tell you.

The Family

You'd think, in the middle of all that, you wouldn't notice one more couple coming in, but everybody did. You couldn't help but notice the girl – she was just a little thing, but she was *so* pregnant. And you could tell she was hurting. Her eyes were sunk in about as far as her belly was poked out.

The man kept beggin' Lumas to give them a room, but he could see for himself that they'd have to throw out two other families to make space. When Lumas saw me come by with the wheelbarrow, he had an idea, and told me to take 'em down to the hay shed and clear out a corner where they could rest. "It's really the best I can do," he told them. "I'll send someone to help you soon."

That had to be me, because old Lumas promptly forgot about it. He was about wrung out, and I guess I don't blame him. It didn't matter: the man seemed very grateful to have any sort of roof over their heads.

Joseph was his name, he said, and he called his young wife "Mary" – good, honest names. Anyway, I took them down the hill and told them where to watch their step, and I pitched enough hay out of a corner for them to have a cozy little place for the night, but I wouldn't let their donkey inside lest he stink up the place.

They spread their blankets over a pile of hay, and I dragged in a small feed trough and cleaned it out for them, just in case. It didn't really take long for things to happen after that – the young woman must've been in labor for some time before they got here, and she squatted down and had that baby birthed almost before I could get back with some clean water and soft rags. She had brought her own swaddling to wrap the baby in, and before long the little fellow was nursing and I think his mama slept right through it.

The Shepherds

Once things settled down, I pushed the wheelbarrow back up the hill to shovel out the courtyard one more time, and almost got run over by Cousin Joram and his boys comin' down the road. They all had this wild look, like a lion had

---

Census: Luke's purpose in locating Jesus' birth in Bethlehem is clearly to emphasize that he was a descendant of David. The tradition must have developed long after Jesus' birth, because the story appears to have some problems. We have no record of a census conducted under Augustus, for one thing. For another, his timing is off: Quirinius did not become governor of Syria until 6 CE, probably 10 years after Jesus was born.

Historical quibbles should not undercut the theological importance of the story: Jesus was born in a time of political uneasiness, and into a world hailed by the emperor Augustus not only as "lord" (*kurios*), but also as "savior of the whole world."

Luke intends to contrast the earthly "lord" with the true "Savior, who is the Messiah (Christ), the Lord" (v. 11).

been after 'em. I knew they were supposed to be up in the high meadows outside of town – but here they were, all flustered and out of breath.

"What's wrong, Joram?" I asked. "Did bandits steal your sheep? What's going on?"

He looked at me and wheezed, *"You mean you don't know?"*

"Know what?" I said.

"Didn't you hear about the baby? We're lookin' for him."

"Well," I said, "There was a baby boy born here tonight, but his folks are from Nazareth and I don't think you'd know them."

"Oh," Joram said, "If he was born here at the inn, I guess he couldn't be the one."

"Well," I told him, "He wasn't exactly born in the inn. His folks are staying in the hay shed out back. The little fella's sleeping in a manger I cleaned out for 'em."

Oh, you would have thought I had handed Joram a million shekels. He almost jumped out of his sandals, and I swear he turned a flip before he came down. He and his boys started slapping each other on the back and grinning and saying, *"It's true! It's true!"*

The Angels

And finally, I asked, *"What's true?"*

And Joram calmed down a bit and said, "When the baby was born, did the angels sing?"

And I said, *"What angels? That girl made a lot of noises, but it sure didn't sound like angels singing."*

And he said, "Did the heavens open wide?"

And I said, "You've been drinking, haven't you?"

And he said, "Oh, no, cousin. If I'm drunk, I'm drunk on joy! Let me tell you what happened to us!"

Then the other boys all gathered around and nodded their heads so I wouldn't think he was tellin' a story.

"We were out in the fields watching over the sheep, like we always do, and the night was dark since there's not much of a moon tonight, and everything was quiet, and then 'boom!' The night exploded and right there in front of me was an honest-to-God angel, all big and shining white, and the air crackled and fizzed when he moved … "

I looked at the other boys, and they were all still nodding their heads and grinning like they had seen it, too.

"And then the angel spoke to us," Joram said, "and his voice was like music walking. He said 'Don't be afraid, but listen: I'm bringing you great and happy news for everybody; for *this very day* in David's town a baby was born who will be the Savior, the Messiah, the Lord.'"

"Domen!" he said, *"the Messiah we've been hoping for! He said the Messiah was born today in David's town, and we all know that means Bethlehem!"*

"So," I said … "then why ain't you lookin' for him up on the hill where the grand old families live? You wouldn't expect the Messiah to be born down here by the road!"

The Manger

"That's what I thought, too," said Joram, "but the angel said 'And this will be a sign for you: you will find a baby wrapped in swaddling clothes and lying in a manger.' And you said this baby was sleepin' in Lumas' hay manger! *It's the sign!* It's *what the angel said! Are you sure the angels didn't sing?"*

And again, I said, *"What angels?"* And Joram said, "when the first angel finished speaking to us, it was like the clouds rolled back and the sky lit up like morning, and we could see *angels everywhere.* There were hundreds of them, thousands! And they were all singing 'Glory to God, and peace on earth!' Are you *sure* you didn't see 'em?"

"Of course, I'm sure," I said. "All I saw was a man and a woman and a baby. I think if there had been angels around, I woulda noticed!"

"Oh," said Joram. "I'm sorry you didn't, but *we did,* didn't we boys?" And they all nodded. "And he *did say,* 'This will be a sign, that you'll find the baby in a manger,' didn't he?" And they all said, "That's right."

"Domen," he said, "we want to go down and see this baby. Do you think it will be alright?" And before I could answer or tell them how tired young Mary was, they were already down the hill and all I could do was follow behind.

When Joram and his friends got to the manger, I stopped in the shadows while they crept up close, and every one of them knelt down, and Mary and Joseph didn't seem to mind. When the shepherds told the man and woman what they had seen and heard, Mary smiled and Joseph fell right back in the hay with a big grin. Seems like an angel had talked to them, too, and said their child came from the Holy Spirit and would be the Son of God, come to save people from their sins. They both had thought they might have been crazy, but the angel had spoken to the shepherds, too, so it must be true! And right then and there, they said "Then we really will give him the name Jeshua, 'salvation of God,' because the angel said he will deliver his people from their sins."

Then Joseph hugged Mary, and Mary hugged the shepherds, and then the shepherds all pounded Joseph on the back the way men do when they're happy but self-conscious about hugging. It was a very pretty picture, but there was only one thing wrong with it.

The Complaint

And what was wrong was that *I* didn't see any angels. If that was the Son of God, born in the manger I cleaned up for them, why shouldn't I get to see an angel, too?

How could I know what they said was real? How could I know that Mary and Joseph and Joram's boys were not all having the same delusion? Could I believe that this child was the Messiah of God if I didn't see any angels, if God didn't speak to me as he spoke to them?

Well, I never did see angels, but I did keep an eye and an ear out for that boy while he grew up. He made quite a name for himself. Bethlehem ain't far from Jerusalem, you know, and I heard all about what happened there.

Now, you … you didn't get to see the angels or the baby either one. You may wonder if you can truly believe that God would come to earth in such a way. You may not see angels. You may not see the baby. But look around and you *can* see the difference he has made: churches everywhere, millions of people changed – people who are different because they trusted what the angels said.

In this day and age, can *you* believe? I hope you will.

The Hardest Question
Is it "good will toward men," or "to men of goodwill"?

Luke 2:14 relates the angelic blessing "Glory to God in the highest heaven, and on earth peace among those whom he favors!" We may be more familiar with the King James' rendition of "peace on earth, good will toward men."

Some interpreters have suggested "peace on earth toward men of good will." Which is correct?

Our first observation is that *'anthropois* (the root of "anthropology" or "Anthropocene") is masculine in form, but intended as a generic reference to all people. That much is clear.

The question hinges on the word translated as "good will," and whether it should be read in the nominative or genitive case. The KJV reading, based on considerable manuscript evidence – but some by corrections added to the originals – has the nominative reading *eudokía*, which makes "good will" the subject: "good will toward people."

The reading in most modern translations follows manuscript evidence for a reading of *eudokías*, the genitive form. The genitive form has slightly stronger support in the manuscripts, and is also the more difficult reading, meaning that later scribes would be more likely to try and smooth it out. With *eudokías* as a genitive, the phrase could be translated as "toward people of good will," or "toward people of (God's) favor."

The reading "toward people of good will" would imply that God's grace and peace was intended only for those whose own good intentions would welcome it, which is theologically questionable.

The word *eudokía* occasionally refers to human goodwill (as in Phil. 1:15), but more commonly refers to divine favor. For this reason, most modern translators assume it means something such as "toward people of God's good favor." The NRSV, as noted, has "among those he favors," while NET has "among people with whom he is pleased," and NIV11 has "to those on whom his favor rests."

Christ did not come for well-intentioned people alone, but God's gracious favor is directed to all – recall that the angel's first words were "Do not be afraid. I bring you good news that will cause great joy for all the people" (v. 10).

Christmas 2

First Reading
Isaiah 62:1-12*

New Days and New Names

… but you shall be called "My Delight Is in Her," and your land "Married" … (Isa. 62:4b)

Metaphors are a mainstay of biblical writing, especially when it comes to relationships. In the Old Testament, Israel is like a vine that produces worthless grapes (Isa. 5:1-7), an ox that doesn't know its owner (Isa. 1:3), or a wild donkey in heat (Jer. 2:24). Despite their recalcitrance, God carries the wayward Hebrews as an eagle bearing its young (Deut. 32:11), and cares for them as a mother nursing her children (Isa. 49:14-15, 66:12-13). In the New Testament, Jesus tells parables about mustard seeds and stony soils, and broods over Jerusalem as a mother hen fretting over her chicks (Matt. 23:37, Luke 13:34).

One of the more surprising metaphors – one that would be shocking if it were not so familiar to regular churchgoers – is the image of God and Israel as husband and wife. **[God's bride]** Nowhere is that metaphor presented more forcefully than in this oracle from the prophet often called "Third Isaiah" (or "Trito-Isaiah"), who was responsible for chapters 56–66 in the larger book of Isaiah. Long after Isaiah of Jerusalem's prediction of Israel's downfall had come to pass, this prophet preached amid the ruins of Jerusalem after a small vanguard of Israelites had returned under Cyrus' patronage to rebuild their home.

It was a depressing time. Second Isaiah (responsible for Isaiah 40–55) had spoken beautiful prophesies of how Jerusalem would be rebuilt (44:28), enriched with the wealth of the nations (45:14), and bursting at the seams with new growth (45:19-23, 54:1-3). The physical reality was a far different story, however, as the hopeful exiles

> **God's bride:** The metaphor of Israel as God's bride appears several times in Isaiah (54:5, 61:10, 62:5). In the book of Hosea, the prophet is called to act out the marriage, taking a wife "of harlotry" and remaining faithful, though she was not faithful to him. The comparison to God and Israel is made clear in Hos. 2:16, 19-20.
>
> Some interpreters have sought to find a similar metaphor in the lovers of the Song of Songs, but the book contains no mention of either God or marriage, making it an unlikely allegory.
>
> In the New Testament, John the baptizer spoke of Jesus as the "bridegroom" who "has the bride" (John 3:29), and Jesus spoke of himself as a bridegroom (Mark 2:19-20 and parallels). Paul compared the love of a husband and wife to that of Christ for the church in Eph. 5:25-26.

returned to find overgrown ruins, opposition from their neighbors (Ezra 4:1-5), and heavy taxes to pay (Neh. 5:15).

The people grew discouraged. Some of them wanted to give up, but the prophet pressed a new and hopeful vision.

A new relationship
(vv. 1-3)

The latter Isaiah spoke out of his own determination to offer a brighter prospect: "For Zion's sake I will not keep silent, and for Jerusalem's sake I will not rest, until her vindication shines out like the dawn, and her salvation like a burning torch" (v. 1, NRSV).

"Zion" could refer to the temple mount in Jerusalem, where God was thought to dwell, or to the city of Jerusalem as a whole. It could also be personified as a stand-in

---

*Isaiah 62:6-12 is a reading for Christmas 2 in Years A, B, and C. Isaiah 62:1-5 is the Old Testament reading for the second Sunday of Epiphany in Year C. This study incorporates both texts, Isaiah 62:1-12.

for the people of Israel. Zion also came to symbolize the eschatological center of God's kingdom on earth (Micah 4–5; Isaiah 2, 11). Christians adopted the language in their own future hopes, looking forward to God's establishment of a heavenly Zion (Revelation 14).

In our text, Zion refers to the city, which the prophet saw as dark and despairing. He was confident, however, that God had not forgotten Jerusalem, and that God's own work of salvation would again bring light and hope to the ancient city.

Other nations would witness Israel's coming vindication, Isaiah believed, when God established a new relationship symbolized by a new name and by treatment fit for royalty (vv. 2-3).

Isaiah described the future Jerusalem as a "crown of beauty" and a "royal diadem" in the hand of God, suggesting a beautiful city on a hill with its rebuilt walls and parapets looking like a giant crown. The crown was not yet complete, for God was still about the task of redemption.

When people today trust in Christ for salvation, we also take on a new name. In America, a common name is "Christian." Unfortunately, hurtful and judgmental actions by some who tout the name "Christian" have given the term a negative connotation in some circles. As a result, some believers prefer terms such as "Christ-followers."

New names
(vv. 4-5)

The theme of a new name for Jerusalem (symbolic of Jerusalem's people) emerges with force in vv. 4-5. The abandoned and desolate city would see better days, Isaiah declared: "You shall no more be termed 'Forsaken' (*Azubah*), and your land shall no more be termed 'Desolate' (*Shemamah*), but you shall be called 'My Delight Is in Her' (*Hephzibah*), and your land 'Married' (*Beulah*); for the Lord delights in you, and your land shall be married" (v. 4).

We know what it is like to change a name. Children who are called by diminutive nicknames as children often revert to their given names as adults. Persons entering marriage typically take a common name, whether it is the husband's surname (in line with tradition) or a hyphenated version that preserves both. In either case, the change of name is significant. It indicates a change of relationship.

> **Who's getting married?** Some translations have the very difficult reading "so shall your sons marry you" (KJV, NIV, NASB95, NET). This is a straightforward translation based on the Masoretic text (the standard Hebrew text), which is supported by other ancient versions. The earliest text contains no vowels, so some translators emend the vowels traditionally associated with the noun *bnk* so that it reads "your builder" instead of "your sons." This was adopted by the NRSV as the original author's most likely intent.
>
> Another option, suggested in a footnote of the NET, is to translate the verb *ba'al* as "possess" rather than "marry," since it can have that connotation. In this case, the reading would be "so your sons will possess you" or "dwell in you," the reference being Jerusalem.

In v. 5 Isaiah employed the marital metaphor for Jerusalem: "For as a young man marries a young woman, so shall your builder marry you, and as the bridegroom rejoices over the bride, so shall your God rejoice over you." **[Who's getting married?]**

Prayer and peace
(vv. 6-9)

Having indicated his own determination not to be silent or to rest until Jerusalem was restored, the prophet called on others to join him in the task, to "remind the LORD, take no rest, and give him no rest until he establishes Jerusalem and makes it renowned throughout the earth" (vv. 6-7).

Hebrew kings had a court official whose duties included reminding the king of his responsibilities and appointments. The official was called a *mazkîr*, or "reminder" (cf. 2 Sam. 8:16). Isaiah used the same word (in the plural) to speak of "you who remind the Lord." He instructed them to do so repeatedly, without rest. Like watchmen, they were to stand on the ruined walls of Jerusalem and cry out for the promises of God to be fulfilled.

What an audacious instruction! And yet, this is not the only time the Bible speaks of importunity in prayer. Jesus told stories about a needy and determined man who kept on knocking until his friend opened the door (Luke 11:5-10), and about a dogged widow who badgered an uncaring judge until justice was done (Luke 18:1-8). Jesus related the stories to prayer, even as he commended the Syro-Phoenician woman for her tenacity in seeking his blessing (Matt. 15:22-28).

Is it irreverent to imagine that God will not hear us without persistent pestering? Perhaps the best interpretative approach is to realize that postexilic Israel was facing a crisis, and there was little hope other than for them to cry out to God. Jesus was known to pray all night long when facing important decisions (Luke 6:12). Such prayer may serve to purify or focus our own hearts more than to bend the will of God, but like Alfred Lord Tennyson's portrayal of the insistent ascetic Simeon Stylites, we have a biblical mandate for "battering the gates of heaven with storms of prayer."

One of the promises Isaiah declared was that God would no longer allow enemies to rob Israelites of the food and wine for which they had labored (vv. 8-9). We should recall that when the exiles returned, they were not given rights to all of Israel or even of Judah. In fact, their new borders stretched only a short distance beyond Jerusalem itself. The "new Israel" was a tiny province called "Yehud," where the former exiles lived under Persian jurisdiction. Fierce and antagonistic neighbors inhabited the surrounding provinces. When the early returnees put crops in the fields around Jerusalem, nearby "armies" or gangs of bandits could have shown up at harvest time and robbed them.

Isaiah dared to claim that Yahweh had sworn an oath to end such larceny. Ancient persons typically swore that they would (or would not) do something by calling on a god to strike them down if they did not perform their oath (e.g., 2 Kgs. 6:31). While mortal persons swore by the deity, Yahweh had no "higher power" to appeal to, but swore by God's own self (Isa. 45:23; Jer. 49:13, 51:14), or by divine attributes such as God's holiness (Ps. 89:35), great name (Jer. 44:26), or here, "by his right hand and by his mighty arm."

Homecoming
(vv. 10-12)

The prophet concluded with an appeal for the pioneering refugees to prepare the way for other Israelites to come home. These verses are sometimes interpreted as a missionary text, but their primary concern is the coming manifestation of God that will bring salvation to the people and reunite the scattered people of Israel. The inhabitants of the new and future Jerusalem are called to raise the flag, proclaim the salvation of God, and call God's scattered people home (vv. 10-11).

Then, Isaiah declared, the people and the city would receive yet more new names, including "The Holy People," "The Redeemed of the Lord," "Sought Out," and "A City Not Forsaken." By these new names, the people would reflect their new character and exert their attraction for others to join them.

When God's people demonstrate true holiness of character, when they demonstrate through loving living that they are indeed "the redeemed of the Lord," then others will naturally want to "come home" and join them. When this happens, the renewed city of Jerusalem (or the faithful church) will no longer be called "Ignored" or "Desolate." Instead, the restored city will be "Sought Out" by those who seek to know God.

Every day, we come into contact with people who have no relationship with God, but who may be seeking a divine connection. Is there anything about our lives that would make us "Sought Out" as fitting guides to God?

The Hardest Question
What's in a name?

We should not overlook the significance of the "new name" – actually several new names – that are promised to Israel in this text, though we often do. It's easy enough to glide over the strange-sounding names, but the people who heard Isaiah preach would have understood that names – especially changed names – can bear great consequence.

In the biblical world, names were not typically a pleasant assortment of sounds, but had real meanings. Names could have simple meanings or connote entire sentences: "Dan" means "judge," while "Daniel" means "God is my judge." "Saul" means "asked" and "David" means "beloved," while "Elijah" means "My God is Yahweh" and "Isaiah" means "Salvation of Yahweh."

When Isaiah promised that God would grant Jerusalem/Israel a new name, his audience might have remembered how Abram's name was changed to Abraham, and how Jacob's name was changed to Israel. Both name changes came at times of transition, as an indication of a new relationship with God.

Hosea's daughters were given unhappy names: Lo-Ruhammah ("Not Pitied"), and Lo-Ammi ("Not My People"). These spoke of Israel's unfaithfulness before God. Yet, Hosea declared a coming day when they would get new names, when they would be called "Pitied" and "My People" (Hos. 2:21-23).

For Isaiah, Israel's new names would celebrate a new status, no longer as desolate and unloved, but as the subject of God's delight, indeed God's own bride. In the course of Isaiah 62, aside from the reference to Israel as God's bride, six new names are attributed to Jerusalem and its people, two in v. 4 and four more in v. 12:

1. *Hephzibah* – "My delight is in her"
2. *Be'ulah* – "Married"
3. *Am-haqodesh* – "Holy People"
4. *Ge'ulei-Yahweh* – "Redeemed of the LORD"
5. *Derusha* – "Sought out"
6. *Ir-lo-ne'ezava* – "A city not forsaken"

The Hebrew versions of these names have little significance for us other than an understanding of how "Hephzibah" and "Beulah" came into English (the KJV transliterated those names from Hebrew without translation, but rendered the final four names as their English equivalents only).

The meaning of the names, however, has great importance, demanding that we who call ourselves God's people ask ourselves some hard questions. Is God delighted in us? Would God acknowledge a committed, lifelong relationship with us? Would others recognize us as a holy people redeemed by God? Would they seek us out as people who are in touch with God?

"What's in a name?" asks only the abstract. "What's in *your* name?" gets personal.

Christmas 2

Second Reading
Psalm 97*

A God Who Reigns

Rejoice in the LORD, O you righteous, and give thanks to his holy name! (Ps. 97:12)

A common theme in the readings for the Christmas season is the celebration of Christ as king. We do this when singing the chorus of James Montgomery's familiar "Angels from the Realm of Glory," which calls believers to "Come and worship, come and worship, worship Christ, the newborn king."

It comes as no surprise, then, that psalm readings for the three Christmas liturgies come from Psalms 96, 97, and 98. All three belong to a collection (Psalms 93–99) known as "royal psalms" because they each, in their own, honor God as king.

We may not like the idea of having a king, or for anyone to have control over us. We learn as children to cry "You're not the boss of me!"

But the psalmist believed that we need a boss over our lives, and the boss was no earthly ruler, but the one and only heavenly king.

A God of power
(vv. 1-5)

The psalm begins with images of divine power that rules over the world: "The LORD is king! Let the earth rejoice; let the many coastlands be glad!" (v. 1). Most ancients had never traveled far, and the world they knew was very small. Even merchants who traveled long distances had no concept of the earth as we know it. For Hebrews who may have seen the Mediterranean Sea, word of the "coastlands" beyond was the ambiguous extent of the known world.

No matter how large or small the world may have seemed in their minds, the psalmist believed God was in charge of it all. The Hebrew words for "king" and "reign" have the same consonants (*mlk*), and the psalmist would have written with consonants alone. If written as *malak*, it's the verb "to reign." Written as *melek*, it means "king." The commonly used Masoretic text points to it as the verb, so most versions translate it as: "The LORD reigns" (NIV11, NET, NASB20, HCSB). The NRSV, surprisingly, renders it as the noun: "The LORD is king." Fortunately, the meaning is unchanged: Yahweh is king. By definition, a king reigns.

Yahweh's sovereignty includes the sky: "Clouds and thick darkness are all around him; righteousness and justice are the foundation of his throne" (v. 2) The Hebrew Bible commonly envisions God as being present in a cloud, from stories of God leading by a cloud in the wilderness, to appearing in a cloud on Sinai, to enveloping the temple at its dedication, to surrounding the disciples when Jesus was transfigured. It was thought that no one could see God "in person," so God's presence was typically thought to be wrapped in clouds.

Fire, like clouds, was often associated with God, generally as a symbol of destructive power: "Fire goes before him, and consumes his adversaries on every side, His lightnings light up the world; the earth sees and trembles. The mountains melt like wax before the LORD, before the Lord of all the earth" (vv. 3-5).

The description is largely metaphorical, especially the idea of mountains melting like wax, but the ancients believed that gods controlled the weather and directed lightning bolts where they would. The psalmist may have seen or heard of lightning that sparked a destructive fire: the story of Job recounts the loss of his flocks when "The fire of God fell from heaven and burned up the sheep and the servants, and consumed them" (Job 1:16).

Images of the Caananite god Ba'al, whether cast in bronze or carved on stone, routinely portrayed him striding forward, with a club in his uplifted right hand (thunder) and a spear sometimes made to look like a lightning bolt in his left.

Yahweh's control of fire was not limited to lightning. The psalmist may also have recalled stories from Numbers in which God punished people by sending fire to consume them (Num. 11:1, 16:35). Similar stories were associated with Elijah, who called down fire from heaven to consume a sacrifice (1 Kgs. 18:38) and to immolate groups of his enemies (1 Kgs. 1:10, 12).

A primary image associated with divinely sparked fire is that it becomes uncontrollable. God, as king, determines when it will begin and end, prompting humans to stand in awe before God's power. [**Uncontrollable**]

A God of righteousness
(vv. 6-9)

Fortunately, God is not only powerful in capability, but also righteous in nature: "The heavens proclaim his righteousness; and all the peoples behold his glory" (v. 6).

God is no despot, whose rule is based on power alone, but one whose kingdom is undergirded by principles of justice: "righteousness and justice are the foundation of his throne" (v. 2, see also Ps. 89:14). When prophets such as Micah charged Israel to "do justice" (Mic. 6:8) and Amos

challenged people to "let justice roll down like waters, and righteousness like an ever-flowing stream" (Amos 5:24), they were upholding the same values on which God's reign is based.

For the psalmist, Yahweh's rule was superior to all others. Those who bowed down before "worthless idols" were wasting their time, because "all gods bow down" before Yahweh (v. 7).

God's righteous "judgments" bring joy to God's people. Verse 8 declares "Zion hears and is glad, and the towns of Judah rejoice, because of your judgments, O God." The same sentiment occurs in Ps. 48:11, in a Song of Zion.

Just what "judgments" the psalmist has in mind are not stated, and unnecessary. It is likely that he was thinking of justice in general rather than specific verdicts or punishing interventions. The word for "judgments" is the plural form of *mishpat*, which means "justice" in v. 2. [**Doing justice**]

Only Yahweh could bring justice on a global level, the psalmist held, "For you, O LORD, are most high over all the earth; you are exalted far above all gods" (v. 9).

The poet's confidence in God's rule over all things echoes a theme from Israel's wisdom tradition. The sages behind Proverbs, the wisdom psalms, Job, and Ecclesiastes did not ground human and divine relationships on salvation history or covenants, as most Old Testament writers did. Rather, they believed that God as creator had set up a right order of things. For them, righteousness was found in the wisdom to seek out the divine order and follow it.

A God of love
(vv. 10-12)

The psalmist likewise trusted that Israel's powerful and righteous God cared about the lives of people on earth. "The LORD loves those who hate evil" he wrote, and "he guards the lives of his faithful; he rescues them from the hand of the wicked" (v. 10).

Like other Old Testament writers, the poet believed that God would bless those who chose just behavior over wicked living. Thus, he insisted, "Light dawns for the righteous, and joy for the upright in heart" (v. 11). In Old Testament teachings based on Deuteronomy, the promise of prosperity to the righteous served as motivation for obedience to God's teachings. Though Christian believers do not live under the same covenant, we can still trust in God's care, even when facing hard trials.

Confidence in living before a just God and hope for a happy life when following God's teaching gave the psalmist reason to enjoin others to "Rejoice in the LORD, O you righteous, and give thanks to his holy name!" (v. 12).

Though some people cynically argue that "no good deed goes unpunished" (as in the musical *Wicked*), righteousness brings its own reward. Learning to practice justice may not be repaid with worldly wealth or acclaim, but it honors the divine king, makes our world better, and brings the satisfaction of knowing that we have done what is right.

The Hardest Question
Why is God typically pictured as being surrounded by clouds?

The Hebrews believed that no one could see God and live (Exod. 33:20), though there were exceptions. Jacob boasted that he had seen God but did not die, naming the site of his memorable wrestling match "Peniel," meaning "face of God" (Gen. 32:30). Gideon feared death when he met the "angel of Yahweh," but was assured that he would not die (Judg. 6:22-23). Similarly, God – or at least an image of God's feet standing on a clear pavement – appeared to Moses and the elders of Israel, but "God did not lay his hand on the chief men of the people of Israel" (Exod. 24:11). When Moses went further up the mountain to meet God, however, "the cloud covered the mountain" (Exod. 24:15).

Many other instances depict God in a cloud. Yahweh was thought to be present within a "pillar of cloud" by day and the "pillar of fire by night" that led the people of Israel in the wilderness (Exod. 13:21-22; 14:19, 24). The cloud would rest on the tabernacle as long as God wanted them to stay in one place, and when it lifted, they would venture on (Exod. 13:21, cf. Exod. 16:10, 40:36-39; Num. 9:15-22; 10:11-12, 34).

God appeared to Moses in a "dense cloud" (Exod. 19:9-16) when the people arrived at Sinai, and again when Moses climbed up to meet Yahweh: "the cloud covered the mountain, and the glory of the LORD settled on Mount Sinai, and the cloud covered it for six days; on the seventh day he called to Moses out of the cloud. Moses entered the cloud, and went up on the mountain" (Exod. 24:15-18).

When Moses entered the tent of meeting, "the pillar of cloud would descend and stand at the entrance of the tent, and the LORD would speak with Moses" (Exod. 33:9-10). When Moses returned to the mountain, "the LORD descended in the cloud and stood with him there, and proclaimed the name, 'The LORD'" (Exod. 34:5). When the tabernacle was dedicated, "the cloud covered the tent of meeting, and the glory of the LORD filled the tabernacle," to the extent that even Moses was unable to enter (Exod. 40:34-35). God told Moses to instruct Aaron not to come into the holy of holies, lest he die, "for I appear in the cloud upon the mercy seat" (Lev. 16:2).

When Moses grew weary of leadership and uttered an agonized prayer, God told him to call out 70 elders to help share the load of settling disputes. "Then the LORD came down in the cloud and spoke to him, and took some of the spirit that was on him and put it on the seventy elders …" (Num. 11:25).

When Aaron and Miriam complained against Moses because his wife was a "Cushite" and because they believed God had spoken to them also, God summoned all three to the tent of meeting. "Then the LORD came down in a pillar of cloud, and stood at the entrance of the tent, and called to Aaron and Miriam; and they both came forward" (Num. 12:5).

These are a few of the many references to God's characteristic appearance in a cloud during the wilderness period, later recalled by Nehemiah (9:12, 19), in the Psalms (78:14, 97:2, 99:7, 105:39), and by Isaiah (4:5).

The wilderness was not the only place God was said to have appeared in a cloud, however. When Solomon's temple was dedicated, "a cloud filled the house of the LORD, so that the priests could not stand to minister because of the cloud; for the glory of the LORD filled the house of the LORD" (1 Kgs. 8:10-11, cf. 2 Chron. 5:13-14).

In Ezekiel's inaugural vision of God, he described "a great cloud with brightness around it and fire flashing forth continually, and in the middle of the fire, something like gleaming amber" (Ezek. 1:4). In a later vision of the temple, Ezekiel also spoke of a cloud as indicating God's presence (10:3).

The psalmists saw God's being surrounded by "clouds and thick darkness" in a positive way, but prophets used the image in a threatening manner. In describing judgment that would come on the "day of the LORD," they spoke of God's approach "in clouds and thick darkness" (Joel 2:2, Zeph. 1:5).

Although God is seen in Christ in the New Testament, the image of God in a cloud is still found. Matthew's account of Jesus' transfiguration says that as Jesus was speaking to Peter, "… suddenly a bright cloud overshadowed them, and from the cloud a voice said, 'This is my Son, the Beloved; with him I am well pleased; listen to him!'" (Matt. 17:5).

Christmas 2

Third Reading
Titus 3:3-7

Why Christmas Matters

He saved us, not because of any works of righteousness that we had done, but according to his mercy, through the water of rebirth and renewal by the Holy Spirit. (Titus 3:5)

When Sunday falls on Christmas Day, it creates a conundrum for church leaders. On the one hand, we'd like to go full force with every service, thinking "What better day than Sunday to celebrate Christmas?" On the other hand, we are aware that Christmas in America has strong cultural as well as religious dimensions. Church leaders know that many parishioners will be traveling or hosting family celebrations at home, and church attendance is likely to be skimpy at best.

Would it be more charitable to take the pressure off families and have an abbreviated service or cancel Sunday worship altogether? It can be a tough and sometimes unpopular call, but most churches will take the approach that if there are people who want to worship on Christmas, they should have the opportunity.

Christmas next occurs on a Sunday in 2033, 2039, 2044, and 2050.

Why choose the little epistle of Titus for a Christmas text? Today's selection doesn't tell the Christmas story, but it tells why the Christmas story matters.

The official lectionary text from the epistles is Titus 3:4-7, but we've expanded the text to include v. 3 and incorporated a look back at chs. 1–2 to set the context more fully.

A sinful people
(v. 3)

The letter to Titus is presented as a message from the Apostle Paul to a colleague and "child in the faith we share" named Titus (1:4). Though scholars often question whether Paul wrote the letter or if a close disciple wrote it in his name,

---

The letter to Titus: The letter of Titus is one of the "Pastoral Epistles." They all claim to have been written by Paul, and are traditionally attributed to him. Some modern scholars cite evidence to suggest that the letters come from a later period, perhaps penned by a disciple writing in Paul's name. While that is a possibility, the theology of the letters, and especially Titus, is in harmony with the views expressed in other letters in which Pauline authorship is not questioned. For simplicity's sake, we will refer to the author as Paul.

The letter to Titus presumes that Paul had traveled, preached, and established churches on the island of Crete, and that he had left Titus in charge of them. This presents a bit of a quandary because Paul's only known visit to Crete came when he was being carried as a prisoner to Rome (Acts 27:8), and likely had limited time or freedom to travel and preach. The account in Acts is concerned mainly with bad weather that blew them away from Crete, leading to two weeks at sea and a shipwreck on Malta (Acts 27:9–28:1).

It is often proposed that Paul was released from his imprisonment in Rome at some point, and that he resumed his travels and preaching before being arrested a second time. In 2 Tim. 4:16-17 we find a reference to Paul's "first defense," which may imply that he was then facing a second defense, though that need not require a second arrest. He could have been speaking of his first defense, before Felix in Caesarea, knowing that his appeal to Caesar would lead to a second defense in Rome.

Whether before or after his arrest, it is entirely possible that Paul traveled to places not mentioned in Luke's account of his itinerary in the book of Acts. Whether Paul had spent much time in Crete or not, he was clearly concerned about the churches there, and took some responsibility for them.

we'll refer to the author as Paul. According to the letter, Paul had left Titus on the island of Crete to bring order to the churches and appoint elders to guide them (1:5). This seems curious, because the description of Paul's journeys in Acts does not include a sojourn in Crete other than a port call as he was being shipped to Rome as a prisoner. **[The letter to Titus]**

Crete must have been a challenging church field, for Paul cited a self-ascribed reputation of Cretans for lying, violence, and gluttony (1:12). Even today, "Cretan," like "Philistine," is sometimes used as a pejorative term. As a result, Titus was challenged to be especially careful in teaching sound doctrine while vetting and choosing good leaders for the churches.

After an extended self-introduction emphasizing his identity as an apostle (1:1-5), Paul quickly got down to business, beginning with a list of requirements that Titus should follow in selecting church leaders (1:6-9). He then offered quite patriarchal advice for older men and women (2:1-5), for younger men (2:6-8), and for slaves (2:9-10). He encouraged all believers to be obedient to God, respectful of governing authorities, and courteous to one another, avoiding the evil behaviors they had once practiced (2:11–3:3).

This is where our text begins, with a reminder that none of us are free from sin. All of us know what it is like to hold misguided beliefs and to make bad choices. "For we ourselves were once foolish," Paul wrote, "disobedient, led astray, slaves to various passions and pleasures, passing our days in malice and envy, despicable, hating one another" (v. 3).

That's quite a depressing portrait. The catalog of sins seems to follow an intentional progression from disobedience to deception to desires so dishonorable that they cause alienation from others. When we become sufficiently disconnected from others, we begin to operate from a position of malice and even hate. Some of us may feel that we have not ventured to the end of that path, but most of us have spent time on the road to ruin.

The word "foolish" means exactly that, but in this context it may also suggest ignorance with regard to the gospel. "Disobedience" points to those who have heard the message and know what is right, but choose not to follow, "led astray" by faulty teachings or enslaved by their own "various passions and pleasures." Such self-focus can lead to

a life dominated by evil (a better translation than "malice") and envy, which might make one seem "despicable" to others. People who feel despised may respond with hatred of their own.

A loving God
(vv. 4-5)

Such a sorry state to be in! But Paul rejoiced that God had other, better plans for us. He expressed that good news through a succinct recital of the what, the how, and the why of the gospel. Verses 4-7, though broken up in English translations, constitute one long sentence in the Greek text. Critical editions of the Greek New Testament typically set the text in verse, as poetry. There is a certain rhythm to it when read in Greek, leading some scholars to propose that it might have been an early hymn. Whether sung as a hymn or not, the text's dense doctrinal content suggests that it was almost certainly recited in worship as an early creed or statement of basic beliefs.

Though the human condition is uniformly sinful (v. 3), God desired a better outcome for us, so "when the goodness and loving kindness of God our Savior appeared, he saved us, not because of any works of righteousness that we had done, but according to his mercy, through the water of rebirth and renewal by the Holy Spirit" (vv. 4-5). This is the "what" of salvation, and a reminder of why the text is appropriate for Christmas worship.

Paul spoke of God's character in terms familiar to the Hebrews, who thought of Yahweh as "a God merciful and gracious, slow to anger, and abounding in steadfast love and faithfulness" (Exod. 34:6, reflected in Num. 14:18; Neh. 9:17; Ps. 86:15, 103:8, 108:4; Jonah 4:2). Paul spoke of God's "goodness and loving kindness" that led to the appearing of Christ as Savior, one whose saving grace is not dependent on our works or worthiness, but on God's merciful love alone. **[Philanthropy]**

Philanthropy: The Greek word translated as "loving kindness" (NRSV) or "love for mankind" (NET) is *philanthropos*, a combination the words *philos* (love) and *anthropos* (human). The English word "philanthropy" is a direct derivation. In our time the word is used mainly in relation to charitable donations for human good, but it speaks of a loving disposition toward others, not limited to financial gifts.

In v. 6, the creed turns to the "how" of salvation. We experience God's mercy "through the water of rebirth and renewal by the Holy Spirit," Paul said. This expression has given rise to multiple interpretations. The word translated as "water" (*loutron*) more typically refers to the act or place of washing (as in NET, NIV11, and KJV), usually for ceremonial purposes. Some readers see this as a reference to baptism, though Paul may have simply used "washing" as a metaphor for the work of the Holy Spirit, who God "poured out on us richly through Jesus Christ our Savior" (v. 6).

Some interpreters see "rebirth" and "renewal" as two different aspects of our salvation experience, with baptism marking our rebirth into a new relationship with God and the Spirit bringing renewal through the change in our lives. Others argue that the two terms should be read as synonyms, with renewal added to clarify the meaning of rebirth (or "regeneration"), rather than to suggest a separate stage of experience.

A blessed hope
(vv. 6-7)

Regardless of how we parse the terms of relationship in v. 5, the obvious agent of change is the Holy Spirit, "poured out on us richly through Jesus Christ our Savior." God is not stingy with grace: the word translated "richly" could also be rendered "generously" (NIV11) or "in full measure" (NET). The Holy Spirit is available – fully available – to all who repent and trust in Christ for salvation.

Note the Trinitarian feel of v. 6. A clear doctrine of the Trinity did not develop until well beyond the New Testament period, but Paul's language here speaks of God in three ways: *God* poured out the *Holy Spirit* through *Jesus Christ*. Texts such as this led to the later development of the belief that the Father, the Son, and the Holy Spirit exist in a triune reality as one God.

The rebirth and renewal we receive through God's grace working in Christ and empowering us with the Spirit has a purpose that includes our transformed lives on this earth, but also extends beyond it. Here is the "why" of salvation: "so that, having been justified by his grace, we might become heirs according to the hope of eternal life" (v. 7). The presence of the Spirit, as Paul told the

> **Sure sayings:** Titus 3:8a marks one of several "sayings" texts in the Pastoral Epistles, each marked by a phrase such as "The saying is sure," or "the saying is sure and worthy of acceptance." This is one of two instances in which "The saying is sure" follows the saying in question (the other is 1 Tim. 4:9). In four other cases, all of them shorter, "the saying is sure" comes first, followed by the saying (1 Tim. 1:15, 3:1, 4:9; 2 Tim. 2:11).

Ephesians, is the present guarantee of our future life with God (Eph. 1:13-14).

To be "justified" is to be made right with God. Hulitt Gloer describes "justified" as being "right-wised," taking lives that sin had turned upside down and turning them right side up: "… in Christ we have caught a glimpse of what right-side up really looks like and, reborn and continually being renewed by the Spirit, we can begin to live 'right-wised' lives" (*1&2 Timothy, Titus*, Smyth & Helwys Bible Commentary [Smyth & Helwys, 2010], 84-85).

Those who have become right with God become "heirs according to the hope of eternal life." Here Paul speaks of an inheritance that is not just "pie in the sky by and by," for it has both present and future dimensions. We experience the comforting and inspiring presence of God in our lives now, empowering us to live different and "renewed" lives. We also live with the assurance of a coming day when we will know God's amazing grace even more fully, and for eternity.

"The saying is sure," Paul concluded (v. 8a). [**Sure sayings**] You can believe it.

And that's why Christmas matters.

The Hardest Question
How should we understand the relationship between "rebirth" and "renewal"?

As mentioned above, scholars have proposed a variety of ways to interpret Paul's statement that salvation comes "through the water (washing) of rebirth and renewal by the Holy Spirit" (v. 5). Remembering that the term translated "water" in the NRSV is better translated as "washing," and that the word for "rebirth" could also be rendered as "regeneration," let's take a closer look at the options:

- To read "rebirth and renewal" as two different stages in the Christian experience, with water/washing being a reference to rebirth through baptism, and renewal being the ensuing work of the Holy Spirit: This reflects a literal reading of the Greek *kai* ("and") as a connective between two different things. Some denominational groups interpret this to speak of the two steps of conversion and confirmation. Those in Pentecostal/Holiness traditions lean toward this view, believing that one's initial baptism/conversion should be followed by a second "baptism in the Spirit."

- To read the *kai* as what scholars call "epexegetical," meaning that the second term is intended to explain the meaning of the first: In this case, "renewing" would not indicate a different experience, but would clarify the term "rebirth" – rebirth is renewal that comes through the Holy Spirit, an initial experience with ongoing effects.

- To read "washing" as the primary subject, with both rebirth and renewal explaining its significance: God saves us through the washing, that is, through the rebirth and renewal that comes through the Holy Spirit being poured out on us. A variation on this theme is to see "washing" through baptism as the symbol of one's rebirth and renewal. Those who take a sacramental view of baptism as actively conveying grace might see "washing" as the effective event of rebirth and renewal, preferring the former option. Believers who regard baptism as a symbolic act would opt for the latter.

Some scholars parse the options even further, but the important thing remains unchanged: people who once lived in sin can be cleansed and "reborn" as new people in Christ, with the Holy Spirit effecting daily renewal in the lives of those who seek God.

(For more, see Donald Hagner, *1&2 Timothy, Titus*, Smyth & Helwys Bible Commentary [Smyth & Helwys, 2010], 81-82; William D. Mounce, *Pastoral Epistles*, vol. 46, Word Biblical Commentary [Zondervan, 2000], 448-449; Gordon D. Fee, *1 and 2 Timothy, Titus*, Understanding the Bible Commentary Series [Baker Books, 2011], 204-206.)

Christmas 2

Fourth Reading
Luke 2:1-20*

A Different Angle

**A similar form of this text (Luke 2:1-14, [15-20]) is used for the first Christmas option.
A study of Luke 1:1-20 appears in this volume at that point.*

Christmas 3

First Reading
Isaiah 52:1-12

Beauty on the Hills

How beautiful upon the mountains are the feet of the messenger who announces peace, who brings good news, who announces salvation, who says to Zion, Your God reigns. (Isa. 52:7)

Christmas readings turn often to the book of Isaiah and its several promises of a coming king. Deriving mainly from the writer we call "Second Isaiah" or "Deutero-Isaiah," they emerged in the latter years of exile for the people of Judah.

Judah had lived as vassals to the Babylonians for some time when Judah's king Jehoiakim rebelled against the Babylonians in 601 BCE. Three years later, Nebuchadnezzar soundly conquered Judah, but did not destroy Jerusalem. He replaced the young king Jehoiahin, who had ruled only three months, with his uncle Mattaniah, changing his name to Zedekiah. Jehoiachin, along with many Judahites from royal or wealthy families, or people with good education or particular skills, was marched as a captive to Babylon.

Late in his 11-year reign, Zedekiah rebelled against Babylon. Nebuchadnezzar returned in 587/586 BCE, and this time his forces leveled the city of Jerusalem, looting and burning both the temple and the city. More people were taken to exile, and in succeeding years, further waves of captives were taken, leaving only the poorest people to farm the land.

Life in exile was not like being in prison. The people were assigned places to live and allowed to work in paid jobs. They could marry, own property, and conduct their own business, but were not allowed to leave.

Hebrews born in exile may not have been eager to leave the fertile land, but older people who remembered Jerusalem longed for the right to return and to have their own king again.

> **The text:** The lection of Isa. 52:7-10 makes for an inspiring reading during worship, but it needs more context for study. It is part of a prophetic poem that begins with Isa. 51:17 and continues through 52:12, one in a series of poems that alternate with the "Servant Songs" in Isaiah 49–54. The first three Servant Songs are found in Isa. 42:1-4, 49:1-6, and 50:1-11; the fourth (52:13–53:12) follows immediately after our text.

Out of this situation, a new Isaiah arose to proclaim comfort and hope to the people. Oracles attributed to Second Isaiah are found in chs. 40–55. His encouraging predictions of a coming king did not take place in his lifetime, though the exiles were allowed to return to Jerusalem under a Persian governor around 538 BCE.

In time, Second Isaiah's oracles about a coming king came to be regarded as prophesies of a messiah, and they were adopted by the early church as predictions of Christ as the coming king. Not surprisingly, such texts are commonly chosen for the Advent and Christmas season. [The text]

A ringing alarm
(vv. 1-2)

Chapter 52 follows a rousing call for attention (51:17-23) in which the prophet appears to address the city of Jerusalem, but is in reality speaking to the exiles. Fallen Jerusalem and, alternately, Zion, are personified images of the exiles themselves. The prophet promised that their suffering would end; the tables would be turned and the "cup of staggering" the city had drunk would be handed to its tormentors.

Verses 1-2 take up the theme: "Awake, awake, put on your strength, O Zion!" The people/city are called to put on festal attire as they rise and shake the dust away, loosening the figurative bonds from their necks.

An amazing promise
(vv. 3-6)

The following oracle promises redemption with the interesting statement "You were sold for nothing, and you shall be redeemed without money" (v. 3). The people had not been sold into captivity as slaves: they had been defeated in battle and taken as captives. No price had been paid to put them in exile, and no ransom would be required to bring them out.

Verse 4 mentions two earlier exiles: Jacob, whose 12 sons were named as ancestors of Israel's tribes, had gone willingly to Egypt out of necessity in a time of famine, and his offspring had lived there long enough to multiply considerably, but they had not been allowed to leave. Many years later, Israelites living in the northern kingdom had been conquered by the Assyrians and scattered among other nations "without cause."

In v. 5 Yahweh asks a surprising question, "What am I doing here?" The answer will be forthcoming: the exiles' oppressors may howl against Yahweh, but "my people shall know my name; therefore in that day they shall know that it is I who speak; here am I" (v. 6).

The oracle may raise a question in our minds. Had not the earlier prophets tied the coming exile to Israel's disobedience, threatening defeat and captivity if they did not repent and follow Yahweh faithfully? Didn't they insist that the exiles had brought their punishment on themselves due to their persistent rebellion? Wouldn't that qualify as "for cause"?

Perhaps we are to imagine that, though God used the armies of Babylon as instruments of punishment or discipline for Israel, the Babylonians themselves had no cause, no good reason, to assume that they could run roughshod over the people and dominate their land. Their despising of Yahweh's name (v. 5) showed that they had no sense of their role in God's plan. The oppressors would be put in their place, and "Jerusalem" would both know Yahweh's name and recognize that God was at work: "they shall know that it is I who speak; here am I."

A beautiful message
(vv. 7-10)

This promise brings us to the stated text for today, a happy oracle of good news for Judah: "How beautiful upon the mountains are the feet of the messenger who announces peace, who brings good news, who announces salvation, who says to Zion, 'Your God reigns'" (v. 7). The emphasis is not about how attractive the messenger's feet might be, but about how delightful it would be to see his approach and hear the message of peace and the good news of salvation. [**How beautiful**]

The prophet speaks from the perspective of Jerusalem, whose sentinels or watchmen would be the first to see the peace-bearing messenger. In response, Isaiah said, "together they sing for joy, for in plain sight they see the return of the LORD to Zion" (v. 8). Here the emphasis has switched from the sight of the messenger to the vision of the restored city.

But the watchmen would not be the only ones singing. Still addressing the people as Jerusalem personified, the prophet called his hearers to "Break forth together into singing, you ruins of Jerusalem; for the LORD has comforted his people, he has redeemed Jerusalem. The LORD has bared his holy arm before the eyes of the nations; and all the ends of the earth shall see the salvation of our God" (vv. 9-10).

Note that the city has not been rebuilt: the "ruins of Jerusalem" are challenged to rejoice. Redemption might have come, but restoration still lay ahead.

How beautiful: The term translated as "beautiful" (in various forms of the verb *n'h*) is also used in the Song of Songs to describe various parts of their partner's body. In Song 1:5 the woman says she is "black but beautiful," while in 1:10 others describe her cheeks as "comely" with ornaments. The male lover speaks in 2:14, admiring the woman's sweet voice and "lovely" face. In 4:3 he insists that the woman's mouth is "lovely," and in 6:4 he speaks of her overall appearance: "You are beautiful as Tirzah, my love, comely as Jerusalem, terrible as an army with banners." Here the word *yafah* is rendered as "beautiful," and *na'uwah* is translated as "comely."

A strong charge
(vv. 11-12)

Restoring Jerusalem would require the faith, the investment, and the hard work of people who were willing to return to their ancestral home and take up the immense task of rebuilding. As v. 1 began with "Awake, awake," v. 11 begins "Depart, depart, go out from there!" The prophet saw a day when the people would be told to leave the unclean land of Babylon, to purify themselves, and make their orderly way (not in haste or in flight) back to Jerusalem (vv. 11-12a).

They could make their journey home with confidence that "the LORD (Yahweh) will go before you, and the God (Elohim) of Israel will be your rear guard" (v. 12b). Using two different names for God, the prophet assured the people of divine protection from both the front and the rear.

A transformed text

In context, it is clear that the prophecy has to do with a prediction that God would bring the exile to an end so the people could safely return to Jerusalem and begin the long process of rebuilding.

In 539 BCE, Cyrus led his Persian army to sweep over Babylon with hardly a fight, and the promise entered the first stages of reality. Unlike the Babylonians and Assyrians, Cyrus believed that vassal people would be happiest and serve best in their own homeland, with freedom to serve their own gods.

They would live as a sub-province of Persia and be obligated to pay taxes to their overlords. They would be ruled by a governor who was appointed by the Persians, but at least he would be one of their own, and possibilities remained.

Israel did not reach the happy heights that this and other prophesies seemed to predict, but they did not stop longing for the promises to come true. In time, oracles such as this one became associated with the hope for a messiah who would yet arise and lead Israel to glory.

Some Jews still hold to the hope of those promises, interpreted in that way.

Early Christians saw it differently. They came to believe that Jesus had come as the fulfillment of all the messianic prophecies, though he was a different kind of messiah than what they had expected. He did not establish an earthly kingdom, but came to inaugurate the kingdom of God, bringing a message of salvation for all people, to fulfill the prophet's assurance that "God reigns."

The Hardest Question
Can we see God "in plain sight"?

Texts for Christmas and Epiphany often emphasize the revelation or appearance of God or Jesus in ways that humans can see with their eyes, whether in a cloud or in person. Today's text follows that theme, and we may profit from looking back to v. 8, where the prophet spoke of Jerusalem's sentinels seeing the coming (and reigning) king "in plain sight."

The English idiom translates the Hebrew phrase "eye to eye" ('ayin b'ayin), which KJV renders literally. The NET and NASB20 translate "with their own eyes."

The prophet did not describe any physical appearance of Yahweh when "they see the return of the LORD to Zion." Whether we are to imagine Yahweh as wrapped in smoke or cloud, or perhaps enveloped in a cloud of dust kicked up by the royal procession, is not clear.

Whatever they were to see, it would convince them that the king had come with evidence from their own eyes.

Those who connect this text with Christ believe that his followers did indeed see him with their own eyes: saw him teach, saw him heal, saw him die, and saw him on the other side of the tomb.

We don't see Jesus in the flesh now, but we can see evidence of Christ's presence in the love and the lives of those who serve him well.

Perhaps we would do well to consider the idiomatic meaning that English assigns to the phrase "eye to eye." For us, to see eye to eye involves more than looking into each other's visual orbs: it means to connect with one another in one accord. To see eye to eye is to agree on something, often in mutual support.

The question we should ask is not about seeing Jesus in the flesh, but about whether we see eye to eye with the king who rules, and our role in the kingdom.

Christmas 3

Second Reading
Psalm 98*

A New Song for a Lasting Love

O sing to the LORD a new song, for he has done marvelous things … (Ps. 98:1)

Do you know anyone who doesn't enjoy at least some type of music? Music "soothes the savage beast," so the saying goes, but can also comfort us in melancholy times or lift us from the ordinary to the sublime. We enjoy familiar songs, but there's something special about hearing a new song that rings our bell. We may need to hear or sing it more than once, but soon the catchy melody or compelling words have us adding the new song to our playlist of favorites.

What are some occasions that might call for a new song? New movies, Broadway shows, or albums by musical artists call for new songs. Social campaigns such as the Civil Rights Movement often birth new songs. In a church context, the dedication of a new building or the retirement of a long-time staff member may lead to the commissioning of a new hymn.

Can you name one or two new songs that you first heard in the last year? What makes songs memorable to you?

A new song
(vv. 1-3)

Psalm 98, which is similar in many ways to Psalm 96, would have been used in Israel's formal worship, whether at the temple or in festival settings. It is one of several psalms (24, 47, 93, and 95–100) that celebrate Yahweh as king over all things. Psalms 96, 97, and 98 are traditionally read during the Christmas season as we celebrate Christ as the "king of kings."

The poet's summons to "sing to the LORD a new song" (v. 1a) may suggest that the psalm was written for a special occasion, perhaps to celebrate a military victory or the enthronement of a new king. It could also have been sung at an annual festival celebrating Yahweh as king. Some writers suggest the psalm would have been appropriate for a day when the Ark of the Covenant might have been brought out for public admiration, then marched at the head of a joyous procession before returning to its honored place in the Holy of Holies, an earthly analogue to the heavenly throne room.

The psalm falls naturally into three sections: an initial call to praise with reasons for why such praise is appropriate (vv. 1-3), a further and more detailed summons for people to give joyful praise to Yahweh as king (vv. 4-6), and a closing call for creation itself to celebrate the coming of Yahweh as a righteous judge (vv. 7-9).

Why was divine praise so timely and essential? Because God "has done marvelous things," the psalmist said. He does not cite specifics, but vv. 1b-2 suggest that the new song may have been composed on the heels of a military victory in which Yahweh was thought to have played a crucial role. "His right hand and his holy arm have gotten him victory," the author sang. "The LORD has made known his victory; he has revealed his vindication in the sight of the nations."

The term translated as "victory" three times in vv. 1-3 (NRSV) is derived from the Hebrew verb *yāsh'a*, and is more commonly translated as "deliverance" (NET11) or "salvation" (NET). Israel's historical memory often centered on military victories, so the translation is not inapt.

This text also occurs as a reading for the sixth Sunday of Easter in Year B, and for Proper Sundays 27 and 28 of Year C.

The Israelites believed that Yahweh had ordained certain battles to be fought, and that Yahweh would fight for them when they were faithful, assuring victory against any odds. **[Yahweh war]**

We cannot know whether the psalmist had in mind a particular victory, perhaps a recent one, or if he was celebrating Yahweh's ongoing role in creating and delivering Israel as a people, then empowering leaders such as David and Solomon to expand the kingdom through military means. The generic terminology suggests that the psalm celebrates the ongoing heritage of God's mighty acts rather than a particular victory. The psalmist's concept of divine deliverance certainly went beyond success in battle: he was aware that salvation comes in many forms.

The psalm appears to have come from a time of strength for the Hebrew people, for the psalmist claims that God's righteousness (NRSV has "vindication") has been revealed "in the sight of the nations" (v. 2b), and "All the ends of the earth have seen the victory of our God" (v. 3b), presumably through the ascendance of Israel on the international stage.

The psalmist credited this to God having "remembered his steadfast love and faithfulness to the house of Israel" (v. 3a). This affirmation of Yahweh's character, drawn from Exod. 34:6 and often recalled (2 Sam. 2:6, 15:20; Ps. 25:10, 61:7, 86:15, 89:14), was a reminder of the special covenant between God and Israel, one in which Yahweh promised to show steadfast love and faithfulness to Israel, expecting loyalty in return. There was no question in the psalmist's mind that Yahweh was living up to the divine end of the arrangement. **[A divine covenant?]**

Yahweh war: The Hebrew concept of "Yahweh war" connected covenant obedience with divine favor in war: when the people kept the covenant and obeyed the law, they believed God would fight for them. Thus, the narratives explain, it was Yahweh's intervention that enabled Joshua and the invading Israelites to defeat the walled city of Jericho (Joshua 6). Likewise, Israel's repentance and Samuel's intercession had roused Yahweh to "thunder with a mighty voice" against an overwhelming army of Philistines, enabling Israel to rout them (1 Samuel 7). Later victories, especially under David, were attributed to divine favor, for "Yahweh was with him" (1 Sam. 18:14).

A divine covenant? The covenant between Yahweh and Israel is explicitly described in the Pentateuch (especially Exodus and Deuteronomy), and is a major theme in the Hebrew Bible.

In the covenant, established at Sinai and renewed through periodic ceremonies, Yahweh promised to be faithful to Israel and bless the people in many ways. The blessings, however, were contingent on Israel's obedience to the covenant guidelines described in the law, especially the command to serve Yahweh only and eschew any other gods. This theme is illustrated repeatedly in the narratives of the Deuteronomistic history (Joshua–2 Kings, with the exception of Ruth) and forms the basic theology behind much prophetic preaching.

Many Americans hold to a belief that God has a covenant with America as the "new Israel" and quote scriptures directed to Israel as promises (or threats) to America. Other see this as exegetical overreach. Do you believe God has entered such a covenant with America? If so, on what basis?

A joyful noise
(vv. 4-6)

A faithful and loving God is worthy of praise, and the psalmist called for a jubilant response. He addresses "all the earth" in v. 4, focusing on the earth's people in vv. 4-6 and the forces of nature in vv. 7-9.

Note the author's use of repetition as a connective device: worshipers are to "… break forth into joyous song and *sing praises. Sing praises with the lyre, with the lyre* and the sound of melody."

Modern translations sometimes mask the ebullience of this text. "Make a joyful noise" is much tamer than the text's imperative "Shout!" The assumption that it was a joyful shout has to be drawn from the context. "Break forth into joyous song" translates "Break out with a ringing cry!" Since the shouting and loud cries are associated with the last verb, "sing praises," we assume that the shouting and ringing cries would be exuberant counterpoints amid a congregation of people singing joyfully at the tops of their voices.

The ancients had no pipe organ to amplify the sound of singing, but trumpets and horns joined the chorus, according to v. 6. The word for "trumpet" indicates a narrow instrument made from hammered silver rolled into a tube (Num. 10:2). **[Trumpets]** The "horns" were

Trumpets: The word translated as "trumpet" occurs 29 times in the Hebrew Bible, with 16 of those in 1–2 Chronicles. The Jewish/Roman historian Josephus described a trumpet used by the Hebrews as a narrow tube a little less than a cubit (about 18 inches) in length and slightly thicker than a flute (*Antiquities of the Jews* 3.12.6). The sound produced by such an instrument would have been high and shrill.

Trumpets were used by priests in a variety of ceremonies, but could also be sounded as an alarm in time of war (Hos. 5:8), to summon the tribes, or as a signal to break camp (Num. 10:2-4).

In 1968, excavations around the southwest corner of the temple mount in Jerusalem uncovered a broken stone that would have marked the place on the parapet where priests would have stood to blow the ceremonial trumpets. Its inscription says literally, "for the house of the blowing (of trumpets)," meaning "the place of trumpeting." The stone fragment, now in the Israel museum, is pictured above.

ram's horns, which are largely hollow, with a tiny mouthpiece cut into the pointed end. Called a *shōfar*, the ram's horn can still be heard accompanying bar mitzvahs or weddings in some Jewish circles. Though hard to blow, the *shōfar* produces a high, piercing wail.

One can only imagine how the combination of loud singing, stringed instruments, and untuned horns and trumpets must have resulted in a raucous tribute to God. The "joyful noise" associated with temple worship must have rivaled that of soccer matches in South Africa, where excited fans punctuate their cheers with long plastic horns called "vuvuzelas." Try to imagine the reaction if such uninhibited praise should erupt during Sunday worship in most of our churches.

A coming judge
(vv. 7-9)

Caught up in a frenzy of adulation, the psalmist imagined the natural order joining the chorus of people singing praise to God: "Let the sea roar, and all that fills it; the world and those who live in it. Let the floods clap their hands; let the hills sing together for joy at the presence of the LORD …" (vv. 7-9a; note the similarity to Ps. 68:11-13).

The NRSV, perhaps overly influenced by the familiar KJV translation, underplays the psalmist's intent. The word translated as "floods" – which might connote an occasional rainstorm spawning happy puddles – is the standard word for "rivers," and the term rendered as "hills" typically means "mountains." The psalmist's image was not of pastoral hills and rills, but of majestic mountains and mighty rivers pouring out praise for the God who both creates and continues to act in the world.

Why should all the world's people and even the earth itself reverberate with praise to God? Because "… he is coming to judge the earth. He will judge the world with righteousness, and the peoples with equity" (v. 9b). This confession acknowledges that life before God has three tenses: God's creative and saving work of the past has significance for the present and extends into the future, when God will one day come in judgment to set all things right – not only with the peoples of the earth, but also with the earth itself.

The psalmist intuitively understood that the earth and its people are interconnected: God's people have a responsibility to care for both. If we wreck the environment through careless exploitation, we make life hard for the people who depend on clean water, fresh air, and fertile soil – including ourselves. If we act in socially unjust or prejudicial ways against others, we diminish opportunities, disregard human rights, and run roughshod over the spirits of people who were created in God's image.

The psalmist imagined a day when God would "judge the world with righteousness and the peoples with equity." That is a glorious thought, and one deserving of boisterous praise. In the meantime, however, the psalm reminds us that those who live in this world have a responsibility to treat the earth rightly and act justly toward others – divinely inspired actions that are likewise worthy of praise.

The Hardest Question
Was God right-handed?

The Bible attests that God is Spirit, so it would seem entirely inappropriate to attribute "handedness" to Yahweh. Nevertheless, Hebrew literature, both in narrative and poetry, often spoke of God in anthropomorphic terms, using human language to speak symbolically of divine actions.

One of the more common metaphors imagined Yahweh exerting divine power through an upraised arm and a mighty right hand. Most humans are right-handed, and most soldiers would throw a spear or wield a sword with their right arm. It was only natural to assume that gods would also favor the right hand.

A song attributed to Moses celebrated God's deliverance over the Egyptians: "Your right hand, O LORD, glorious in power – your right hand, O LORD, shattered the enemy … You stretched out your right hand, the earth swallowed them … Terror and dread fell upon them; by the might of your arm," (Exod. 15:6, 12, 16).

The author of Deuteronomy spoke of God's powerful hand, without designating it as the right one. He asked "has any god ever attempted to go and take a nation for himself from the midst of another nation, by trials, by signs and wonders, by war, by a mighty hand and an outstretched arm, and by terrifying displays of power, as the LORD your God did for you in Egypt before your very eyes?" (Deut. 4:34). Similar references to God's mighty hand and outstretched arm are found in Deut. 5:15, 7:19, 9:29, 11:2, and 26:8, along with 1 Kgs. 8:42, 2 Kgs. 17:36, and 2 Chron. 6:32.

David famously conquered Jerusalem, according to 2 Samuel 5, but Ps. 78:54 insists it was by the power of God's right hand: "And he brought them to his holy hill, to the mountain that his right hand had won." Psalm 118:15-16 celebrates divine victories in similar fashion: "There are glad songs of victory in the tents of the righteous: 'The right hand of the LORD does valiantly; the right hand of the LORD is exalted; the right hand of the LORD does valiantly.'"

Jeremiah attributed creation to Yahweh's powerful arm, again without designating which one: "It is you who made the heavens and the earth by your great power and by your outstretched arm" (32:17, see also 27:5). But he

also saw Yahweh's arm at work in battle, whether in Israel's favor (Jer. 32:21), or against a rebellious people (Jer. 21:5).

The image of God acting in creation or fighting with an upraised arm and mighty right hand is consistent with iconography common in the ancient Near Eastern world, where gods thought to be active in the world were often portrayed as standing erect with the right arm raised, typically holding a club or thunderbolt. These are known to archaeologists as "smiting gods," and a quick Google search for "smiting god images" will bring up a number of examples from Egyptian, Canaanite, Syrian, Hittite, and other contexts.

While participating in the Fourth Expedition to Lachish in 2015, I was fortunate enough to uncover a small bronze image of a smiting god in a Canaanite context: the pointed crown indicates divinity, and the right arm, though broken off, is clearly upraised. What appear to be large feet include corroded prongs that would have been inserted into a stone or wooden base so that the image would stand. Found in a Late Bronze Age Canaanite context, the image probably represented one of the several manifestations of Baal, such as Baal Resheph.

The Israelites were warned not to make graven images of Yahweh, but they were frequently exposed to the images used in the religion of their neighbors, and it is only natural that their mental image of God would be similar to the one they had often seen depicted: God as a warrior, with an upraised right arm indicating divine might.

Third Reading
Hebrews 1:1-14

Who's the Boss?

But of the Son he says, "Your throne, O God, is forever and ever,
and the righteous scepter is the scepter of your kingdom." (Heb. 1:8)

No one compares to Jesus – both traditional hymns and contemporary songs wax poetic on the theme. In doing so, they reflect a belief emphasized by the New Testament book known as Hebrews.

Though Hebrews was traditionally attributed to Paul, its eloquent Greek and somewhat differing theological themes suggest another author. In form, the book is not so much a letter, despite the epistolary ending, but a sermonic appeal for all to trust and honor Christ with highest praise. **[Form]** It appears to be directed primarily toward believers who had adopted a hybrid version of Christianity that retained many teachings and practices transferred or adapted from Judaism – or aberrations of Judaism. They were probably diaspora Jews who had come to faith in Christ. Otherwise, some of the author's arguments would have no point: the sermon challenges readers to put traditions associated with Judaism behind them and to trust in Christ alone.

In any case, the people addressed appear to have been facing some measure of persecution, to the extent that some were in danger of apostatizing, "falling away from the living God" (3:12). The author believed that the people addressed needed to "be moved on" to maturity in Christ. This is especially evident in the last few verses of ch. 5, where he describes them as babies who still needed milk when they should be grown up and teaching others.

The author was writing to people whom he believed had strayed from the path of right doctrine. They had confused their worship of Christ with the worship of angels and with worship through the temple. They had confused the priesthood of Christ with the priesthood of Melchizedek. They had allowed folk-religion and local customs to twist the meaning of faith in Christ and of life in Christ's behalf.

With these things in mind, perhaps, the writer began the letter, not with an extended greeting or a prayer of thanks as Paul was prone to do, but with a straightforward, Christocentric confession of faith.

The lectionary text for the epistle is Heb. 1:1-4, (5-12). While scattered verses serve very well as liturgical readings, for study we will gain more understanding by considering the entire first chapter of Hebrews, vv. 1-14.

God has spoken …
(1:1-2a)

The writer held that God in former times had spoken through the prophets, "in many and various ways." The alliterative phrase *polumerōs polutrōpōs* asserts that God has many ways of speaking. What might these be?

We often think of creation as one manner of God's self-revelation. Job, for example, marveled at the majesty of

---

Form: Hebrews has some characteristics of a letter, at the end, but it primarily has the form of a lengthy and eloquent sermon designed to proclaim the supremacy of Christ and to challenge the recipients to put all else behind, grow in their faith, and serve Christ alone.

It is generally assumed that the book originated as a sermon that was put in written form and sent to a group of Christians who needed to hear its message. Being found helpful, the letter was copied and circulated to other churches, growing in popularity and acceptance until it was accorded a place within scripture.

creation, saying "These are indeed but the outskirts of his ways; and how small a whisper do we hear of him! But the thunder of his power who can understand?" (Job 26:14).

Both Old and New Testament accounts insist that God also spoke via the medium of angels (the Greek word *angelos* means "messenger") – for example, to Abraham, to Jacob, to Balaam, to Gideon, and to others. The target audience of Hebrews had apparently exaggerated the role of angels beyond that of messenger, however, so the author did not overemphasize their role.

Creation speaks, but indirectly. We seek and need a more specific word. Thus, the author insisted that God had spoken directly through the prophets. The writer would have had in mind the patriarchs through whom God spoke in the Pentateuch and the leading religious figures of the Bible's historical books (also called "former prophets"), in addition to those persons we think of as the writing prophets. New Testament figures such as John the Baptizer were also considered to be prophets, newly come after a long absence of the prophetic word.

God spoke to and through the prophets in different ways. God spoke in thunder to Moses, but in a still, small voice to Elijah. In Old Testament thought, a true prophet was one who had access to God's inner council, being privy to God's plans. A prophet was one who understood the hearts of the people, the plans of God, and how the two might intersect – or collide.

For the author, all of that was preliminary: the clearest and most powerful means of divine speech had come in the form of the divine Son, Jesus Christ. The writer's implication is that God had revealed Godself progressively: through creation, through the prophets, and now, "in the last of these days," through the Son. Only in the person of Christ could the progressive self-revelation of

God be fully manifest. No message could be more powerful than the life, the words, the actions, the death, and the resurrection of Jesus Christ.

Christ as supreme
(1:2b-3)

In the space of a verse and a half, the writer made seven impressive claims about Christ. Each affirms some aspect of Christ's divinity.

Jesus is described as God's appointed "heir of all things," the one through whom God "created the worlds." This calls to mind John 1:1-3a: "In the beginning was the Word, and the Word was with God, and the Word was God. He was in the beginning with God. All things came into being through him, and without him not one thing came into being."

Emphasizing Christ's supreme status, the writer spoke of Christ as "the reflection of God's glory," one who bears the "exact imprint of God's very being." Whatever divine "essence" one might attribute to God, the writer believed, belonged also to Christ.

Furthermore, Christ "sustains all things by his powerful word," an insistence that Christ's involvement in creation continues.

Christ's work is not limited to the physical aspects of creation, the author wrote, but had a more personal role in human lives leading to his divine enthronement: "when he had made purification for sins" – the work of atonement being seen as Christ's crowning achievement – "he sat down at the right hand of the Majesty on High," an image from Ps. 110:1 reflected often in the New Testament. [**Right-hand man**]

In case readers did not get the point about Christ's supremacy over all things, including angels, the author adds "having become as much superior to angels as the name he has inherited is more excellent than theirs" (v. 4).

Angels as subordinate
(1:4-12)

As mentioned above, the recipients of this letter appear to have been entranced by angelology. Perhaps they prayed to certain "guardian" angels in hopes of protection or success, or honored angels in other ways. Whatever the

---

Right-hand man: References to Christ being at the right hand of God are frequent, not just in Hebrews, but throughout the New Testament. Luke 22:69, Acts 2:33, Rom. 8:34, Col. 3:1, and 1 Pet. 3:22 are just a few of many examples.

In the ancient world, when a king sat on the throne to deal with matters of state, his most powerful court official would be positioned at his right hand. The image persists today in the description of a leader's "right-hand man" (or woman) as being most important or influential in the work.

Sons of God: Although they are not addressed as sons, beings called "angels" in the New Testament were sometimes called "sons of God" in the Hebrew scriptures. Genesis 6:2-4 claims that certain "sons of God" were so attracted to human women that they left heaven and cohabited with the women, giving rise to a race of giant warriors known as the "Nephilim."

The story of Job includes two scenes in which the "sons of God," supernatural beings created by God, gather in council with God to discuss the affairs of humans (Job 1:1, 2:1).

Likewise, the account of creation in Job 38 insists that, when God set the foundations of the earth, "the morning stars sang together and the sons of God shouted for joy" (Job 38:7). The NRSV translates "sons of God" as "heavenly beings," while the NIV11 has "angels." The NET, NASB20, and CSB render it literally as "sons of God."

practice, it was common enough – and serious enough – that the author found it necessary to emphasize Christ's supremacy above all angels. He did this via seven quotations from the Old Testament that support three primary points.

First, he insisted that Jesus alone was regarded as God's son. Verse 5 asks "For to which of the angels did God ever say, 'You are my Son; today I have begotten you'? Or again, 'I will be his Father, and he will be my Son'"? The two questions reflect Ps. 2:7 and 2 Sam. 7:14. Both were originally directed to earthly kings, but came to be thought of as messianic prophecies. **[Sons of God]**

The divine command to "Let all the angels worship him" is drawn from the Greek versions of Deut. 32:43 (the Hebrew text is quite different) and Ps. 97:7, in which the Hebrew term for "gods" is translated with *angeloi*, meaning "angels."

Verse 7 describes angels, clearly subordinate to Jesus, as "winds" or "flames of fire." The word translated "wind" is *pneumata*, which can also mean "spirits." The reference is a quotation from Ps. 110:4: "you make the winds your messengers, fire and flame your ministers." The text speaks metaphorically, and not necessarily of angels, though the Hebrew terms translated as "messengers" and "ministers" could be used of angels.

In contrast to the servant role of angels, the writer of Hebrews insisted that God had raised Christ above all: "God, your God, has set you above your companions

by anointing you with the oil of joy" (vv. 8-9). Again the author has quoted from the Psalms, this time from Ps. 45:6-7. In context, the psalm was addressed to Israel's king, who was thought of as God's adopted son and could even be referred to in royal hyperbole as "God." Earthly kings were not set above angels, but Christ was.

Verses 10-12 speak to Christ's role in creation. The earth and heavens are wonderful but perishable, but Christ's rule would be eternal. This is a quotation from Ps. 102:25-27, where it was clearly addressed to Yahweh, but the writer of Hebrews attributes it to Christ in his efforts to show that Christ, with God, is not only supreme, but also eternal.

A summary statement
(1:13-14)

The chapter closes with a summary attempt to put angels in their proper place. "But to which of the angels has he ever said, 'Sit at my right hand until I make your enemies a footstool for your feet'?" (v. 13). As in v. 3, this looks back to Ps. 110:1, which was originally addressed to Israel's king as God's adopted son, but later applied to Christ.

God, of course, had never made such a statement to angels. Rather, their perpetual function is one of service: "Are not all angels spirits in the divine service, sent to serve for the sake of those who are to inherit salvation?" (v. 14).

Just how angels "serve for the sake of those who are to inherit salvation" is not stated, but that is not the author's concern. The point is that angels are not to be worshiped: their role as servants – even in our behalf – continues. Christ's eternal nature and earthly service have brought him to the highest of all thrones, as king of all kings.

Despite the spiritual nature and powerful attributes associated with angels, we don't worship them, or anything else: Christ alone deserves our ultimate allegiance.

The Hardest Question
Who wrote the book of Hebrews?

The author of Hebrews chose to remain anonymous. Paul always identified himself clearly in his letters, and even letters thought to have been written by others but attributed to Paul spell out the supposed author's name, but this is not the case with Hebrews.

What can we surmise? The author was clearly an early Christian leader, but with a strong Old Testament background and some apparent affinities with ideas common among Christian teachers in Alexandria, a city in northern Egypt that was home to a thriving Christian community by the late first century.

As early as 180 CE, some leaders of the Eastern churches claimed Paul as the author of Hebrews, arguing that it was written to the Christians in Alexandria. The Western church did not claim Pauline authorship until the fourth century. Indeed, the book was slow to be accepted as scripture in the Western churches, largely because of its lack of attribution to a known and respected author.

Several factors mitigate against Pauline authorship, the most notable being that the book is written in excellent Greek, comparable only to Luke-Acts in the New Testament, and clearly different from the prosaic style of writing in Paul's letters. Clement of Alexandria, writing in the third century, recognized that the Greek was different from Paul's style, but explained the discrepancy by claiming that Paul wrote the book in Hebrew and Luke translated it into Greek. Given that Paul was apparently quite comfortable writing or dictating his other letters without a translator, however, the argument is not convincing.

The themes explored in the book have some relation to Pauline thought, but also show notable differences. For example, the writer spends a great deal of time discussing Melchizedek and the priesthood of Christ, a subject that Paul does not address. Charles Trentham suggested that the writer was both "more Jewish than Paul on the one hand, and more Greek than Paul on the other" (*Hebrews*, vol. 12, Broadman Bible Commentary [Broadman Press, 1969], 5).

The eloquent Apollos is frequently mentioned as a possible author, and a joint authorship by Priscilla and Aquilla has some support. Other early believers have also been mentioned, but none convincingly. Apparently, the writer did not find it important to identify himself or herself, which provides a clue as to how much time modern readers should spend in worrying about the matter.

Fourth Reading
John 1:1-18*

The Word That Reveals

In the beginning was the Word, and the Word was with God, and the Word was God. (John 1:1)

It seems to be universal. Throughout the ages, humans have looked beyond the bounds of observable life and experience to explain why the world exists, and why things are the way they are. Wherever we go in time or place, we find people looking to the gods – singular or plural – as their culture has come to think of them.

Christians hold to a belief that there is one and only one God, a single deity revealed as Creator, Redeemer, and Spirit. We believe that God wants to be known, and can be glimpsed through the stories, teachings, letters, and other materials that make up the Bible.

The author: The Fourth Gospel, commonly called the gospel of John, was written anonymously. Tradition holds that it was written by the apostle John, brother of James and a son of Zebedee. A concluding note to the gospel identifies the author as "the apostle Jesus loved" (21:20-24).

Many scholars doubt that John the son of Zebedee could have been the author, citing significant differences between the Fourth Gospel and the earlier synoptics of Mark, Matthew, and Luke. It appears to have been written late in the first century, and takes a more philosophical approach that seems uncharacteristic of a Hebrew fisherman.

Some scholars attribute the book to a man known as "John the Elder," who spent the last years of his life in Ephesus. Others believe multiple "Johannine" authors may have contributed to the Fourth Gospel; the letters of 1, 2, and 3 John; and Revelation. The puzzle has no clear solution. Fortunately, the truths we learn from it do not depend on knowing the identity of the author.

The Bible *begins* with the radical claim that God has created humans in God's own image (Gen. 1:27), suggesting that there is something godlike in us, some spark of the divine, some shadow of God's face. That is a mind-boggling idea: that God could be revealed through human flesh or personality.

The Bible *ends* with an even more remarkable claim that God and human believers will live together face to face, that in eternity "God himself will dwell among them, and they shall be his people" (Rev. 21:3).

In between, John's gospel declares that God is revealed most perfectly in the human life of Jesus Christ. Christ not only shows us the way to God: the gospel declares that he *is* God, the very essence of God, the embodied word of God in human form. [**The author**]

New Testament writings challenge us to model our lives and views after those of Jesus, God's ultimate revelation. Rather than adopting social norms masquerading as "biblical worldviews" based on prooftexts and prejudice, we are called to a "Jesus worldview."

Christ as the Word
(vv. 1-9)

In the memorable and poetic prologue to the Fourth Gospel (1:1-18), the author describes Christ as the divine *logos*, the Word of God incarnate. "In the beginning was the Word, and the Word was with God, and the Word was God" (v. 1).

While John 1:1-14 appears in Christmas 3 readings for all years, a similar text (John 1:[1-9], 10-18) is read on the second Sunday after Christmas, when that occurs. For purposes of textual continuity, the study presented here encompasses all of John 1:1-18.

The basic meaning of the term *logos* is "word," but it could also carry connotations such as "reason," "wisdom," "matter," or even the "reckoning" of an account. Greek philosophers used the word in different ways. Some, such as Aristotle, used the term in the sense of reasoned discourse or the body of an argument, while the Stoics associated *logos* with a supernatural principle that pervades the universe and animates living things. In the Jewish philosopher Philo's thought, the *logos* was the means by which God created the world and holds all things together. Scholars have often noted some similarities between the Fourth Gospel and Philo's concept of the *logos*.

Writers have often assumed that John used the *logos* concept to make the gospel more appealing to Gentile audiences familiar with Hellenistic philosophy, but the word would communicate well with readers from a variety of backgrounds.

Jewish readers could have thought of *logos* in terms of the Hebrew Bible's witness to God's words as a creative power that could speak the world into being (Genesis 1; Ps. 33:6, 9) or accomplish any divine purpose. Isaiah declared of God, " … so shall my word be that goes out from my mouth; it shall not return to me empty, but it shall accomplish that which I purpose, and succeed in the thing for which I sent it" (Isa. 55:11).

Greek readers could have imagined the *logos* as a philosophical principle, the projected thought of the transcendent God, giving stability to life and forming a divine-human bond of rational thought.

Early Christian readers might have interpreted *logos* as the proclamation of Christ through the preaching of the gospel as a "ministry of the word" (Acts 6:4), whose content was Christ himself (Luke 1:2, Acts 1:21-22). Jesus' very life was a sermon on the nature of God who offers the gift of relationship to the human world.

Christ the Word was not only present from the beginning (v. 2): the author insists that Christ was intimately involved with the creation of the world as the source of both life and light (vv. 3-5).

How did the world first come to know of Christ? The first witness to understand and proclaim Jesus' special nature as the anointed of God was a man named John, Jesus' cousin and the one who came to be known as "the baptizer." He is introduced in vv. 6-8 as the one who came "to testify to the light," namely, "the true light that enlightens everyone" (v. 9). The light "was coming into the world" – a reference to the incarnation – but the connection between Jesus as the light and as the Word was yet to be spelled out.

The power of Christ
(vv. 10-13)

Although the Word created the world and became incarnate within the world, the author comments, the world did not know him (v. 10): creation did not recognize its creator. John found it heartbreaking that the people of Israel did not recognize Christ as their own long-awaited Messiah: "He came to what was his own, and his own people did not accept him" (v. 11).

Still, there were individuals who did recognize Jesus as Lord, who believed in him, and who accepted him as savior. "To all who received him," the author wrote, "who believed in his name, he gave power to become children of God, who were born, not of blood or of the will of the flesh or of the will of man, but of God" (vv. 12-13).

To believe in Christ's *name* is to believe that Jesus is who he claims to be – the Son of God, the Word of God, indeed, one with God. To those who believed in his name, Christ "gave power to become children of God" – the divine Son of God empowered human persons to become the mortal children of God. The word translated as "power" can also be rendered as "right," "privilege," or "ability." Without Christ we are mortal persons in a mortal world with no hope for anything beyond. With the coming of the *logos*, however, those who acknowledge Jesus as the divine Word can enter a special relationship with God.

As the human Jesus was connected to God, the writer taught, mortals who become children of God enter the relationship "not by blood or the will of the flesh or the will of man" (a threefold reference to human birth), but by God's will and God's work alone. Jesus' earthly birth by the will of God is the pattern for our spiritual birth (cf. John 3:1-16). Thus, John defines Christianity purely in terms of God's grace: God loved the world enough to become incarnate in Christ so that we might believe and become children of God.

Circumlocutions: Although we tend to think of John's gospel as being written largely for people well versed in Greek philosophical categories, v. 4 reflects John's desire to communicate with literate Jews also. Readers familiar with rabbinic writings would immediately notice that John used three common references to God in a single verse.

In Jewish writings such as the Targums (Aramaic paraphrases of the Old Testament) and the Mishnah (collected teachings and commentaries of the rabbis), there was a strict prohibition on using God's name – even the Hebrew versions of "God" and "Lord" – because it was thought to be presumptuous. Therefore, several circumlocutions were used to speak of God without naming God.

In the Targums, the most frequent terms used to indicate God's activity included "Word," "Presence," and "Glory." In describing God's work, the rabbis would say, for example, that the Word spoke, the Presence dwelt, the Glory appeared.

Notice John's use of similar terms in v. 14: "the Word was made flesh, and dwelt among us, and we beheld his glory." For any literate Jew, the obvious presence of these common circumlocutions would make a clear claim that Jesus Christ was the living embodiment of God himself (see G.B. Caird, *The Revelation of Saint John the Divine* [Harper & Row, 1966], 264).

The custom of avoiding any public use of God's name continues among observant Jews, who avoid either saying or writing "Yahweh," "God," or "Lord." Instead, they are likely to refer to God as "the Holy One, blessed be He," or "the Name" (in Hebrew, *HaShem*). When writing God's name, they will intentionally misspell it as "G-d."

The glory of Christ
(vv. 14-15)

The Fourth Gospel begins with Christ as the eternal *logos*, then shifts to the earthly incarnation: "And the Word became flesh and lived among us, and we have seen his glory, the glory as of a father's only son, full of grace and truth" (v. 14). [**Circumlocutions**]

The meaning of "as of a father's only son" is subject to debate. The word used is *monogenēs*, which can suggest the idea of "only begotten," but can also mean "singular" in the sense of "the only one of its kind." Jesus certainly was the only one of his kind, but the added phrase "of the father" leads many interpreters to choose "only begotten" as the best translation. In a sense, God is the Father and begetter of all persons, but God's relationship with Christ, the "only begotten," is unique.

God's self-revelation through the incarnate Christ enabled humankind to see and appreciate God's true glory. The human Christ revealed God's matchless glory, declaring it most clearly through his nature, being "full of grace and truth." John preserves a careful balance by coupling these terms. *Grace* is God's free gift of love and forgiveness. *Truth* reflects God's desire to be consistent and trustworthy in dealing with humankind. In Christ, we see the depths of God's compassion combined with a devotion to what is right.

John offers further testimony of Christ's glory in the parenthetical remark of v. 15, where he quotes John the Baptist as saying "This was he of whom I said, 'He who comes after me ranks ahead of me because he was before me'" (cf. Matt. 3:11). Many people expected John to reveal himself as Israel's messiah, but John pointed to Jesus as the true Anointed One: the name "Christ" (*Christos*) is a Greek form of the Hebrew "Messiah" (*mashiach*) which means "anointed." The Fourth Gospel further argues that even John the baptizer did not recognize Jesus' importance at first, but God revealed it to him (cf. John 1:25-34).

The grace of Christ
(vv. 16-18)

Since Christ is "full of grace and truth," it follows that, for believers, "from his fullness we have all received grace upon grace" (v. 16). The grace we receive comes from God, through Christ. Perhaps John is suggesting that our human propensity to sin always leaves us in need of more grace, which we can receive "from his fullness … grace upon grace." [**Grace upon grace**]

The prologue comes to an end with a brief comparison between the way God was seen through the eyes of the law and through Christ: the law was given to humans through Moses, the writer said, but "grace and truth came through Jesus Christ" (v. 17).

Grace upon grace: In the phrase "grace upon grace," the word translated as "upon" could also mean "over against" or "instead of." Perhaps John is suggesting that the grace we have received for past sins can be "exchanged for" new grace to deal with our present failure. We can experience God's grace time after time because it comes from an inexhaustible source, "from his fullness."

God has been gracious from the beginning, but laws engraved on stone or written on parchment could not communicate divine grace as effectively as the human person of Jesus. Jesus was grace and truth in the flesh, the living embodiment of divine character.

Moses had once begged to see the Lord's glory, but was only allowed to catch a brief glimpse of God's "back" or "afterglow" (Exod. 33:23). The most interesting thing about this story is that, while passing by, God revealed the divine nature in words: "The LORD, the LORD, a God merciful and gracious, slow to anger, and abounding in steadfast love and faithfulness" (Exod. 34:6).

Although the story claims that Moses spoke with God "face to face" (Exod. 33:11), it also quotes God as saying "you cannot see my face; for no one shall see me and live" (Exod. 33:20). Thus, John insisted that no one had truly seen God until the coming of Christ, for "it is God the only Son, who is close to the Father's heart, who has made him known" (John 1:18).

The face Moses longed to see was the face beloved by John and Mary and Peter and James. It is the face of Christ, the living embodiment of divine grace, God with us – and the face in which we see reflected a view of the world we are called to follow.

The Hardest Question
How should we use the phrase "the Word of God"?

Many people habitually refer to the Bible as "the Word of God," going so far as to capitalize "Word." We often conclude a public scripture reading, for example, saying "The word of God for the people of God."

This is typically done as a sign of respect, and I don't wish to criticize those who practice it, but the question is worthy of more thought than we typically give it. My personal preference is to reserve "Word" with a capital "W" as a term for Christ, after John 1:1 – "In the beginning was the Word, and the Word was with God, and the Word was God." Capitalizing "Word" in this instance recognizes the divinity of Christ as the incarnate Word of God.

The Bible, although it claims to contain words of God, does not present itself as "the word of God." The prophets often spoke what they believed to be direct words from God, using formulas such as "this is what God says"

(Isa. 42:5), or "thus says the LORD" (Isa. 37:6; Jer. 37:7, 44:25; Ezek. 45:9). More commonly, however, they insisted "the word of the LORD came to me …" (Jer. 1:11, 13; 2:1; Ezek. 3:16, 6:1; among many others) or told their listeners to "hear the word of the LORD …" (Isa. 1:10, 28:14; Jer. 7:2, 17:20; Amos 7:16; et. al.).

Narrators telling stories about the prophets often used similar language. "The word of the LORD" is said to have come to Abraham (Gen. 15:4), Samuel (1 Sam. 15:10), Elijah (1 Kgs. 17:8), Nathan (1 Chron. 17:3), Isaiah (Isa. 38:4), Hosea (Hos. 1:1), Joel (Joel 1:1), and others. Similar permutations appear: Moses taught "the words of the LORD" (Exod. 24:3, Num. 11:24, others). "The word of the LORD" came to all Israel (Deut. 5:22) and was even spoken of as being heard by a "stone of witness" (Josh. 24:27).

We could cite many similar instances, but the point is that the Bible contains *some* words that it claims were spoken *by* God, but most of the Bible consists of words *about* God, or about the ongoing and usually troubled relationship between God and God's people. It is a witness to Hebrew and Christian efforts to explain their understanding of God, the beginning of a long story of divine-human relationships in which we continue to play a part.

The Bible as a whole, then, does not claim to be "the word of God" (with or without an uppercase W), though it does purport to contain words from God. Although it's commonly done, to speak of the Bible as "the Word of God" – especially when "Word" is capitalized – could be seen as a stretch. Moreover, for some believers it may come perilously close to "bibliolatry," to making of the Bible an idol, ascribing to it a sacred or divine status that it does not claim for itself.

The collection of writings that we call the Bible did not name itself. The word "Bible" comes from the Greek *biblia*, meaning "scrolls" or "books." Titles such as "Holy Bible" were ascribed by people, not claimed by the text itself.

The Bible is a vehicle for divine revelation, but it is not in itself divine.

While we clearly should have deep respect for the Bible and may properly speak of it as "sacred" Scripture, that is because of its testimony that points us to God, not because it possesses divinity.

First Reading
Isaiah 63:7-19

When Prayer Makes Bold

I will recount the gracious deeds of the LORD, the praiseworthy acts of the LORD,
because of all that the LORD has done for us, and the great favor to the house of Israel that he has shown them
according to his mercy, according to the abundance of his steadfast love. (Isa. 63:7)

Do you ever grow impatient when facing hard times or unpleasant circumstances, longing for the difficulty to pass and easier times to arrive?

As a boy, it seemed as if time must have slowed down between two and three o'clock in the afternoon. I would watch the minutes creep by on an institutional wall clock and long for the bell that would deliver me from school.

Waiting is hard – especially when we are waiting through a period of life that we consider difficult, unpleasant, or painful. In those times we may pray for deliverance and hope for healing. Sometimes it seems that our prayers go no further than the ceiling, and we may wonder if God is still around, or still cares.

The post-Christmas season can be prime time for feeling down. Even a "good Christmas" filled with family and gifts and Christmas cheer can leave us in the dumps once the house empties out and we are left with piles of trash and plates of stale cookies. How will we pay the bills? When will we see some of our family again?

Celebrating Christmas does not make the troublesome issues of life disappear, and in those days we need a reminder that God is still around.

Such was the situation for Israel in the text for today.

Disappointment and hope
(vv. 7-14)

The lectionary text for the day encompasses only Isa. 63:7-9, a woefully small excerpt cherry-picked for liturgical reading. Read in isolation, it might suggest a triumphant return and happy days in a beautifully restored city. The text is part of a larger unit extending from 63:7 through at least 64:14, however. We'll follow the text through v. 19 to get a larger picture.

The exiles' return to Jerusalem was one of the great disappointments of all time. In messages designed to offer hope to the people, Isaiah of the Exile had announced boldly that Jerusalem would be rebuilt (44:28), enriched by the wealth of the nations (45:14), and so prosperous that the borders of Jerusalem would have to be expanded (49:19-23, 54:1-3).

Such prophecies led many Hebrews to expect nothing but prosperity when they returned. Instead of a land flowing with milk and honey, however, they found a devastated city in a desolate countryside. They encountered opposition from neighboring provinces when they tried to rebuild (Ezra 4:1-5). They experienced famine and drought (Hag. 1:6, 9-11; 2:16-17). They existed only as a very small sub-province of Persia and were forced to pay heavy taxes to support the local government and provide tribute to Persia (Neh. 5:15).

In the face of such hardship, many of the people concluded that God must not love them anymore. They apparently decided that the practice of their faith was a waste of time (Mal. 1:2a, 3:14). How could God's spokesperson deal with a people such as this? The prophet responsible for our text chose to pray for them. **[Isaiah: Part Three]**

Today's text is part of an intercessory prayer (63:7–64:12) that follows a depiction of God as a blood-stained warrior taking vengeance against Edom (63:1-6), and

Isaiah, Part Three: The lengthy and complex book we call "Isaiah" covers a broad period of more than two hundred years in Israel's turbulent history.

The book begins in Judah before the exile, when Isaiah of Jerusalem was called by God "in the year that King Uzziah died" (742 BC, cf. Isa. 6:1). He was largely responsible for Isaiah 1–39 (with some exceptions), where the primary theme is judgment: God's people had sinned, and would be punished.

When we come to Isaiah 40-55 (possibly including chs. 34–35), the historical context leaps forward more than a hundred years. The people of Judah were enduring the predicted exile (587–538 BCE) when a new prophet in the tradition of Isaiah arose to bring comfort and hope. This prophet is often called "Second Isaiah," "Deutero-Isaiah," or "Isaiah of the Exile." His prophesy that Babylon would fall to Cyrus the Persian came to pass in 539 BCE, and within a year Cyrus allowed the Hebrew captives to return home.

Isaiah 56–66 seems to presuppose the early part of this period, speaking to the particular needs of the struggling restoration community. These words may be from yet another prophet ("Third Isaiah," or "Trito-Isaiah"), though it is possible that Isaiah of the Exile was a part of the returning group, and continued to prophesy. In any case, as James Leo Green once wrote, "the thing that really matters most about any book in the Bible is not who wrote it but whether the voice of God is heard in it" (*God Reigns* [Broadman Press, 1968], 10).

preceding a comforting divine response in 65:1-25. The prayer is offered on behalf of the people – expressing their pain, asking their questions, pleading their case. The prophet prays, not necessarily as *he* would pray, but as the *people* would pray. Then, he responds to the people with the words of God.

The prayer sounds very much like a psalm, and for good reason. Most of the psalms were prayers, and many were prayers of lament, like this one. Our own prayers in times of deep pain rarely follow a logical progression of thought, and the same is true of biblical petitions, where prayers of lament typically include elements of complaint, entreaty, confession, and trust, though not always in that order.

Isaiah initiated the prayer with a burst of praise (v. 7) not unlike Pss. 89:1-2, 105:1-2, and 106:1-2. The prophet recalled how God had blessed Israel and called the Hebrews into covenant. In times of distress, God had delivered them.

Even when their rebellion led to promised discipline, God had again bestowed favor on the people and "became their savior in all their distress." God's divine presence, love, and compassion had "redeemed them ... lifted them up and carried them all the days of old" (vv. 8-9).

Perhaps the praise was intended as an appeal that would incite God to recall past love and be moved to deliver the people from their current distress. The opening words of praise would also remind the Hebrews that God had been faithful before, and God could be counted on to deliver again despite their rebellious and unbelieving behavior (v. 10).

Isaiah recalled Mosaic traditions of how God had delivered Israel from Egypt in miraculous fashion. Despite the people's intransigence along the way, God had led them "like a horse in the desert" that does not stumble, giving them rest "like cattle that go down into the valley."

"Thus you led your people," Isaiah prayed, "to make for yourself a glorious name" (vv. 11-12). Note again how the prophet appealed to the divine ego: if the people who struggled during the lean early years of the postexilic period didn't deserve to be delivered, perhaps God would intervene nevertheless for the sake of preserving a reputation as being just and faithful, having "a glorious name."

Disillusionment and sorrow
(vv. 15-16)

But deliverance had not come. In behalf of the suffering people, Isaiah cried, "Look down from heaven and see!" (63:15a, cp. Ps. 80:14). In so many words, he was asking "Can't you see what kind of trouble we are in? Are you so caught up in your holy and glorious habitation that you can't take the time to look upon our sorrows?"

"Where are your zeal and your might?" Isaiah asked. "The yearning of your heart and your compassion? They are withheld from me" (v. 15). **[Deep compassion]**

Deep compassion: The NRSV has converted a graphic Hebrew idiom to a more palatable English expression: a literal reading of "yearning of your heart" would be "the tumult of your bowels." The ancients often associated deep feelings, especially of compassion, with the bowels. See also Phil. 2:1 and Col. 3:12, which appeal to Christian believers' "bowels of compassion."

> **Parental language:** Biblical terminology referring to God as "father" derives from a period of patriarchy when virtually all authority figures were male, and Yahweh was largely assumed to be male, too. The Old Testament does contain some feminine imagery for God, however.
>
> God appears as a mother bird sheltering Israel beneath her wings (Ruth 2:12; Ps. 17:8, 57:1, 91:4). Three times, Isaiah portrays God in feminine terms: God is like a woman in childbirth crying out in pain (42:14), God will comfort Israel as a mother comforts her child (66:13), and God will not forget Israel any more than a mother could forget the baby at her breast (49:15).
>
> We understand that God is beyond gender as humans know it. And, in our culture, though true equality remains elusive, we have become more sensitive to issues of equality between men and women. Thus, while biblical language for God is predominantly male, in our culture it can be more helpful to think of God as "parent" without the need for a gender identifier.

People of every age have asked this question. When trouble comes and prayers aren't answered as we like, we may think God isn't listening or doesn't love us anymore.

The prophet turns to the metaphor of a parent and child in v. 16, adding "For you are our father." The parental imagery of God as father seems familiar to us because it is common in the New Testament, but it is quite rare in the Hebrew Bible, where "Creator" is more commonly used. Thus, Isaiah's emphasis on the parental nature of God and the relationship responsibilities implied by it is a notable claim.

Israelites commonly spoke of "Father Abraham," and they revered Jacob (also called Israel, cf. Gen. 32:28) as the father of the 12 tribes, but those ancestors were long dead and gone, unable to help: "Abraham does not know us and Israel does not acknowledge us," Isaiah said (v. 16a). In contrast, he prayed, "You, O LORD, are (still) our father; our Redeemer from of old is your name" (v. 16b). The implication is: "You're our parent. We're in trouble. *Do something!*" [**Parental language**]

Doubt and blame
(vv. 17-19)

Have you noticed that children have a way of blaming their troubles on their parents? Sometimes, of course, parents *are* culpable, and many children suffer because of parental abuse or neglect. But, in the everyday course of life, short-sighted and immature children often accuse their parents in unjust ways. "You hate me!" "You don't want me to have any friends!" "You're trying to ruin my life!" "It's all *your* fault!"

Children who are reprimanded for "talking back" may blame their parent(s) for making them mad and thus "forcing" them to misbehave. Sometimes our ultimate parent gets the same sort of treatment. In the old story of Genesis 3, when Adam was confronted with his sin, he blamed it on both Eve *and God*: "the woman whom *you gave* to be with me, *she gave* me from the fruit of the tree" (Gen. 3:12).

Isaiah's prayer, reflecting the mood of the dispirited people, made the same kind of charge against God. "Why, O LORD, do you make us stray from your ways and harden our heart, so that we do not fear you?" (v. 17a).

Was Isaiah thinking of how God had hardened Pharaoh's heart prior to the Exodus (cf. Exod. 7:3), and charging the Lord with hardening the Hebrews' hearts also? The prayer calls on God to "turn back for the sake of your servants" (v. 17b). The word translated "turn back" (*shuv*) is often translated as "repent," but it was not God who needed to repent.

Israel had enjoyed the bounty of Canaan in the past, but the people had come to believe those days were past (v. 18). After years of exile and a troubled return, the people felt as far removed from God as those who were "not called by your name" (v. 19). They didn't feel like the people of God at all.

Isaiah shifted to a challenge, pleading with God to act in the present as in the past: "Oh, that you would tear open the heavens and come down!" Isaiah wanted God to appear with such power that the mountains would shake, Israel's enemies would quake in fear, and Israel would once again experience God's compassionate presence (64:1-4).

Haven't we had similar longings? It's not unusual for us to feel distance from God, recalling an earlier sense of closeness and wondering if God has forgotten us. Isaiah would suggest that God is not the one who moved.

The Hardest Question
Why read this text during the Christmas season?

A text such as Isa. 63:7-19, largely a lament, may seem a strange choice for the Christmas season, but a feeling of sadness and loss is not at all unusual during late December. Some people remember happy Christmases from years past, but age or changing family situations have left them on the outside looking in. Others stay busy through the frantic preparations for the season, but as it passes they may feel as let down as needles falling from a dried-out Christmas tree. For those who have lost a loved one or suffered ruptured relationships during the year, Christmas inevitably brings a sadness that is the flip side of former happy times together.

Isaiah's intense longing and hoping for the revelation of God is an appropriate text for such days, though we also have the benefit of the good news we celebrate at Christmas. We long for Christ to be reborn with power in our own lives. In the strong symbols of Advent and Christmas seasons we may find reminders that God has not forgotten.

Isaiah heard a similar reminder in God's response to his plaintive prayer in Israel's behalf. The Lord had been there all along: "I was ready to be sought out by those who did not ask, to be found by those who did not seek me. I said, 'Here I am, here I am,' to a nation that did not call on my name. I held out my hands all day long to a rebellious people, who walk in a way that is not good, following their own devices …" (65:1-2, NRSV).

Believers old and new can easily fall into the trap of looking for God only in the wind and the fire, the loud and the powerful, the holiday spectaculars. As a result, we may fail to hear the still, small voice of the God who has been there all along.

Second Reading
Psalm 148*

Praise Squared

Praise the LORD! Praise the LORD from the heavens; praise him in the heights! (Ps. 148:1)

Have you ever walked out into a beautiful rain-fresh morning, or looked out over a stunning mountain vista, or watched a puppy at play, and felt moved with gratitude that we live in such an amazing world?

Our daily outlook is often tinged with busyness related to work or home, or with frustration over some aspect of life, or with sorrow that has left us feeling vaguely disappointed. Moments of pure praise are likely rare – but for those moments, Psalm 148 is a perfect text.

Israel's praise was commonly mixed with lament, because that's the way life is. No one stays on top all the time. Occasionally, though, a poet was moved to declare unadulterated thanksgiving to God, pure praise such as that echoed in hymns such as Charles Wesley's "Love Divine, All Loves Excelling." The chorus ends with the redeemed standing before God, "lost in wonder, love, and praise."

A hallelujah hymn

Psalm 148 is one of five "Hallel" or "hallelujah psalms" that conclude the book (Psalms 146–150). All of them focus purely on praise, beginning and ending with the words "*hallelu-yah*." The term is a combination of two Hebrew words: *hallelu* is a plural imperative form of the verbal root *hll*, meaning "Praise!" and the object "*yah*" is an abbreviation of the divine name *Yahweh* – so "hallelujah" literally means "Praise the Lord!" **[Hymnic variety]**

The composite expression came to be used, not only as exhortation to energetic praise, but also as an exclamation of praise itself. As such, the early translation known as the

> **Hymnic variety:** Why do some Christian songs use the term "Hallelujah" and others use "Alleluia"? Both expressions mean the same thing: "hallelujah" is an English transliteration of the Hebrew *hallelu-jah*, and *alleluia* is an English version of how the Greeks transliterated it, which was taken over into the Latin Vulgate and thus is the predominant form in classical or "high church" music.
>
> Today, whether we sing the revivalist "Hallelujah, thine the glory, hallelujah, amen" or a stretched-out version of "alleluia" in "Christ the Lord is Risen Today," we're saying the same thing. Song writers choose the form of the word that best fits the rhythm, meter, and mood of the song they're writing.

Septuagint often simply transliterated the Hebrew phrase into Greek letters as *allelouia*. We continue that practice today. Whether we exclaim "Hallelujah!" in praise or sing "Alleluia" in a more formal hymn, we are proclaiming "Praise the LORD," where "LORD" stands for Yahweh, the special covenant name God revealed to Israel (Exod. 3:15).

The church father Augustine took note of this. He wrote that when people say "Praise the Lord," they are doing precisely what they are telling others to do (*Expositions on the Psalms 121–150* [New City Press, 2004], 6:477).

While the classic form *hallelu-jah* appears only at the beginning and the end of Psalm 148, the verb *hallelu* appears 10 more times, encouraging worshipers to "praise the LORD" (spelled differently), to "praise the name of the LORD," or simply to "praise him!" This gives a sense of continuity to the psalm, leaving no doubt about its central theme.

*Psalm 148 also occurs as the Psalm reading for the fifth Sunday of Easter in Year C.

Heavenly praise
(vv. 1-6)

Psalm 148 has a distinctive structure. While the overriding concern is that all creation should praise God, vv. 1-6 call on all aspects of the heavens to pay tribute to God, while vv. 7-14 issue the same challenge to every attribute and inhabitant of the earth. Can we find ourselves in this psalm?

The first verse utilizes the verb for "praise" no less than three times: "Praise the LORD! Praise the LORD from the heavens; praise him in the heights!" The psalmist then begins an inventory of heavenly inhabitants that owe praise to God, beginning with "all his angels … all his host" (v. 2).

Anyone who claims to understand either the number or hierarchies of heavenly beings overestimates his or her abilities. The Hebrew word translated as "angels" is *mal'achim*, which means "messengers" (the prophet Malachi's name means "my messenger"). The word for "hosts" is sometimes used in the sense of heavenly armies in the expression "LORD of hosts" (1 Sam. 17:45), sometimes as heavenly attendants (Ps. 103:20-21), and sometimes as a reference to stars that accompanied the sun and moon (Deut. 17:3, 5). These were often associated with pagan deities. Israel was forbidden to worship these, but sometimes did, leading to judgment (2 Kgs. 23:4-5, Jer. 19:13, Zeph. 1:5). Verse 2 of our text clearly addresses heavenly beings thought to attend God in various ways, for heavenly bodies come next.

"Praise him, sun and moon; praise him all you shining stars!" (v. 3). The author of the creation story in Genesis 1 refused to use the words "sun" and "moon" because neighboring nations worshiped the heavenly bodies as gods, with similar names ("sun" is *shemesh* in Hebrew, *shamash* in Babylonian/Assyrian). Here the writer names the "sun, moon, and shining stars," but in a category that is clearly a step down from "God's heaven" to the visible "heavens" above the earth, where they inhabit the sky. They are God's creation, not gods in themselves. **[Wordplay]**

The Hebrews' pre-scientific view of the universe held that a cosmic ocean existed above the "firmament" that defined the limits of the heavens above the earth, and that windows opened to allow rains to fall (Gen. 1:6-8, 7:11, 8:2; Mal. 3:10). This is probably behind the expression

> **Wordplay:** Hebrew readers can observe an impressive use of wordplay in the first few verses. The consonants from Yahweh's "name" (*shem*) are reflected in the Hebrew words for "the heavens" (*hashemayim*) in v. 1, "sun" (*shemesh*) in v. 3, and both "the highest heavens" (*shemē-hashemayim*) and what is above the "heavens" (*shemayim*) in v. 4.
>
> A similar wordplay is found in v. 13, which employs "name" (*shem*), "his name" (*shemō*), and "heavens" (*shemayim*).

"waters above the heavens" (v. 4). Atmospheric clouds appear in the next section.

Calls to praise often conclude with a reason for praise. Why should heavenly beings and bodies "praise the name of the LORD"? Because "he commanded, and they were created. He established them forever and ever; he fixed their bounds, which cannot be passed" (vv. 5-6). Through their very existence and fulfillment of their divinely ordained function, the heavenly hosts and cosmic luminaries reflect praise to their creator.

My wife owns a beautiful "lazy Susan" turntable that her grandfather handcrafted with an inlaid checkerboard on the top. The checkered squares are made from sycamore and mahogany wood, while the border comes from red oak. The quality of the craftsmanship reflects honor due to the crafter. In a similar way, the majesty of the universe speaks to the power of its creator and the glory that is due.

Earthly praise
(vv. 7-14)

With v. 7, the psalmist turns from the heavens to the earth, along with its oceans and atmosphere. He begins with the sea: "Praise the LORD from the earth, you sea monsters and all deeps." Here "sea monsters" may call to mind whales or other large sea creatures that had been seen or imagined by sailors. The word is *tanninim*, a loan word from Aramaic. It is variously translated as "serpent," "dragon," or "monster," related both to land and water, and may have been inspired by sightings of whales, crocodiles, or other imposing creatures. In most cases its use is metaphorical, and not intended to describe a specific animal. Both sea monsters and the depths of the sea they inhabit are personified as capable of voicing praise.

The storm God? Believing Baal to be the god of storms and weather, the Canaanites typically depicted him, and his consort Anat, with an upraised right arm holding a club or spear and sometimes symbolizing thunder and lightning. "Baal with Thunderbolt," 15th-13th century BCE, from Ras Shamra. Now in the Louvre. Public domain via Wikimedia Commons.

The atmosphere takes the stage in v. 8, where the psalmist calls for praise from "fire and hail, snow and frost, stormy wind fulfilling his command!" The imagery suggests all kinds of powerful storms. "Fire" in this context calls to mind lightning, which often accompanies hail-producing storms. NRSV's "frost" would be better rendered as "clouds" (as in NIV11, NET, and HCSB): the word more commonly describes thick smoke, which clouds resemble. Israel's Canaanite neighbors depicted

Baal as the storm god, but the psalmist believed Yahweh alone reigned over all the earth, from ocean depths to highest heaven. [**The storm God?**]

In vv. 9-10, the psalmist shifts to the earth's surface with an intentional movement from geological features ("mountains and hills") to prized vegetation ("fruit trees and cedars"), then to animal life ("wild animals and all cattle, creeping things and flying birds"). The list does not distinguish between "clean" and "unclean" animals: every creature that lives and moves is a part of God's good creation and owes praise to the Lord.

We are not surprised that humans make up the final category called to praise God (vv. 11-12). Once again we see a purposeful progression, this time from royalty ("kings of the earth and all peoples, princes and all rulers of the earth") to common folk ("young men and women alike, old and young together").

How can cosmic bodies, ocean depths, land formations, standing trees, and living creatures join human beings in giving praise to God? Even unconscious entities give praise to exalt God's glory "above earth and heaven" precisely by existing and fulfilling the function God designed for them (v. 13).

On one hand, then, the psalm pictures humans as one part of the larger web of creation. We, like stars, clouds, trees, and animals, give praise to God by being and doing what we have been called to be and do. That is an important lesson, but there is more.

Why should people praise God? The final verse turns to Israel as God's covenant people, especially blessed by God and thus even more obliged to offer abject praise: "He has raised up a horn for his people, praise for all his faithful, for the people of Israel who are close to him. Praise the LORD!"

"Horn" in this instance is probably a metaphor for a special position of dignity or privilege. The psalmist believed Israel had been chosen as God's special people, to live in a covenant relationship that would serve as a shining example and draw other peoples to God. The mark of Israel's honor was seen in their praise to God.

Christians are not Israelites – but we also claim to live in a special relationship with God, a new covenant made available to all through the salvific work of Christ. We also are called to live in such a way that our attitudes and behaviors reflect the goodness of God and attract others to have faith. There is no better way – or greater reason – to praise the Lord.

Hallelujah?

The Hardest Question
What was Israel's "horn"?

Psalm 148 concludes: "He has raised up a horn for his people, praise for all his faithful, for the people of Israel who are close to him. Praise the LORD!" I noted above, that "horn," in this context, probably serves as a metaphor for honor or dignity. But what is its background? Are there other possibilities?

Peoples of the ancient Near East, having observed powerful horned animals, typically saw horns as a sign of power. Mesopotamian gods were routinely portrayed with horns curled around their heads as a crown, and kings who claimed to be divine likewise included horns on commissioned images of themselves. [Divine horns]

The Israelites used animal horns as containers for liquids such as anointing oil, and punctured the small end

Divine Horns: Atop the *Hammurabi Stele*, the Babylonian king Hammurabi receives the contents of his law code from the enthroned sun god Shamash, whose head is wrapped with stylized horns. The stele, found in Susa in 1901, is now in the Louvre in Paris. (Photo of facsimile in the Oriental Institute, Chicago)

to make the trumpet-like *shofar*, used for signaling in war or in temple worship.

Sacrificial altars typically bore symbolic horns at each corner as prominent features to which blood was applied during ceremonies (Exod. 27:2, 29:12, and others). Accused persons seeking asylum could take hold of the horns of the altar for sanctuary (1 Kgs. 1:50, 2:28). Amos spoke of the horns of the altar at Bethel being cut off as a punishment for Israel's sin (Amos 3:14).

Metaphorically, horns spoke of a king or country's power, strong in victory (1 Kgs. 22:11) or broken in defeat (Jer. 48:25). Ephraim and Manasseh were described as having "horns like the horns of a wild ox" as a symbol of their might (Deut. 33:17). Hannah's song of praise says Yahweh will give strength to the king and "exalt the horn" (NRSV "power") of the anointed (2 Sam. 2:10). A similar metaphor is found in Ps. 89:17: "For you are the glory of their strength, by your favor our horn is exalted." The same psalm says that God's steadfast love and faithfulness will bless the king, so that "in my name his horn shall be exalted" (Ps. 89:24).

Psalm 75 warns against promoting one's own "horn," an image of excessive pride (Ps. 75:5), leaving such exaltation to God: "All the horns of the wicked I will cut off, but the horns of the righteous shall be exalted." Similar themes are present in Ps. 92:10 and 112:9.

Similar imagery is behind Ps. 148:14, though with a twist: Israel's dignity and power are here not connected with a mighty king or with a military victory, but identified with their position of closeness to God and their call to praise Yahweh: "He has raised up a horn for his people, praise for all his faithful, for the people of Israel who are close to him."

James Luther Mays describes it this way: "The LORD has given his faithful praise as their dignity and power. They are the ones who are 'near' to him, know and can speak his exalted name. They are given the praise with which to voice the unspoken praise of all creation. Praise is their place and purpose. In the praise of the people of the LORD, the name that is the truth about the entire universe is spoken on behalf of all the rest of creation" (*Psalms*, Interpretation: A Bible Commentary for Teaching and Preaching [Westminster John Knox Press, 2011], 445).

First Sunday after Christmas

Third Reading
Hebrews 1:1-14*

Who's the Boss?

*This text is also the epistle reading for the third set of Christmas readings.
A study on the text appears in this volume at that point..*

Fourth Reading
Matthew 2:13-23*

A Strange Beginning to a Happy Ending

A voice was heard in Ramah, wailing and loud lamentation, Rachel weeping for her children;
she refused to be consoled, because they are no more. (Matt. 2:18)

Christmas, as many people have experienced, has a dark side. With its blatant commercialization, emotionally charged memories and gift-enhanced anticipation, it's easy to expect so much of Christmas that the season cannot help but be disappointing.

Families who have experienced a recent death or divorce may focus on the empty spot under the Christmas tree where the loved one's presents used to go. Those who are alone at Christmas may feel more lonesome than any other time of the year.

The original Christmas story also had a dark side – a very dark side. We don't like that part of the story, so we tend to gloss over it, but there it is, hiding behind the manger scenes and fireplace stockings, haunting the narrow streets of Bethlehem.

The dark side of Christmas is about insanity and brutality and death. It is about pulling up stakes, running through the night, and living on the edge. It is the story of baby Jesus, boy fugitive.

A stealthy escape
(vv. 13-15)

Only Matthew tells us this story, which differs in many respects from the version told by Luke, in which Joseph and Mary were natives of Nazareth who returned there soon after Jesus' birth. Matthew, in contrast, portrays them as living in a house in Bethlehem.

Matthew alone recounts a series of terrifying events surrounding Jesus' early life, each foretold by an angel

> **Matthew's perspective:** Luke's infancy narrative implies that Mary and Joseph remained in Bethlehem for two to three months (long enough for all the purification rituals to be completed), then brought Jesus to Jerusalem to offer appropriate dedication sacrifices (Luke 2:21-38) before returning to their home in Nazareth of Galilee (Luke 2:39-40).
>
> Matthew, whose birth and infancy narratives derive from another source, portrays the holy family as living in a house in Bethlehem when they were visited by wise men from the East.
>
> We note also that Matthew's narrative is seen through Joseph's eyes, whereas Luke's account is told from Mary's perspective. The theme of fulfillment is very important to Matthew, and constantly recurs as he seeks to show how Jesus' life, death, resurrection, and offer of salvation were a fulfillment of Old Testament prophecies. Although the prophecies in context often referred to temporal (and past) events, Matthew saw an eschatological fulfillment in Jesus.

who appeared in Joseph's dreams, with each event fulfilling some Old Testament prophecy. [**Matthew's perspective**]

Only in Matthew do we hear of the magi who traveled far in search of a baby king they had seen in the stars. Assuming that King Herod would know of such an auspicious event, they stopped in Jerusalem to inquire about the new king's birth – unintentionally alerting the paranoid ruler to a potential rival.

Herod was a harsh and unstable potentate described as an Idumean, meaning he was of Edomite descent. Known as "Herod the Great" for his many impressive building projects, he knew that he was unpopular and feared a potential overthrow.

This text also appears as an optional gospel reading for the second Sunday after Christmas in the Episcopal tradition.

In his later years, around 6 BCE, Herod grew so suspicious of an internal coup that he ordered his own sons Alexander and Aristobulus to be executed, along with his favorite wife, a Hasmonean princess named Mariamne. Later, he executed another son, Antipater.

The Jewish historian Josephus claimed that Herod, wanting to ensure that the land would mourn his passing, left orders that a member of every family in his kingdom should be killed on the day of his death (*Antiquities of the Jews*, 17.6.6).

It's no wonder, then, that Herod would go off the deep end when "wise men from the East" alerted him to the predicted birth of a future "king of the Jews" (vv. 1-2). Herod responded with fear – and when Herod was upset, everyone around him was on edge: "he was frightened, and all Jerusalem with him" (v. 3).

After dismissing the magi for the moment, Herod consulted his religious advisors concerning any prophecies regarding a future king, and they recalled Micah's prediction that "a ruler who is to shepherd my people Israel" would arise from Bethlehem (vv. 4-6, citing Mic. 5:2).

Later, meeting secretly with the magi, Herod learned when they had seen the surprising star that led them to believe a new king had been born. He bade them to find the child and to inform him of the boy's whereabouts, feigning a desire to go and offer his own homage to the future king (vv. 7-8).

After the wise men found the house where Jesus and his parents lived, they paid their respects and presented the family valuable gifts (2:9-11). Warned in a dream to bypass Herod and return by "another way" (2:12), they foiled Herod's efforts to learn the child's specific location.

Joseph also had a portentous dream, instructing him to flee with his family to Egypt because Herod was seeking to kill (literally "destroy") the child (v. 13). Joseph packed

---

Ancient exegesis: The practice of drawing connections based on surface similarities is a far cry from modern exegetical standards, but it was common in the first century, when Roman rule made life hard for the Jews, and messianic expectations were rife.

Donald A. Hagner describes the practice this way: "What we have here is a matter of typological correspondence – that is, a substantial similarity is seen to exist between two moments of redemptive history, and therefore the two are regarded as interconnected, forming one larger continuity; the earlier is thus seen to foreshadow or anticipate the latter, which then becomes a kind of realization or fulfillment of the former. ... Matthew sees Jesus as living out and summing up the history of Israel. In Egypt, in the exodus, and in the wilderness (see 4:1-11), Jesus is the embodiment of Israel, not only anticipating her victories but also participating in her sufferings (cf. Isa. 63:8-9)" (*Matthew 1-13*, vol. 33A, Word Biblical Commentary [Word Books, 1993], 36).

---

up his family and left "by night," presumably the same night in which the dream had come (v. 14). **[Jesus, boy fugitive]**

This was done, Matthew said, to fulfill the prophet's words: "Out of Egypt I have called my son" (v. 15, from Hos. 11:1). When Hosea spoke those poignant words, he was thinking about how God had called Israel out of Egypt, not about a future messiah. But that did not bother early Christians, who were diligent in searching for connections between the Hebrew Scriptures and the life of Christ, and who didn't hesitate to employ a popular Jewish practice of searching for hidden meanings, drawing typological connections between ancient and present days.

While the prophet clearly had an entirely different intent, early interpreters believed they could perceive a deeper meaning that the prophet himself may not have understood. **[Ancient exegesis]**

An angry attack
(vv. 16-18)

Herod's reaction was merciless and swift, but not swift enough. Having learned the time of the star's appearance, he ordered a mass execution of young boys in and around Bethlehem. The NRSV and some other versions say that Herod "sent and killed all the children," but this

---

Jesus, boy fugitive: How does it make you feel to think of Jesus, the son of God, being hustled through the night as a young political fugitive? The late Malcolm Tolbert once pointed to the paradox that in this instance, God's purpose was not accomplished through a spectacular miracle, but through an ignominious flight. What does this suggest about God's ability (and inclination?) to work in hidden or unexpected ways?

> **Popular, but not biblical:** Reading Matthew's account alone offers a needed reminder that our modern manger scenes are a poor attempt to harmonize two very different gospel stories. Matthew, the only writer to mention the wise men, portrays them as arriving at a house up to two years after Jesus' birth. There is no scriptural support for the idea that the magi appeared at the manger alongside shepherds and livestock on the night Jesus was born.

translation ignores the masculine gender of *tous paidas*, which clearly indicates male children. When masculine words obviously stand as representative for all, inclusive language is appropriate, but there would have been no reason for Herod to kill baby girls: his fear of a foretold rival king would almost certainly have been directed toward a potential male usurper.

Herod's command to include all boys under two years old – "according to the time that he had learned from the wise men" (v. 16b) – suggests that they did not appear on the scene until at least a year after Jesus' birth. This is understandable, as considerable preparation would have been required for a very lengthy journey by foot, camel, or donkey. In other words, there would have been no wise men at the manger. [**Popular, but not biblical**]

Bethlehem, about six miles south of Jerusalem, was a small town at the time, and the number of male infants in the lightly populated area could have been as few as 20, which may explain why the atrocity did not attract the attention of historians: we have no extrabiblical accounts of such an act, though it is fully consonant with Herod's reputation for brutality.

But even the massacre of 20 infants is a crime beyond imagining, as Americans learned in December 2012 when a deranged man gunned down first graders at Sandy Hook Elementary School in Connecticut, killing 20 children and six adult teachers and staff members.

The slaughter of the innocents is truly a dark side of Christmas: an episode as black with death as Jesus' birth is bright with hope and life. How could early Christians hope to explain why God would allow such an atrocity to accompany the birth of Jesus?

Matthew again took refuge in scripture, seeing the awful calamity as a fulfillment of prophecy (v. 17-18), though he carefully refrained from attributing the horrific

massacre to God. Normally he introduced scripture quotations with statements such as "This was done to make come true what the Lord said …," or "this was to fulfill …" The present text, however, begins with a simple passive: "then was fulfilled what had been spoken through the prophet Jeremiah."

The quotation comes from Jer. 31:15, where it plainly refers to the Hebrews who were killed or carried away in the Babylonian exile, an occasion for sustained and abundant weeping: "A voice was heard in Ramah, wailing and loud lamentation, Rachel weeping for her children; she refused to be consoled, because they are no more" (v. 18).

In context, the quote from Jeremiah derives from a joyful section of consolation, a promise that the exiles whose loss had occasioned such weeping would yet return. Matthew, however, focuses on the intense grieving associated with the murders.

A safe return
(vv. 19-23)

The final chapter of Jesus' early journeying follows the death of Herod, which would not have been long in coming: Jesus' birth is often dated to between 6 and 4 BCE, and Herod died in 4 BCE.

Again, Matthew tells us, an angel appeared to Joseph, this time with the good news that Herod was dead, the coast was clear, and it was safe to return home (vv. 19-21).

When the weary travelers neared Bethlehem, however, Joseph learned that Herod's son Archelaus had taken control of Judah. Herod the Great had ruled all of greater Palestine as a client king for the Romans, but none of his sons were deemed worthy of ruling the entire area. Thus, the territory was divided between three sons: Herod Antipas, Herod Phillip, and Herod Archelaus.

Archelaus was widely regarded as the least capable of the three, known for having inherited all of his father's vices and none of his virtues. The Romans endured his heavy-handed rule until 6 CE, then gave in to citizen complaints and deposed him because of his general incompetence and unneeded brutality.

Joseph was warned in yet another dream to avoid Archelaus' reach, so the holy family skirted Judah and journeyed into Galilee, settling in the obscure village of

> **The Nazorean:** How do we explain this unusual name – and its unique spelling? One position suggests that Matthew was referring to a text such as Judg. 13:7 (cf. 13:5 and 16:17), in which Samson's mother was told that she would give birth to a son, who "will be a Nazirite of God."
>
> Some scholars believe there was a time when "Nazirite" and "Nazarene" were thought to be equivalent terms. Thus, Matthew may have confused the words and quoted a text about Nazirites, thinking that the word could also refer to a native of Nazareth.
>
> A problem with that argument is that Jesus did not act like a Nazirite. Nazirites were forbidden to drink wine, but Jesus freely joined in eating and drinking with sinners to the point that he was called "a glutton and a drunkard" (Matt. 11:19).
>
> A second option is that Matthew may have had in mind Isa. 11:1, which says "A shoot shall come out from the stump of Jesse, and a branch shall grow out of his roots." In that oracle, widely regarded as a messianic prophecy referring to a future king, the word for "branch" is *netser*. Since early believers (including Matthew) thought that Jesus was the intended messiah and ultimate fulfillment of the "righteous branch" prophecy, they may have stretched the word *netzer* to *natsorean*. This is a reasonable suggestion, though it does not explain the unusual spelling. Nazareth is not mentioned in the Old Testament, but the Hebrew equivalent of the "z" in Nazareth would be the letter *tsade*, transliterated as "ts" in *netser*.
>
> In cases such as this, we must sometimes simply admit that we cannot know for sure what Matthew had in mind, except that he intended to cast yet another line among the many ties that bind Jesus to the Hebrew scriptures.

Nazareth, where the more lenient Herod Antipas ruled (vv. 22-23a).

Unlike Luke's gospel, which presumes that Nazareth had been Joseph and Mary's hometown (Luke 1:26-27; 2:1-4, 29), Matthew's story does not indicate that the family had previous roots in Nazareth, suggesting that they chose to go there in order to live away from the tyrant Archelaus, and in fulfillment of a prophecy that "he would be called a Nazorean" (Matt. 2:23).

Again, Matthew connects this move with the Old Testament – or attempts to. In v. 23b, he speaks as if he is quoting scripture: "… so that what had been spoken through the prophets might be fulfilled, 'He will be called a Nazorean.'" This might lead to raised eyebrows, because neither that prophecy nor the word "Nazorean" appears anywhere in the Old Testament.

Matthew must have been citing a general tradition when he referred generally to "what had been spoken by the prophets." Efforts to explain this conundrum reach no certain conclusions, though several possibilities have been advanced. Matthew may have confused the Hebrew word "nazarite" with "Nazarene" in recalling a tradition that Jesus was called "the Nazarene," as were his followers (Acts 24:5). [The Nazorean]

Matthew's account suggests that Jesus' early years were spent in a dangerous world and with no permanent home. Today we live in an increasingly mobile society where it's less likely that people will spend their entire lives in the same locale. Even for those who do, perhaps this story will remind us that we are also pilgrims and wanderers on this earth, beset by dangers but called to make the world a better place as we make our way toward a more lasting home.

And, even though we may find his exegetical methods suspect, Matthew's account also challenges us to trust in Jesus as the final fulfillment of all prophecy that pointed to a messiah who would come to deliver God's people from the exile of their sins.

The Hardest Question
Why does this story sound familiar?

Those who read the text closely may notice several similarities between Matthew's story of Jesus' birth and the older story of Israel in Egypt. The parallels are almost certainly intentional, as Matthew sought ways of showing that as Moses saved the Israelites from Egypt, Jesus saved God's people from their sins. Notice these parallels:

The Pharaoh ordered all Hebrew male infants killed (Exod. 1:22), while Herod ordered all male infants in and around Bethlehem to be killed (Matt. 2:16). Moses was saved by his parents' action (Exod. 2:3-10), and Jesus was likewise saved by his parents' action (Matt. 2:13-15).

Moses fled Egypt when the Pharaoh threatened his life, but returned when that Pharaoh died (Exod. 2:15, 4:19-20). Jesus' family fled their home when Herod threatened his life, but returned when Herod died (Matt. 2:13-15, 19-21).

Hosea spoke of Israel as God's son in saying "Out of Egypt I called my son" (Hos. 11:1). Matthew quotes that text as a foretelling of Jesus' return from Egypt (Matt. 2:15).

Moses was sent to deliver the Israelites from bondage to the Egyptians, while Jesus came to deliver God's people from their sins.

In some cases, as in Exod. 4:19 and Matt. 2:20, the wording is nearly identical. It seems clear that Matthew saw Herod as a type of Pharaoh, and Jesus as a new and greater analogy to Moses.

Matthew also saw similarities between Jesus' life and the time of the exile, as he quoted Rachel's weeping for the exiles in conjunction with the mothers of Bethlehem weeping for their slaughtered sons (Jer. 31:15, Matt. 2:18-19).

Matthew went on to cite many other Old Testament texts that he perceived to be fulfilled in Jesus (Matt. 4:14, 8:17, 12:17, 13:14, 13:35, 21:4, 26:54, 26:56, 27:9). To modern readers, Matthew's linking of specific scriptures about Israel with the story of Jesus may stretch the Old Testament's original meaning, but his overall purpose is clear: all that Israel had hoped for finds its culmination and resolution in the life and work of Jesus.

As Donald A. Hagner put it, "For Matthew, all Israel's history finds its recapitulation in the life of Jesus" (*Matthew 1-13*, vol. 33A, Word Biblical Commentary, [Word Books, 1993], 34).

Second Sunday after Christmas*

First Reading
Jeremiah 31:7-14**

Saving Grace

For thus says the LORD: "Sing aloud with gladness for Jacob, and raise shouts for the chief of the nations; proclaim, give praise, and say, 'Save, O LORD, your people the remnant of Israel.'" (Jer. 31:7)

Have you ever felt like giving up hope? We all may have felt beyond hope at some point, but we didn't give up. Even in the worst of times, so long as we wish for a good future, or pray – or even complain – we are expressing hope for better days.

The prophet Jeremiah offered hope to a people living under judgment. Jeremiah believed that God had already exiled the northern kingdom of Israel, and would soon bring the Babylonians to defeat the southern kingdom of Judah and send them into exile, too. **[Jeremiah the prophet]** He had no patience with people who violated their covenant with Yahweh and turned to other gods, or who failed to keep the law by mistreating one another.

Jeremiah lived to see Jerusalem destroyed and several waves of leading Hebrew citizens forced to leave their homes and take up residence in Babylon. The prophet Ezekiel, who was also a priest, had been carried away among the exiles, and did not begin his prophetic career until he arrived in Babylon.

Jeremiah had counseled submission to the Babylonians as God's will, and possibly for that reason he was not forced into exile. Jeremiah remained in the land with the new governor Gedaliah for some time, but a rebellious cabal assassinated the governor and made plans to lead many remaining Judeans to Egypt. Jeremiah predicted trouble if they went to Egypt, but the rebels paid no heed. They not only migrated to Egypt but also carried Jeremiah with them, where he continued to prophesy (Jeremiah 40–44).

A prayer
(v. 7)

Today's text is found in a hopeful section of Jeremiah sometimes called the "Book of Consolation" (chs. 30–31, 33), words of assurance directed to the exiles. Three consecutive oracles (vv. 1-6, 7-9, and 10-14) promise that God would not forget those who remained from Israel and Judah, but would look past their former rebellion and return them to the land of promise.

The oracle begins in typical fashion: "For thus says the LORD …" One of the marks of a true prophet was the belief that he or she heard from God directly and related God's word without altering it.

The message begins with a call to "Sing aloud with gladness for Jacob, and raise shouts for the chief of the nations" (v. 7a). Jacob was remembered as the one whose name was changed to "Israel," and whose sons gave rise to the 12 tribes.

"Chief of the nations" seems an odd way to describe Israel, which at that time was no nation at all, at least from a political standpoint. Still, there was a bond that held the people together, an ethnic heritage with one another despite being scattered across the known world, and a covenant connection with the God they believed ruled over all. From a theological or covenant perspective, then, Jeremiah could speak of the dispersed Israelites as the "chief of the nations."

The point was that God had promised to return them from exile and bring them back together as a people: Jeremiah

---

Texts for the second Sunday after Christmas are the same for years A, B, and C.

**A shorter version of this text (vv. 7-9) also appears as the Old Testament reading for Proper 26 in Year B*

Jeremiah the prophet: Jeremiah lived and ministered during a difficult time in Israel's history. Judah had been a vassal to Assyria for a century, but Assyria's strength waned as Babylon became ascendant. Egypt continued to be a major power with designs on Palestine, and Judah found itself caught in the middle of these struggles between larger nations.

Jeremiah was active during the reigns of five Judean kings: Josiah (640–609), Jehoahaz (609), Jehoiakim (609–598), Jehoiachin (598–597), and Zedekiah (597–587). He is one of the few prophets whose actual writing ministry is explicitly mentioned. While the oracles of other prophets have been preserved, we rarely read of them taking quill to parchment.

Jeremiah 36:1-5 describes how Jeremiah dictated his prophesies against Judah – perhaps the first 25 chapters – to Baruch, a scribe and close associate. When the scroll was read to Jehoiakim, the angry king cut it up and burned it bit by bit. Afterward, Jeremiah had Baruch write the oracles again, and added many other choice words.

The book of Jeremiah includes both first person accounts in which Jeremiah speaks, along with third person accounts that describe Jeremiah's activities. God also speaks in the book of Jeremiah, and sometimes it is difficult to determine whether the author intends for us to understand that God or Jeremiah is speaking. Jeremiah also speaks in behalf of the people or their kings, often as a sarcastic means of criticizing their actions – but not always with clear attribution.

The first half of the book is dominated by poetic oracles, though some narrative exists to put them in context. The latter half is primarily in the form of narrative, more frequently describing the prophet's actions. Baruch may have been responsible for much of the narrative that describes Jeremiah and his various activities.

The book grew in the hands of editors in later years: the LXX version is one-seventh longer than the Masoretic text, and it contains many more references to Jeremiah as a prophet.

In the previous oracle, Jeremiah declared Yahweh's continuing care for Israel, saying "I have loved you with an everlasting love; therefore I have continued my faithfulness to you" (v. 3). Jeremiah's oracle is a plea that the people should cry out in repentance and hope in a God who would not let them go. [**Jeremiah's message**]

A promise
(v. 8)

Have you ever longed for good news, and rejoiced when it came? Verse 8 declares the good news the exiles had been waiting for. Speaking for Yahweh, Jeremiah declared "See, I am going to bring them from the land of the north, and gather them from the farthest parts of the earth, among them the blind and the lame, those with child and those in labor, together; a great company, they shall return here."

Babylon was located slightly north, but mostly east of Jerusalem. One could not journey from one to the other in a straight line, however, because the great stretch of the Arabian desert could not be crossed, even with camels. Travelers from Babylon to Palestine used roads that followed the "Fertile Crescent" north along the Euphrates River and east toward Phoenicia before turning south to the narrow land bridge that Israel had occupied.

Since both armies and peaceful travelers from the east arrived from the north, Jeremiah sometimes referred to Babylon as the "land of the north" – but he did not stop there. While exiles from Judah had been relocated to Babylon in the early sixth century, and some (including Jeremiah) had migrated to Egypt, they were not the only displaced Hebrews.

The larger northern kingdom of Israel had been conquered by the Assyrians in 722 BCE. Though many fled to Judah, most of Israel's people were scattered across a wide area: the Assyrian practice was to shuffle conquered peoples among other defeated territories rather than bringing them all to Nineveh.

Jeremiah believed that God cared about all of Israel's dispersed descendants, and would "gather them from the farthest parts of the earth."

God's promise did not extend to the strong alone: those who returned would include the blind and the lame, women who were pregnant and even in labor – people one

called the scattered exiles to "proclaim, give praise, and say, 'Save, O LORD, your people, the remnant of Israel'" (v. 7b).

His oracle, then, begins with a call for hope and trust that God would reverse their fate and redeem them from captivity, instructing the people to pray for that very thing to happen. The prayer, which calls upon God by the covenant name Yahweh, is a reminder that the remnant had been exiled, but not excommunicated: they were still Yahweh's people, and Yahweh was still a God of steadfast love.

Jeremiah's message: Jeremiah's preaching and actions were predicated on the belief that God was alive and at work in the world, relating directly and purposefully with people. He portrayed God as both intensely angry and mournfully compassionate, a God of both wrath and weal, a God of both judgment and of salvation.

Jeremiah, sometimes described as the "weeping prophet," believed that God felt deeply the pain of the Israelites and the groanings of creation. God could also express anger, heartache, regret, and even hate. The same emotions were displayed in the words and actions of the prophet, who resonated with both God's love for the people and disappointment in their behavior.

The sin that most frequently caught Jeremiah's eye was Israel's penchant for going after other gods and failing to trust in Yahweh. Like Hosea, Jeremiah often described this rebellion through the metaphor of marital infidelity.

Jeremiah echoed the basic theme of Deuteronomy and the Deuteronomistic History in asserting that sin inevitably leads to judgment. Because the people had chosen evil, evil would be visited upon them. Thus, Nebuchadnezzar and the conquering Babylonians could be seen as God's unwitting agents of judgment, even as Cyrus the Persian would later become a medium of salvation.

Despite his focus on judgment for Israel's sin, Jeremiah also saw a new day coming when God would forgive recalcitrant Israel and return the people from exile. Most of the hopeful prophesies are found in Jeremiah 30–31 (some include ch. 33), often called the "Book of Consolation."

The blind and the lame: Leviticus 21:16-20 excluded priests who were blind and lame, among other things, from entering the temple and drawing near to the presence of God. Women were categorically excluded from the temple. Jeremiah, however, saw a day when God would reach out to and restore all people, even those one might not expect to be included. Later, Jesus would make a point of showing similar concern for all people.

While one might imagine joyful tears at the prospect of returning home, Jeremiah had in mind the sorrowful weeping of people who had realized the gravity of their sins. Later, he spoke of Ephraim (the largest of the tribes) pleading with God, admitting past wrongs, and repenting in shame (vv. 18-19).

Thus, the prophet saw God offering consolation to a sorrowful, penitent people, assuring them of forgiveness and hope for a new day. Indeed, God would ease their journey, Jeremiah said: "I will let them walk by brooks of water, in a straight path in which they shall not stumble; for I have become a father to Israel, and Ephraim is my firstborn" (v. 9b).

There is no straight path along brooks of water between Babylon and Jerusalem, so we must read Jeremiah's promise as a metaphorical vision of God leading the people directly home, providing for them and encouraging them along the way.

The NRSV's "for I have become a father to Israel" may appear misleading, as it seems to imply that God had only recently adopted the people. A more literal translation is "because I am Israel's father" (NIV11, NET, HCSB, KJV, and NASB95 have variations on this).

It was God who had called Abraham to begin a new nation, and God who had entered a covenant relationship with Israel. Stories in Exodus, Leviticus, and Numbers describe how God had brought Israel through the desert wilderness and into the promised land: now Jeremiah saw God bringing the exiles through another desert and back to their homeland.

The reference to Ephraim as "my firstborn" is metaphorical: Ephraim was one of Joseph's two sons, second born but given the firstborn's blessing by his grandfather Jacob (Gen. 49:22-26). Ephraim became the most populous and

would not expect to set out on a long and arduous journey by foot. [**The blind and the lame**]

Jeremiah's promise offers hope to anyone who feels distant from God. We may sometimes think of ourselves as spiritually blind or crippled, or so burdened by other things that we can't see through the fog to find God. This verse assures us that no one is so far from God or so handicapped by circumstances that God cannot find us when we cry out with Israel, "Save, O LORD, your people …"

A return
(v. 9)

Jeremiah believed that God's promised deliverance would take place in connection with the repentance of God's people. "With weeping they shall come," Jeremiah said in Yahweh's behalf, "and with consolations I will lead them back" (v. 9a).

influential tribe in the northern kingdom, and its territory encompassed the capital city of Samaria.

Jeremiah was not suggesting that the descendants of Ephraim would get special treatment, or that the northern kingdom would dominate the southerners from Judah. Here, as in vv. 18-19, Ephraim symbolizes all the Hebrew children that God would bring back home.

A hope
(vv. 10-14)

The oracle in vv. 10-14 repeats the promise in different words: Jeremiah called for all nations to hear that God would gather Israel and keep them as a shepherd looks after a flock (v. 10). God had "ransomed Jacob," he said, "and has redeemed him from hands too strong for him" (v. 11). The people could not save themselves, but they could trust God to bring them home.

The people would return to Zion and sing on its heights, Jeremiah said, "and they shall be radiant over the goodness of the LORD" (v. 12a). He then pointed to specific areas of restoration: grain, wine, oil, flocks, and herds. They would pass from the desert of exile to "become like a watered garden, and they shall never languish again" (v. 12b).

Women would dance and both old and young would be merry, Jeremiah said in Yahweh's behalf, for "I will turn their mourning into joy, I will comfort them, and give them gladness for sorrow" (v. 13). Priests and people alike would leave scarcity behind and be satisfied with the bounty God would provide (v. 14).

How do we read a text like this? While the exiles were indeed allowed to return when Cyrus led the Persians to victory over Babylon in 539 BCE, they found Jerusalem in shambles and the land in a famine. The lavish promises of Jeremiah were not fulfilled, at least in the way one might expect.

Still, the oracles served their purpose. They gave people hope. Today we may read texts such as Revelation 21 in anticipation of a glorious home in heaven. We cannot know just what eternity will be like, but the extravagant imagery gives us hope of a better world beyond this one.

For all who feel isolated from God, exiled by sinful choices, or overwhelmed by circumstances, today's text offers hope for forgiveness and a renewed fellowship with God, whose steadfast love never changes.

The Hardest Question
Has Jeremiah's prophecy been fulfilled?

The hopeful words of Jeremiah's prophecy continue to inspire, but were they fulfilled? In one sense, we can answer in the affirmative, because the exiles in Babylon were free to return to Jerusalem after the Persian king Cyrus conquered Babylon in 539 BCE. Cyrus' philosophy, different from that of the Assyrians or the Babylonians, was that people were more likely to be loyal to the empire if allowed to live in their homelands and worship their own gods.

So, the Hebrews, like other conquered nations, were free to return if they wished. Several waves of Hebrews made the long and arduous journey to Jerusalem and the small area of "Jehud" Cyrus had granted them, but many others chose to remain in Babylon, the only home they had known. There was no great migration of Israelite exiles from other parts of the world, and certainly no easy journey along brooks of water.

Some people today claim that the formation of the secular State of Israel in 1948 fulfilled the promise, because Jews from all over the world have returned to inhabit parts of the land, though they remain a small minority of Jews the world over. God's presence is not limited to the former lands of Judea and Samaria, however, but extends to wherever people are. The modern State of Israel is a secular state created by the United Nations in response to the Holocaust. That declaration forced many Palestinians into exile, and often violates the inclusive spirit of Jeremiah's promise, so it can hardly be seen as a fulfillment of Jeremiah's prophecy.

One may suggest that the ultimate fulfillment of Jeremiah's prophecy is found, not in a return of a Hebrew remnant to Jerusalem, but in the opportunity for all people to come to God through Jesus Christ, who reached out to all people, whatever their gender or physical capabilities or nationality.

In Christ, God's reconciling love and abundant forgiveness is available from the farthest parts of the earth, calling all people to "come home" to the land of communion with God – and with all of God's children.

Second Sunday after Christmas

Second Reading
Psalm 147*

A Good Way to Begin

Praise the LORD, O Jerusalem! Praise your God, O Zion! For he strengthens the bars of your gates; he blesses your children within you. (Ps. 147:12-13)

Themes of the Christmas season bring heaven and earth together: The Son of God surrenders heavenly prerogatives to become incarnate on the earth. A new star appears to celebrate his birth and guide the magi. An angelic chorus sings from the sky to shepherds keeping watch in their fields.

The beginning of a new year is also an appropriate time to remember that the Creator of the universe has offered to live in personal relationship with people of the earth, and Psalm 147 provides an effective reminder of that dual reason for daily praise. Although the RCL text calls for vv. 12-20 alone, we will consider the entire psalm. [**How many psalms?**]

God's restorative power
(vv. 1-6)

Psalm 147 was probably written at some point after Hebrew exiles were allowed to return to Jerusalem around 537 BCE, fortified by a decree from King Cyrus authorizing them to rebuild the temple of Yahweh. The early years of the return brought hard times, however. The former exiles found the city in ruins, the people of neighboring towns were hostile, and a period of famine made it difficult to survive, much less prosper.

The excitement of the return soon faded. Governor Sheshbazaar had workers to clear the site of the temple, and priests built an altar that enabled them to reinstitute the cultic practices surrounding sacrifices and annual festivals. Heavy opposition from surrounding provinces and a daily struggle for survival soon brought construction efforts to a halt, however. Residents focused on building houses and establishing farms for themselves, leaving the temple unfinished.

When the prophets Haggai and Zechariah arrived with the new governor Zerubbabel in 520 BCE, they were appalled at the lack of progress. They lambasted the people for not having rebuilt the temple and restoring proper worship as a first priority. Haggai, in fact, claimed that Yahweh had sent the famine as punishment because the people had failed to put God first (Haggai 1). Urged on by the prophets' preaching, Zerubbabel corresponded with Persian leaders to overcome legal challenges brought by neighboring governors and renew the Hebrews' authorization to build a new temple. A five-year construction effort culminated with the dedication of the new temple in 515 BCE. [**The Second Temple**]

A later editor apparently wanted to credit Haggai and Zechariah's influence, for the LXX adds the names Haggai and Zechariah after the introductory "Hallelujah" in vv. 1 and 12: "Hallelujah, Haggai and Zechariah; sing praises …" The awkward construction may be a tribute to them

> **How many psalms?** Some commentators believe Psalm 147 is a combination of what were originally two or three psalms, and the LXX (an early Greek translation) divides it into two parts, with the first 11 verses numbered as Psalm 146 and vv. 12-20 as Psalm 147 (other psalms in the LXX are also numbered differently). Psalm 147, like all of Psalms 146–150, begins and ends with the word "Hallelujah."

The Episcopal tradition uses Psalm 84 for this occasion.

The Second Temple: The dedication of the rebuilt temple in 515 BCE marked the beginning of the "Second Temple Period," though most scholarly references to the Second Temple focus on the greatly expanded and remodeled temple of the late first century BCE and the first 70 years of the first century CE. That temple was razed by the Romans in 70 CE.

for their role in promoting the postexilic rebuilding of the temple, referenced in v. 2.

Psalm 147 celebrates the rebuilding of the temple, and it reinforces the importance of offering praise to God – an activity typically associated with the temple, where a professional order of temple singers led in worship. After the opening "Hallelujah," a call to worship that literally means "Praise Yahweh," the psalmist declares that singing praises to God is a good and proper response to God's ongoing display of grace (v. 1).

As evidence of Yahweh's beneficence, the psalmist praises Yahweh for building up Jerusalem and gathering those who had been exiled from their home, healing their broken hearts and bandaging their wounds (vv. 2-3).

Translating v. 2 calls for a bit of interpretation. The verb translated as "build up" in the NRSV simply means "to build." If we are correct in setting the psalm in the postexilic period, however, the translation "rebuilds" (as in NET) would be appropriate.

With v. 4 the psalmist changes gears, amazed that the God who cares for the hard-pressed people of Jerusalem is the same God who could count and name every star (v. 4). One might expect a God of such immense power and immeasurable wisdom to be unconcerned with human struggles, but not so: Yahweh intervenes to lift up the downtrodden – such as the returning exiles – and to cast down wicked people such as the neighboring officials who had sought to prevent the temple from being built (vv. 5-6).

When you think of your own life and perhaps your church, do similar thoughts ever occur to you? How amazing it is to sit outside on a clear night to ponder the stars in their number and magnitude – or to pore over amazing images of distant galaxies from the Hubble Space Telescope – while imagining that the same God who created the universe also cares for humankind and desires to live in a relationship of covenant love with us.

God's dependable provision
(vv. 7-11)

The second strophe of Psalm 147 begins with a renewed call to praise God with song. The word translated as "sing" in the NRSV usually means "to answer" or "to respond." In this way, the psalmist reminds us that our prayers and songs of praise are a human response of gratitude for God's goodness to us (v. 7).

And how has God been good? The psalmist considers the gifts of clouds and rain that make the grass to grow on Israel's fertile hills (v. 8). Like other ancients, he did not consider wind or rain to be the result of global meteorological phenomena: he believed that the seasonal rains were a gift of God's sustaining grace, not only to humans, but also to the animals and birds (v. 9).

As God looks upon the earth and considers its inhabitants, what sparks divine pleasure? It is not the impressive beauty of a muscled horse in full gallop or the efficient stride of a human runner (v. 10), the psalmist says, but the response of "those who fear him, in those who hope in his steadfast love" (v. 11).

Some writers think the reference to strong horses and swift runners could be a military reference to chariots and infantry, but that is not a necessary assumption. The point is that God may find satisfaction in gazing upon the wonders of creation at its best, but what really brings God pleasure is the grateful response of those who have put their hope in the promise of God's love.

The injunction to "fear the LORD" is especially common in Israel's wisdom literature, which insists: "the fear of the LORD is the beginning of wisdom" (Prov. 1:7, 9:10; see also Ps. 111:10 and Prov. 4:7). "Fear" in this context does not suggest abject fright, but a sense of reverence and respect for God that goes deep enough to affect one's behavior in keeping the commands and honoring the covenant relationship between God and Israel.

God's covenant word
(vv. 12-20)

With each section, the psalm goes a little deeper into the joys and challenges of an ongoing relationship with God. As in the first two stanzas, the third section begins with a call to praise Yahweh. Here it utilizes two different

> **Gates and dates:** The reference to God's strengthening Jerusalem's city gates suggests that Psalm 147 was written during or after the governorship of Nehemiah, who not only led efforts to rebuild the city's protective walls and gates (Nehemiah 2–6), but (with Ezra's help) to re-educate the people on the history and significance of the covenant ordinances guiding their relationship with God (Nehemiah 8–9).

words for "praise," two different terms for God, and two different names for Jerusalem: "Praise (*shavchi*) the LORD (*Yahweh*), O Jerusalem," the psalmist called. "Praise (*haleli*) your God (*Elohim*), O Zion" (v. 12).

Again, the call to praise God is followed by reasons for why adoration is due. The first cause for praise addresses the renewed Jerusalem specifically: with God's help the city's gates have been reinforced so children can find safety and people can live in peace, enjoying the earth's bounty that God provides (vv. 13-14). **[Gates and dates]**

But God's work extends beyond Jerusalem to all of nature, including the ability to control the seasons by divine command. With delightful imagery, the psalmist declares that "his word runs swiftly" to bring snow, frost, hail, and cold (vv. 15-17). But winter ends: as God's word brings on the frozen precipitation of winter, so God also "sends out his word, and melts them; he makes his wind to blow, and the waters flow" (v. 18). Many residents of ancient Jerusalem had farms and family members living outside the city. They understood the importance of the alternating seasons for growing needed crops.

But divine care goes beyond the physical: God has provided both a covenant of relationship and the instructions needed to follow it: "He declares his word to Jacob, his statutes and ordinances to Israel" (v. 19).

In drawing to a close, the psalmist highlighted Israel's unique place in God's order: no other nation had been granted the opportunity to live in such a relationship with God, whose ordinances should be understood as gifts rather than demands, keys that could open the door to lives of peace and of praise (v. 20).

The psalm is impressive, but can it speak to people who are not Israelites, who don't live in Jerusalem, at a time when the temple no longer exists?

The answer, of course, is *yes*. Followers of Jesus live under a new and different covenant, but it is rooted in the same God who loved and blessed and disciplined and forgave the people of Israel. Our relationship is not based on keeping the law, but in trusting the One who fulfilled the law and did for us what we could not do for ourselves, in Jesus who offers grace beyond measure.

This is not to say our relationship is devoid of demand: as Israel was called to love God and keep the commandments, Jesus challenged his followers to love God and keep *his* commandments – namely, to love one another as we love ourselves. Every commandment is bound up in this: when we see the world as Jesus does, and love as Jesus loved, positive actions will follow.

Followers of Jesus are not promised that the faithful will always prosper or that hardships will not come our way: good behavior is no guarantee of financial freedom, and wrongdoing will not automatically bring punishment. Our motivation in following Jesus goes beyond the selfish desire for personal prosperity: it is a longing to see the world with Christlike compassion and to do our part to bring peace and wholeness to others.

Praising God with our voices and songs is one response to the grace we have received: offering praise through our love and our lives is even better.

The Hardest Question
What was God's "word" to Israel?

The psalmist's various references to God's "word" in Ps. 147:15-20 are interesting in their variety, and in what they suggest to us about our own use of the term "God's word." Some Bible readers and interpreters through the years have tended to take virtually every mention of "God's word" as a reference to the Bible, but the Bible as we know it did not exist in the time of the psalmists or the prophets – and no biblical author wrote with a conscious awareness that he or she was contributing to something that would later be considered holy scripture.

Hebrew has two primary terms that can be translated as "word," *'amar* and *dabar*. Both can also take on the meaning of "command" or "order." The word *dabar* can also be translated as "thing," and sometimes has the connotation of a promise.

The poet behind Psalm 147 used both terms, commonly in the sense of a "command." The NRSV translation of v. 15 says "He sends out his command (*'amar*) to the earth; his word (*dabar*) runs swiftly." Later, God "sends out his word (*dabar*)" to melt the ice and snow (v. 18). In these verses, God's word is God's command to the forces of nature.

When we come to v. 19, we find two lines in synonymous parallel: "He declares his word to Jacob" is equivalent to "his statutes and ordinances to Israel." Here the psalmist would have had in mind things such as the covenant commands found in the Ten Commandments of Exodus 20 and Deuteronomy 5, in addition to other legal materials scattered throughout the books of Exodus, Leviticus, Numbers, and Deuteronomy, all of which claim to be words from God.

The heart of the covenant with Israel, as taught in the book of Deuteronomy, is that God's people should love Yahweh with all their being and teach their children to do the same (Deut. 6:4-9), with the understanding that God had promised blessings to those who lived in covenant obedience, and trouble to those who chose idolatrous ways instead.

The books of Joshua through 2 Kings built on the teachings of Deuteronomy to relate Israel's history from that singular perspective, noting the times when either individuals or the nation prospered or floundered, based on their willingness to live within the covenant and honor Yahweh. When prophets such as Samuel, Elijah, or Elisha remind them of the covenant, they use terms akin to "thus says (*'amar*) the LORD" (Judg. 6:8, 1 Sam. 10:18, 2 Sam. 12:7, 1 Kgs. 20:42, 2 Kgs. 7:1, and many others).

Pre-exilic prophets such as Amos, Micah, and Isaiah warned the Hebrews that trouble would come if they did not honor God, speaking in oracles that likewise claimed to be "the word of God" (Isa. 7:7, Amos 5:4, Mic. 4:6, plus scores of other examples). The exilic prophets Jeremiah and Ezekiel explained to the exiles – as a word from God – how they had rebelled and why they deserved their fate, but that they could still have hope through repentance (Jer. 2:5, Ezek. 5:5, and others). Postexilic prophets such as Haggai and Zechariah urged the Hebrew remnant that returned to Jerusalem to be a faithful and holy people if they expected to prosper (Hag. 1:2, 5, 7; Zech. 1:3; and many more).

Psalmists such as the author of Psalm 147 reflected this same theology in calling the former exiles to not only praise God for blessings given, but also to live in such love and obedience that future benisons would be assured.

The Bible speaks often of the "word of the LORD," or "God's word," always in the sense of God sending a prophetic word or declaring a command that the people should follow. Modern readers should be skeptical of taking that term and automatically applying it to the Bible as a whole. Rather, we should take the Bible seriously enough to recognize what it claims to be God's word, and what it does not.

Second Sunday after Christmas

Third Reading
Ephesians 1:3-14*

Where Hope Belongs

... so that we, who were the first to set our hope on Christ, might live for the praise of his glory. (Eph. 1:12)

Hope. Thank God for hope. We have all experienced years we would probably like to forget, so that we come to a new year hoping the next 12 months will be better than the last. Perhaps this is one of those years for you.

Today's text was written to a people who desperately needed hope. It comes from the introduction of Paul's letter to the struggling church at Ephesus on the west coast of Asia Minor. Paul insisted that with their hope fixed on Jesus, they still could fill their lives with days of praise.

Ephesus was an important port city in the first century, though silting of the Cayster River now leaves it landlocked. It was a sizable city with impressive temples, government buildings, health centers, residential areas, a massive theater, and even a large library. It was a major trade center with a cosmopolitan population.

Ephesians is widely regarded as one of Paul's "prison letters," perhaps written from Rome after 59 CE (Acts 28:14ff), or from his earlier imprisonment in Caesarea (Acts 23:31ff). **[Authorship]**

Authorship: Paul worked among the Ephesians for quite a while (Acts 19), so it is surprising that there are very few personal references in the letter, and he speaks more of having heard about them (1:15) than of having known them. This has led some scholars to suggest that a later admirer of Paul wrote the letter. Thomas B. Slater, writing in the Smyth & Helwys Bible Commentary, calls it "deutero-Pauline" (*Ephesians* [Smyth & Helwys, 2012], 20), and Andrew T. Lincoln, author of the Word Biblical Commentary on Ephesians, is even more convinced that a disciple of Paul wrote the letter, drawing heavily on Paul's letter to the Colossians for his imagery (*Ephesians* [Thomas Nelson, 1990]).

Other writers attribute the letter to Paul, arguing that the stylistic differences may be due to his use of an *amenuensis* (scribe), who may have flavored Paul's dictation with his own style. Some also suggest that the lack of personal references may indicate that Paul was writing mainly for new converts who had come into the church since his time there. For purposes of simplicity, we'll refer to the author as Paul while remaining aware that Paul's thought may have been reflected in the words of a close disciple.

The oldest and best Greek manuscripts do not include the words "in Ephesus" (1:1), leading some interpreters to believe that the letter was written as an encyclical, to be passed around and read among all the churches, with a blank space in the first sentence to be filled in with the name of each local church.

Paul's reference to himself as a "prisoner for Christ Jesus" (3:1) or "prisoner in the Lord" (4:1) probably suggests that he was writing at a time when he had been imprisoned because of his activities in openly proclaiming the gospel. Paul was imprisoned briefly on several occasions (2 Cor. 11:23), and after being arrested in Jerusalem (Acts 21:27-36), he was held for trial in the coastal city of Caesarea (about 58–60 CE, Acts 23–26) before appealing to the emperor and being taken to Rome, where he remained in prison for at least two years and may have been executed there (60–62 CE, Acts 27–28).

Four of Paul's letters are known as "prison epistles," and include references to his captivity. These include Philippians (1:7, 13-14); Colossians (4:3, 10, 18); Ephesians (3:1, 4:1, 6:20); and Philemon (1, 9, 10, 13, 23). Second Timothy, more commonly regarded as a "pastoral epistle," also claims a prison setting (2 Tim. 1:8, 16; 2:8).

This text is also used on Proper 10 in Year B.

In Christ we are blessed
(vv. 3-6)

Ephesians 1:3-14 is written as one incredibly complex sentence – a grammatically challenging but breathless call for Christian people to give thanks for all that God has done. Fortunately, English translations tend to break the sentence into more digestible bits.

The text follows the pattern of a Jewish blessing, a blessing to God for God's blessing of humans. Paul begins with multiple reminders of divine beneficence. Throughout the text, "in him" and "in Christ" are key words. The work that has changed our lives and can change others through us has come through the one we call Jesus, the Christ.

Paul rejoices that God has blessed those who trust in Christ with "every spiritual blessing" (v. 3). The first of these is that God chose to adopt believers as children through the work of Christ (vv. 4-6). The phrase "he destined us for adoption" is a favorite of those who believe in predestination, interpreting it to suggest that God has chosen certain persons to be saved and others lost, even before the foundation of the world.

Such a view is highly problematic, for it robs humankind of any meaningful freedom while also undermining the missionary imperative of the gospel. That mission mandate is taught far more clearly than the few ambiguous references used to support a belief that God predetermines our destiny before birth.

If God has already chosen every person who will be saved, there is little point in spreading the gospel, because God would need no help from us. In the early part of the mid-19th century, Baptists, for example, engaged in a heated conflict between "Particular Baptists," who believed that Christ died only for those particular "elect" persons, and "General Baptists," who believed that Christ died for all. The missionary vs. anti-missionary controversy split many churches, sometimes resulting in side-by-side "Missionary" and "Primitive" (or "Anti-missionary") churches. **[Good seed or bad]**

Some non-predestinarians deal with the troublesome phrase by appealing to divine omniscience, asserting that God knows who will choose to trust Christ, but there is a better way to interpret the text. The point is not that God has foreordained Charles and Chantrese to be saved

> **Good seed, or bad?** In America, a prime mover in the anti-mission movement was a preacher named Daniel Parker. In an 1826 pamphlet titled "Views on the Two Seeds," he taught that every person was born with either a "good seed" of godliness (equivalent to "the elect" of Calvinist teaching) or a "bad seed" of the devil (equivalent to the "non-elect"). Some early Baptist churches came to be known as "Two Seed in the Spirit Baptists," while others were described with terms such as "Old School," "Predestinarian," or "Primitive."

and adopted as God's children, while rejecting Maggie and Marvin. Paul is writing to *the church* – to a group of people who have chosen of their own free will to follow Christ. God has in fact foreordained that every person who trusts in Christ can be saved, can become a part of the church, can experience all the blessings that God wants his children to have.

God saves us not only as individuals, but also as a community of faith. Paul is not teaching that God's eternal plan has a roster of predetermined believers, but that God's eternal providence has a place for every person who chooses to accept the gift of divine grace. Those who believe this cannot help but give praise to God.

In Christ we have redemption
(vv. 7-10)

Following his introduction of the theme in vv. 3-6, Paul begins three of the remaining sections of this lengthy 12-verse sentence with the words "in him." Some translations substitute the word "Christ" for "him" as a means for clarifying that the pronoun always refers back to Christ.

In vv. 7-10, Paul affirms that in Christ we have redemption. We have forgiveness. We have access to an amazing grace that is beyond our comprehension. We are all guilty of sin, guilty of rebellion against God's way, guilty of living for self with little thought for others. At some point, most of us have been guilty of lying, cheating, lusting, and worse.

And yet Paul says, "In him we have redemption through his blood, the forgiveness of our trespasses, according to the riches of his grace that he lavished on us" (vv. 7-8a). We could never make up for our wrongdoings on our own, but Christ has declared us forgiven. In some marvelous way far beyond our comprehension, we can experience redemption through his blood – the forgiveness of our sins.

The word Paul uses for "forgiveness" (*aphesis*) is the technical Greek term that refers to a legal pardon. It is a mystery to us that God would love us so and take pleasure in redeeming us – and no wonder that Paul would celebrate it.

In Christ we have an inheritance
(vv. 11-12)

Paul goes on to make the remarkable claim that God not only loves us enough to save us and adopt us as children, but also has set aside a surprising inheritance for those who set their hope in Christ: that we "might live for the praise of his glory" (vv. 11-12).

Paul was born into a Jewish family. He would have grown up hearing or reading about the inheritance of the land that God had promised to Israel, but through Christ he had learned of a greater inheritance, an eternal one, offered to those who trust in God. This inheritance doesn't come when someone else dies, in the normal order of events. The inheritance belongs to us even now, and we experience it in full when *we* die.

Paul makes a point of saying that this is one reason God has planned such a glorious future for us – that we might be motivated to live in praise to God: "so that we, who were the first to set our hope on Christ, might live for the praise of his glory" (v. 12).

Paul believed the first generation of Christian believers had a notable privilege and a special responsibility. They were the first to set their hopes on Christ, and their lives of praise would set a pattern for others to follow as they called them to lives of faith. Many generations of believers later, we share the same hope and the same calling to bear witness through our own grateful living.

If you've ever helped to put shingles on a house, you learned that every row of shingles is a guide for those that come after. The man who instructed me in the art of roofing first cut a piece of scrap shingle to the proper length so I could check that each succeeding row was just the right distance above the one below: he called the handy guide a "preacher."

In a similar fashion, every generation of Christians provides a pattern for the next to follow, and sometimes

> **Days of praise – and service:** As a practical exercise, think of specific ways that you can show praise to God both through service and worship. Consider this: in Hebrew, the same word is used to mean both "service" and "worship" – and we typically speak of a "worship service." What are some ways we can express our worship of God through service to others?

we need a good "preacher" to keep us straight. If we would lead those who come after us rightly, then we will lead them to offer praise to God, not just with their words, but with their actions.

We don't praise God through Sunday worship alone, but when we show love to a child on Monday, when we feed the hungry on Tuesday, when we listen to a hurting friend on Wednesday. We praise God with our lives when we visit the sick on Thursday, when we repair a toilet on Friday, even when we enjoy wholesome family recreation on Saturday. Because Jesus Christ has filled our hearts with amazing grace, we fill our lives with days of praise. **[Days of praise – and service]**

In Christ we know the Holy Spirit
(vv. 13-14)

All of this sounds good, but we know that there are days when we don't feel so full of praise. Some days, we may question how real this eternal inheritance might be. Paul's response was to insist that God offers a taste of heaven on earth as we open our hearts and lives to the presence of the Holy Spirit that marks us like an indelible seal.

The Spirit is the "pledge of our inheritance toward redemption as God's own people," Paul said, "to the praise of his glory" (vv. 13-14).

Jesus no longer walks with us as he walked with Mary and Martha and Peter and John. Even in Paul's day, Jesus was no longer present in that physical way. But Paul believed Christ's promise to be present through the Spirit. Paul had experienced the touch of God's Spirit, and he believed that the Spirit's touch today is the guarantee of God's embrace tomorrow.

The Spirit of Christ in our lives works not only as an internal guide to direct our living, but also as a reminder of our hope that God can continue to sustain us even in difficult days.

In Jesus Christ we have redemption from our sins. We have an inheritance in eternity. We have a present comforter and guide, and we have *hope* that no matter what comes, we can trust that the God who loves us has good things in store, an inheritance beyond our imagining.

The Hardest Question
What about predestination?

Predestination beliefs, often described as "Calvinism," are held more of less strictly within various denominations, and often interpreted differently. In some, the notion of predestination is de-emphasized in favor of affirming divine sovereignty.

So what do we mean by "Calvinist"? The name comes from John Calvin, a 16th-century French theologian who was among the second-generation leaders of the Protestant Reformation. Calvin strongly emphasized the absolute sovereignty of God in matters of salvation, a teaching that God has predestined who will be saved and who will not.

Though some modern Calvinists prefer different terminology, the central beliefs of classic Calvinism are traditionally described by the acronym "TULIP." They are:

Total depravity – All humans are so tainted by sin that they are not capable of responding to God on their own.
Unconditional election – God has foreordained who will be saved and who will be condemned; humans have no choice in the matter.
Limited atonement – Christ's death provided atonement for sin, but it is limited to those "elect" whom God has designated for salvation.
Irresistible grace – When God calls the elect through the Holy Spirit, they are incapable of resisting the gospel.
Perseverance of the saints – Those whom God has elected to salvation will persevere and not turn away from their faith.

A few biblical references can be cited in support of double-decree predestination, albeit out of context, including one from today's text, which says "He destined us for adoption as his children through Jesus Christ, according to the good pleasure of his will" (Eph. 1:5). Romans 8:29-30 expresses similar sentiments. Other verses, such as John 6:44, are sometimes cited: "No one can come to me unless drawn by the Father who sent me." But none of those verses rules out the possibility that God's call and desire for human salvation extends to all persons, not just a select group of "elect."

While a few texts may be cited in support of limited atonement, many others are clear calls for all people to respond to Christ, not just "the elect." We are familiar with John 3:16, for example: "For God so loved the world that he gave his only Son, so that *everyone who believes* in him may not perish but may have eternal life." Jesus' teachings do not suggest that only certain people may believe, but "whosoever," as the KJV puts it. The next verse emphatically makes it clear that the gospel is for the entire world: "Indeed, God did not send the Son into the world to condemn the world, but in order that the world might be saved through him." Many other texts could be cited: think, for example, of Jesus' "great commission" of Matt. 28:19-20, or Acts 1:8. The good news is for every nation, "to the ends of the earth." Nothing about that calling suggests that anyone is excluded from hearing and responding to the gospel.

Second Sunday after Christmas

Fourth Reading
John 1:1-18*

The Word That Reveals

*John 1:1-14 appears in Christmas 3 readings for all years, and the similar text of John 1:(1-9), 10-18 is read on the second Sunday after Christmas, when that occurs. For purposes of textual continuity, the study presented encompasses all of John 1:1-18. It is found under Christmas 3. An Episcopal adaptation offers optional readings from Matthew and Luke for the second Sunday after Christmas.

New Year's Day*

First Reading
Ecclesiastes 3:1-15

It's Always Time

For everything there is a season, and a time for every matter under heaven … (Eccl. 3:1)

We've heard today's text before. Maybe it was at a funeral, where the reminder that "there is a time to be born, and a time to die" was intended to bring a sense of order and solace into a trying time. Perhaps it was in Pete Seeger's adaptation of the text, which became a hit for the Byrds as "Turn! Turn! Turn!" in 1965.

With the Civil Rights Movement ringing cultural change and the war in Vietnam sparking widespread unrest, the song came across as a hopeful assurance that, if there's a time for everything, peace must be on the horizon. [**Turn! Turn! Turn!**]

It may be surprising to learn that the person responsible for this memorable poem – the only part of Ecclesiastes that many people can recall – found little comfort in his belief that life is so ordered and predictable.

A classic poem
(vv. 1-8)

The author of Ecclesiastes called himself Qoheleth, which is often translated as "Preacher" or "Teacher." He does not come across as a happy man. [**Qoheleth**] An old tradition identifies the author as Solomon, but David's son could

> **Qoheleth:** Qoheleth is an unusual name formed from the feminine *qal* active participle of the verb *qahal*, "to assemble." It could mean "one who assembles," or "convener." The feminine ending was sometimes used to indicate a title rather than a personal name.
>
> The notion of Qoheleth as one who assembles a group, presumably to teach them, led the Septuagint translators to use the equivalent Greek word *ecclesiastes*. The term is related to *ekklesia*, the Greek word often used for the church. Perhaps this connection inspired the fourth-century Latin scholar Jerome to call him *Concianator*, and Martin Luther to use the German word *Prediger*, both meaning something akin to "preacher," a translation reflected in the King James Version.
>
> Most readers would not think Qoheleth was much of a preacher. He was a sage, a philosopher of sorts whose reflections on life were often at odds with traditional teaching, but nevertheless drew an audience and were considered valuable enough to be preserved as scripture.

hardly have written Ecclesiastes. The author was a sage and probably a person of some means, but certainly not the richest man who ever lived, though he pretended to be in a brief royal fiction designed to emphasize his frustration with life (1:12–2:26).

Ecclesiastes 1:1 and 12:9-12 were almost certainly added by a later hand, someone who sought to balance Qoheleth's radical cynicism and *carpe diem* musings with traditional beliefs. Qoheleth's contribution is framed by the same sentence in 1:2 and 12:8, identical brackets that underscore his belief that humans might find some joy and profit in life, but could never find true meaning or understand the ways of God.

> **Turn! Turn! Turn!:** Seeger claimed that he leafed through the Bible and wrote the song in 15 minutes after his publisher complained that he couldn't sell the protest songs that Seeger preferred. The Byrds' cover of the song can be found at http://www.songfacts.com/detail.php?id=246.

---

*The studies for New Year's Day are provided for years when January 1 falls on Sunday, or when emphasizing the New Year is preferred. Texts are the same for Years A, B, and C.

And how did he begin and end? "Meaningless! Meaningless! Says the Teacher: All is Meaningless!" Or, in the more familiar KJV: "Vanity of vanities, says the Preacher, vanity of vanities. All is vanity."

The word in question is the Hebrew word *hevel*, which describes a breath or vapor that quickly disappears, as on a cold day. Some translators render *hevel* with words such as "perfectly pointless" (CEB) or even "absolute futility" (HCSB). Robert Alter's translation lets the metaphor speak for itself without interpretation: "Merest breath, said Qoheleth. Merest breath. All is mere breath" (*The Wisdom Books: Job, Proverbs, and Ecclesiastes* [W.W. Norton, 2010], 346).

Qoheleth was not the typical wisdom teacher. He wrote beautifully, mostly in a sort of lyric prose that occasionally morphed into poetry. More notably, he did not share the optimism of traditional wisdom teachers: he was not convinced that any amount of wisdom, wealth, or human experience could lead to true satisfaction in life.

Qoheleth began his loosely organized teachings with a reflection on the cyclical futility of life (1:3-11). He observed that generations of people, like seasons of the year, come and go. The sun comes up and goes down, while cycles of wind and weather repeat themselves year after year. All the streams run to the sea, but the sea is never full. People live only to be forgotten, he concluded.

The old sage followed that reflection with a story of a rich and powerful king who could do, have, or try anything he wanted. After various adventures in excess – the sort of things people might expect to make for a happy life – he concluded there was nothing new under the sun and nothing to be gained from human toil, for "all was vanity and a chasing after wind, and there was nothing to be gained under the sun" (2:11).

That pessimistic note brought Qoheleth to the first formal poetry in his book, and our text for the day. Whether Qoheleth composed the lyrical observations or quoted previously existing verse is unknown. The textual unit, found in vv. 3-8, explores the notion of a time and season for everything.

The poem consists of 14 antithetical pairs arranged into seven couplets in which the first and second lines are related. Each pair includes two things that seem mutually exclusive at any given moment, but all of which are common life experiences.

There is "a time to be born and a time to die," the poet said, "a time to plant, and a time to pluck up what is planted" (v. 2). Like crops that are sown and later harvested, human life is marked with a beginning and an ending. No one is exempt.

Verse 3 reflects a reality of human culture in which conflict seems inevitable, so that there is "a time to kill, and a time to heal; a time to break down, and a time to build up" (v. 4). The words for breaking down and building up are drawn from construction, especially the building or breaking down of protective walls (Isa. 5:5, 49:7; Ps. 80:12). Neither killing people nor destroying good walls is desirable, but in this world, it happens.

Both weeping and laughter have their place and appointed time, often related to mourning and dancing (v. 4). There is much in this world to make us sad or melancholy, but also much to cause rejoicing. Neither puritanical seriousness nor excessive frivolity would fit Qoheleth's reality, in which both sorrow and gladness have their place. [**Wordplay**]

The imagery of v. 5 has given rise to much speculation. The poet compares times for throwing or gathering stones to "a time to embrace, and a time to refrain from embracing." Farmers typically cleared stones from a field to prepare for planting (Isa. 5:2), often using them to build a protective wall. A war story in 2 Kgs. 3:19, 25 reflects a custom of ruining enemies' fields by throwing stones into them, but neither custom has an apparent connection with human hugs or the lack of them. Rabbinic interpreters took "throwing stones" as a euphemism for ejaculation during sexual intercourse, and "gathering stones" as a reference to periodic abstinence (*Midrash Rabbah Qoheleth* 3.5.1). The remainder of the poem avoids metaphors, but this interpretation offers an apt comparison to embracing or refraining.

Verse 6 contrasts seeking and losing with keeping and throwing away. On the surface, both relate to personal

> **Wordplay:** In v. 4 the poet utilizes a playful combination of words that share similar sounds. "Weeping" and "laughing" are *libkōt* and *lishōq*, while the words for "mourning" and "dancing" are *sepōd* and *reqōd*.

property. If something has been lost, there is a time to seek it, but also a time to give it up as lost. As possessions of differing values or usefulness pile up in our homes, we must decide what to keep and what to discard. One might extend the truism to abstractions such as ambition or love: there is a time to go after something (or someone), and a time to let go. That may be beyond the poet's intent, however.

The opposing pairs of ripping/sewing and silence/speaking (v. 7) may seem unrelated, but it helps to recall that the tearing of one's garments was a public symbol of mourning (see Gen. 37:29, 34; 2 Sam. 1:11-12; 2 Kgs. 2:11-12; Job 1:20; and others). Clothes were handmade and not easily replaced: when mourning was over, torn clothing would be repaired. Perhaps the poet had in mind the loud ululations and other cries of grief that often accompany mourning: a time would come when weeping would give way to silence.

The poem concludes with a more obvious pair of antithetical behaviors: "a time to love and a time to hate; a time for war and a time for peace" (v. 8). We would like to live in a world where love and peace thrive, but the cold reality is that there are things that inspire hatred, and there are times when war is not only the lesser of two evils, but also necessary to preserve the liberty to enjoy peace and love. [**Chiasm**]

Chiasm: Some interpreters see a structure within the poem that literary scholars call a chiasm: various thematic elements that appear in one part of the text are balanced by similar statements later in the text, but in reverse order. A line drawn along the left margins of the diagram would look like the left half of the Greek letter *chi* (X), hence the name "chiasm." Recognizing the elements of chiasm in vv. 2-8 reinforces the view that in v. 7, which corresponds to v. 4, the rending of clothes should be seen as a symbol of mourning.

vv. 2-3 – Life and death, killing and healing
    v. 4 – Mourning and joy
        v. 5 – Throwing away and gathering
        v. 6 – Throwing away and gathering
    v. 7 – Mourning (ripping clothes) and silence
vv. 8 – Love and hate, war and peace

An eternal puzzle
(vv. 9-15)

While the poet's ponderings on time and human actions may be assuring to readers, it was no comfort to Qoheleth. God is not mentioned in the poem, but Qoheleth presumed that God had set the world and its realities in place, leaving humans to live in a situation they could not understand.

Human toil (v. 9) could be seen as a reference to the ordinary activities of going through life, "the business that God has given to everyone to be busy with" (v. 10), and Qoheleth wondered what gain or profit anyone could find at the end of it. While there was a time for everything, it was God who "has made everything suitable for its time," not humans (v. 11a). As in 1:4-11, where he bemoaned the cyclical nature of life, Qoheleth knew that he might bounce between mourning and dancing or tearing down and building up, but if it was God who determined the times, Qoheleth could see no gain in it.

The real kicker for Qoheleth, however, was that God "has put a sense of past and future into their minds, yet they cannot find out what God has done from the beginning to the end" (v. 11b). The NRSV's "past and future" translates a word that usually means "eternity," and the phrase "a sense of" is not in the text, but is added for clarity. A more literal translation could be "eternity, too, he has put in their hearts, but so that humans cannot find out what God has done from beginning to end."

But is that reading correct? The Hebrew text was written without vowels, which were added many centuries later, based on the way rabbis were commonly pronouncing the text at that time. Some scholars believe the word *'ōlam* in v. 11 should be read with different vowels, as *'elem*, which can mean "darkness." Thus, they would translate the verse to say that God has put darkness or ignorance into human hearts, so they cannot understand what God is doing (see, for example, NET).

This led the sage to find some comfort in the pleasures of life that he *could* understand: "I know that there is nothing better for them than to be happy and enjoy themselves as long as they live; moreover, it is God's gift that all should eat and drink and take pleasure in all their toil" (vv. 12-13, see also 2:24, 5:18-19, 8:15, 9:7-10).

Qoheleth's philosophy was not limited to "eat, drink, and be merry," but he firmly believed that God intended for humans to enjoy what pleasures they could, even if they could not understand the full meaning of their existence. Trying to comprehend God's work leads more to awe than to understanding (v. 14), he said, for only God can stand in the present while seeing into the past and the future (v. 15). The human task is to revere God and appreciate the lives God has given.

Qoheleth's conclusion may seem depressing – or encouraging for those who enjoy a party – but he was skeptical of the wisdom tradition's certainty, and he lived long before the time of Jesus. If Qoheleth had known the gospel message of eternal life through Christ that we learn from the New Testament, perhaps he would have sung a different tune.

The Hardest Question
Why couldn't Solomon have written Ecclesiastes?

The book of Ecclesiastes appears to have been written sometime during the postexilic period, hundreds of years after Solomon's time. Modern scholars hold differing opinions of whether Qoheleth wrote during the rule of the Persians (538–333 BCE), or after Alexander the Great conquered Palestine in 333 BCE, bringing the area under Greek rule and expanding the influence of Hellenistic thought. There are few, however, who would date the book earlier than 400–350 BCE.

But what about the traditional belief, held by many, that Solomon was the author? This came about because of the editorial superscription in 1:1 ("The words of the Teacher, the son of David, king in Jerusalem") and Qoheleth's use of royal fiction as a teaching method in 1:12–2:26.

It is unlikely that Qoheleth expected anyone to believe he really was "king of Israel in Jerusalem," though countless people have done so, including the person who added the superscription and identified him as a "son of David," since all the kings who ruled in Jerusalem were Davidic descendants. Solomon, of course, had a reputation for great wisdom, so it is not surprising that traditions

arose that Solomon was the author of both Ecclesiastes and Proverbs, even though much of Ecclesiastes directly contradicts the traditional wisdom of Proverbs, which contains attributions to a variety of authors.

Solomon, however, could hardly have written the book of Ecclesiastes. Why?

First, the royal fiction is found only in a small part of the book. In most of the book Qoheleth makes no pretension about being king. In fact, his attitude toward kingship is more critical than friendly. He sometimes connects kingship with injustice (3:16, 4:1-2, 5:7) and often makes comments about how to deal with kings, but not how to rule (8:2-4; 10:4-7, 16-17, 20). A king would hardly write in this way.

Second, the themes and language of the book are manifestly unlike what one would expect from a book written in the 10th century, as it would have to be if Solomon was the author. The Hebrew text has all the characteristics of the postexilic period, a time when the Hebrew language showed influence from Aramaic, which had become the *lingua franca* of the period. The presence of Aramaic and Persian style or loan words is strong evidence that the work was written in a later period. Qoheleth's grammar is unlike classical Hebrew and has often been described as reflecting the transition period between biblical Hebrew and the Mishnaic Hebrew of the rabbis that developed in the last couple of centuries before Christ. Franz Delitzsch once quipped: "If the Book of Koheleth were of old Solomonic origin, then there is no history of the Hebrew language" (cited by Roland E. Murphy, *Ecclesiastes*, vol. 23A, Word Biblical Commentary [Zondervan, 1992], xxvii).

Thus, there is little to substantiate the idea that Qoheleth and Solomon were the same person. Qoheleth could pretend to be Solomon for the sake of teaching his students, even as a modern preacher might present a dramatic monologue in the guise of an ancient prophet, but he was a sage from a much later period. He appears to have been a person of some wealth (and frustrated that he could not take it with him), but he was neither a king nor the richest man who ever lived.

New Year's Day

Second Reading
Psalm 8*

Not Quite Angels

O LORD, our Sovereign, how majestic is your name in all the earth! (Ps. 8:1)

We all face the challenge of finding our place in the world. For some people, it's less difficult because it's more limited: local culture or parents tell children what their place is, and opportunities are few. Some people may assume from childhood that they will live in the same village and watch cattle or plant rice until they grow old, with their own children following them. Other children may grow up obeying their parents' instructions to do well in school and become a doctor or an engineer, to take over the family business, or even to marry a person of their parents' choosing.

> **What's a *gittith*?** The superscriptions in the psalms are ancient notations added by scribal copyists at an early date, but they are not original to the psalm. Many of them suggest a setting for the psalm or associate it with an author or collection. Some, such as Psalm 8, include musical instructions.
>
> In Psalm 8, the note is addressed "To the director: according to (or 'upon') the *gittith*." The Hebrew word is not translated because we don't know what it means. Some scholars believe the *gittith* was a type of stringed instrument such as the lyre, and would translate "upon the *gittith*." Optionally, the word could indicate the name of a tune, and translate "according to 'the *gittith*.'" The word is similar to the plural form of *gat*, which means "wine-presses" (*gittoth*), so some think the tune may have been sung at harvest time, perhaps during the Feast of Booths.
>
> The superscription identifies the psalm as a "psalm of/by/to David." Whether the annotator believed David wrote the psalm or simply associated it with a collection dedicated to David is unclear.

Those who live in freer circumstances have more opportunities and options, but sometimes feel overwhelmed and at a loss to find and establish their identity. In America, young adults are waiting longer and longer to get married, have children, or settle into a career. Many feel lost even into their 30s or 40s, unsure of who they want to be, what they want to do, or where they belong.

Psalm 8 cannot point us to a career or a mate, but it does help us to understand where we fit in the larger scheme of things – indeed, in the *largest* scheme of things – in relation to God and the world.

An editorial superscription associates the psalm with David, in addition to something called a *gittith*. [**What's a *gittith*?**]

A majestic God
(vv. 1-2, 9)

Have you ever stood beneath a clear night sky studded with stars, feeling overcome by how big the universe is and how puny we are? As impressive as it is just to look at the stars – which the ancients believed were fixed into a dome over the earth – those who have even a hint of our current understanding of the universe must feel even smaller. We live in a small solar system near the edge of a massive galaxy containing more than 100 billion stars, and it's just one of an estimated *100 billion* galaxies.

The psalmist had no way of understanding that the earth is a planet rather than the center of the universe, or that there are untold billions of star systems surrounded

---

*Psalm 8 is also read on Trinity Sunday in Years A and C, and on Proper 22 of Year B.

How to translate? The closing words of v. 1 offer an interesting translational conundrum. The word translated "You have set" in the NRSV, or "You have revealed" in NET, is an imperative form of the word meaning "to give." Translators generally regard the text as corrupt and read it as another form of the word, nuanced as "set" or "reveal." The unusual word is preceded by another word that normally means "which" or "that," but seems a bit out of place here. Some translators now prefer an option, first suggested by Mitchell Dahood, in which the two three-letter words are put together, forming a longer word that means "to minister" or "to serve." This leads to a potential translation "I will worship your majesty above the heavens." (For more on this, see Peter C. Craigie, *Psalms 1–50*, vol. 19, Word Biblical Commentary [Zondervan, 1983], 104.)

by other worlds, but he didn't need that knowledge to appreciate human smallness.

If we consider the size of the universe, and we also believe that God created all things, how could we think of God as anything other than possessing magnificence beyond our comprehension? Thus, the psalmist writes "O LORD, our Sovereign, how majestic is your name in all the earth! You have set your glory above the heavens" (v. 1).

Those who recall the familiar KJV may remember the opening words as "O LORD, our Lord." The initial "O" is not in the text, but added for English style. Literally, the text has "Yahweh, our Lord." Yahweh is the personal, covenant name that God revealed to Israel (Exod. 3:15), always rendered in English by LORD, or occasionally GOD, in all upper-case letters. The word translated as "Sovereign" or "Lord" comes from the word *'adonai*, which means "lord," or "master." In different contexts, it could be used of human persons in positions of authority, but here clearly refers to God.

English translations don't convey it, but the word translated as "our Lord/Sovereign" (*'adonēnu*) is a plural form of the word. Grammarians refer to this term as a "plural of majesty," a way of making God's lordship even more emphatic. The term usually appears in the singular form, but here the psalmist is particularly interested in emphasizing God's greatness, so he uses the plural.

Having addressed God by the covenant name "Yahweh," the psalmist connects divine splendor to the divine name: "How majestic is your name in all the earth!"

As high as the heavens might be, said the psalmist, God's glory is elevated even higher. [**How to translate?**]

With v. 2, we come to the most puzzling part of the text, an apparent declaration that God can use even the praise of infants to silence all foes. The verse is clearly designed to expand upon the theme of God's magnificence, but its imagery interrupts the main flow of the psalm, so we'll leave a further discussion of that thorny verse for "The Hardest Question" below.

A privileged people
(vv. 3-5)

The central appeal of Psalm 8 is the question found in vv. 3-4: "When I look at your heavens, the work of your fingers, the moon and the stars that you have established; what are human beings that you are mindful of them, mortals that you care for them?"

The psalmist struggled with the mindboggling notion that God could create something as massive as the heavens and earth and still care for human beings. We can't know if the psalmist conceived of God in anthropomorphic terms, or just happily employed the metaphor, but he used the idea that God created the universe using only fingers as a way of emphasizing Yahweh's limitless power. If such a God could be bothered to care about puny, squabbling humans, how amazing is that?

But God does care, he concluded, because Yahweh not only created human beings, but also "made them a little lower than God, and crowned them with glory and honor" (v. 5). Again, those who grew up reading the KJV will remember a different translation: "For thou hast made him a little lower than the angels …"

Which is it? Are we to think of ourselves as a little lower than God, or than angels? As usual, the answer is a matter of interpretation. The word is *'elohīm*, the plural form of a word meaning "god" that could be translated as "gods" in a generic sense, as in Exod. 18:11, "Now I know that the LORD is greater than all gods." Most of the time, however, it was used as an alternate term for the God of Israel, with the plural form being a "plural of majesty" designed to indicate that no singular term for God would be adequate.

The Old Testament also speaks of supernatural beings, created by God, who served on a divine council and did

To whom was God speaking? Some readers mistakenly assume that when God said "let us make mankind in our image" (Gen. 1:26), it was an early reference to the Trinity, in which God the Father was speaking to God the Son and God the Holy Spirit. The author of Genesis (like the psalmist) had no such concept, but shared the ancient Near Eastern belief, common in many religions, that the high god often met in council with lower-level supernatural beings. Israel adapted the concept to think of Yahweh's divine council as consisting of heavenly beings who were clearly supra-human, but not considered gods. They, too, were part of God's created order.

God's bidding, often as intermediaries between heaven and earth. Hebrew commonly refers to these beings as "sons of God" (benē-'elohīm), as in Job 1:6, where the NRSV uses the term "heavenly beings." We typically think of such beings as "angels," and the Septuagint translators read it in this sense, using the Greek term 'aggelous (the double gamma [g] was pronounced as "ng"), the root of the English word "angel."

How do we decide? The psalmist almost certainly had Gen. 1:26-27 in mind, where God spoke to the divine council and said "Let us make humankind in our image" before creating humans, both male and female. Thus, the idea is that humans were created not only in the image of God, but also in the image of the angelic assembly. [To whom was God speaking?] Thus, some interpreters prefer to translate 'elohīm as "angels," while others prefer the more common meaning of "God."

At the end of the day, the meaning is little different. Humans not only are made by God, but also share in God's image, and in making them this way God has "crowned them with glory and honor."

A responsible dominion
(vv. 6-8)

The poet's recollection of the creation story continues in vv. 6-8, which recall Gen. 1:28, in which God instructed humankind to "Be fruitful and multiply, and fill the earth and subdue it; and have dominion over the fish of the sea and over the birds of the air and over every living thing that moves upon the earth."

The psalmist had seen such dominion in action, and praised God for having given humans charge "over the works of your hands," putting "all things under their feet" (v. 6). Sheep and oxen, the beasts of the field, the birds of the air, fish and everything living in the sea had come under human control (vv. 7-8). [Not just sheep] The psalmist's point is that all life, from land to sea and sky, was subordinated to humankind: the work of God's hands was put into human hands.

For the psalmist, the idea that God had not only taken notice of humans, but also given them control of life on earth, was such an astonishing notion that he could not resist bursting into praise once again, closing the psalm by repeating his initial thought: "O LORD, our Sovereign, how majestic is your name in all the earth!" (v. 9).

How do you think the psalmist might have responded if he could see just how greatly humans have multiplied, and to what extent they have exercised dominion? We must remember that God's granting control of the earth to humans in Gen. 1:28-30 includes both accountability and authority. God did not put the earth into our hands so that we might exhaust its resources, pollute its water, and overheat its atmosphere.

The psalmist lived in a time when the earth's population was small, air pollution was limited to cooking fires, and animals were not being forced into extinction on a regular basis. If he could catch a glimpse of what humans have done – and are doing – to the planet, he might not have thought it was such a good idea to put them in charge.

The poet has testified that God's greatness is beyond comprehension, and yet God cares enough for humankind not only to grant them stewardship of the earth, but also to desire a relationship with them. When you contemplate the beautiful poetry of Psalm 8, what challenges you the most?

Not just sheep: Translators typically render v. 7 as "all sheep and oxen, and also the beasts of the field," mainly for lyrical purposes: it sounds better. The word translated as "sheep," however, is tsōneh, which refers to a mixed flock of sheep and goats. Such mixed flocks were typical: sheep were raised mainly for their wool, while goats provided meat and milk.

The Hardest Question
What do babies have to do with it?

Verse 2 is the most difficult part of Psalm 8 to interpret: The NRSV has "Out of the mouths of babes and infants you have *founded a bulwark* because of your foes, to silence the enemy and the avenger." The NET renders it differently: "From the mouths of children and nursing babies you have *ordained praise* on account of your adversaries, so that you might put an end to the vindictive enemy" (italics added).

What could baby noises have to do with establishing strength (the literal meaning of "bulwark"), or with silencing enemies and avengers? The verse has perplexed interpreters from at least the third century BCE, when early Greek translations were being done.

How do we interpret this puzzling text? Some writers suggest this approach: As a baby's cry leads to a response from the parent to deal with the problem, so Israel could cry to God, who would deliver them from their foes.

Another approach looks back to the previous emphasis on God's name and glory to propose that God's name is so powerful that even babies could pronounce the divine name and God would silence Israel's enemies.

One may also think of the baby's cry as a metaphor for weakness, and as a reminder that God often used weak or unassuming people to accomplish great things: the Old Testament contains many examples of "little come big," when unexpected heroes such as Ehud (Judg. 3:12-30), Deborah (Judges 4–5), or Gideon (Judges 6–8) arose to lead Israel to victory over their foes.

Yet another approach notes that the Septuagint, an early Greek translation, used the word "praise" instead of "strength," suggesting that the translators' copy of the text had a different word. This leads to the idea that God displayed divine greatness by drawing praise even from infants.

Whatever nuance we put on the psalmist's precise meaning, his purpose was clearly to magnify the glory and power of God over all creation, from infants to enemies.

New Year's Day
Third Reading
Revelation 21:1-6*

A New Day

And the one who was seated on the throne said, "See, I am making all things new." (Rev. 21:5a)

Do thoughts of heaven cross your mind very often? I suspect most of us go through the majority of our days without a thought of heaven – but if someone we love dearly should die, it may be all we can think about.

When my seven-year-old daughter fell victim to a drunk driver many years ago, I fantasized about whether heaven would offer hot dogs and fish sticks and pony rides.

When we come to fear that our own death might be near, heaven will surely be prominent in our thoughts.

The Bible speaks descriptively of heaven in a few places, and uncounted sermons have been preached on its wonders. The truth, however, is that we have no real idea what heaven is like, though our imaginations can run wild. We may visualize heaven as a homecoming where loved ones live together in harmony, or as a place where angels sing, ambrosia abounds, and we can play every day.

Those thoughts are about as helpful as the book of Revelation. John's apocalyptic writing is metaphorical and symbolic throughout, so we should not regard his language-stretching vision of jeweled walls and pearly gates and golden streets as a literal description, but mainly as a place of beauty beyond human imaginings.

Secondly, what John describes in Revelation 21–22 is pointedly denoted as a "new heaven and a new earth." Whatever heaven might be like now, John suggests, it is not the same place or dimension to be experienced in eternity. What the present heaven and the new heaven have in common is that God is at the heart of them.

The Bible does not tell us all we *want* to know about heaven, but it tells us all we *need* to know. It tells us that we can hold to the hope that life for the believer does not end with our last breath, but remains open to joy.

A new dwelling
(v. 1-2)

We can imagine that heaven had been on John's mind for a long time. He had experienced hardships and persecution. Perhaps he had known people who were killed because of their faith. Sporadic episodes of persecution reportedly included public torture, with Christians being burned as torches or fed to the lions in the Coliseum. One early church legend says that Roman officials tried to kill John, but could not, and so they banished him to the island of Patmos. **[Boiled in oil?]** It's not hard to imagine why John thought so much about heavenly things.

Hebrew traditions held that God created the earth so that everything was "very good" (Gen. 1:31), but it fell under a curse when humankind turned against God's way

---

Boiled in oil? An early church tradition, recorded in Tertullian's *The Prescription of Heretics*, claims that John was dunked in boiling oil before a Roman audience, but not harmed. Supposedly all who saw the miracle were converted to Christianity, and since the Romans couldn't kill John, they shipped him off to Patmos.

While there is certainly no evidence to support this unlikely legend, there is little question that John must have experienced and witnessed the kind of severe persecutions that typically gave rise to apocalyptic writings.

This text is also used for All Saints Day in Year B and on the fifth Sunday of Easter in Year C.

No more sea: The overwhelming and destructive power of the sea contributed to its association with chaos. No human could hope to control the sea, and few gods were thought to have such power. In the Babylonian creation myth, the god Marduk proved his supremacy by battling and defeating the sea-dwelling goddess Tiamat in order to stabilize the world and create humankind.

In Hebrew thought, the sea could also suggest separation from God. In the biblical concept of a "three-story" universe, the flat earth was covered by a dome-like "firmament" that held back the great cosmic sea above, with heaven thought to be beyond the sea.

In John's first vision of heaven (Rev. 4:6), the throne of God seemed to be set beyond "something like a sea of glass, like crystal." But in the new heaven and the new earth, there is no more sea. Chaos is no longer a threat. There is nothing to separate the faithful from God.

(Genesis 3). When injustice reigned or enemies threatened and the situation looked particularly bad, Israel's prophets sometimes spoke of a new or renewed earth where closeness to God would be restored. Isaiah of Jerusalem, for example, envisioned a new age of peace in which all creation would live in harmony with God (Isaiah 11), and a later prophet writing in Isaiah's name predicted an entirely new creation: "For I am about to create new heavens and a new earth; the former things shall not be remembered or come to mind" (Isa. 65:17).

John was certainly familiar with these ancient hopes, and amid the dire straits of his day, he believed they were about to be fulfilled. "Then I saw a new heaven and a new earth," he said, "for the first heaven and the first earth had passed away, and the sea was no more" (v. 1).

John was convinced that God would soon draw earthly history to a close and set everything right. All that had become cursed and crooked would be restored and made straight, for there would be a new earth. The reasons for a new heaven are less obvious, but the ancients thought of the two as being created together. "A new heaven and a new earth" is John's way of emphasizing God's creative power to make all things new.

A new heaven and earth would be necessary, John said, because the old heaven and earth "have passed away." Earlier, while describing a judgment scene in which God would sit on a great white throne, John said "the earth and

the heaven fled from his presence, and no place was found for them" (Rev. 20:11b).

Of special significance is John's insistence that "the sea was no more." The sea was a prominent source of fear in the ancient world. Maritime travel was dangerous and uncertain. Sea dragons or serpent-like monsters such as Leviathan were thought to inhabit the depths (Job 26:12; Isa. 27:1, 51:9-10), making the sea a fearful place.

The sea symbolized chaos and the threatening power of un-creation, which could only be held in check by God. In the new heaven and earth, the frightening sea would be no more. [**No more sea**]

In addition to a new heaven and earth, John's vision included a new Jerusalem: "and I saw the holy city, the new Jerusalem, coming down out of heaven from God, prepared as a bride adorned for her husband" (v. 2, cf. Rev. 19:7-8).

The author envisions the perfect union of Christ and his bride as about to take place, but believed that only God could fully prepare the bride for the moment. Other New Testament passages also use the wedding metaphor to describe the relationship of Christ and the church (2 Cor. 11:2), and Jesus himself once told a wedding parable about the kingdom of God in which being properly dressed was a significant issue (Matt. 22:1-14).

The Jerusalem of old was the city of David, the home of the temple, the heart of every major Hebrew religious festival. But it was also a city that could stone prophets and crucify Jesus. Luke's gospel portrays Jesus as weeping for the recalcitrant people of Jerusalem (Luke 13:31-35). Perhaps the new Jerusalem's descent from heaven is a reminder that only God can restore the city's holiness and transform it into a dwelling place fit for eternity. [**God's dwelling**]

At first (and maybe, at last), this text seems confusing, and it is helpful to remember that John is using word pictures, metaphorical language that often shifts its boundaries.

John speaks of a new heaven and a new earth. He speaks of a new and holy city of Jerusalem coming down out of heaven to the new earth. After this, however, the distinctions fade, and the new heaven, earth, the city, and believers seem to meld together. The new Jerusalem is not a city but is the bride of Christ, the body of believers. Through all the shifting images, the point is that, in the new age, God's dwelling will be with God's people.

> **God's dwelling:** The word translated as "home" in the NRSV can also be rendered as "dwelling" (NIV) or "tabernacle" (KJV, NASB). The Greek word is *skēnē*, which literally means "tent." When the author of John's gospel claimed that "the Word became flesh and dwelt among us," he used the verbal form of the same word (lit., "tabernacled"). *Skēnē* is probably derived from a Semitic loan word such as the Hebrew *shakan* (to dwell), which gave rise to words such as *mishkan* (tent, tabernacle) and *shekinah* (dwelling). The rabbis often used the word *Shekinah* to refer to the presence of God's glory thought to pervade the temple's most sacred space, the holy of holies.

A new presence
(vv. 3-4)

John describes a loud voice from the throne saying, "See, the home of God is among mortals. He will dwell with them as their God; they will be his peoples, and God himself will be with them; he will wipe every tear from their eyes. Death will be no more; mourning and crying and pain will be no more, for the first things have passed away."

Here is the most important aspect of John's message. What the new heaven and new earth look like or where they are located or how big they are is immaterial. God will live among God's people: that is what truly matters.

That God's "tent" or "dwelling" would be among mortals is a mind-boggling concept. To imagine God's presence, we will no longer need a tabernacle or an altar, the Ark of the Covenant or the holy of holies, a cross on a steeple or stained-glass windows. Rather, God will dwell among humans in some way beyond our present ability to imagine. The covenant relationship so longed for between God and Israel will finally be fulfilled (Exod. 6:7, Lev. 26:12, Jer. 7:23).

Living in the full presence of God would mean living in the absence of death, John says. Mourning and crying and pain, in one way or another, all have a connection with death – the death of relationships, the death of dreams, the death of innocence, the death of trust, the death of loved ones, the death of self. Death, in some form, is at the heart of every pain.

The Bible has nothing good to say about death. That's why it is such good news to hear that God will do away

with it. Without the deathly fear of darkness and separation, there is no more cause for mourning or tears or pain. The ultimate sign of the presence of God is the absence of death. [**Death as an enemy**]

A new word
(vv. 5-6)

God's final word is always a word of hope. "See, I am making all things new." The New Testament speaks of how Christians become a "new creation" when we trust in Christ and ask Christ's spirit to live in us (2 Cor. 5:17, Gal. 6:15). We do not become immediately perfect, but despite human weakness, we grow in the "inner person" as a new creation, secure in Christ until the day of his appearing (2 Cor. 3:18, 4:16-18; Col. 3:1-4). John now envisions this same transformation on a cosmic scale as all things are redeemed and made new.

G.B. Caird once described John's vision of a corrupt world's miseries giving way to a future hope this way: "the agonies of earth are but the birth-pangs of a new creation" (*The Revelation of St. John the Divine* [Harper & Row, 1966], 266).

John declares as God's own testimony that "these words are trustworthy and true" (v. 5). There will come a day when all the former things are past, when God will bring all things to an eternal conclusion in which the greatest needs of his children are eternally met: "To the

> **Death as an enemy:** Biblical accounts portray death coming into the world as an unwanted invader following humankind's sin (Genesis 3, Rom. 5:12), with the result that mortals became not only subject to death (Heb. 9:27), but also are enslaved by the fear of it (Heb. 2:15, cf. Robert H. Mounce, *The Book of Revelation*, New International Commentary on the Old Testament (Eerdmanns Publishing Co., 1977], 372).
>
> The author of Ecclesiastes expresses great sorrow and frustration because he understood the ugliness and finality of death and saw nothing positive beyond. Isaiah looked forward to a day when death would be swallowed up forever (Isa. 25:8), and Paul announced that the longed-for day had come through the work of Christ (1 Cor. 15:54-56). Death, then, is seen as an enemy to be conquered, and "the last enemy to be destroyed is death" (1 Cor. 15:26). This is precisely what John declares in Rev. 21:4.

thirsty I will give water as a gift from the spring of the water of life" (v. 6).

John has more to say about the believer's eternal home (Rev. 21:7–22:21), but the most important thing has already been said. God is present. Death is absent. The noise of running water is not the sound of tears, but the eternally bubbling spring of the water of life.

The Hardest Question
Many of the images in Revelation are simply stupefying, and some of them seem impossible. How do we understand these things?

We noted above that Rev. 20:11b declares "… the earth and the heaven fled from his presence, and no place was found for them," while in 21:1 John says "Then I saw a new heaven and a new earth, for the first heaven and the first earth had passed away."

How could this be? Biblical writers had no concept of a universe such as we do, an unmeasurable space inhabited by uncounted galaxies containing millions and billions of stars. For John, "heaven and earth" would represent all there was – yet he declares that heaven and earth fled from God's presence.

This is one of several places where John is using word pictures, speaking in metaphorical language. Where could heaven and earth go apart from God? Where in the universe could the universe flee? The psalmist testified that he could not flee from God's presence (Ps. 139:7). How could heaven and earth do so?

Similarly, John describes a new heaven, a new earth, and a new Jerusalem that appear to begin as separate entities, but they ultimately combine into a different image. This is not uncommon: various elements of John's vision may shift in their shape or meaning. At other times, multiple characters (such as two strange beasts and a dragon) may represent the same evil power.

To understand this, think about how things work in our dreams: we may find ourselves moving instantly from one place to another, or discover that a classroom has turned into muddy marsh or a doctor's office. Dreams often defy logic and morph from one thing to another, though we may learn something from the symbols that show up in them.

Perhaps it would be helpful for us to remember that John's revelations came to him in visions that he would have written later, and visions were much like dreams thought to be sent from God.

New Year's Day

Fourth Reading
Matthew 25:31-46*

Wait. What?

And the king will answer them, "Truly I tell you, just as you did it to one of the least of these who are members of my family, you did it to me." (Matt. 25:40)

How do you feel about the word "judgment"? We may be good at judging others (though we rarely admit it), but we don't want anyone judging us. One of the nicest things we might say about someone is that they are "not judgmental."

But the Bible has much to say about judgment, especially in writings of the prophets. Today we are reminded that Jesus also talked about it. While we prefer to think of Christ's love and grace rather than judgment, our mental picture of Jesus is incomplete if we do not include his teachings about personal responsibility.

Matthew 25 follows an apocalyptic passage in which Jesus speaks of an eschatological judgment not unlike the Old Testament concept of the "Day of the LORD" (Matthew 24). The chapter consists of three sections, each with a judgment theme. [**Three teachings on judgment**]

The third section speaks of a judgment to take place when Christ, as the glorified "Son of Man," comes into his kingdom. Some scholars consider this to be a parable, like the parable of the bridesmaids and the parable of the talents that precede it. Some read the text as direct discourse describing a literal event. Others read it as a prophecy with parabolic elements.

Sheep and goats
(vv. 31-33)

Jesus spoke of the "Son of Man" coming in glory, surrounded by angels, to sit on his throne. Jesus often used "Son of Man" as a self-ascription to suggest his solidarity

---

> **Three teachings on judgment:** Matthew 25 follows an apocalyptic teaching in ch. 24 with three different teachings related to judgment. The first section is a parable concerning 10 bridesmaids who awaited the coming of the bridegroom (25:1-13). Five had brought sufficient oil for an extended wait, but the other five missed the bridegroom when he arrived after they had left to replenish the oil in their lamps. It is a reminder of the importance of being prepared.
>
> That second section is the familiar parable of the talents (25:14-30), in which Jesus again speaks of returning after an extended absence. It stresses the importance of using our God-given gifts wisely and faithfully as we await Christ's return.
>
> The third section is our text for today, the account of the "sheep and goats" judgment, which many readers also consider to be a parable.

---

with humankind, but here it takes on images of power and glory characteristic of earlier apocalyptic usage of the term (Dan. 7:13).

As "all the nations" gathered before him, Jesus said, he would distinguish between those who belonged with him and those who did not, utilizing a metaphor of separating sheep and goats. The sight of a shepherd separating his flocks was common in Palestine. Sheep and goats commonly pastured together as a mixed flock, but they occasionally needed to be separated for shearing, milking, or shelter.

There is nothing inherently good about sheep or bad about goats. Both were highly prized in the pastoral economy. Goats tended to be more self-sufficient than

---

sheep, which were more reliant on the shepherd. On the annual Day of Atonement, Hebrew priests sacrificed one goat as a purification offering while symbolically transferring the sins of the people to a second goat, which was then driven into the wilderness – the original "scapegoat" (Leviticus 16). This may have contributed to goats having a more negative reputation than sheep.

In Jesus' metaphorical image, the "sheep" would be culled out and positioned at the king's favored right hand, while the "goats" would be consigned to his left. In Semitic thought, the right hand was commonly favored. The king's most trusted advisor would stand at his right hand, even as Jesus could be depicted at the right hand of God (Acts 2:33, 5:31, 7:55-56).

Being left-handed did not imply that someone was evil, but instead different, out of the ordinary. Ehud used left-handedness to his advantage in assassinating the king of Moab and rising to lead Israel as a judge (Judg. 3:15-25), while a cadre of 700 left-handed Benjaminites were known for their accuracy with a sling: "each one could sling a stone at a hair and not miss" (1 Chron. 12:2). While the narrator praised the warriors' skill, the tribe of Benjamin was often presented in a negative light. [Sketchy southpaws]

Surprise No. 1
(vv. 34-40)

The important question here is not about sheep and goats or left and right, but about the criteria Jesus will use for judgment. Humans come in many shapes and shades, but none of our differences are as distinctive as that between sheep and goats. It cannot be ethnicity or gender that determines our place with Jesus: some other characteristic must come into play.

We must begin with a note of caution: a literal interpretation of this text alone – without reference to other revealed truths about the gospel – could lead to a works-righteousness theology in which one earns his or her way into heaven. Other scriptures make it clear that salvation is a gift of God, not an earned payment for good works (e.g., Eph. 2:8-9).

The difference in emphasis provides needed balance. Salvation is offered freely, but the mark of those who have truly experienced that gift is a genuine and faithful life of

> **Sketchy southpaws:** Many cultures ascribe a negative connotation to being left-handed. Even though about 10 percent of the world's population is left-handed, the much larger proportion of right-handed people determine the norm. In some cultures, left-handed people are considered clever; but in others, unlucky.
>
> Some cultures, such as Islam, insist on using the right hand for eating and social interactions, reserving the left hand for cleaning oneself with water after defecation. Using the left hand to eat, to hand over payment to a merchant, or even to present a gift can be considered offensive.
>
> The Latin word *sinistrum* originally meant "left," but also came to be associated with evil or bad luck, and that connotation remains in derivative languages such as English, where "sinister" means "evil" or "menacing." In French, the word for "right" is *droit*, which also means "straight" or "correct," while *maladroit* (also in the English) means "clumsy," as does the word *gauche*, which also means "left."

service to God. The book of James puts special stress on this point: faith without works is dead (Jas. 2:17-26).

Many people imagine that one day we will be given some sort of a doctrinal test to determine fitness for the kingdom, but salvation is not dependent on orthodoxy. A common folk belief asserts that everyone's good and evil works will be weighed in a cosmic scale, with those whose deeds tip the scale toward the good gaining a ticket to eternity. Of course, virtually all people who hold that view also believe their good deeds outweigh the bad.

Jesus, however, will not base judgment on whether we can pass a doctrinal exam or demonstrate sufficient piety. Nor will he ask whether we have "walked the aisle" and experienced baptism. In the context of this discourse, the criteria for judgment lie elsewhere. Jesus said, "the king will say to those at his right hand, 'Come, you that are blessed by my Father, inherit the kingdom prepared for you from the foundation of the world'" (v. 34).

Who are the chosen? Jesus identified the favored ones as those who had ministered to him when he was hungry or thirsty, homeless or naked, sick or in prison (vv. 35-36). The chosen "sheep" would be surprised, Jesus said, being unaware that they had done any of those things for Jesus and wondering how they could get credit for ministering to him (vv. 37-38).

The king would respond, Jesus said, "Truly I tell you, just as you did it to one of the least of these who are members of my family, you did it to me" (v. 40).

The identity of "the least of these" is a bigger question than one might expect. Readers commonly assume Jesus was talking about ministry to any who are poor, needy, or oppressed. Most recent scholars, however, believe the qualifying word 'adelphōn mou ("my brothers," but understood without gender) points to Jesus' followers. With that interpretation, the issue is not so much how people treat needy folk in general, but how they respond to the followers of Jesus sent on mission into the world – and thus to Jesus himself.

If this is the correct interpretation, it takes nothing away from the importance of caring for the poor and working for justice as central aspects of Jesus' teaching (Luke 4:18-19). It remains true that we cannot truly love God without also loving our neighbor, but the focus here puts the emphasis on one's response to the community of Christ.

Surprise No. 2
(vv. 41-46)

The remainder of our passage is the flip side of the previous verses. The "goats" shuffled off to the left side – reportedly to face "eternal fire prepared for the devil and his angels" – will also be surprised (v. 41). They could feel certain that if they had seen Jesus facing afflictions of hunger, thirst, homelessness, nakedness, illness, or imprisonment, they would surely have reached out and provided for him, and asked when they could have ignored his need (vv. 42-44).

As before, Jesus said: "Truly I tell you, just as you did not do it to one of the least of these, you did not do it to me" (v. 45). If "the least of these" refers to Jesus' followers, these are rejected because they responded negatively to Christ's family. If we follow the more common view that "the least of these" could describe any poor or marginalized people, we are reminded that the way we treat others reflects our relationship with God. If our love for Jesus is genuine, it will manifest in love for others.

In reading this passage, we must be careful to focus on the main point without getting hung up on the contrast between eternal fellowship with Jesus for some and an eternal torment for others (vv. 34, 41, 46). Matthew 24 and 25 follow a confrontation between Jesus and some religious leaders he considered to be hypocrites because they threatened others with the emerging idea of hell while failing to practice justice in their own lives. When Jesus talked about hell, he was turning their own language against them, not necessarily endorsing the idea that God intends to torture the unfaithful throughout eternity – a concept that seems out of character for a God whose deep love for humanity was revealed in Jesus. Here it is likely that Jesus' words have been shaped by the early church, and it is certain that the idea has been reinforced by early interpreters.

We don't have to believe God will roast unbelievers in hell to appreciate the heart of Jesus' message in this text: the best way to be close to Jesus is to get close to "the least of these," his family. This is an important reminder that church matters: Jesus' "sheep" are those who support Christ's family, the community of faith in which we live out our calling.

The Hardest Question
Who did Jesus mean by "the least of these who are members of my family"?

As noted in the lesson, most readers of this passage tend to assume that Jesus was talking about anyone who was hungry or thirsty, homeless or naked, sick or in prison, especially the poor or those who are unable to look after themselves. The gospels make it clear that Jesus' own mission included feeding the hungry, healing the sick, and proclaiming liberty to those who were in various types of bondage. But does that mean Jesus considered all people in need to be among the "least of these who are members of my family"? Who were Jesus' 'adelphōn? The word literally means "brothers," but was commonly used in a generic sense that modern translations render as "brothers and sisters" or, as here, "members of my family."

Three options are generally considered: the "least of these who are members of my family" could refer to the Jews, to the poor and needy in general, or to Jesus' followers.

There is little support for the idea that Jesus had fellow Jews in mind, though some Christians who take a "premillennial" view of the end times believe the text refers to how Gentiles treat the Jews during the so-called "millennium," which they view as a literal 1,000-year period after an initial return of Christ, when 144,000 Jews will act as witnesses. Most scholars believe that view, which is based mainly on a literal reading of Revelation 7, 14, and 20, does not stand up to serious scrutiny. And, there are no other biblical references in which Jesus refers to the Jews as his family. This is clearly not a good option.

The more popular view, that "the least of these" refers to all who are poor and downtrodden, has more going for it. The qualifier "who are members of my family" is added in v. 40, but not in v. 45. Jesus' actions and teachings clearly favored the poor and ministered to them. This view has some scholarly support, and was championed by Mother Teresa, who often spoke of the poor as "Jesus in disguise." But this view also runs into problems.

Nowhere else in the New Testament does Jesus refer to the poor as his family, or use kindness to the poor as a measure of faith. Jesus said far more about "fishing for people" (Mark 1:17), about winning and making disciples (Matt. 28:19-20), than about feeding the hungry. In one instance, without downplaying the importance of ministry to the needy, Jesus suggested that spending time with him took precedence: "For you always have the poor with you, and you can show kindness to them whenever you wish; but you will not always have me" (Mark 14:7).

Now consider the possibility that "the least of these who are my family" refers to Jesus' disciples and other followers. First, when Jesus uses the term "brothers" elsewhere in Matthew, he is speaking of his disciples. When asked about his mother and brothers, Jesus pointed to his *disciples* and said: "Here are my mother and my brothers! For whoever does the will of my Father in heaven is my brother and sister and mother" (Matt. 12:49-50). After his resurrection, Jesus was speaking of the disciples when he told two amazed women followers, "Do not be afraid; go and tell my brothers to go to Galilee; there they will see me" (Matt. 28:10).

For an even closer comparison, Matthew 10 describes how Jesus commissioned his disciples for a mission of evangelism and healing. He intentionally sent them without money, provisions of food, or extra clothing – thus subject to hunger, thirst, homelessness, and nakedness – while warning that they would be in danger of persecution and imprisonment. Not everyone would receive them, Jesus said, but "Whoever welcomes you welcomes me, and whoever welcomes me welcomes the one who sent me" (Matt. 10:40).

He then continued the theme: "Whoever welcomes a prophet in the name of a prophet will receive a prophet's reward; and whoever welcomes a righteous person in the name of a righteous person will receive the reward of the righteous; and whoever gives even a cup of cold water to one of these little ones in the name of a disciple—truly I tell you, none of these will lose their reward" (Matt. 10:41-42).

The language is strikingly similar – Jesus promises rewards to those who bless his disciples ("these little ones") with as much as a cup of cold water.

Although not immediately self-evident, the identification of "the least of these who are members of my family" as Jesus' followers is most in line with the evidence.

This view offers an added benefit: if we think of the criterion for judgment as being based entirely on our response to the poor, the passage appears to support a works-righteousness theology that is in tension with scriptures that speak of salvation as the gift of God, based on grace (Rom. 3:23, Eph. 2:8-9, among others).

Judgment, instead, is based on one's response to Christ's challenge as mediated through "the least of these members of my family."

Again, this interpretation does not relieve Christ-followers of their responsibility to work for justice and care for those in need: other texts make clear our call to self-sacrificial service, loving God and loving others. We do this best when we begin by caring for those within a community of faith, learning and living out what it means to be one of "the least of these who are members of my family."

Epiphany of the Lord*
First Reading
Isaiah 60:1-9

Rise and Shine!

Arise, shine; for your light has come, and the glory of the LORD has risen upon you. (Isa. 60:1)

As Christ-followers embark on a new year, it is appropriate that we celebrate the season of Epiphany, which centers on the appearance of Christ among us. "Epiphany" comes from a Greek word that means "appearing."

During the first few centuries of church history, after December 25 came to be observed as the birthday of Christ, it became customary to identify January 6 with the visit of the magi and Jesus' consequent revelation to the Gentiles. Some church fathers even held that Jesus' public revelation through baptism and his initial demonstration of power at the wedding in Cana occurred on the same calendar date, though years later. **[Special seasons]**

So, if Epiphany is all about Jesus, why is today's text from Isaiah?

Isaiah 60 is one of the most beautiful and hopeful passages in the Hebrew Bible, promising an amazing age of salvation for God's people and glory for God. From a Jewish perspective, the hope of a light that would draw all nations to Jerusalem has yet to be fulfilled.

The early church, however, thought of Christ as the promised light of the world sent to draw all people to God. Thus, readings from Isaiah 60 became a regular part of the liturgy for Epiphany.

The Revised Common Lectionary suggests Isa. 60:1-6 as the recommended Old Testament text. The initial textual unit goes at least through v. 7, however, or possibly v. 9. As a result, we'll include vv. 1-9 in our study.

> **Special seasons:** Some Christian groups celebrate the period between December 25 and January 6 as "the 12 days of Christmas," a time to celebrate the incarnation of Christ (Nativity) and his manifestation to the world (Epiphany). Armenian Apostolic and Armenian Catholic churches, which developed separately from the Eastern Orthodox, observe January 6 as the date of Jesus' birth.
>
> Churches that follow the Revised Common Lectionary celebrate a "Season of Epiphany" that ends on Transfiguration Sunday, the last Sunday before Lent. Since the date for Easter (and hence, the beginning of Lent) may vary by several weeks from year to year, the Season of Epiphany can last from five to nine weeks.

A light in the darkness
(vv. 1-3)

Isaiah 60 almost certainly dates from the early postexilic period, long after the eighth-century Isaiah of Jerusalem inspired the book that bears his name, and shortly after the Persian king Cyrus allowed Jewish exiles to begin returning to Jerusalem around 538 BCE. **[Third Isaiah?]**

One would expect an exuberant era as the former exiles exulted in their return to Jerusalem, but those who made the long journey from Babylon were distraught at what they found: the glorious city their grandparents remembered lay crumbled and overgrown, a home for foxes and not for people.

Even though the Persian king had provided financial assistance and other exiles contributed funds, reconstruc-

---

* The Season of Epiphany can have up to nine Sundays, depending on where Easter falls. Texts for the first five Sundays are provided here, even though all will not be used in all years. Texts for Epiphany 6–9 are the same as the texts for Proper Sundays 1–4, and are provided in Volume 3 of Year A.

Epiphany always falls on January 6, the traditional date the magi arrived in Bethlehem. Studies are provided for years when Epiphany falls on Sunday, or if preferred for use on the first Sunday after Epiphany. The texts are the same for Years A, B, and C.

Third Isaiah? Modern scholars often note that the book of Isaiah had multiple authors, because it clearly addresses at least three distinct historical settings: the book begins in Judah before the exile (mid-eighth century BCE), moves to the Babylonian captivity (c. 587–537 BCE), and concludes with the Jews back in Jerusalem, remembering former days in exile.

Scholars typically posit at least two, if not three, different prophets who contributed to the traditions we now know as the book of Isaiah. In ancient times, the practice was not uncommon: issues of authorship were not as important as they are today. Someone who belonged to a postulated "School of Isaiah" (Isa. 8:16 indicates that there were disciples who followed him) might have felt led by God to contribute to the Isaiah traditions without worrying about adding an additional signature.

While the book addresses three different historical settings, some scholars propose that the same author who brought comfort during the exile could also have been one of those who first returned from Babylon to Jerusalem, and thus could have written both of the last two sections. In this case, there would have been two prophets addressing three periods in the Hebrews' history.

Whether there are two authors or three, we generally speak of the book as comprising three sections, "First Isaiah" (chs. 1–39, written mainly for an eighth-century audience in Judah), "Second Isaiah" (or "Deutero-Isaiah," chs. 40–55, speaking to exiles in Babylon in the mid-sixth century), and "Third Isaiah" (or "Trito-Isaiah," chs. 56–66, addressing the needs of former exiles who had returned to Jerusalem and struggled to rebuild an Israelite identity in Jerusalem). These three sections are not as neat as we would like: some parts of chs. 1–39 appear to have been written later, for example, but they provide a rough guide to the development of the book.

There are some similarities, but also distinct differences in style, vocabulary, and theology between the first and last parts of the book. This reinforces the explanation that one or more later disciples, steeped in Isaiah's basic ideas and responsible for preserving Isaiah's work, continued his prophetic tradition in later years.

While "Second Isaiah" and "Third Isaiah" share some vocabulary and themes, they typically differ in that Second Isaiah's oracles of hope are generally tied to anticipated historical events, while the promises of Third Isaiah have no temporal connections.

---

tion was a slow and painful process, made more difficult by the enmity of neighboring peoples.

The Babylonians had left behind residents thought too poor or uneducated to prove a threat, and through the years they had intermarried with neighboring residents of differing ethnic backgrounds. The returning exiles considered themselves to be the only "pure" Jews remaining, and they wanted nothing to do with their ethnically mixed cousins, which provoked intense animosity between the groups.

It was a dark time for a struggling population badly in need of a word of hope.

Into this discordant and discouraged setting, the prophet injected a timeless promise, calling the dejected people to "Arise, shine; for your light has come, and the glory of the LORD has risen upon you" (v. 1, NRSV).

What do we make of the verbs translated "has come" and "has risen"? Tangible evidence of God's restored favor remained lacking. The verbs are both in the perfect tense, which is often translated as the English past tense, but can sometimes be translated as present or even future. Thus, the NET Bible renders them as "arrives" and "shines." The perfect also appears in oracles as a "prophetic perfect," describing an as-yet-unfulfilled future, but using the past tense to indicate the certainty of fulfillment.

The prophet switches to the imperfect (uncompleted) tense in v. 2, making it clear that his vision was not yet fulfilled. Note the sharp contrast between darkness and light. "Darkness shall cover the earth," he said, "and thick darkness the peoples," while "the LORD will arise upon you and his glory will appear over you" (v. 2).

This verse helps us to understand that "the light" of v. 1, where it appears in parallel with "the glory of the LORD," must refer to the presence of God made manifest among God's people. "Yahweh will arise upon you," said the prophet. An alternate meaning of the word rendered as "arise" is "shine" – it was used in conjunction with the dawn, when the sun appears to both "rise" and "shine."

God's appearing spoke to a time of salvation, a common theme for Third Isaiah (see also 56:1, 59:11, 60:1, 62:11, 63:4, and 66:15). A similar connection is found in the prophecies of Second Isaiah (40:10, 50:2).

Herein is the connection to Epiphany: reading this text through the lens of Jesus' life and work, the church interpreted the promise of light as a sign of the incarnation. God had come to dwell with humankind: as we read in the gospel (John 8:12, 9:5) and celebrate in song, "the light of the world is Jesus." It should come as no surprise that Jesus' birth would be marked by the appearance of a bright star.

Isaiah envisioned a time when foreign nations, blanketed in darkness, would be drawn to the light of God shining over Jerusalem, and they would come streaming to the city, both kings and their peoples (v. 3). This calls to mind the eschatological hopes of Isa. 2:2-3 and Mic. 4:1-2, in addition to the New Testament emphasis on the gospel being for all nations.

A global response
(vv. 4-9)

While modern interpreters look at Isaiah's promise through a New Testament lens, we can't ignore the fact that the dispirited exiles would have heard the oracle quite differently.

For Israel, the hoped-for sign of God's appearing would be the return of all the exiles who had been scattered across the known world, so that Jerusalem would once again be populated by the faithful. We recall that, while the leading citizens of Judah had spent about 50 years in Babylon, their kindred from the much larger northern kingdom had fallen to the Assyrians in 722 BCE, and its people had been dispersed to other lands.

Thus, the promise of v. 4 that "your sons" and "your daughters" would return to Jerusalem and draw other nations would have come as welcome news. The image suggests that the peoples among whom the exiles had lived would now treat them as honored guests as they escorted them home. [**Nurses, or guardians?**]

What is more, the exiles would not return empty-handed: the nations would also bring an influx of wealth to Jerusalem, riches that could be used to rebuild the city and restore its glory. "Wealth on the seas" speaks of distant peoples who would travel to Palestine by ship, while "riches of the nations" encompasses all who would come to Jerusalem (v. 5b).

Such good news would cause the grieving Jerusalemites' grieving hearts to tremble and swell, leaving them radiant with joy (v. 5a) – highly appropriate for people who have been bathed in the light of God's presence.

The wealth flooding into Jerusalem would be so great that the city would be inundated with the camels required to carry it all, according to v. 6. But the prophet appears to assign the camels more than a task-bearing role: the beasts appear to come "proclaiming the praise of the LORD"!

Nurses or guardians? While the NRSV says "your daughters shall be carried on their nurses' arms" (v. 4), other translations vary. KJV has "thy daughters shall be nursed at thy side," while NIV reads "your daughters are carried on the arm," and NET has "your daughters are escorted by guardians."

The verb comes from the root *'amn*, from which we get the word "Amen." Its basic meaning is "to confirm" or "to support." In the niphal stem, used here, it carries passive meanings such as "made firm," "confirmed," or "established." In some cases, building on the sense of "support" and when used in conjunction with the word for "side" (or "hip"), it can mean "carried on the hip," which could suggest "carried by a nurse." That is the usage here.

Though the daughters are metaphorically described as infants, returning exiles of both genders would have been of all ages. The diminutive image of infant daughters adds a touch of tenderness to the prophecy. The point is that they are escorted home by the other nations as they followed the light of God's presence in Jerusalem.

Another way to read the text is to assume the subject of "praise" is "all those from Sheba," meaning the merchants would be praising God, not the camels.

This metaphor of animal praise is amplified in the following verse, however, where Isaiah announces to Jerusalem that the "flocks of Kedar" and "rams of Nebaioth" will "serve you" and "go up on my altar with favor" (v. 7).

Kedar and Nebaioth could refer to geographical areas of uncertain location, but more commonly describe tribes from Arabia, where Sheba (from the previous verse) was also located. Arabia was considered to be an area of great riches.

Translators usually gloss over the poet's apparent intent by saying the rams would "be acceptable on my altar" (NRSV) or "be accepted as offerings on my altar" (NIV), but the text suggests that the rams willingly climb the altar to offer themselves as a sacrifice.

The image of animals from foreign lands coming to praise God and offer themselves as sacrifices builds on the theme that all creation will recognize and pay homage to God's presence in Jerusalem.

While vv. 6-7 imagined wealth flowing in from southern and eastern regions, vv. 8-9 look westward to the "coastlands" of the Mediterranean Sea and the "ships of Tarshish" that would bear both long-lost Hebrews and their accumulated wealth back home. Here, the coastlands and the ships do this "for the name of the LORD your God, and for the Holy One of Israel," a further indication that both the earth and inanimate objects would contribute to the praise of God.

Two perspectives

Isaiah's vision of a day when God's presence would bathe Jerusalem and its environs with light, a day when foreigners would escort the exiles home and bring treasure by the boatload and camel load, has yet to occur in a literal sense. Jerusalem remained a rather nondescript place and never regained its former majesty until Herod the Great expanded and enlarged both the city and the temple nearly 500 years later. The temple and much of the city were destroyed again in 70 CE.

For Jewish readers the prophecy remains a matter of hope and promise.

Christian believers who know Matthew's nativity stories, however, see an obvious hint of its fulfillment in the visit of the wise men (Matt. 2:1-12). The magi came from the East (a long journey that would have required them to ride camels), and they brought gifts of gold and incense, precisely what the camels deliver in Isa. 60:6. The purpose of the wise men's visit was to pay respect to one they believed would be king over the Jews – the one whom Christians believe embodied the very epiphany of God.

The Hardest Question
What good does it do?

The prophecy found in Isaiah 60, like other visions of a glorious future when God reigns on earth and all happily worship, has yet to occur – though more than 2,500 years have passed. Should we still expect Isaiah's words to be fulfilled in a literal sense? If not, what good are they?

Isaiah's preaching was designed to bring hope to a despairing people. Surely we understand the importance of hope. Sometimes we encourage each other with assurances that things will get better, at times imagining amazing but unlikely futures, as a way of lifting our hopes. Whether everything turns out as we hope may not be as important as the way hope keeps us going in troubled times.

The late Vaclav Havel, a poet, author, and playwright who became the first president of the Czech Republic, had this to say about hope:

> Hope is a state of mind, not of the world. Either we have hope or we don't; it is a dimension of the soul, and it's not essentially dependent on some particular observation of the world or estimate of the situation. Hope is not prognostication. It is an orientation of the spirit, and orientation of the heart; it transcends the world that is immediately experienced, and is anchored somewhere beyond its horizons ... Hope, in this deep and powerful sense, is not the same as joy that things are going well, or willingness to invest in enterprises that are obviously heading for success, but rather an ability to work for something because it is good, not just because it stands a chance to succeed. The more unpropitious the situation in which we demonstrate hope, the deeper the hope is. Hope is definitely not the same thing as optimism. It is not the conviction that something will turn out well, but the certainty that something makes sense, regardless of how it turns out.
> (from *Disturbing the Peace: A Conversation with Karel Hvížďala* [Knopf, 1990], 181).

Give this quote some thought. How might it help us understand how Isaiah's prophecies could be meaningful, even if they're not fulfilled to the letter?

Epiphany of the Lord
Second Reading
Psalm 72*

Praying for Justice

A similar text, Psalm 72:17, 18-19, is used for the second Sunday of Advent in Year A. A study incorporating all of Psalm 72:1-19 appears in this volume at that point.

Epiphany of the Lord

Third Reading
Ephesians 3:1-13

The Mystery of the Ages

In former generations this mystery was not made known to humankind,
as it has now been revealed to his holy apostles and prophets by the Spirit... (Eph. 3:5)

Do you like mysteries? Many people love nothing better than a week at the beach with a new mystery novel, or watching a dramatic crime drama on TV, or researching a question for which they don't know the answer.

We like to see mysteries solved: whether we're reading Agatha Christie novels, or watching another remake of Sherlock Holmes, or working in a lab in hopes of discovering a cure for cancer, solving the puzzle is part of the appeal.

Our text for the day concerns a mystery that Paul both resolved and explained in his letter to Christians in the city of Ephesus. **[Ephesians]**

A dangerous mystery
(vv. 1-4)

Reading ch. 3 requires some familiarity with previous chapters, for v. 1 begins with "This is the reason that I Paul am a prisoner for Christ Jesus for the sake of you Gentiles" (v. 1).

What does he mean by "this"? The first two chapters of Ephesians reflect on Paul's conviction that God's grace had been made available to Gentiles as well as Jews. Modern readers may have a hard time imagining it being any other way, but most of the Bible was written from a Jewish perspective that divided the world into Jews and everyone else. The Hebrews believed God had called them out through Abraham to live as a special covenant people. Rabbinic Judaism, as developed during the postexilic period, had promoted an increasingly isolationist mindset. **[An exclusive club]**

> **Ephesians:** For more background on Ephesus, see "Digging Deeper" entries for the lesson from Eph. 1:1-14 that appeared earlier in this volume.
> I once found it helpful to write an imaginative short story as a way of introducing this text. It can be found in a collection of similar efforts called *Telling Stories: Tall Tales and Deep Truths* (Smyth & Helwys, 2008), 80-89.

When Jesus came along, he declared that God loved all peoples and that sincere faith in God was more important than rabbinic law. Jesus called upon fellow Jews to accept this new revelation of God and some did, but the religious establishment saw Jesus as more of a threat than a savior.

Paul had been among those who did not accept the legitimacy of Jesus' teaching, and he had led efforts to arrest and punish Jews who had chosen to follow the crucified teacher. This he continued until Jesus stopped him in his tracks on the road to Damascus. Through a blinding vision, Jesus challenged Saul to have faith in him and called him to spend the rest of his life reaching out to the very persons he once had hated: he was to become an apostle to the Gentiles (Acts 9).

> **An exclusive club:** As Judaism developed during the postexilic period, by the first century many Jews believed they were the exclusive inheritors of God's favor. It was possible for Gentiles to convert to Judaism and thus choose to become God's chosen, but it wasn't easy: they had to swear off their past and adopt Jewish customs, including circumcision and the adherence to Jewish rules for living, which the rabbis had expanded considerably.

As Saul began his missionary work, he used the Greek version of his name, Paul. He committed himself to reaching all people, enduring many sufferings and persecutions to proclaim the gospel among the Gentiles. One of his most compelling visions was to foster reconciliation between Jews and Gentiles (described in Ephesians 1). Toward that end, Paul had gone throughout Asia Minor, collecting a relief offering from Gentile churches to aid poor Jews in Jerusalem. Paul hoped that the show of Gentile generosity would encourage Judaism's leaders to be more accepting of Gentiles, so he brought the offering to Jerusalem. While there he used some of his own money to assist several Jewish men in the costly requirements of fulfilling vows they had made (Acts 21:27-36). **[Vows]**

As Paul labored to bring about reconciliation, however, Jewish detractors falsely accused him of breaking the law by bringing Greeks into the temple. They created such a riot that Roman soldiers who kept watch at the temple

took Paul into custody for his own safekeeping. When the Jewish authorities brought formal charges against Paul, the Romans kept him in prison until the charges could be settled. Paul was moved from Jerusalem to Caesarea, then later transported to Rome. This letter may have originated in a prison cell in Rome.

Paul knew that God's inclusion of Gentiles in the kingdom was a radical idea to traditional Jews. To help them understand, he described it as a mystery that had just come to light, one that Jesus had revealed to him along with his commission (vv. 2-4).

A mystery revealed
(vv. 5-6)

Paul declared that the mystery had been unknown to previous generations, but that through divine action it "has now been revealed to his holy apostles and prophets by the Spirit" (v. 5).

And what is the mystery? Paul stated it bluntly: "that is, the Gentiles have become fellow heirs, members of the same body, and sharers in the promise of Christ Jesus through the gospel" (v. 6).

Lest anyone harbor notions that God accepted Gentile believers as anything less than Jews, Paul spells it out in three ways, using three words that employ the same prefix, *sun-*, which means something akin to "together with." **[Shape shifter]**

First, Gentile believers "have become fellow heirs" – they could jointly share in all that it meant to be "heirs of salvation" and all the blessings that come with it. The word Paul uses for "joint heirs" is *sugklēronoma*, the same word he uses elsewhere to describe Christians as heirs of God and joint heirs with Christ – inheritors of all the good blessings God has in store (Rom. 8:17; Gal. 3:29, 4:7).

Second, Gentile believers are "members of the same body." The word Paul used to describe this (*sussōma*) is not found anywhere else in the New Testament, in the LXX, or in Greek classical literature, so it is likely that Paul coined the word himself by combining *sun-* with the word for "body" (*sōma*) to suggest that Jewish and Gentile believers are "co-bodied" or "bodied with" one another.

A heart, lung, or kidney transplant patient receives organs that originated with other persons, but they all become part of one body that functions well if the host

---

Vows: In early Jewish life, vows consisted of conditional promises to God that were considered sacred. In a vow, a person asked God for something, and promised that if God provided, he or she would give something to God in return. Hannah, for instance, asked God for a son and promised to return him to God (1 Sam. 1:1-11). Israelites traveling from Egypt promised that if God would give them victory over the Canaanite king of Arad, they would devote all the spoil to God and keep nothing for themselves (Num. 21:1-3). It was also possible to promise that one would respond to answered prayer with a public testimony, or by living as a Nazirite for a certain period of time.

A number of rules governed the practice of vow-making (see Leviticus 22 and Numbers 30). Among these was a requirement that persons were not released from their vow until they had not only given to God what was promised, but had also offered certain sacrifices at the temple – a practice that could be costly. In the first century additional requirements had been added, including the shaving of one's head at the temple, for which there was a fee. The process could be expensive, and it was considered a virtuous act of charity for someone with means to pay the cost of sacrifices for persons who had made vows. This is what Paul was doing in Acts 21: he was completing rites for a personal vow, but also footing the bill for four other Jewish men who had made vows. His attempt at building bridges backfired when certain Jews from Asia wrongly accused him of bringing Greeks into the temple. They stirred up an angry mob, and the Romans originally took Paul into custody for his own protection.

Shape shifter: The Greek prefix *sun-* may change its form based on which consonant or syllable it is attached to (note: some Greek scholars prefer to transliterate the *upsilon* as *y* rather than *u*). Thus, in the three "together with" words Paul uses in v. 6, *sun-* appears first as *sug-*, then as *sus-*, then as *sum-*. In each case, the meaning is the same, but the final letter *nu* shifts to a different form to facilitate pronunciation.

body doesn't reject the new implants. Fighting rejection is a challenge for modern medicine, and it was a struggle in the early church for Jews to accept Gentiles as full participants within the body of God's chosen people.

Third, Gentiles could become "sharers in the promise in Christ Jesus." Here the word is *summétochos*, which suggests a partnership in which people share everything equally. Both Jews and Gentiles have equal access to every promise that comes through the gospel – the good news of Jesus Christ.

A mystery proclaimed
(vv. 7-13)

It was that gospel, Paul said, that called him into God's service (v. 7). Paul was clearly proud of what he had accomplished, but described himself as "the very least of all the saints," thinking of his calling as a gift of grace that allowed him to bring the good news of "the boundless riches of Christ" to the Gentiles (v. 8), revealing "the mystery hidden for ages in God who created all things" (v. 9).

Don't we enjoy being the bearer of good news? As children or even adults, we may have competed to be the first to share some bit of happy tidings with others. Paul thought it a gift of grace that God allowed him to be a pioneer among those who brought the good news of Christ to the Gentiles.

The hoped-for result, Paul said, was that "through the church the wisdom of God in its rich variety might now be made known to the rulers and authorities in the heavenly places" (v. 10). By "rulers and authorities in the heavenly places," Paul was referencing a common first-century belief that angelic or demonic powers existed in various heavenly spheres between God and the earth.

Modern believers are less likely to think of angels and demons ruling among the planets, but can appreciate Paul's grand point that the mystery of the gospel has come

full circle: in a light from heaven, the Spirit revealed it to Paul (3:3), and then to "apostles and prophets" (3:5), who helped carry the message to all people (3:9), who would create such a church that even the heavenly "rulers and authorities" could see what God was up to (3:10).

The mystery was no new thing, Paul said, but "in accordance with the eternal purpose" that God had carried out through Jesus (v. 11), enabling all people to "have access to God in boldness and confidence through faith in him" (v. 12). Paul gladly declared that it was no longer a mystery.

The privilege of sharing such good news was a continual comfort to Paul even in the face of hardship and imprisonment. Readers should not "lose heart over my sufferings," he said. Paul considered his own sufferings to be for the sake of those who came to believe, and thus well worth the price: "they are your glory" (v. 13).

This was Paul's message: through the mystery of the ages, God had a plan to put the fractured peoples of the world back together again by including *everyone* who wanted to belong in the kingdom. That was the good news: God's love extends to all people, no matter what we have done or what bad habits we have. We are included, even if we don't yet know much about the Bible or have all our questions answered – and we never will in this life. We're included because God's love extends to all humankind.

As newly accepted people of God, Jesus' family of faith is called to spread that good news in both word and deed, confident that God's grace and love are sufficient for our present and our future.

The mystery has been revealed: God's love extends to every person, including each of us.

The Hardest Question
Who are the "rulers and authorities"?

To understand v. 10, we must understand that Paul was speaking of an ancient understanding of the cosmos. Before Copernicus figured out that the earth orbits the sun – in the 15th century – people generally believed that the earth existed as the unmoving center of the universe.

The creation story of Genesis 1 describes a dome-like structure called "the firmament" over the earth, with the sun, moon, and planets following set paths across the sky, then traveling beneath the earth to come back around.

By the first century CE, especially within the Roman world, many people believed that the earth was at the bottom of a complex structure of up to seven "spheres" in which the heavenly bodies moved around the earth, with each sphere being governed by supernatural beings described with terms such as "rulers and principalities" or "authorities in the heavenly realms."

God was thought to inhabit "the highest heaven," which existed above the other spheres. The "rulers and principalities" were thought to be both good and evil, aware of life on earth and capable of affecting it. In some belief systems, one could only gain the highest heaven by advancing through the other spheres. A popular teaching called Gnosticism, for example, taught that one must gain the knowledge of certain mysteries in order to pass by the various rulers and authorities and move toward the highest heaven.

Paul spoke from the context of this popular understanding of the universe, arguing that Christ had defeated all evil powers through his crucifixion and resurrection, so that they had no further authority over humans who have trusted in Christ. For example, Paul questioned the Colossians: "If with Christ you died to the elemental spirits of the universe, why do you live as if you still belonged to the world? Why do you submit to regulations, 'Do not handle, Do not taste, Do not touch?' All these regulations refer to things that perish with use; they are simply human commands and teachings. These have indeed an appearance of wisdom in promoting self-imposed piety, humility, and severe treatment of the body, but they are of no value in checking self-indulgence" (Col. 2:20-23).

We find similar ideas in Ephesians, where Paul spoke of God's power to save: "God put this power to work in Christ when he raised him from the dead and seated him at his right hand in the heavenly places, far above all rule and authority and power and dominion, and above every name that is named, not only in this age but also in the age to come" (Eph. 1:20-21). Though Christ had defeated them, Paul taught, Christians must still confront the powers: "For our struggle is not against enemies of blood and flesh, but against the rulers, against the authorities, against the cosmic powers of this present darkness, against the spiritual forces of evil in the heavenly places" (Eph. 6:12).

Modern believers are not bound to accept the same worldview as the ancients. Our view of the universe has vastly changed, as we understand the earth to be part of a solar system that moves within a galaxy containing billions of stars, among billions of other galaxies. We may no longer need to believe we are separated from God by heavenly spheres inhabited by "elemental spirits," but we can recognize that endemic systems of evil within our own society – such as racism, sexism, and economic injustice – are still an impediment to the ideals of the kingdom, and the witness of the church has power to fight them.

Epiphany of the Lord
Fourth Reading
Matthew 2:1-12*

Meaningful Gifts

On entering the house, they saw the child with Mary his mother; and they knelt down and paid him homage. Then, opening their treasure chests, they offered him gifts of gold, frankincense, and myrrh. (Matt. 2:11)

In the early days of the new year, as we come back to an even keel from the highs and lows of Christmas and post-Christmas and New Year's Eve and back-to-back bowl games, the season of Epiphany calls us back to the Christ child, and in particular to the story of the "wise men" who came to pay him homage.

They brought gifts, as we recall, gifts that inspired the tradition of Christmas gift giving that has pushed the baby Jesus aside and become the primary focus of Christmas in our culture.

Gifts can be valuable, but the most expensive gifts are not necessarily the most meaningful. You may have received amazing gifts that could not be put in a box and were not under the tree. The love of our family is a gift, as is the kindness of friends. But this season reminds us of the greatest gift, of how God came to us through Jesus Christ, a child born to be our Savior. The first Bible verse many of us learn says "God so loved the world, that he *gave* his only begotten son, that whosoever believeth on him should not perish, but have everlasting life" (John 3:16, KJV).

A rising star
(vv. 1-2)

But let's return to those wise men. We begin with an awareness that many of our ideas about them are based far more on imagination and tradition than on the scriptural record, which tells us very little. There is nothing, for example, to suggest that the wise men were kings, as

---

Wise kings? The tradition that the wise men were kings arose from the early church's very loose association of Isa. 60:1-3 with their magi's visit. In its original context, the postexilic prophet who contributed to the book of Isaiah acknowledged Israel's distress and predicted that God would have more glorious things in store. The prophecy came to be associated with the arrival of a future messiah:

"Arise, shine; for your light has come, and the glory of the LORD has risen upon you. For darkness shall cover the earth, and thick darkness the peoples; but the LORD will arise upon you, and his glory will appear over you. Nations shall come to your light, and kings to the brightness of your dawn."

The prophecy does not speak of a specific ruler, but of a transcendent Israel that would attract other nations to come and learn the ways of God. The text goes on to insist that the kings of surrounding nations would come bearing gifts including camels and flocks, plus gold and frankincense (Isa. 60:4-7).

---

they're portrayed in the popular carol "We Three Kings of Orient Are." **[Wise kings]**

The text doesn't even call them "wise men," using the ordinary words, but refers to them as *magoi*, commonly translated as "magi." The Greek term is also the root of the word "magic." Then as now, astrologers who look for portents in the stars were popularly associated with sorcery or magical powers.

The magi were a class of scholars who labored, often within royal courts, as astronomers and astrologers, as observers and catalogers of the natural order. They were, to a degree, the scientists of the ancient world.

This text can also be used for the second Sunday after Christmas in some traditions.

A careful reading shows that most manger scenes ever constructed are almost certainly wrong, because Matthew clearly implies that the magi did not arrive in Bethlehem until up to two years after Jesus was born. Matthew's version does not mention a census, a journey from Nazareth, or a birth in a manger; it appears to assume that Bethlehem was Mary and Joseph's home. When the magi came calling, their destination was a house (*oikía*).

An old church tradition assigns the names Gaspar, Melchior, and Balthazar to the magi, but we really have no way of knowing. Another tradition says they came from Parthia, the general area of Iran. The text says only that they were from "the East," which could have implied anywhere from Mesopotamia to Arabia.

Again, tradition holds that there were three wise men, but Matthew says only that they brought three gifts, leading to an assumption that there were three of them. There could have been just two, or a dozen.

Whatever their number, names, or place of origin, the author said the men had journeyed far to visit the child, because "We observed his star at its rising and have come to pay him homage" (v. 2). [A star is born]

A star is born: How did the magi come to associate the rising of a star with a prediction of a king born in Israel? They would not have been Jews, of course, and probably did not have access to the writings that came to be regarded as Hebrew Scripture. They did not know, for example, about Micah's prediction that a future ruler would be born in Bethlehem.

They may or may not have known stories associated with Balaam, a man who lived east of Israel and was widely known as a shaman or sorcerer. When the people of Israel were passing through on their way from Egypt to Canaan, the king of Moab hired Balaam to curse them. God would not allow it, requiring Balaam to speak a blessing over Israel instead. The oracular blessing found in Num. 24:15-19 included a prophecy that "a star shall come out of Jacob, and a scepter shall rise out of Israel …" (Num. 24:17b).

In its context, the oracle predicted Israelite mastery over Moab and other nearby peoples, but the poetic assertion that "a star shall come out of Jacob and a scepter shall rise out of Israel" was later interpreted as a messianic prophecy. Although "star" and "scepter" are clearly metaphors, some early believers saw an association between a rising star and Jesus' birth.

Many inquiring individuals have searched for evidence of a supernova or planetary conjunction that might fit the time frame of Jesus' birth, generally thought to be between 6 and 4 BCE. While some arguments are appealing, we cannot firmly identify any celestial phenomenon that attracted their attention.

A paranoid king
(vv. 3-8)

To find the future king, the travelers first visited the current monarch: Herod. Also known as "Herod the Great" because of his extensive building programs, Herod was known as a cruel and suspicious man who never hesitated to kill anyone who got in his way, including his own family members.

There's no way of pretending that Herod was a nice man, though he might have argued that he only did what was required to remain in power. When the magi came to ask the whereabouts of a newborn Jewish king, his suspicions were raised to a fever pitch. The NRSV says he was "frightened," but the root word more commonly means "disturbed" (NIV11, HCSB) or "troubled" (NAS95). NET has "alarmed."

Herod's distress, Matthew wrote, extended to "all Jerusalem." Perhaps we are to assume that the magi did not go to the palace first, but had asked about the city for information about a new king, leading to public curiosity and possible celebrations, which Herod might have dealt with harshly, troubling the city.

Apparently, Herod found a way to stall the magi, perhaps by offering them a bath and a bed, then called for the Jewish priests and scribes. He quizzed them to learn if there were Hebrew prophecies dealing with a new king, and they responded with a quotation from Mic. 5:2 that spoke of one who would be born in Bethlehem and become "a ruler who shall shepherd my people Israel" (v. 6).

Herod sent the priests away and "secretly" summoned the magi to question them concerning the precise time they had seen the portentous star. Having gained that information – which he would later use to order the murder of every boy baby in Bethlehem under two years old (vv. 16-18) – Herod sent the magi to Bethlehem with instructions to return with news of what they had found, "so that I may also go and pay him homage" (v. 8).

A mad king: Herod was ethnically an Idumean – meaning his ancestors were from Edom – but his family had been forcibly converted to Judaism when the Maccabees led the Jews to a period of relative independence in the mid-second century BCE, beginning a short-lived dynasty of the Hasmonean family.

After the Romans regained control of Israel some years later, Herod's father Antipater managed to win enough favor to get himself named king, and his son after him. Later, Herod inherited Galilee while his brother Phasael was appointed ruler of Judea. Phasael soon lost the land to a Parthian force, but in 37 BCE, after a three-year struggle, Herod overthrew the Parthian-appointed Antigonus II. The Romans allowed him to add Judea to his kingdom.

Herod was a master politician, siding with Mark Antony as long as it was beneficial, then switching allegiance to Octavian after Antony and Cleopatra were defeated.

To curry favor with the Jews, Herod married a young Hasmonean princess named Mariamne, fathering two sons, Alexander and Aristobulus. As he grew old and sick and increasingly mistrustful, Herod had all three of them executed, along with Mariamne's mother, Alexandra. Herod had 10 wives and 15 children altogether, making for a complicated and conflicted family life. He was suspicious to the end: just five days before he died, Herod ordered that Antipater, his oldest son, be put to death.

Herod suffered from a disease that made his last few years miserable. He died in 4 BCE, and was buried just south of Jerusalem at a fortress he had built for himself and named Herodium.

No one would want to receive the sort of "homage" that Herod would offer. [**A mad king**]

A memorable visit

(vv. 9-12)

Once the wise men departed Jerusalem for Bethlehem, just six miles to the south, the same star that had instigated their journey reappeared, leading them until it stopped "over the place where the child was" (v. 9). The image of a moving star may suggest that star was a temporary vision or image, divinely created, rather than a celestial phenomenon.

Little is said about the magi's visit. They were overcome with joy, Matthew said (v. 10). They entered the house and saw Jesus with Mary. If Joseph was present, Matthew's source does not say. The magi knelt before the baby and "paid homage" to him (v. 11a, NRSV), or

"worshiped him" (NET, NIV11, HCSB). The verb translated as "knelt down" actually means "to fall," which could suggest that they fell on their faces before the baby, though that seems unlikely.

The visitors' intention was probably not to "worship" the baby so much as to pay respects. The magi were not Jews, and would have worshiped the gods of their home country. Since they typically worked within royal courts, their visit would have had diplomatic overtones. As ancient visitors typically bowed in the presence of a ruling king, the wise men's respectful appearance before the child probably had this purpose. Nothing other than the terminology "pay homage/worship" suggests that they thought of the baby as divine: They saw him as a future king with whom good relations for their country would be important.

We have more clarity regarding the gifts the magi brought. We can't know if each of the men brought a gift, as popularly portrayed, or if they collectively delivered the contents of a chest or saddlebag. In either case, the gifts consisted of gold, frankincense, and myrrh. None would have been overly large.

The gift of gold needs little explanation. Gold is a traditional symbol of royalty, and a fitting gift for one who would be king. The story insists that the wise men believed Jesus was born to be king of the Jews, and this gift endorsed their belief.

The second gift was frankincense, an aromatic spice that had various uses. In some circles, it symbolized immortality. Perhaps the wise men were expressing a wish that the future king would enjoy a lengthy reign.

The last gift was myrrh, a more puzzling choice. Myrrh has a strong spicy scent, and its most common use was as a burial spice. Why bring a bag or box of burial spices to a baby boy? Perhaps it was a traditional gift in their country. Perhaps it was simply something valuable and easily portable that Joseph could sell for cash when needed. It is unlikely that the magi would have understood the gift as a foreboding symbol of the suffering Christ would face, though later believers assigned it such significance.

The saddest thing about the story of the wise men is that we cannot read it without its context, remembering that the wise men unwittingly put King Herod on the trail of a new king reportedly born in Bethlehem. They were divinely warned to depart by another way rather than reporting to Herod (v. 12), as was the holy family (vv. 13-15). Nevertheless, their whereabouts became known to the paranoid king, who ordered the slaughter of every baby boy under two years old throughout the entire town of Bethlehem and the country around it (vv. 16-18).

Even the giving of God's best gifts does not guarantee that life will be easy, that evil will not exist, that wicked people will not do bad things, that the innocent will not suffer.

Life is like that. Our greatest joys can be tempered with sorrow, but the Christmas story helps us to realize that they are all of a piece. As C.S. Lewis wrote in *Surprised by Joy*, sorrow and happiness are two sides of the same coin. The laughter we share now will be remembered in mourning later: we wouldn't feel sorrow if we have not known joy.

The gift of God in Christ and the tragic aftermath of the magi's visit helps us to realize that life is not a dress rehearsal, but the real thing. There is both joy and pain for all, but the gift of God in Jesus Christ gives us assurance that we are not alone in this life, and hope for a life beyond this one in which pain has passed, and every tear will be wiped away.

The Hardest Question
How do we explain the Christmas star?

Matthew says that the same star that had alerted the wise men to the birth of a king suddenly reappeared after they left Herod, leading them directly to Jesus. This leads us to ask what sort of "star" could have moved about and stopped over a particular house – but that's one of many questions we can't answer.

Those who look for known events to correlate with biblical stories have pointed to any number of stellar conjunctions, comets, or the occasional supernova as explanations for the Christmas star, but none of those can explain Matthew's contention that the star moved ahead of the magi and stopped directly over the house where Jesus could be found.

Such a "star" – or bright light that appeared as a star – has no physical explanation that we know of. Perhaps we are to imagine that God sent an angel to guide the magi, and they perceived its bright light as a star.

More likely, perhaps we are to think of the star as a visionary phenomenon revealed to the magi alone. If a literal star-like light had been moving about over the countryside and hanging low enough to mark a specific house, we'd expect great crowds to have noticed and followed it, leaving no opportunity for the magi to have a quiet visit with Mary and the child.

In particular, we'd expect that Herod's henchmen would have been alerted to watch for anything unusual in Bethlehem. If a moving star that marked a house had been visible to all, they would not have missed it, and the night would have had no happy ending.

In the end, we must admit that the Christmas star is one of many things in the biblical record that must rest in the arms of faith.

First Sunday after Epiphany
First Reading
Isaiah 42:1-9

A Time for Justice

Here is my servant, whom I uphold, my chosen, in whom my soul delights;
I have put my spirit upon him; he will bring forth justice to the nations. (Isa. 42:1)

An old saying holds that good preaching should "afflict the comfortable and comfort the afflicted." Do you experience (or provide) that in your church? Biblical prophecy provides a helpful model of such proclamation, and a prime example is the book of Isaiah, which spoke to Israel in times of both security and distress.

God's servant

Events and life-situations described in the book of Isaiah reflect at least three distinct settings: The book begins in Judah during the eighth century BCE, shifts to Babylon during the sixth-century exile, and concludes with the Jews back in Jerusalem following the exile. As different challenges arose during this extensive period, at least two or three different prophets preached in the name of Isaiah, addressing needs that arose in their varying historical contexts. [**Multiple Isaiahs?**]

Isaiah 42 falls within a section commonly known as "Second Isaiah." Isaiah of Jerusalem, responsible for much of Isaiah 1–39, preached during the eighth century, when the wealthy and powerful were comfortable and in need of affliction. He promised judgment if the people did not repent and change their ways. Judgment came when the powerful Babylonians conquered Judah, destroyed Jerusalem, and marched many of its citizens into exile.

> **Multiple Isaiahs?** A more detailed discussion of Isaiah's authors can be found in "Digging Deeper" notes for the Epiphany lesson from Isa. 60:1-6 and the Second Sunday after Christmas lesson from Isa. 62:6-12, in this volume.

> **Servant Songs:** The "Servant Songs" are often identified as Isa. 42:1-4, 49:1-6, 50:1-11, and 52:13–53:12, but scholars disagree on their precise limits. Some, for example, consider the first song to be comprised of Isa. 42:1-4 only, while others see it as 42:1-7 and others stretch it to 42:1-9. The second song is often delimited as 49:1-6, but some scholars see it continuing through v. 13. Some identify the third song as 50:1-11, but others include only 50:4-11. There is little question about the limits of the fourth song, marked as 52:13–53:12. Some scholars interpret Isaiah 55 as a fifth servant song.

During the latter years of the exile, when the people had suffered judgment and were bogged down in Babylon, a prophet in the model of Isaiah began to preach, offering hope to a bedraggled people who may have wondered if they would ever see their homeland again. Commonly known as "Second Isaiah," his message is found in chs. 40–55. His preaching included four poems commonly called "Servant Songs," the first of which is this week's text. [**Servant Songs**]

A song of justice
(vv. 1-4)

People understand the power of armies, force, and control. When ancient prophets spoke of better days and a restoration for Israel, many imagined that a military messiah such as David would arise and lead them to conquer their enemies in battle. Some prophecies seem to speak of this type of king, including oracles in Isaiah (chs. 9, 11). They speak of a coming king who would be great and would bring peace to the earth, but they say little about how he would accomplish the task. Many assumed that the deliverer would be a military messiah.

They were wrong.

Isaiah of the exile speaks of a coming ruler as God's *servant*: "Here is my servant, whom I uphold, my chosen, in whom my soul delights; I have put my spirit upon him; he will bring forth justice to the nations" (v. 1).

That one sentence packs a lot of information. First, the coming one is to be God's servant. It was not uncommon for prophets to describe Israel as God's servant people, or to criticize them for being prideful and self-indulgent, rather than living humbly before God.

Hebrew poetry is based on repetition, often using parallel statements for emphasis or explanation. Here, "my chosen" is parallel to "my servant," underscoring God's intentional choice of the servant. Likewise, "in whom my soul delights" parallels "whom I uphold." God would not only support the servant, but also take delight in doing so.

The second couplet of the verse describes how God would empower the servant: "I have put my spirit upon him," and the end result of their work, that "he will bring forth justice to the nations."

The Hebrew word underlying "spirit" literally means "breath" or "wind." The scriptures speak of rare individuals who experienced the power of the "spirit of the LORD" (*ruah-Yahweh*); people such as Gideon (Judg. 6:34), Samson (Judg. 13:25), Saul (1 Sam. 10:10), and David (1 Sam. 16:13).

The spirit of the LORD came upon such people during times of oppression, empowering them to prevail over Israel's enemies and, ideally, to restore justice. In Hebrew, the idea of justice (*mishpat*) is more than a legal concept. True justice involves faithfulness to God and fairness toward others. To bring justice is not just to make sure all people get what they deserve, but to ensure that everyone has what they need. The text literally says that the servant will "make justice go out to the nations."

While the first verse might lead hearers to expect a spirit-emboldened warrior-servant like David, the next two indicate that he would not bring justice through ruthless force, but with gentle tenderness toward the "bruised reed" and "smoldering wick," graphic references to a weak and downtrodden people. The exiles were like wetland reeds that had been bent but were not dead, or a smoldering

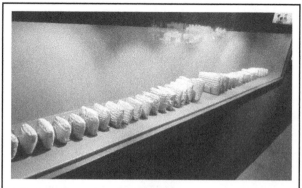

Life in exile: While we often think of the exiles as facing great suffering, their most serious loss was their homeland. A variety of cuneiform texts from ancient Babylon attests that the Babylonians provided regular rations for the Hebrews, assigned them places to live, and allowed them to participate in regular commerce. For an interesting recap of these, see Laurie E. Pearce, "How Bad Was the Babylonian Exile?" *Biblical Archaeology Review* 43:5 (Sept.-Oct. 2016), 48-64.

An informative collection of cuneiform tablets describes commercial activities of Jews living in various places in Babylon, including a settlement known as "Judah-town." Pictured here from a display at the Bible Lands Museum in Jerusalem in 2015, they include records of business deals made by the Jewish family of Samak-Yama, including his son, grandson, and his grandson's five sons. A brief video of the exhibit can be found at http://www.reuters.com/article/us-israel-archaeology-babylon-idUSKBN0L71EK20150203. Photo courtesy of Wikimedia Commons.

flame that has not died out (vv. 2-3). The servant would encourage them appropriately. [**Life in exile**]

Such words would have been comforting to the people of Israel, who remembered proud traditions of having once been a great nation. As Isaiah of the exile proclaimed God's word, he recognized their weakened, wounded, and uncertain condition. The servant would understand the needs of his people and bring justice coupled with tenderness.

Believers in our own time might become more compassionate people and more effective servants for Christ if we could begin to understand that justice involves far more than getting – or giving to someone – what they deserve. God's justice is always tempered by grace to offer what people need most. Often, their greatest need is forgiveness. Sadly, even those who delight most in singing "Amazing Grace" can be remarkably stingy when it comes to extending grace to others.

One might think a servant who is characterized by gentleness might be weak or easily defeated, but Isaiah insisted that "He will not grow faint or be crushed until he has established justice in the earth" (v. 4a). The servant's justice would involve more than the liberation of Israel: it would pervade the entire world.

The promise of justice is good news for any people. The expectation that "the coastlands wait for his teaching" (v. 4b) extends hope that the servant's work would extend beyond Israel to the coastlands on either side, and beyond. In the ancient world, where few people traveled far, a seafaring journey to "the coastlands" expressed a thought not unlike "to the ends of the earth."

A call from God
(vv. 5-9)

With v. 5, the divine speech shifts from a third person description of what the servant would do to a direct address from God: "Thus says God, the LORD," the one who created the heavens, the earth, and the people upon it. [**The God**]

Some scholars see this as a wholly different oracle, while others perceive it as a continuation of the song. The God who has created all things speaks in v. 6: "I am the LORD, I have called you in righteousness, I have taken you by the hand and kept you; I have given you as a covenant to the people, a light to the nations …"

Who is God addressing in these verses? The pronoun "you" is singular, and some see vv. 5-9 as a direct address to the servant. John D.W. Watts has argued that the "servant" in this case is Cyrus, the Persian king who would soon conquer Babylon and set the Israelites free (*Isaiah 34–66*, vol. 25, Word Biblical Commentary [Zondervan, 2005], 660).

Others judge that the oracle addresses the people of Judah and Israel. John Goldingay notes: "The last singular 'you' was Jacob-Israel in 41:8-16, who has presumably been the implicit addressee throughout. In other words, in verses 1-4 God was saying to Jacob-Israel, 'You know you are my servants? Well, this is what my servant is destined to be and do'" (*Isaiah*, Understanding the Bible Commentary Series [Baker Books, 2012], 241).

Since neither Cyrus nor the Hebrew people fully carried out the commission given in vv. 6-7, later Jewish

> **The God:** Isaiah 42:5 is unusual in that it refers to God (here called *'El*) with the direct article attached: *ha'ēl yhwh* means "the God, Yahweh," an apparent affirmation of the monotheistic belief that there is only one God, Israel's God, whose name was revealed as Yahweh. This is one of the earliest clear statements of monotheism. Assertions such as the first commandment insist that Israel should have no other gods before Yahweh, and earlier prophets and priests pleaded for the people to worship Yahweh rather than the Baals or other gods, but the eighth-century prophets may have been the first to insist that Yahweh was not just the mightiest God and the one Israel should worship, but the only true god.

interpreters moved the message forward and pictured the one addressed as a future messiah. Early Christians believed Jesus to be that messiah, one who came as "a light to the nations, to open the eyes that are blind, to bring out the prisoners from the dungeon, from the prison those who sit in darkness" (vv. 6b-7). Note the similarity of this text to Isa. 61:1-2, which Jesus cited as a sort of mission statement in Luke 4:16-21 – adding "recovery of sight to the blind" to the release of prisoners, a combination found in Isa. 42:7, but not in Isa. 61:1-2.

The passage closes with an affirmation of Yahweh's identity as the only true god, the one who controls the earth's destiny, and who can declare "new things … before they spring forth" (vv. 8-9).

The first Servant Song speaks of one chosen and empowered by God to bring about justice, not by rude power, but by gentle grace. It expresses a hope that begins in every hurting, wounded heart, and it extends as far as the mind can imagine.

The people of Israel saw this as a mystery wrapped in a riddle. The people of Christ see it as the foretelling of one who could die on a cross but not be crushed by it, one who would rise even beyond the grave to establish justice through all the earth.

Though Christ-followers focus on the Suffering Servant they see in Jesus, there remains a corporate aspect to the text: if Christ's justice is to extend throughout the earth, it will be through the gracious and compassionate presence of Christ's persistent followers.

The Hardest Question
Who was the "servant" in the Servant Songs?

Who did Isaiah have in mind when speaking of this servant? The answer is not as obvious as one would like, as the various texts do not always refer to the servant in the same way, and may not always have the same concept in mind.

Early on, Israel's rabbis interpreted the songs as predictions of the hoped-for Davidic messiah, tending to discount the aspects of suffering. After Jesus' life and ministry, New Testament writers described Jesus as a new and different kind of messiah ("Christ," like "Messiah," means "anointed one"). They embraced the suffering of the servant as a foreshadowing of Christ's afflictions in bringing about redemption for humankind.

The servant sometimes seems to be Jacob-Israel in a corporate sense. The book of Isaiah often uses language similar to that of the Servant Songs to describe Israel as a whole: "But you, Israel, my servant, Jacob, whom I have chosen" (41:8), or "But now hear, O Jacob my servant, Israel whom I have chosen" (44:1; see also 44:21; 45:4; 49:3, 5-6). Today, many Jewish and some Christian scholars also think of the servant as describing the corporate personality of the Israelites, who suffered on the way to becoming a cleansed and better people. Some have argued that the prophet saw himself as the servant, standing in for the people.

It is possible to see Isaiah's prophecy as multivalent: God's challenge to Jacob-Israel might be fulfilled in different ways by all Israel, or by a lone servant playing a particular role. Some scholars even see the servant in 42:1-9 as Cyrus, the Persian king who would conquer Babylon and set the Israelites free. Isaiah calls Cyrus by name and calls him God's shepherd who will carry out his purpose (44:28), and even God's "anointed" or *meshiach* (45:1), the same word that became "messiah."

For the most part, Isaiah seems to portray Jacob-Israel as God's intended servant, though the people are disinclined or unable to fulfill their calling. Thus, another must stand in for them and carry out the mission the people have failed to accomplish.

New Testament writers saw Jesus as the ultimate "servant of Yahweh" who fulfilled the purpose Isaiah described. Matthew 12:18-21 connects the ministry of Jesus with the fulfillment of Isa. 42:1-4, and Philip explained to an Ethiopian seeker that Jesus was the suffering servant described in Isa. 53:7-8 (Acts 8:26-35). It is likely that Jesus, who introduced his ministry with a quotation from Isa. 61:1-2 (Luke 4:16-20), saw Isaiah's "Suffering Servant" as a model for his life and ministry. Indeed, the disciples might never have understood Jesus if not for Isaiah's servant imagery. Even with that scriptural testimony, they struggled long and hard to understand a God who suffered.

Verses from the Servant Songs are quoted verbatim eight times in the New Testament, and apparent allusions to the texts are found another 18 times.

In sum, from Isaiah's perspective, God had chosen the Hebrews to live in covenant as God's representative in the world, living obediently as a light to the nations, calling others to trust in Yahweh, too. Through the centuries, it became apparent that Jacob-Israel (indicating the two kingdoms of Judah and Israel) was either incapable or unwilling to live out that calling. The servant in Isaiah, then, can be seen both as the corporate people and as the one who would ultimately accomplish what they could not.

First Sunday after Epiphany

Second Reading
Psalm 29*

A Prayer for Peace

May the LORD give strength to his people! May the LORD bless his people with peace! (Ps. 29:11)

Most of us know what it is like to stand on the ocean's shore, on a mountain peak, or beneath a powerful waterfall – and to feel very small as we contemplate the incredible scope and splendor of creation. If a major thunderstorm should catch us there, we would feel even smaller.

Thunderstorms are powerful, fearsome, and dangerous. Lightning, wind, and flooding can wreak widespread destruction, and there is nothing we can do to stop them. The best we can do is seek shelter, ponder the awesomeness of nature's fury, and wait for the storm to pass so peace might return.

The Hebrews, like other ancient peoples, associated storms with divine power. Polytheistic cultures usually identified one member of their pantheon as the weather god. Because the land's fertility depended on regular rains, they gave extra attention to gods thought to control the weather.

Many of Israel's closest neighbors worshipped weather-related gods. The Sumerians honored Isshkub as the storm god, while the Assyrians called their weather god Adad (or Addu), and the Hurrians named theirs Tesshub. The Syrians worshiped Hadad as the god of storms, and most familiar to Bible readers, the Canaanites believed that Baal was the power behind thunder, lightning, and rain.

While the church's season of Epiphany is designed mainly to commemorate the manifestation of Christ to the Gentiles, lectionary texts also reflect the manifestation of God's power and presence in other ways – as in powerful storms as an aspect of creation.

The author of Psalm 29 celebrated a belief that Yahweh controlled all aspects of nature as well as the lives of humans. The psalm testifies that a God who can wreak havoc with the weather is also capable of bringing peace amid all the storms of life.

A call to worship
(vv. 1-2)

The psalm was likely sung as a hymn in worship, led by a priest or designated singer standing before the congregation on a Sabbath or festival day. The psalm may have been performed as a solo, or possibly chanted one line at the time, with the people repeating it in a "call and response" fashion.

In the opening verse, the psalmist calls not only the earthly congregation to worship – but surprisingly also invites the heavenly court to join Israel in praising Yahweh's glorious attributes. [**Heavenly beings**]

The first three lines begin with the same phrase, "Ascribe to the LORD," a call to acknowledge God's

---

Heavenly beings: Ancient Near Eastern peoples commonly believed that earthly events were directed by a heavenly council of gods, presided over by the chief god. For the Canaanites, the chief god was El. For the Babylonians, it was Marduk. The Israelites also envisioned a heavenly council, but in a different fashion: in their minds the council was composed of angelic "sons of God," presided over by Yahweh, who had created them along with everything else in heaven and earth.

Psalm 29 is also used for the first Sunday of Epiphany in Years B and C, and for Trinity Sunday in Year B.

majesty as an act of worship. The pattern of "incremental repetition" is characteristic of older Hebrew poetry such as the Song of Deborah in Judges 5, suggesting that this might be one of Israel's oldest psalms.

The word translated "worship" is a specialized term that means to bow down or prostrate oneself in humility before God. Here, it means to praise God's "glory and strength," and "the glory of his name." The root meaning of the word translated "glory" is "heaviness," which leads to the idea of glory or majesty.

To worship the LORD "in holy splendor" (v. 2) could possibly mean "in holy attire," suggesting that one be properly dressed for the occasion. Since the prior emphasis has been on God, however, the phrase more likely refers to divine grandeur. We are called to worship the LORD who is characterized by holy splendor.

A God who speaks with thunder
(vv. 3-9)

Have you ever watched a thunderstorm approaching over an ocean or lake? With v. 3 the psalmist praises God's "voice" that is heard in thunder, first "over the waters … over mighty waters." One may envision a thundercloud building offshore, visible for a great distance, booming over the ocean waves before washing ashore. Land to the east of Israel is mostly desert, so thunderstorms typically come from the West, sweeping in from the Mediterranean Sea.

Readers might also imagine the large Sea of Galilee as the locus of a storm. The "sea" is a large, harp-shaped lake about 13 miles long and seven miles wide. It is located at 700 feet below sea level with mountains both east and west, where a wind tunnel effect can produce huge waves and frightful conditions when storms arise.

The verse may have a more metaphorical intent, however: the ancients thought of the sea as great waters of chaos that had to be restrained by the gods. The scriptures acknowledged Yahweh's power to control the seas, especially in creation, where God's spirit brooded over the waters (Gen. 1:2), created a dome-like "firmament" to separate the waters above from the waters below (Gen. 1:6), then drew limits for the waters beneath the solid sky so that dry land might appear (Gen. 1:9-10). [Controlling chaos]

So, while v. 3 may carry the visual image of a thunderstorm blowing across the sea or a lake, it also carries a

> **Controlling chaos:** Job 38:8-11 speaks eloquently of God's power to control the powerful seas and bring order from chaos: "Or who shut in the sea with doors when it burst out from the womb? – when I made the clouds its garment, and thick darkness its swaddling band, and prescribed bounds for it, and set bars and doors, and said, 'Thus far shall you come, and no farther, and here shall your proud waves be stopped'?"

reminder that Yahweh alone controls the waters of chaos and brings order to the world.

Verses 4-9 celebrate God's "voice" that is heard both in thunder and in the frightening din of a strong wind. The cedars of Lebanon were known for their towering strength, yet Yahweh's voice had the power to snap them like twigs (v. 5). Anyone who has observed the aftermath of a tornado, hurricane, or even a severe thunderstorm has seen tall trees twisted and splintered.

How could "Lebanon skip like a calf and Sirion like a young wild ox"? (v. 6). The mountains of Lebanon were heavily forested with cedars and other trees. "Sirion" is an alternate name for Mount Hermon, a large northern peak from which snowmelt feeds the headwaters of the Jordan River. When storms blow through, trees covering the mountains shift and dance in the wind, making it appear that the entire mountains are moving. Thus, the poet could compare the roiling, windswept mountains to energetic young bovines at play.

Thunder is the sound that lightning makes, so it is not surprising that the psalmist connects God's thundering voice to "flames of fire" (v. 7). The word translated as "flashes forth" normally means "chops" or "hacks," so the NET translates it as "the LORD's shout strikes with flaming fire." This appropriately recalls the violence of a lightning strike that accompanies the thunder.

When thunder and lightning are booming overhead, the very ground seems to vibrate. Even the uninhabited wilderness, lacking large trees, "shakes" in response to the LORD's resounding voice (v. 8). Since previously mentioned locations (Lebanon and Sirion) were beyond the northern reaches of Israel, the "wilderness of Kadesh" probably refers to a northern location. Some scholars argue, however, that the writer has in mind the wilderness surrounding an area known as Kadesh in the southern

Laboring deer, or twisting oaks? The preserved words of v. 9 are problematic: they don't seem to fit precisely, and most translations depend on some speculative emendation of the text. The word "oaks" (NRSV), for example, does not appear in the text. The word is "deer," which may or may not make sense. Taking note of the parallel word "forest" in the next line, the NRSV translators arrived at "oaks" by emending the word "deer" (*'ayyalot*) to *'ēlot*, which could mean "large trees." The word "writhe" can be used of a female animal in labor, however, so a number of scholars have proposed that Yahweh's voice "causes the deer to writhe," creating such a fright that the animals go into premature labor. The problem there is that the form of the verb means "give birth" rather than "cause to give birth," so the reading remains uncertain.

Negeb, better known from stories in the Old Testament (Gen. 20:1, Numbers 20, etc.). If that is correct, the psalmist's intent would be to portray the mighty storm as sweeping across the entire nation, from its northernmost to the southernmost extremities.

Verse 9 is difficult to translate, though the author clearly intends to further illustrate God's power as seen in the storm. **[Laboring deer, or twisting oaks?]** The precise translation of certain phrases is debatable, but the over-riding imagery is as obvious as a storm: God's thunderous voice overpowers both land and people, leading all who worship to say "Glory!"

Note how the shout of "Glory!" in v. 9 reflects the call to ascribe to God "glory and strength" and "the glory of his name" in vv. 1-2.

A closing word of praise
(vv. 10-11)

The final two verses bring the psalm to an end with a four-line blessing or affirmation from the worship leader. The subject of each line is Yahweh. The first two lines declare that Yahweh sits above the flood, as king, forever.

There is no Hebrew referent for "enthroned," which appears twice in the NRSV's translation of v. 10. The text simply says that Yahweh "sits" or "dwells" over the flood, and as king. To "sit as a king" is to sit on a throne, however, so it is not a great stretch to translate the phrase as "sits enthroned" in both lines, as the second is parallel to the first. **[The flood]**

The final stanza can be read as a simple affirmation, as reflected in NIV11, NET, HCSB, and others. The NRSV translators, however, chose to render the two verbs as precatives, as a twin entreaty asking God to give strength to the people and bless them with peace.

This is grammatically justified, as the imperfect and jussive forms of the verb are identical. Throughout the psalm, the author has expressed full confidence that God has power over the forces of nature, leading one to assume that Yahweh's power extends to people, too.

So, translating as an affirmation, "The LORD gives his people strength, the LORD grants his people security" (NET) is entirely appropriate. Since v. 11 is the first time the poet mentions God's people, however, it is also legit-imate to read the verse as a wish that the Lord who rules the forces of nature will grant strength to God's people and bless them with peace.

How do we read this psalm today? Some might see in it a promise that the all-powerful God will provide perfect protection for those who trust, but if so, they miss the point. The psalm reflects the setting of a frightening storm – an awe-inspiring manifestation of God's power over nature, which can be destructive.

God's people will experience storms. The psalm itself is evidence of that: bad weather is not our only trouble. We may also face storms of financial disaster, lingering disease, emotional heartache, or other difficulties.

The psalmist knew this, and declared that through all the storms of life, we can trust in the God whose power extends over all, the God in whom we can find strength to endure the fiercest of storms and yet experience the blessing of peace.

The flood: The word translated as "flood" (*mabbul*) appears only here and in the stories of the Noahic flood in Genesis 6–8. We can't be sure if the psalmist intended for worshipers to recall the story of that ancient flood, or if his description of "surging waters" (an alternate translation) primarily goes back to the stormy waters of v. 3. In either case, it is a reminder that Yahweh is Lord over all creation, including the mighty waters that humans cannot begin to tame.

The Hardest Question
Is Psalm 29 adapted from a hymn to Baal?

Two words found in v. 1 have sparked considerable specu-lation. They are *benē 'elim*, which could be translated either "sons of God" or "sons of gods," with a lower-case "g." The NRSV's translation ("O heavenly beings") obscures the underlying text.

What's unusual is that this form is more characteristic of the Ugaritic language than ancient Hebrew. The politi-cal state of Ugarit, which was centered in the coastal city of Ras Shamra in northern Syria, came to an end in the 12th century, about the same time Israel was emerging as a rather cohesive tribal league. Although conclusions must be tentative, many scholars see strong similarities between the people of northern Syria and related people groups further south. Their languages are similar enough that Ugaritic and Canaanite can be considered dialects of the same tongue. Both cultures praised Baal as one of the leading gods.

When biblical writers describe heavenly beings in other texts (e.g., Gen. 6:2, 4; Job 1:6, 2:1), they typically use the Hebrew expression "*benē ha'elohim*," because Israel's more generic name for God was *'elohim*. The spell-ing used in v. 1, found also in Ps. 89:6 (and possibly in Deut. 32:8, according to some ancient versions), is closer to the spelling found at Ugarit, *bn 'ilm*, for "sons of El."

Both Hebrew and Ugaritic are Northwest Semitic languages, with Ugaritic being the older of the two. Hence, though there are identifiable differences between them, they are quite similar in many ways, and much of the vocabulary – like that of Romance languages such as Italian and Spanish – overlaps.

The opening "*benē 'elim*" is the first of several phrases in the psalm that are similar to vocabulary found in Ugaritic, possibly Canaanite mythology. The combina-tion of parallel terms and northern place names led H.L. Ginsberg to propose in 1935 that the psalm was originally a Canaanite hymn to the storm god Ba'al that had been adapted for Yahwistic use.

Several reputable scholars have supported Ginsberg's contention, but most agree that firm evidence is lacking: while we do have some religious texts used by the people of Ugarit, we have no similar examples of Canaanite hymnody. So, while this hymn about Yahweh appearing in a thunderstorm can be expected to reflect the same sort of language that might be found in a hymn to Baal, we cannot assume that the authors have taken over an old Canaanite hymn and substituted "Yahweh" for "Baal."

First Sunday after Epiphany

Third Reading
Acts 10:34-43[*]

Who Converted Whom?

*This text is also used on Easter Day for Years A, B, and C. A study appears at that point in Year A, Volume 2.

Fourth Reading
Matthew 3:13-17

A Son Who Pleases

And a voice from heaven said, "This is my Son, the Beloved, with whom I am well pleased." (Matt. 3:17)

What does it take to get your attention? Suppose your church had a guest preacher who read the sermon in a monotone. Or, let's say the guest was an academic who droned on about the political interplay between seventh-century Judah and the Assyrian Empire. Would that keep you engaged?

Then again, imagine a Sunday morning when the choir door opened and a bushy-haired wild man dressed in burlap came out and started calling the deacons a bunch of snakes. No one would sleep through that sermon – *if* they let him finish it.

An unusual preacher

No one drifted off when John the baptizer preached, either. **[Baptist, or baptizer?]** John famously made his abode in a wilderness area near the Jordan River, yet people reportedly came a full day's walk from Jerusalem and even beyond to hear his message and to be baptized by him (vv. 5-6).

Baptist, or baptizer? The most common name for Jesus' preaching cousin is "John the Baptist." I prefer the term "John the baptizer" for two reasons.

First, the word translates a participle that means "one who baptizes" or "the one baptizing." Second, "Baptist" has come to mean something entirely different. It refers to a broadly diverse denomination that (for the most part) believes in practicing baptism by immersion, but Baptists are also known for other things, not all of them appealing. It's not appropriate to hang a label on John that implies more than it means.

Although Landmark Baptists contend that the Baptist denomination started with John the Baptist, that is a false and unfortunate view. The John who immersed Jesus was a baptizer, but not a Baptist.

Elijah: John's rugged appearance and rustic dress reminded contemporaries of Elijah because the crusty prophet's appearance was so distinctive that anyone who had seen him remembered it. A story in 2 Kgs. 1:1-8 says that King Ahaziah of Israel once injured himself and sent messengers to inquire of the god Baal-Zebub whether he would live.

Elijah intercepted the messengers and sent them back with this word: "Is it because there is no God in Israel that you are sending to inquire of Baal-zebub, the god of Ekron? Therefore you shall not leave the bed to which you have gone, but shall surely die."

When this was reported to Ahaziah, he asked, "What sort of man was he who came to meet you and told you these things?"

The servants answered: "A hairy man, with a leather belt around his waist."

The king probably groaned as he said, "It is Elijah the Tishbite."

John's unruly appearance, ascetic behavior, and harsh preaching was a clear echo of the ancient prophet Elijah, an eccentric preacher who wore rough clothing cinched with a strip of leather and who lived in the wilderness, eating what the land provided (2 Kgs. 1:8).

The Jewish people of Jesus' day were anxiously awaiting a messiah to end Roman domination and put the promise back in the promised land. Isaiah had predicted that a messenger would appear in the wilderness to prepare the way (Isa. 40:3, Matt. 3:3), and Malachi had prophesied that Elijah would return to earth just before the climactic "day of the LORD" (Mal. 4:5-6).

A tradition in 2 Kings 2 held that Elijah did not die, but had been carried to heaven in a whirlwind, so it wasn't a great stretch to imagine that God might send him back.

When John showed up dressed in a camel's hair garment with a leather belt, living in the wilderness and subsisting on locusts and wild honey, people with eschatological hopes thought Elijah had returned. **[Elijah]**

John not only looked like Elijah, but he also sounded like him. He had one single, simple message: "Repent, for the kingdom of heaven is near!" (v. 2). Elijah of old had called for the leaders of Israel to repent of their idolatry and return to Yahweh. The word "repent," in biblical language, means to turn around. It means to turn away from selfishness and idolatry so one can turn toward God and experience forgiveness and right living.

According to vv. 7-12, John accused Pharisees and Sadducees – even those who sought baptism – as being like snakes squirming away from imminent danger, but not really changing their ways.

Few things cause more stress than change, whether it is changing jobs, changing houses, changing schools, changing churches, or dealing with change brought by separation or death. Change causes all sorts of alarms to go off in our heads. The hardest change to make is a change in the way we think, a change in our personal behavior, a change in our lifestyle.

John called for repentance accompanied by change, declaring "the kingdom of heaven is near!" The "kingdom of heaven" (or "kingdom of God") refers not to a place but to the rule or reign of God. God rules whether we like it or not, but we can choose whether we will trust in God and play an active role in God's kingdom.

John's preaching took on special urgency because the Messiah was coming, and in the Messiah the promise of God's kingdom had become incarnate in the form of a human being. Through Jesus, God was about to reveal just what the kingdom was all about – what it meant to know God and to be known, to love God and to be loved.

From his encampment at Bethany Beyond the Jordan, John called on people to demonstrate repentance through the radical step of public baptism in the Jordan River. His authoritative preaching led some to wonder if John was the expected Messiah, but he insisted that his purpose was to prepare the way for Jesus, the true Messiah, the one who would ultimately separate the wheat from the chaff (vv. 11-12). **[Bethany Beyond the Jordan]**

Bethany Beyond the Jordan: The Jordan River has shifted its course over the years, partly due to earthquakes, since it runs through the northern part of the Great Rift Valley, which extends into Africa.

The remains of two ancient churches (under modern shelters), along with steps leading down to the former water level, testify to an early belief that this now-dry channel was the place where Jesus was baptized at "Bethany Beyond the Jordan," and where early pilgrims came to be baptized in the same place.

A surprise candidate
(vv. 13-15)

John's odd appearance and forceful preaching had shocked many others, but he was the one caught off guard on the day when Jesus showed up, having traveled many miles from Galilee, and asked to be baptized. The two men were cousins, according to Luke 1:36, and God had apparently revealed to him that Jesus was the Messiah, so he was baffled at why Jesus would want to join the crowds in seeking baptism.

John tried to dissuade Jesus. "I need to be baptized by you," he argued, "and do you come to me?" (v. 14).

We might also question why Jesus chose to be baptized. He had committed no sin and had no need to repent, or so Heb. 4:15 insists. He told John it needed to happen in order "to fulfill all righteousness" (v. 15). That simply means to do what is right, what God wants to be done. Why? What would Jesus' baptism accomplish? One common guess is that Jesus chose to be baptized as a way of identifying with humankind, symbolizing the fullness of his humanity.

Perhaps he also wanted to indicate that baptism is important, that it matters. **[Why was Jesus baptized?]**

Why was Jesus baptized? Why did Jesus choose to undergo a public baptism by John? John baptized with water, utilizing the power of symbol to indicate the need for sinners to repent and have their sins washed away. Like an Old Testament prophet, John called members of the established religion to account for their failures. The gospels suggest that many people were convicted by his preaching, and they sought John's water baptism as a symbol of cleansing, as a way of declaring their intention to turn away from sin and turn toward God.

Jesus, however, reportedly lived without sin. The Bible (Heb. 4:15) and church tradition insist that Jesus, though tempted as humans are tempted, did not sin. Thus, John's baptism would hardly be necessary. Jesus had no need of liquid lustrations to symbolically wash away sins that did not exist.

Why, then, did he pursue baptism? John himself wondered, insisting that he was more in need of Jesus' baptism than the other way around (Matt. 3:14).

It is often suggested that Jesus chose to be baptized as a way of expressing solidarity with humankind. Although he did not need to be baptized as a symbol of repentance, perhaps Jesus desired to be baptized as a sign of both humility and humanity. As he did not think his divinity was something to be exploited, but "emptied himself" (Phil. 2:6-7), so he did not regard himself as "too good" to be baptized.

There is also a sense in which the act of baptism served as Jesus' public ordination to the ministry that lay ahead.

In submitting to John's baptism, Jesus also endorsed John's work and showed that he was not in competition with him. John's call for repentance was appropriate. Jesus brought an entirely new dimension to the gospel, but repentance would remain important. Jesus began his preaching ministry by calling on others to repent and believe the gospel (Mark 1:15).

The most important reason Jesus chose to be baptized, however, may be found in his own words. When John objected, Jesus said "Let it be so now; for it is proper for us in this way to fulfill all righteousness" (Matt. 3:15). "To fulfill all righteousness" means, ultimately, to do God's will. Jesus apparently believed it was right for him to experience baptism.

A major introduction
(vv. 16-17)

Jesus' decision to seek baptism also provided an opportunity for John to introduce him to his followers, and for God's Spirit to confirm publicly that Jesus truly was the chosen Messiah sent by God as the hope of Israel – and of the world (vv. 16-17).

Some Christian groups believe that Jesus was baptized by immersion and follow that practice, while other denominations baptize by dribbling, sprinkling or pouring water over one's head. The text offers no clear description of the mode by which Jesus was baptized. It says only "And when Jesus had been baptized" before adding "just as he came up from the water, suddenly the heavens were opened to him and he saw the Spirit of God descending like a dove and alighting on him" (v. 16).

The text could be read to imply that Jesus alone saw the Spirit descending, but the symbolic appearance "like a dove" and the significance of the message that followed would have been lost if others could not have seen and heard it, too. Luke added that the Spirit appeared "in bodily form" as a dove. Whether he intended to suggest that a dove was tangibly present, or only to indicate that the Spirit appeared in the form of a dove's body, is not clear.

An interesting wordplay helps paint the image: as Jesus came up (*'anabaino*) from the water, the Spirit came down (*katabaino*) from heaven to meet him. In rabbinic tradition, the dove was sometimes used as a symbol for Israel. The Old Testament includes a number of allusions to doves, but none in which the dove symbolized God's Spirit.

As a point of interest, the word translated as "dove" was also used to describe the common pigeon, but translators have uniformly preferred the image of a dove.

While Mark wrote only of "the Spirit" descending (Mark 1:10), Matthew specified "the Spirit of God."

The Spirit is most commonly pictured as wind, and Hebrew uses the same word for both "Spirit" and "wind." The avian image of the dove may recall Gen. 1:2, in which the Spirit of God hovered or moved over the waters of chaos as creation commenced.

The purpose of the Spirit's appearance was not just to demonstrate divine support for Jesus' ministry, but to symbolize the active presence of the Spirit in Jesus' life.

While some first-century Jews believed that God's Spirit had been withdrawn following the age of the prophets, Jesus was reportedly conceived by the Spirit. Jesus' baptism not only marked his identity with humans, but also a clear affinity with the Spirit. [**Surprise!**]

> **Surprise!** Many years ago, the late Frank Stagg observed that the appearance of the Spirit as a dove may have been a surprising revelation to John. John's proclamation about Jesus was laced with terms of judgment: the ax was at the root of the tree, and the winnowing fork was prepared to sort the wheat and the chaff. John predicted that Jesus would baptize with the Spirit and with fire (Matt. 3:14-15).
>
> The Spirit, however, appeared in the form of a dove, a symbol of peace. Judgment would come, but not before mercy. Jesus would call others to repentance, but his ministry would be marked primarily by acts of compassion and mercy ("Matthew," vol. 8, *Broadman Bible Commentary* [Broadman Press, 1969], 95)

The visual symbol of God's Spirit was accompanied by a heavenly voice. Matthew's version of the story suggests that the voice spoke to all, publicly attesting divine approval of Jesus. For Mark (1:11) and Luke (3:22), the words were directed to Jesus: "You are my beloved son …," but Matthew presents it as a third person testimony: "*This* is my beloved son …"

The divine speech reflects two Old Testament texts. "You are my beloved son" comes from a coronation psalm used to indicate God's figurative adoption of each new king: "You are my son, today I have begotten you" (Ps. 2:7).

The reference to Isa. 42:1 spoke of a coming Messiah, of whom God would say: "Here is my servant, whom I uphold, my chosen, in whom my soul delights; I have put my spirit upon him; he will bring forth justice to the nations."

The voice from heaven spoke few words, but with great importance. By drawing inferences from Psalm 2 and Isaiah 42, Jesus was described with images of both royal messiah and suffering servant. This dual identity is reflected in differing perceptions of Jesus as he began his ministry, encountering conflict with even his closest companions (Matt. 16:21-28). Many of his followers expected Jesus to declare himself as a royal messiah and to launch a new day of political power. Jesus, on the other hand, more often described himself in the role of Isaiah's suffering servant.

With the benefit of the New Testament as an interpretive frame, we can see how these apparently opposing roles were complementary. Jesus was indeed the Messiah, but the redemption he brought would come through personal suffering and spiritual power rather than through personal strength and military action. Thus, we know that

our own relationship to Jesus – lived out through sharing Jesus' world view – is best experienced through spiritual humility and service to others.

Jesus humbly submitted to John's baptism, and contemporary believers adopt a position of meekness when following Christ in the baptismal waters. We may not see the Spirit descending in the form of a dove, but the humility we express in baptism is an open invitation for the Spirit's presence in our lives.

The Hardest Question
Was Jesus immersed?

Paintings or stained-glass images of Jesus' baptism rarely show Jesus beneath the water or even dripping wet, but many people assume that John dipped Jesus beneath the water and brought him up in the manner common to their tradition. Ministers typically lean the candidate backward into the water during the rite, though some push the candidate face down into the water (which is easier, though lacking in symbolism). Eastern Orthodox Catholics who come to the Jordan River for baptism dip themselves three times by simply squatting down into the water, with or without the help of the priest's hand on their heads. But how strong is the evidence that Jesus was immersed?

The first part of v. 16 (along with the parallel in Mark 1:10) provides one of several texts often cited as arguments for baptism by immersion: "And when Jesus had been baptized, just as he came up from the water …" Those who practice baptism by immersion have traditionally interpreted the phrase as an indication that Jesus' body had been completely under the water, and that the Spirit of God descended like a dove just as John brought him up out of the water.

Grammatically, however, "as he came up from the water" could also describe the action of Jesus walking out of the water and onto the shore. Indeed, that is the most natural meaning. The Greek verb translated "came up" normally carries the sense of walking or climbing, as in going up a hill or going up to a certain place. The preposition *'apo*, translated "from," also suggests the idea of "away from" rather than "up from" or "out of." That meaning is best conveyed by the preposition *'ek*, which is used in Mark 1:10. It can mean "out of" or "out from."

The point is not to argue that Jesus was not immersed, but simply to indicate that the text does not demand that interpretation. The Greek verb could be used in a literal sense to mean "dip" or "immerse," or in a more figurative sense to describe a religious ritual or initiation. It is quite possible that John invited persons to come and stand in the river while he scooped up handfuls of water and poured it over their heads. But, baptism by pouring or sprinkling could have been done almost anywhere. The fact that John characteristically baptized in the river suggests the need for more (or deeper) water, which implies that he practiced immersion. Likewise, Paul's later analogy of baptism to the act of burial and resurrection best fits with the act of immersion (Rom. 6:3-5, Col. 2:12).

Jews of the day commonly practiced full-body self-immersion in special pools (not unlike baptismal pools) as a purification rite before worship. Although John's baptism symbolized spiritual repentance rather than ritual purity, his hearers were accustomed to the idea of dipping themselves in water.

Some years back, archaeologists excavated the remnants of a small cave traditionally associated with John's camp at Bethany Beyond the Jordan, which John 1:28 cites as the place John was baptizing. The back of the cave was incorporated into an early church, including symbols associated with John and with baptism. A later monastery built at the site contained two pools that could have been used for baptism.

Second Sunday after Epiphany
First Reading
Isaiah 49:1-7

A Light to the Nations

It is too light a thing that you should be my servant to raise up the tribes of Jacob and to restore the survivors of Israel;
I will give you as a light to the nations, that my salvation may reach to the end of the earth. (Isa. 49:6)

How far does God's grace extend? That question lies at the heart of theological debates that troubled Israel and continue to dog the church today. Is God's saving grace limited to a select few, or available to all? Our text suggests that, while God had a special relationship with Israel, God's grace, light, and salvation are intended for all peoples of the earth.

The servant as Israel
(vv. 1-4)

Isaiah 49:1-6 is the second of four texts typically called "Servant Songs" because they speak of a servant of God who will bring deliverance, not just to Israel, but to all people. The first Servant Song (42:1-4, or possibly 42:1-9) speaks *of* the servant and possibly *to* the servant, but in the second Servant Song, the servant speaks for himself and of his relationship with God. That much is clear: identifying the servant is another matter.

The overall message of Second Isaiah assumes that the descendants of Jacob, the people of Israel, are called to be God's servants, living in faithful obedience and serving as a light or a blessing to other nations (recall Gen. 12:3). With the Hebrews unable or unwilling to live out their calling, however, the prophet raised the possibility of another who would do what Jacob-Israel had not done. In the second Servant Song, the prophet speaks for the people and appears to identify himself as the servant, standing in for the people.

The song itself is found vv. 1-6. Verse 1 references all peoples, from "coastlands and peoples from far away," and v. 6 concludes with "the end of the earth." These

> **Coastlands:** While I have taken "coastlands" and "peoples far away" as meaning a reference to nations beyond Palestine, some scholars argue that these terms refer to Israel's immediate neighbors along the coast. John D.W. Watts argues that both the "coastlands" and "peoples far away" should be regarded as other populations within Palestine. "They were also addressed as a part of the great assembly in 41:1," he writes. "They were competitors with Jews for rights in the land and favors from the Persians, as were the Philistines of old, but now the coastlands are simply observers in YHWH's great hall of justice" (*Isaiah 34–66*, vol. 25, Word Biblical Commentary [Zondervan, 2005], 729).

serve as bookends, binding together what comes between and emphasizing the theme of God's grace to all people. The RCL reading includes the divine affirmation of v. 7, though it appears to be a separate oracle, beginning with the typical "Thus says the LORD."

The song opens with a surprising challenge: "Listen to me, O coastlands, pay attention, you peoples from far away!" This clearly addresses nations beyond Israel (v. 1a). The word translated as "coastlands" (NRSV) is sometimes rendered as "islands" (KJV, NIV, NASB). It refers not so much to a beach as to the border of a land that touches the sea, where mariners put into port. From the very small perspective of the world known to ancient Israel, the reference would be to nations bordering the Mediterranean Sea. They could only imagine the "peoples from far away" who were beyond. [**Coastlands**]

A second stylistic touch is that the first verse of each section of the song includes the idea that God's purpose for the servant extended from the womb onward (vv. 1, 5).

> **Israel as sinner and servant:** Regarding the identity of the servant as Israel, Trent Butler suggests a distinction between Israel as sinner and Israel as servant. Israel as sinner would be the nation at large, guilty as charged and whining in failure (vv. 1-4), while Israel as servant would be a righteous remnant within the larger nation, committed to calling all Israel to live obediently before God (vv. 5-6). (For more, see Butler's *Isaiah*, Holman Old Testament Commentary [Holman Reference, 2002], 269-70).

The belief that God had a special relationship with some people "from the womb" is common in scripture (Gen. 25:23, Judg. 16:17, Ps. 22:9, Jer. 1:5, Luke 1:41). It is found with reference to Israel in Isa. 44:2, 24.

"The LORD called me before I was born," said the prophet, speaking as the servant. "While I was in my mother's womb, he named me" (v. 1b). And what was the servant's name? It is not "Isaiah," but found in v 3: "And he said to me, 'You are my servant, Israel, in whom I will be glorified.'" Perceiving the servant as the people of Israel may seem a bit troublesome, because we commonly think of the servant as an individual called to restore Israel, as in v. 5 of this same song. As we've noted previously, it is possible to understand the people of Israel and Judah as God's intended servant, though they had failed to become the nation-blessing witness God wanted them to be. Thus, we might perceive a singular servant being called to do on Israel's behalf what the people could not do for themselves. **[Israel as sinner and servant]**

Tension between the individual and corporate identity of the servant is inherent in the text, and there is no easy solution. While Christians may be prone to see Jesus in every mention of the servant, the fit is better in some places than in others. Jesus' mission, like that of the servant in Isa. 49:1-6, is characterized by a movement from the Jews to the Gentiles (Matt. 10:5-6, 28:19-20). Following Christ's ascension, Paul also spoke of the gospel being given first to the Jews, and then to Gentiles (Rom. 1:16).

Whether we see the servant's identity as individual or corporate, the self-description in v. 2 may seem surprisingly warlike, since other texts describe the servant as gentle and non-combative (Isa. 42:3, 50:6, 53:7). The weapons of war, however, were to be words, and their targets were not to be killed, but converted. The metaphor of the mouth as

a sword when filled with the word of Yahweh is also found in Jer. 5:14, 23:29; Eph. 6:17; Heb. 4:12; and Rev. 1:16. "In the shadow of his hand he hid me" suggests that God had waited until the appropriate time to "draw the sword" of the servant's speech.

Similarly, the servant claims to be like a polished arrow, an archer's favorite and most accurate shaft. Again, the servant had been hidden away in Yahweh's quiver, to be withdrawn and unleashed with the message of salvation when the time was right.

In v. 3, any mystery about the intended identity of the servant is made clear: "And he said to me, 'You are my servant, Israel, in whom I will be glorified.'" Israel had not lived up to God's call, but the prophet still hoped they would become a people who would do God's work.

He was not convinced that the people believed it, though. Speaking on Israel's behalf, he stated a common feeling with apparent sarcasm: "I have labored in vain, I have spent my strength for nothing and vanity; yet surely my cause is with the LORD, and my reward is with my God" (v. 4). **[Israel's complaint]**

Similar laments are found in texts such as Ps. 137:1: "By the rivers of Babylon – there we sat down and there we wept when we remembered Zion." In the prophet's words, the people would admit no guilt and acknowledge no failure. They saw themselves as victims, claiming to have poured out their strength in service to God for nothing, since they remained in captivity. From this perspective, their conclusion was not so much a statement of faith as the wishful thinking of pious and self-interested pretense: "yet surely my cause is with the LORD, and my reward with my God" (v 4b).

> **Israel's complaint:** Isaiah put words in the people's mouths, complaining: "But I said, 'I have labored in vain, I have spent my strength for nothing and vanity ...'" (v. 4a).
>
> The word for "nothing" is *tohu*, the same term used in Gen. 1:2 to describe the pre-creation earth as "formless." The word for "vanity" is *hevel*, a word that literally means "vapor" or "breath," something that doesn't last. The longsuffering prophet Jeremiah expressed similar feelings more than once, as in Jer. 20:18: "Why did I come forth from the womb to see toil and sorrow, and spend my days in shame?"

The servant beyond Israel
(vv. 5-6)

God responded to Israel's lament with a challenge that extended beyond the tasks "to bring Jacob back to him" and to see "that Israel might be gathered to him" (v. 5a). The call was to all nations, and for this calling the prophet believed God would provide both opportunity and ability: "I am honored in the sight of the LORD, and my God has become my strength" (v. 5b).

Restoring Israel alone might seem to be an impossible dream, but the servant learned that when God's grace is involved, restoring Israel alone was too small a goal. Thus, God said "It is too light a thing that you should be my servant to raise up the tribes of Jacob and to restore the survivors of Israel; I will give you as a light to the nations, that my salvation may reach to the end of the earth" (v. 6).

We would do well to ponder those words. God's grace, expressed through the work of the servant, would shine as a beacon of light and hope to all the nations. Servant Israel's job was to stop blaming God for the nation's failures, quit pretending to have been faithful, and start proclaiming God's salvation.

Whether servant Israel would prove faithful or not, God's purpose remained – and remains – unchanged: "that my salvation may reach to the end of the earth." In v. 5, the servant comes across as defeated, unable to do the "small thing" of restoring Israel. Israel had rejected God, but God rejected the people's rejection. Neither God nor God's cause would be defeated. God *would* be glorified, the servant *would* be a light to the nations, God's salvation *would* reach to the end of the earth.

Could it be that God had in mind a salvation that goes beyond the limitations we typically draw around saving grace? In Isa. 45:22-23, the prophet spoke for God: "Turn to me and be saved, all the ends of the earth! For I am God, and there is no other. By myself I have sworn, from my mouth has gone forth in righteousness a word that shall not return: 'To me every knee shall bow, every tongue shall swear.'" Matthew 18:14 credits Jesus with saying "Your Father in heaven is not willing that any of these little ones should be lost." The testimony of Luke 3:6 declares that "All people will see God's salvation" (NIV11). Especially interesting, given the emphasis upon

light in Isa. 49:6, is the claim of John 1:9: "The true light, which enlightens everyone, was coming into the world."

John's gospel also quotes Jesus as saying, "When I am lifted up, I will draw all people to myself" (12:32), and "I came not to judge the world but to save the world" (12:47). Is it possible that God might reject even our rejection, as Phillip Gulley and James Mulholland argue in *If Grace Is True* (HarperSanFrancisco, 2004)? "You did not choose me," John quotes Jesus as saying, "but I chose you" (15:16).

Contemplating such ideas can be unsettling or even downright disturbing for those whose basic view of soteriology is "accept Jesus – or else." Other biblical texts suggest differing destinies depending upon one's response to God, and they must also be considered. God's desire, however, is never in doubt: that all be saved.

It may be helpful to remember that just about everything Jesus said and did was unsettling and disturbing to the religious establishment of his day. In our time, when some who claim the name of Christ seem intent on pulling in the stakes and narrowing the parameters of grace, it is refreshing to be reminded that God's purpose is for God's people to be a light to all the nations, "that my salvation may reach to the end of the earth."

We may not know exactly what those prophetic words mean – but we can *hope* they mean exactly what they say.

The Hardest Question
What about verse 7?

Astute readers may have noticed that the lesson title cites Isa. 49:1-7 as the text, but the Bible study deals only with 49:1-6. The lectionary is more inclined to leave out important verses than to include more than necessary. In this resource, we often add extra verses for needed context, but rarely ignore a verse cited by the RCL.

In this case, the lectionary calls for including Isa. 49:7 when the textual unit, the second Servant Song, clearly ends with v. 6. The following verse appears to begin a new unit – or at least a shift in emphasis. Some scholars do hold that vv. 7-13 should be considered part of the song, but few would break it after v. 7 alone.

We've considered vv. 1-6 only in the Bible study, mainly because v. 7 begins a new theme, but we can briefly explore it here. This verse, spoken as divine speech, identifies Yahweh as "the Redeemer of Israel and his Holy One." But to whom does Yahweh speak?

John D.W. Watts has argued that the servant of 42:1-6 is the Persian ruler Cyrus, who conquered Babylon and granted freedom to the Israelites, while the "Holy One" of 49:7-13 is Darius I, who ruled a generation later after having overthrown Cyrus' successor in a *coup d'etat*. Watts argues that Darius' rise from his position as a court functionary to emperor is reflected in the description of "one deeply despised; abhorred by the nations, the slave of rulers" (*Isaiah 34–66*, vol. 25, Word Biblical Commentary [Zondervan, 2005], 738).

Watts has few followers. In vv. 1-6, Yahweh addressed corporate Israel, apparently through the prophet as the nation's representative. Israel's self-perception was one of utter defeat and captivity – a position aptly described by "one deeply despised, abhorred by the nations, the slave of rulers." Isaiah's hearers would have recognized themselves. But, though dejected and oppressed as they were, Yahweh was not finished with them. "Kings shall see and stand up, princes, and they shall prostrate themselves, because of the LORD, who is faithful, the Holy One of Israel, who has chosen you."

This image suggests that lowly Israel would one day be king of the hill. Yahweh's faithfulness would overcome in spite of their unfaithfulness. The theme continues in vv. 8-13, with promises of divine deliverance, provision, and prosperity for God's people. This sounds more like a promise of hope than the commission of God's servant, and is sufficiently different for us to recognize it as the beginning of a new oracle, rather than as a continuation of the servant song in 49:1-6.

Second Sunday after Epiphany
Second Reading
Psalm 40

Covenant Celebration

You have multiplied, O LORD my God, your wondrous deeds and your thoughts toward us; none can compare with you.
Were I to proclaim and tell of them, they would be more than can be counted. (Ps. 40:5)

Has your life ever felt a bit like a roller coaster? There are times when we feel down, whether due to personal trouble or guilt or illness, but in time we recover and feel better, even joyful. We may feel on top of the world for a while: life couldn't be better – but then something happens. Whether we mess things up on our own, or whether trouble comes from outside, we find ourselves struggling again.

That's the way real life is: it has ups and downs. And that's the kind of reality expressed in today's text, the reflections of one who knows what it is like to experience life's best times and worst times while trusting in God through them all. [**The text**]

Happy days
(vv. 1-10)

The psalmist recalled a time of God's deliverance when he was in deep trouble, described metaphorically as being in a "desolate pit" or a "miry bog" (v. 2a, NRSV), perhaps in danger of death.

The word for "pit" was used to describe deep cisterns commonly dug to collect rainwater in dry lands. The modifier translated as "desolate" normally refers to a great din or crashing sound, such as the sea makes. The psalmist probably intended for the reader to think of the pit of Sheol, sometimes described as beneath the sea.

"Miry bog" translates two words that both refer to mud, like "muddy muck," conjuring an image of someone stuck in quicksand, sinking and in danger of death.

In the face of such trial, the psalmist claimed to have waited earnestly for Yahweh to hear his cry (v. 1), and

> **The text:** Some scholars have regarded Psalm 40 as two psalms that have been combined, in part because vv. 1-10 and 11-17 shift from praise to lament, and partly because vv. 13-17 also appear, separately, as Psalm 70. The combination of praise and lament is not unusual in the psalms, however: whatever their roots, these verses have been put in their present form for a purpose.
>
> Psalm 40:5-10 is also read in Years A, B, and C for the "Annunciation of the Lord," celebrated on March 25. At nine months before Christmas, it is the traditional date of Gabriel's announcement to Mary that she would become the mother of Jesus.

that God had pulled him from the metaphorical mud and set his feet on a rock, returning a sense of security to life (v. 2b). [**Waiting patiently?**]

The poet responded with praise, which he also attributed to God's action: "he put a new song in my mouth, a song of praise to our God" – a testimonial tune that would lead others to stand in awe and likewise put their trust in Yahweh (v. 3).

People who look to Yahweh rather than trusting in human pride or false gods are happy (v. 4), the poet said, a word that can also be translated as "blessed." It describes the state of one who experiences security through trusting in God.

The psalmist's claim challenges us to consider our own state of mind, and to think of who we really count on. Do we trust in God and who God has made us to be, or fall into the trap of living for others' approval? Do we follow God's way, or seek happiness in the false gods of materialism or self-gratification? Where have we found joy?

Waiting patiently? The NRSV's translation "I waited patiently for the LORD" could be misleading. The writer speaks of being stuck in a slippery pit that calls to mind quicksand. Though clearly metaphorical, it suggests a situation of some desperation in which quiet patience would be hard to come by.

A closer look at the Hebrew suggests an alternative: the writer used a special construction in which two forms of the same verb (an infinitive absolute plus an active form) are combined for the purpose of emphasis. Literally, we could read "Waiting, I waited," or "I *really* waited." The construction emphasizes not patience, but the tension involved in a time of desperate waiting–perhaps even *impatience*.

The psalmist ecstatically described the multiplicity of Yahweh's "wondrous deeds and thoughts toward us," incomparable and beyond counting (v. 5). He knew the secret of counting one's blessings and remembering the source from which they come.

Psalms such as this one indicate a movement away from animal sacrifices or other offerings as a means of pleasing God (50:8-15, 51:16-17, 69:30-31), reflecting a prophetic emphasis on obedience as superior to sacrifice. The psalmist's intent in v. 6 was not to criticize the practice of animal sacrifice, but reflects how postexilic psalmists came to think of vocal praise as a preferred alternative to it.

Some of the prophets were more forceful in their opinions. For example, Samuel excoriated Saul for feigning sacrificial intentions after disobeying his commands: "Has the LORD as great delight in sacrifices, as in obeying the word of the LORD? Surely to obey is better than sacrifice, and to heed than the fat of rams" (1 Sam. 15:22, see also Isa. 1:11-17 and Mic. 6:6-8).

Note the conjunction of obedience with heeding or hearing in v. 6. Hebrew has no separate word meaning "obey," relying on the verb "to hear" instead: to truly hear is to obey. The psalmist's "open ear" to hear and heed God's commands demonstrates his willingness to obey. He saw even this ability as a gift of God: the NRSV's "you have given me an open ear" translates an idiom "you have dug out ears for me." **[Digging ears?]**

Having heard God's word, he heeded it: "Then I said, 'Here I am; in the scroll of the book it is written of me. I delight to do your will, O my God; your law is within my heart'" (vv. 7-8).

The meaning of "in the scroll of the book it is written of me" has long puzzled interpreters. Some think it may refer to a belief that God keeps a record book of human behavior. Others imagine a heavenly "scroll of the righteous" in which the names of those who please God are written.

The NET translators suggest that the "roll of the scroll" (literally) could refer to a Torah scroll on which God's instructions were written, such as the "book of the law" mentioned in texts like Deut. 30:10, Josh. 1:8, and 2 Kgs. 22:8.

Perhaps a better view is to imagine that the psalmist has written his testimony on a scroll he intends to deposit in the temple as a witness of his past trust, present praise, and future confidence that God will hear his prayers. This is attested in other settings where vocal or written testimony is promised as the fulfillment of a vow.

The author of Psalm 40 may or may not have posted his praise on the temple wall, but he clearly claims to have proclaimed "the glad news of deliverance in the great congregation" – that is, before worshipers gathered outside of the temple. He had not held back either praise or testimony, and believed that God was well aware (v. 9).

Digging ears? The precise meaning of the expression "you have dug out ears for me" is unclear. Some interpreters see it as an indication that hearing is a gift of God: God's creative purpose for humans includes ears. Others imagine the idiom indicates that God has cleaned out the person's ears so he could hear more clearly. Either could be reflected in the NRSV's "you have given me an open ear."

Isaiah used a similar idiom when he testified: "The Lord GOD has given me the tongue of a teacher, that I may know how to sustain the weary with a word. Morning by morning he wakens—wakens my ear to listen as those who are taught. The Lord GOD has opened my ear, and I was not rebellious, I did not turn backward" (Isa. 50:4-5).

Still others interpret the digging out of one's ears to mean that God made something known in an obvious way: the NET has "You make that quite clear to me!"

The early Greek translators appear to have been puzzled by the phrase, coming up with a translation that seems unrelated to the context: the Septuagint (LXX) has "but a body you have prepared for me." The writer of Hebrews was dependent on this translation when he quoted the verse in Heb. 10:5 as a prophecy of Christ's willingness to obey God in giving up his body as a sacrifice.

Verse 10 repeats the thoughts of v. 9 in more detail. The psalmist did not keep the news of God's blessings to himself, but spoke as an authentic witness of God's faithfulness and salvation. The word curiously translated by the NRSV as "deliverance" in v. 9 and "saving help" in v. 10 typically refers to justice (NET) or righteousness (KJV, NIV11, HCSB). Deliverance has its roots in justice.

Note how the poet piled up terms from Israel's classic descriptions of God's character: in vv. 9-10 he spoke of God's righteousness (twice), faithfulness (twice), salvation, and steadfast love, making public his praise before the worshiping congregation.

Have you ever felt so blessed that you could hardly hold it in? "Testimony meetings" aren't as common as they used to be, but we all have opportunities to speak of what God has done for us, whether to our neighbors, our Bible study classmates, or even on social media. In any of these ways, it's important to express thanksgiving in a way that focuses humbly on God's blessing rather than our own piety.

Troubled days
(vv. 11-17)

The psalmist had been blessed, but no living person is exempt from trouble. The latter part of the psalm shifts to an entreaty from the troubled psalmist, who apparently believed his trials had been self-inflicted. Israel's traditional covenant theology, expressed most clearly in Deuteronomy 28, taught that obedience to God's way would lead to health and prosperity, while rebellion would inevitably result in sickness and woe – and the psalmist had woes aplenty.

In v. 11 the psalmist pleaded "Do not, O LORD, withhold your mercy from me." Calling on the very divine dispositions he had praised in the previous verse, he cried "let your steadfast love and your faithfulness keep me safe forever."

Life had gone sour, as "evils have encompassed me without number" – dangers that the psalmist connected to his own failings: "my iniquities have overtaken me, until I cannot see" (v. 12a).

Have you ever felt blinded by troubles, temptations, or failure, finding it hard to see any way forward? We could all confess that our sins are many: the psalmist compared his transgressions to the number of hairs on his

---

Aha! Aha! The Hebrew word translated as "Aha!" would be pronounced something akin to "he-ah," with a short "e" as in "heh." When pronounced in rapid succession, it would sound much like the English way of expressing laughter: "Hah, hah, hah!"

The word has no other meaning than to express laughter. The term can indicate joy: Isaiah spoke of one who warmed himself by a fire, saying "Aha! I am warm" (Isa. 44:16), but even there Isaiah gives it a negative connotation, for the fire is made from scraps left over from idol carving, which the prophet condemned.

Most commonly, as here, the word is used to indicate the derisive laughter of enemies, as in Ps. 35:21: "They open wide their mouths against me, they say 'Aha, Aha, our eyes have seen it'" (cf. Ps. 35:25; Ezra 25:3, 26:2, 36:2).

---

head, leaving him so weighed down that "my heart fails me" (v. 12b).

The psalmist prayed again for deliverance, with an appeal in vv. 13-17 that is virtually identical to Psalm 70. Whether the present psalmist knew that plea and quoted it here, or whether Psalm 70 was taken from this one, we cannot know.

What we do know is that the psalmist felt oppressed, not only by his own sin, but also by persons who wanted to hurt him. The reference to those "who seek to snatch away my life" suggests a belief that enemies were out to harm him, so he prayed for God to confound, to shame, and to turn back those "who desire my hurt" (v. 14).

Verse 15 calls to mind the sort of bullying common to the playground, when one child falls or fails at a game, and others taunt "Nyah! Nyah!" Had others openly made fun of the psalmist's lowly situation? His plea gives that impression: "Let those be appalled because of their shame, who say to me 'Aha! Aha!'" [Aha! Aha!]

As he prayed for his enemies to be shamed and appalled, the psalmist asked the opposite for the faithful: "May all who seek you rejoice and be glad in you; may those who love your salvation say continually, 'Great is the LORD!'" (v. 16).

The poet wanted to experience God's salvation again. He longed for deliverance and stability that would allow him to continually proclaim Yahweh's greatness, but he still felt "poor and needy." His poverty was not financial, but spiritual; his need was for forgiveness of sin and deliverance from trouble.

Despite his poor state, the poet held to the belief that "the LORD takes thought for me" (v. 17a). That belief led him to close by addressing God with a final plea: "You are my help and my deliverer; do not delay, O my God" (v. 17b).

This psalm is a reminder that no one lives on a constant spiritual high. We may know the joyful relief of forgiveness that brings a sense of cleansing and being right with God – but we also know what it is like to go astray and feel far from God.

Sometimes we, like the psalmist, may connect personal or relational troubles to our spiritual state, thinking that God has left us to experience the natural results of our sins.

Such thoughts may lead to a greater appreciation of Christ's willingness to give his own life as a means for effecting our salvation. We don't have to understand how the atonement works in order to be eternally grateful for the way God has demonstrated the steadfast love and faithfulness the psalmist celebrated, so that Christ has indeed become our help and deliverer.

The Hardest Question
Does Psalm 40 speak of Jesus?

Psalm 40:6-8 may strike readers as familiar because the author of Hebrews quoted it – from the Greek Septuagint translation – as if Jesus were speaking the words:

> Consequently, when Christ came into the world, he said, "Sacrifices and offerings you have not desired, but a body you have prepared for me; in burnt offerings and sin offerings you have taken no pleasure. Then I said, 'See, God, I have come to do your will, O God' (in the scroll of the book it is written of me)." (Heb. 10:5-7, NRSV)

The Greek translators apparently took "you have given me an open ear" (literally, "you have dug out ears for me") as a reference to creation, and rendered the line as "a body you have prepared for me." That was a very large translational stretch, but it appealed to the author of Hebrews, who delighted in reading the Old Testament through a Christological lens.

In supporting his argument that Christ's death on the cross rendered animal sacrifices obsolete, the author seized upon Ps. 40:6-8 as an ideal proof text, imagining that the words had been spoken by the pre-existent Christ, who gave his body as a sacrifice so that "burnt offerings and sin offerings" would no longer be needed.

In typical rabbinic fashion, the author cited the text, then followed it with a *midrash*, or commentary. In vv. 8-10, he argued that God no longer desired animal sacrifices, for Christ had come to do God's will by giving his body as a one-time sacrifice. The author concluded: "He abolishes the first in order to establish the second. And it is by God's will that we have been sanctified through the offering of the body of Jesus Christ once for all" (Heb. 10:9-10).

While the psalmist intended only to declare his belief that God desires obedience more than sacrifice, he could never have imagined that a later writer would interpret his words (including a partial mistranslation) as none other than a declaration of the pre-existent Christ.

For the writer of Hebrews, however, any Old Testament text that appeared to be a foreshadowing of Christ was considered fair game for exposition.

Second Sunday after Epiphany

Third Reading
1 Corinthians 1:1-9

Certain Strength

God is faithful; by him you were called into the fellowship of his Son, Jesus Christ our Lord. (1 Cor. 1:9)

Have you ever been on the receiving end of a backhanded compliment, when someone insulted you with a statement disguised as praise?

"I like your dress: it makes you look so slim" sounds like a compliment, but it could be a left-handed way of observing that you're trying to hide extra pounds beneath vertical stripes.

Sometimes, backhanded compliments can simply be mindless: an old photo may spark a comment such as "Wow, you used to be a real beauty!"

They can also be biting: "The junior senator is well-spoken for someone with so little experience."

And sometimes, they can be carefully calculated attempts to say something nice without giving more credit than is due. That's the sort of thing we find in Paul's greeting to the church in Corinth – a church with a lot of potential for a membership that was so immature, self-serving, and polarized.

A troubled church

The Corinth Paul knew was only 100 years old, a Roman metropolis built on the ruins of an ancient Greek city. [**Corinthian history**] For a variety of reasons, Corinth was a notable city.

Geographically, it was located on a narrow isthmus (4 mi. x 10 mi.) between mainland Greece and a large peninsula called the Peleponnesus. This made it an important stop on the trade route from the East, and a bustling trade city that controlled two ports. Goods or smaller ships brought into the port of Cenchreae from the Mediterranean side of the isthmus could be carted across the narrow

> **Corinthian history:** The Corinth that Paul knew was built upon the ruins of an ancient Greek city called Ephyra. As a leading Greek city, it had survived much of the Roman world's expansion including the Peloponnesian Wars (461–446, 431–404 BCE) and the Corinthian War (395–387), but it was destroyed in 146 BCE by the Roman proconsul Lucius Mummius, who razed the city, killed the men, and sold the women and children into slavery. Mummius did such a thorough job that Corinth lay in ruins for a century, until Julius Caesar ordered that it be rebuilt in 44 BCE and populated it at first with former slaves who were granted both freedom and land as a reward for military service.

land corridor, then shipped from the port of Lechaion into the Corinthian Gulf, allowing faster access to points west.

Politically, Corinth was the center of Roman government for the province of Achaia.

Economically, Corinth was considered the "Fourth City" of the Roman Empire.

Ethnically, Corinth was an eclectic, cosmopolitan city, no longer Greek, but settled by many former Roman soldiers who were given land, along with immigrants from all over, including Jews from the diaspora. The city was known as a rowdy place, famous for its immorality and wantonness. The phrase "to Corinthianize" has been used to mean "to become immoral."

Religiously, Corinth harbored a variety of belief systems, including adherence to the old Greek gods, Roman gods, mystery religions, Judaism, and an incipient form of Gnosticism that would prove to be a serious threat to the early church. Citizens were encouraged to participate in the imperial cult and worship the Roman emperor. Temples to Poseidon-Neptune (Greek and Roman names for the same god), Aphrodite-Venus, Demeter-Ceres and Kore-Persephone were established, along with temples to Apollo and Asklepius. Eastern and Egyptian deities also had adherents in the city. Thus, Christians in Corinth had to contend with many well-established and very tempting religions. Issues raised in Paul's letter indicate that rituals of their pagan neighbors had a strong influence on the church's worship.

The Apostle Paul had a long and uneven relationship with the people of Corinth. Along with Timothy and Silas, he first came to the city around 49 or 50 CE, during his second missionary journey. This is the most securely dated encounter in Paul's known missionary career. The account in Acts 18 says that Paul was brought before proconsul Lucius Junius Gallio (Acts 18), and an inscription found in Corinth dates Gallio's rule to either 50/51, 51/52, or possibly 52/53 CE. Paul was accused of unlawful activity, but Gallio dismissed the charges, showing little regard for the concerns of the Jews (Acts 18:12-17).

In Corinth, Paul met Aquila and Priscilla (called Prisca in Rom. 16:3, 1 Cor. 16:19, and 2 Tim. 4:19), a Jewish-Christian husband and wife who had emigrated from Rome after the emperor Claudius expelled Christians from Italy (Acts 18:2). **[Corinthian immigrants]** Paul may have lodged and worked with them in the leatherwork trade, and remained in Corinth for about 18 months.

After a brief return to Jerusalem, Paul traveled to Antioch before departing on his third missionary effort,

---

Corinthian immigrants: The edict of Claudius mentioned in Acts 18:2 is also known from other sources including the writings of Josephus, Suetonius, and Dio Cassius.

Josephus, a Jewish-Roman historian who would have been a contemporary to the event, said the edict took place in the ninth year of Claudius' rule. Suetonius, who was born after the events, researched and wrote biographies of Rome's first 12 emperors. He said of Claudius: "He expelled from Rome the Jews constantly making disturbances at the instigation of Chrestus" (Suetonius, *Claudius*, 25; from Jerome Murphy-O'Connor, *St. Paul's Corinth: Texts and Archaeology* [Liturgical Press, 1983], 138–39).

Scholars typically assume that "Chrestus" is an alternate spelling for "Christus," but it is not clear whether Claudius was concerned with Jews who were agitating against Christ-followers, or if the work of Christian missionaries had led to an uprising.

Corinthian contacts: An awareness of Paul's contacts with the church offers a guide to understanding the letter's basic structure: chs. 1–6 seem to deal mostly with problems Paul had learned about from the visitors, while sections of chs. 7–16 relate directly to issues raised in the letter requesting his advice.

---

going overland to Ephesus, where he stayed for two years. While at Ephesus, Paul had several contacts with the Corinthian church.

The letter we know as 1 Corinthians was not Paul's first letter to the church, for in 1 Cor. 5:9 Paul speaks of a "previous letter" he had written (some scholars think parts of that letter may be retained in 2 Cor. 6:14-7:1). Individual members of the church such as "Chloe's people" (1:11) had contacted Paul, perhaps through personal visits, telling him of problems at Corinth. Paul also received at least one letter from the church requesting his advice (7:1).

In response, Paul wrote what we now call 1 Corinthians. **[Corinthian contacts]** The letter was not well received, leading Paul to make a visit to the church that he called painful (2 Cor. 2:1). After returning to Ephesus, he wrote another letter that he described as tearful and difficult (2 Cor. 2:3-9, 7:12), sending it by Titus. Some scholars think this "severe letter" may be partially preserved in 2 Corinthians 10–13, which is sterner in tone than the surrounding chapters.

Later, Titus met Paul in Macedonia and told him the Corinthians had accepted his letter and were reconciled to him (2 Cor. 2:12, 7:5-16). Paul wrote 2 Corinthians to express his joy and encourage the Corinthians to raise a worthy offering for the poor in Jerusalem.

Later, Paul seems to have made a third visit, probably around 55/56 CE, writing his letter to the Romans while there (Rom. 15:26).

A greeting of grace
(vv. 1-3)

As Paul wrote to the Corinthian church, he had learned that various factions existed, possibly with parties claiming to follow Paul, Apollos, Cephas, and Christ. Scholars have sought to identify various theological differences among the factions, but it seems clear that a struggle for power and leadership of the church fueled the dissension.

Sosthenes: The Sosthenes that Paul mentions in 1:1 is otherwise unknown to us. The synagogue leader who apparently brought charges against Paul before the proconsul Gallio was named Sosthenes (Acts 18:17). He would have had to undergo a conversion as remarkable as Paul's to have become a companion in ministry, but it is possible, because another synagogue leader named Crispus did become a believer, according to Acts 18:8, and Paul himself baptized Crispus (1 Cor. 1:14). Whether the Sosthenes credited with contributing to the letter was a converted synagogue leader or someone else, Paul probably would not have mentioned him if he had not been someone the Corinthian community would have known and respected.

The church appears to have included members across the spectrum of social classes, from slaves to relative elites, and there is evidence that some members considered themselves to be superior to others on both spiritual and social grounds.

How does one begin a letter to a church in turmoil? Paul followed the standard pattern for letters of the time by naming the sender and recipients, followed by a brief greeting.

Paul first identified himself as the writer, then indicated that someone named Sosthenes was with him, possibly a messenger sent from Corinth. [**Sosthenes**]

Paul cited his credentials as one who was "called to be an apostle of Jesus by the will of God." Some members of the Corinthian church appear to have questioned Paul's authority as an apostle (an issue that later become more explicit, see 2 Cor 10:12-18, 11:5), so he wanted to emphasize from the beginning that his authority lay not in himself, but in his divine calling.

In the address, Paul identified his audience as a church (*ekklesia*) and reminded readers that they were "sanctified in Christ Jesus" and "called to be saints" (v. 2a). The Corinthians were unlikely saints but their calling, like Paul's, originated with God.

Saintly or not, Paul called them "sanctified," using a verb that means "to make holy" in the sense of "to set apart as sacred to God." Believers are to be set apart for holy living, but the Corinthians showed that church members can be perfectly forgiven but imperfect in behavior, saints and sinners concurrently.

Paul tactfully reminded the Corinthians that they were not alone, but called to be saints alongside "all those who in every place call on the name of our Lord Jesus Christ, both their Lord and ours" (v. 2b). This remains a helpful word because it's easy for a church or denomination to become isolated, thinking only of itself. Ecumenical activities remind us that we are not alone, but part of the much larger body of Christ.

While secular letters of the period typically began with the word "greeting" (*chairein*), Paul preferred the word for "grace" (*charis*), and here added "peace" as well – along with the reminder that grace and peace derive "from God our Father and the Lord Jesus Christ" (v. 3).

A faithful God
(vv. 4-9)

In his letters, Paul usually followed the greeting with a prayer of thanksgiving for his readers, often subtly raising issues that would reappear in the letter.

In some cases, Paul affirmed his hearers with words of praise, as in 1 Thessalonians, where he thanked God for "your work of faith and labor of love and steadfastness of hope in our Lord Jesus Christ" (1 Thess. 1:3). Paul also praised the Colossians for their faith, love, and hope in Christ that was bearing fruit among them (Col. 1:3-6).

In writing to the Corinthians, however, the best Paul could offer was backhanded praise. He thanked God for the grace that had been given to the Corinthians, enriching them in every way and blessing them with spiritual gifts – but he extended no congratulations for what they had done with the blessings they had received.

Paul thanked God for the Corinthians, but his focus was clearly on what God had done for them, not what they had done for God. God's grace had enriched them "in speech and knowledge of every kind" (vv. 4-5), even though they had spoken against one another, and some believed they had special knowledge that made them superior to others – issues to be addressed later.

The witness of Christ had been confirmed among them, Paul said (v. 6), so they were not lacking in spiritual gifts (v. 7), though the use and distribution of spiritual gifts had become a matter of controversy that Paul would address in chs. 11–14.

This is a reminder that one's spiritual failings do not necessarily negate spiritual gifts. One can be a spiritually gifted shyster as well as a saint – as demonstrated by charismatic evangelists who draw many followers but use their offerings to enrich themselves.

Paul reminded the church that God is faithful, even in difficult circumstances, even among unfaithful people. God's faithfulness would grant the Corinthians "strength to the end" so they might be found "blameless" when Christ returned (v. 8). God had called them into fellowship on the basis of God's own faithfulness, not theirs: they were not only saved by God's persistent grace, but sustained by it.

Paul's prayer did not praise the Corinthians, but did not condemn them, either. Although they were sinners, he still called them saints. Despite their shortcomings, he acknowledged their giftedness.

We, too, are called into fellowship by God's faithfulness. We also are gifted by God's Spirit. We also may fail and fall short of God's best hopes for us, but our faith is grounded in God's faithfulness, which will remain "to the end."

If Paul were to write a letter to you, to your Bible study class, or to your church, what might he say? Would he have to settle for backhanded compliments, or could he offer unabashed, grateful praise?

What would you like for him to say?

The Hardest Question
What does it mean to be "called"?

Paul often used the language of calling, and nowhere more clearly than in today's text, where he claimed to be "called to be an apostle of Christ Jesus by the will of God" (v. 1). He spoke to the believers in Corinth as being sanctified in Christ Jesus and "called to be saints, together with all those who in every place call on the name of our Lord Jesus Christ, both their Lord and ours" (v. 2). By the faithfulness of God, he continued, they were "called into the fellowship of his Son, Jesus Christ our Lord" (v. 9).

Language about calling reappears in 1:26, and is particularly prominent in ch. 7, where Paul urged the believers to remember the state in which they were called and to be faithful in the new relationship with Christ to

which they had been called. Paul's writings do not provide a comprehensive statement about his theology of calling, but he clearly believed the Christian's calling originates with God and is mediated through Christ.

In modern thought, we often think of "calling" as a belief that God has chosen someone for a particular type of ministry: we say someone is "called to preach" or "called to the mission field." While this individualistic concept has validity with reference to one's seeking a vocational direction that pleases God, professional ministers are no more "called" than any other believers.

Paul reminded the Corinthians that all were "called into the fellowship of his Son, Jesus Christ our Lord" (v. 9). This echoes his earlier reference to all those who in every place "call on the name of our Lord Jesus Christ" (v. 2).

Calling, then, has both personal and corporate components. Paul, perhaps because he expected Christ to return soon, emphasized the importance of living out one's calling in whatever station of life one found himself or herself, even if it was the life of a slave (7:17-24). Paul acknowledged that one's life circumstances could change (slaves could become free, for example), but the exercise of one's calling as a faithful believer was not dependent on changing one's station in life.

Our calling is not so much to *do* something as to *be* the person God has in mind, whatever our life situation. The Corinthians, Scott Nash has written, "were not called to follow a script; they were called to *be* someone … For Paul, this calling *in* life was also a calling *into* a certain quality of life" (*1 Corinthians*, Smyth & Helwys Bible Commentary [Smyth & Helwys, 2009], 71).

Nash goes on to cite Frederick Buechner's frequently quoted observation about calling: "The place God calls you to is the place where your deep gladness and the world's deep hunger meet" (*Wishful Thinking: A Theological ABC* [Harper & Row, 1973], 95). That place might be among the ranks of professional ministers, but it may just as well be expressed in the love of friends or co-workers, through community ministries, through public service, or by whatever means we engage the world around us. Our calling is not just to do things, but to be who we truly are.

Second Sunday after Epiphany
Fourth Reading
John 1:29-42

A Lamb Who Leads

He first found his brother Simon and said to him, "We have found the Messiah"
(which is translated 'Anointed'). (John 1:41)

Andrew first found his brother. If you heard good news, amazing news, the news you'd been waiting a lifetime to hear, what would you do first? Imagine that a universal cure for cancer had been announced, or that Israelis and Palestinians had reached a substantive and lasting peace accord, or that an inexpensive way to trap carbon dioxide and reduce climate change had been discovered.

Any of these things would have major, world-reaching effects. They would enhance security, save lives, and improve living conditions in every part of the globe.

Suppose you just heard such life-changing news. What would you do first?

Andrew went and told his brother, Simon.

Who would *you* tell?

Testimony one
(vv. 29-34)

Our text is concerned with three consecutive testimonies to Jesus. The first two are shared by John, commonly known as "John the Baptist," though "John the baptizer" is more appropriate. The Fourth Gospel does not specifically describe John's baptism of Jesus, but it contains an account of John's testimony to Jesus in a baptism setting that has similarities to those in the other gospels, so it is implicit. **[A different approach]**

John's baptismal remarks were not his first testimony to Jesus. Earlier, in a theological discourse on Jesus' identity, the author parenthetically noted that John had spoken of Jesus without naming him: "This was he of

> **A different approach:** The description of Jesus' baptism in the Fourth Gospel is one of many differences between it and the other three, known as synoptic gospels because they are more similar ("synoptic" means "seen together").
>
> Troy A. Miller offers a helpful reflection on the differences between John and the synoptic gospels:
>
> "John records no birth story but has two temple-cleansing stories. He records no parables and identifies Jesus' miracles as 'signs.' He quite often relates not simply *what* Jesus did or taught, but also *why* or *for what reason* he did such things. When compared to the other gospels, John paints a more divine portrait of Jesus, seemingly not wanting his readers to forget or miss the fact that this earthly Jesus is God's Son who existed before all time" (*Feasting on the Word, Year A*, ed. David L. Bartlett and Barbara Brown Taylor, vol. 1 of Accordance electronic ed. [Westminster John Knox Press, 2010], para. 3327).

whom I said, 'He who comes after me ranks ahead of me because he was before me'" (v. 15).

John later testified to priests and Levites who wondered if he was the Messiah by saying that he was not the one, but had been sent to prepare the way. Quoting from Isa. 40:2, he said "I am the voice of one crying out in the wilderness, 'Make straight the way of the Lord'" (vv. 23).

John went on to say that though he baptized with water, another was coming who was so much greater than he that he felt unworthy to untie his sandals (v. 27). This took place, we are told, "in Bethany across the Jordan where John was baptizing" (v. 28).

Our text begins on "the next day," and presumably in the same setting, when John saw Jesus approaching and

> **How many days?** John 1:29 begins a sequence of days at the beginning of Jesus' ministry. These are not clearly delineated. Some scholars think there are six days, though others see four. Chapter 1 seems to include four days: (1) Jewish officials question John about his identity [vv. 19-28], (2) Jesus comes to be baptized and John recognizes him as the Messiah [vv. 29-34], (3) John again proclaims Jesus as the Lamb of God and two of his disciples follow Jesus [vv. 35-42], and (4) Jesus goes with the new disciples to Galilee, where he recruits Phillip and Nathaniel [vv. 43-51].
>
> Despite this, 2:1 begins with "On the third day." This must refer to the third day following Jesus' baptism, not to the first day mentioned in the book.
>
> Some scholars also read the Fourth Gospel as concluding its account of Jesus' ministry with a sequence of six days.

declared, "Here is the Lamb of God who takes away the sin of the world!" (v. 29). **[How many days?]**

A careful reading suggests that John's testimony in vv. 29-34 does not mention Jesus' actual baptism, because it may have occurred on the previous day, and it was only through divine revelation associated with Jesus' baptism that John came to realize that the mystery Messiah he had been preparing for was Jesus himself.

Only then could John point to Jesus and say, "This is he of whom I said, 'After me comes a man who ranks ahead of me because he was before me'" (v. 30, cf. v. 15).

What did John mean? Wasn't he born before Jesus? According to Luke 1:26, John's mother Elizabeth was six months pregnant with John when the angel first announced to Mary that she would conceive. It's clear that John had more than earthly birth order in mind. The gospel writer, who believed that Jesus as the divine "Word" had existed from the beginning (1:1), apparently attributed to John the shared belief that Jesus had a prior existence in heaven before coming to earth. Thus, John could insist "he was before me."

It may seem unusual that John, at the very beginning of Jesus' ministry, would identify him as "the Lamb of God who takes away the sin of the world." This is the sort of thing one would say in retrospect, after Jesus' crucifixion and resurrection, after he had suffered on behalf of others.

The Fourth Gospel was written many years after Jesus' earthly ministry, but the author credited John with prescience enough to choose that terminology early on, perhaps to identify Jesus as a different kind of Messiah. Some Jewish writings of that period spoke of the anticipated Messiah as a powerful warrior lamb, and the Apocalypse of John (Revelation) also speaks of Jesus as the mighty Lamb of God, slain but victorious, who would judge the world.

Such terminology effectively looks at power in a different way: the Lamb of God would overcome through suffering and willing sacrifice, not through overt expressions of military might.

Verse 31 emphasizes how John learned Jesus' identity as the Messiah only through his baptism: "I myself did not know him; but I came baptizing with water for this reason, that he might be revealed to Israel" (v. 31).

This is an interesting thought: Though the synoptic gospels portray John as challenging people to be baptized as a sign of repentance, the Fourth Gospel implies that the ultimate goal of his baptizing ministry was the revelation of Jesus.

Verses 32-33 have John elaborating further: "I saw the Spirit descending from heaven like a dove, and it remained on him." This apparently was a sign for which he had waited: "I myself did not know him, but the one who sent me to baptize with water said to me, 'He on whom you see the Spirit descend and remain is the one who baptizes with the Holy Spirit'" (v. 33).

Now, John could say, "And I myself have seen and have testified that this is the Son of God" (v. 34).

This must have been a bittersweet time for John: he joyfully recognized and testified that Jesus was the Messiah, but in doing so he fulfilled his primary mission. What would he do now? And would his disciples leave him to follow Jesus?

Testimony two
(vv. 35-40)

John's second testimony took place on the following day, when he was talking with two of his disciples as Jesus walked by, and he declared again "Look, here is the Lamb of God!" (vv. 34-35).

If John came to bear witness to the coming Messiah, and the Messiah arrived, it was only natural that his disciples should then pledge their allegiance to him. It's not surprising, then, that the two disciples left John and followed Jesus (v. 37).

When Jesus noticed that they were following him, he turned and asked, "What are you looking for?" The question could just as easily be translated "What do you want?" These are the first words spoken by Jesus in the Fourth Gospel: "What do you want?" (v. 38).

What do *we* want from Jesus? As Rudolf Bultmann once commented: "It is the first question which must be addressed to anyone who comes to Jesus, the first thing about which he must be clear" (*The Gospel of John: A Commentary* [Westminster John Knox, 1971], 100). Is forgiveness all that interests us, or are we interested in following Christ into a new kind of life?

The disciples' answer seems simplistic, but it has deep implications. They asked: "Where are you staying?" That was not just a request for information; it indicated a desire to spend time with him there.

"Come and see," Jesus said, and they followed him to the unnamed place. Was it a guest room in someone's home? A quiet spot in the shade of a date palm grove? It doesn't matter; it's where Jesus could be found. The author doesn't mention a place, but he notes the oddly specific time of day: it was "about four o'clock in the afternoon" (v. 39). [**What time was it?**]

What time was it? The NRSV's "four o'clock in the afternoon" translates the Greek's "about the tenth hour," which is preserved in the KJV. What does that mean? The Romans reckoned time from midnight, but the writer seems clearly to be following Jewish methods of timekeeping.

The Jewish system considers sundown to be the beginning of a new day: thus, in Genesis 1, the writer says "And there was evening and there was morning, the first day" (Gen. 1:5), and so forth through six days.

In the Jewish system, nighttime hours were divided into four "watches" – sundown to 9:00 p.m., 9:00 p.m. to midnight, midnight to 3:00 a.m., and 3:00 a.m. until sunrise, usually around 6:00 a.m.

Daytime hours were reckoned in accordance with temple activities, beginning with the preparation of the altar for the morning sacrifice at dawn, somewhere around 6:00 a.m. If 6:00 a.m. was the first hour, the tenth hour would be 4:00 p.m.

Why would he include this information? If the disciples followed Jesus to where he was staying at four in the afternoon and then "remained with him that day," the implication is that they remained with him for a while, perhaps overnight, listening and learning.

How much time do we spend with Jesus? How often do we seek his presence and go intentionally to a quiet place where we can listen for his voice and reflect on what we believe he is calling us to do?

Testimony three
(vv. 41-42)

The third testimony is not from John, but one of those former disciples. Only one of the two is named: Andrew, the brother of Simon Peter. We are not told whether the action in vv. 41-42 took place on the following day, or after only a couple of hours with Jesus, but Andrew knew exactly what he wanted to do first.

"He first found his brother Simon and said to him, 'We have found the Messiah.'" Greek did not use exclamation points, but we would be justified in adding one here.

Andrew then led Simon to Jesus, "who looked at him and said, 'You are Simon son of John. You are to be called Cephas' (which is translated Peter)."

Mark's gospel also seems to indicate that Jesus nicknamed Peter early on: "So he appointed the twelve: Simon (to whom he gave the name Peter) …" (Mark 13:6). Matthew associates the new name with a later encounter: not until Peter's confession that Jesus was the Messiah did Jesus say "you are Peter, and on this rock I will build my church" (Matt. 16:18). This may or may not indicate the origin of the name.

The Fourth Gospel's account draws a quite different picture from the synoptics. There, Jesus seeks out the first disciples and calls them to follow. Here, we find some of the disciples seeking Jesus, rather than the other way around.

New Testament writers spoke often of Jesus as a good shepherd who is constantly seeking out the lost. When we defer to the world's ways and wander from Jesus' view of discipleship, believers can also stray from the path. When that happens, we can't just sit around waiting for Jesus to find us and jerk us up by the collar. We need to seek him, too.

The Hardest Question
Would John the Baptist really have called Jesus the "Son of God"?

It is thought that the gospel of John – whose author is anonymous – apparently grew out of a circle of believers typically called "the Johannine Community." The book was probably written late in the first century, perhaps during the 90s CE. As such, it reflects beliefs that had developed over time and may attribute some of those developed beliefs to the life and teachings of Jesus.

If that is the case, we might assume that John the baptizer's early reference to Jesus as the "Son of God" could be a retrojection – a later writer putting words in his mouth, so to speak. But is it surprising to think that John would describe Jesus as the Son of God even this early in his ministry?

John was not the first to speak of someone as God's son. Israel, in a collective sense, is described as God's first-born son in Exod. 4:22, where God reportedly instructed Moses to tell the Pharaoh, "Thus says the LORD, Israel is my firstborn son."

Later, descendants of David who came to the throne were thought of as having been adopted as sons by God.

When Nathan relayed God's promise to David that a descendant of his would rule on the throne of Israel forever, he spoke of when David's son would take the throne. "I will be a father to him, and he shall be a son to me" (2 Sam. 7:14).

Coronation hymns in the book of Psalms spoke of the newly crowned king as having been adopted by God: "I will tell of the decree of the LORD: he said to me, 'You are my son. Today I have begotten you'" (Ps. 2:7).

After the kingdom came to an end and no more sons of David ruled in Jerusalem, a belief emerged that God would fulfill the promise of 2 Samuel 7 by raising up a descendant of David as the one anointed to deliver Israel: both "Messiah" in Hebrew and "Christ" in Greek mean "anointed."

It is unlikely that John the baptizer shared the same beliefs as the later Johannine community, and he would certainly not have thought of Jesus in Trinitarian terms as propounded in Nicea centuries later. Still, since he believed that Jesus was the anointed Messiah, descended from David but also sent by God, he could also think of him as the son of God, though probably without the capital "S."

Third Sunday after Epiphany

First Reading
Isaiah 9:1-7*

A Son Is Born

*Most of this text falls within Isaiah 9:2-7, which is the first reading for Christmas 1. A study incorporating both texts, Isaiah 9:1-7, appears in this volume at that point.

Third Sunday after Epiphany

Second Reading
Psalm 27*

Who Needs a Light?

The LORD is my light and my salvation; whom shall I fear? The LORD is the stronghold of my life; of whom shall I be afraid? (Ps. 27:1)

Do you remember the old TV commercials for Certs breath mints? They were marketed as a double value: twin teenage girls were featured in one ad, arguing over whether Certs was a candy mint or a breath mint. An announcer interrupted to insist "It's both!" The girls concluded that Certs were "two, two, two mints in one!"

Today's text calls the old commercial to mind because Psalm 27 appears to be two, two, two psalms in one. Verses 1-6 comprise a joyful psalm of trust, while the following section (vv. 7-14) has the characteristics of a lament. Some commentators argue that these must represent psalms by two different people, or by one person at different stages of life. Others argue that the psalm should be read as a unity, and it is not unusual for psalms of lament to include elements of praise.

A superscription to the psalm attributes it to David, and there are hints that the protagonist could be a king, but there is not sufficient evidence to identify either the author or the date of the composition.

Praising God
(vv. 1-3)

How confident are you in God's care? How assured are you that God will respond to your prayers? Whether we're dealing with one psalm or two, the first six verses of Psalm 27 form a two-part celebration from the lips of one who expresses total confidence in God as the source of all things good. Countless believers have memorized these

> **Similar psalms:** The first few verses of Psalm 27 are often compared to Psalm 23, and for good reason. As the psalmist spoke of God as "my light and my salvation," Psalm 23 declares: "even though I walk in the darkest valley, I fear no evil, for you are with me …" (Ps. 23:4).
>
> Similarly, as the poet behind Psalm 27 sought to dwell in God's presence forever, the author of Psalm 23 claimed: "I shall dwell in the house of the LORD my whole life long" (Ps. 23:6).

words: "The LORD is my light and my salvation; whom shall I fear? The LORD is the stronghold of my life; of whom shall I be afraid?" (v. 1).

God's beneficent care is described in three ways. First, "light" is an appropriate metaphor for confidence in God. Darkness conjures thoughts of hidden threats, fears, or enemies, but light dispels the darkness with the assurance that God is with us. **[Similar psalms]**

"Salvation" renders a Hebrew word that primarily means "deliverance," and in this context it probably refers to a warrior facing dread enemies with confidence that God will grant victory, no matter what the odds.

"Stronghold" might also be translated as "refuge," a place of such security that the psalmist could portray himself as fearless against all enemies or dangers: "of whom shall I be afraid?"

The terminology of v. 1 suggests a military context, with the protagonist of the psalm likely to be thought of as Israel's king, who was expected to be a commander-in-chief not in name only, but in the forefront of the battle.

This text also occurs on the second Sunday of Lent in Year C. Our study will incorporate all of Psalm 27.

Aiming for Dummies: The imagery of the psalmist's enemies stumbling and falling as they attacked calls to mind the early Star Wars movies, in which hosts of the Empire's masked storm troopers would rush Luke Skywalker, Han Solo, or Princess Leia with laser guns blazing, but never hitting them. I once saw a chalk drawing outside of a bookstore that pictured a storm trooper reading a book called *Aiming for Dummies*.

When the elders of Israel petitioned Samuel for a king it was "so that we also may be like other nations, and that our king may govern us and go out before us and fight our battles" (1 Sam. 8:20).

The military metaphors continue in vv. 2-3, where the psalmist expresses confidence that any adversaries who might assail him would stumble and fall: he could face an entire army with confidence that he would survive their attack. [**Aiming for Dummies**]

Living with God
(vv. 4-6)

From the aggressively confident image of a heroic warrior, the poem turns the page to show a softer side to the psalmist, the inner source of his outward courage: his one plea is to dwell always in the presence of God.

A surface reading of v. 4 suggests that the poet wanted to set up permanent residence beneath the wings of the cherubim before the Ark of the Covenant. The psalmist would have known better than to think such an arrangement would be possible, however, since the Holy of Holies was forbidden to anyone but the high priest, and then only once each year.

We should read the verse as a metaphor, then, the symbolic language of one who longed for God's presence to infuse his life. Verse 5 shifts back to the hope of protection while engaging the world, that God would shelter him in a day of trouble, hide him from enemies when necessary, and set him "high on a rock," out of reach of his foes, or possibly standing in victory over them.

In a similar way, we might recall happy times at church where we sensed God's presence during worship in the sanctuary or felt fully at home during fellowship meals. In times of struggle or uncertainty, especially when far from home, we might long to be back in the church where we have found safety and security – but we know that it's really God's presence we need, and that is not limited to the church building.

Verse 6 combines thoughts of victories on the battlefield and worship in the temple: as a victor, the psalmist declares "I will offer in his tent sacrifices with shouts of joy; I will sing and make melody to the LORD" (v. 6). The word translated as "shout" is *teru'ah*, which describes a cultic shout or battle cry such as soldiers would voice when going into battle. It was no small noise, but a loud exclamation, in this case a shout of joyous praise.

Note the references to God's "tent," as a place of refuge in v. 5 and as a place of sacrifice in v. 6 (though v. 4 speaks of dwelling in the "house of the LORD"). If indeed the psalm originated with David – or if a later psalmist wanted to make it appear that it did – "tent" would be the appropriate term. David brought the Ark of the Covenant to Jerusalem and installed it in a tent, according to 2 Sam. 6:17, where he was prone to pray (2 Sam. 7:18). The temple was not built until the reign of Solomon. [**Tent, or house?**]

The first part of the psalm, then, begins and ends with happy praise from a joyful and confident worshiper. When we come to v. 7, though, we wonder: "Could this be the same person?"

Longing for God
(vv. 7-12)

In vv. 7-14, assurance is but a memory and God's presence a distant dream. In the classic form of a lament, the psalmist longs for a sense of God's presence and pleads for God

Tent, or house? The use of apparently contradictory terms to describe Israel's centralized worship place also occurs with relation to the cultic center at Shiloh when Eli presided as priest. We read of a tent of meeting (*'ohel mō'ed*) in 1 Sam. 2:22, and the temple of the LORD (*hêkal Yahweh*) in 1 Sam. 1:9 and 3:3. According to 1 Sam. 3:15, Samuel rose up to open the doors of the house of the LORD (*bêt Yahweh*).

The imagery suggests that the tabernacle reportedly constructed during the wilderness wandering had come to rest in Shiloh, where it became a more permanent installation.

> **A parent who doesn't forsake:** Some scholars suggest that the psalmist's insistence that parents might forsake, but not God, may reflect a royal setting. We have indicated previously that the first part of the psalm fits well with the image of a king celebrating the confidence of divine protection as he goes into battle. One stream of thought in ancient Israel was that the king was "adopted" as God's son in a sense, as seen in coronation hymns such as Psalm 2 "He said to me, 'You are my son; today I have begotten you'" (Ps. 2:7).

not to turn away, as if he or she feels abandoned by the same God who once had seemed so close (vv. 7-8).

Heart-full of desire, the psalmist pleads to see God's face (v. 9a), leading readers to wonder why the poet believed that God had turned away. Our only clue is the psalmist's plea "Do not turn your servant away in anger, you who have been my help. Do not cast me off, do not forsake me, O God of my salvation!" (v. 9b).

Why would God be angry? Hebrew theology did not consider God to be capricious or easily provoked. Rather, the classic understanding of God's temperament was Yahweh's self-revelation to Moses in Exod. 34:6: "a God merciful and gracious, slow to anger, and abounding in steadfast love and faithfulness …"

Generally, one who feared God's anger did so from an awareness of personal sin, of having turned away from God first. But the Bible also contains accounts of people who felt abandoned by God for no good reason. Job is the classic example, and this poet might be another.

The psalmist was convinced that God, even more faithful than one's parents, would not forsake forever (v. 10) – but that did not preclude the fear of being forsaken in the meantime. [**A parent who doesn't forsake**] Enemies were about (v. 11), false witnesses who were "breathing out violence" (v. 12). If we are to think of vv. 7-14 as deriving from the same postulant as vv. 1-6, who may have been a king, vv. 11-12 summon visions of palace intrigue or propaganda campaigns from neighboring nations.

Such speculation is not necessary, however. The psalmist, like many of us, could have experienced the cold shoulder of former friends who turned against him, or jealous competitors who sought to elevate themselves by bringing him down. Such times might lead us to wonder where God has gone, and why such trouble has come to us. Dealing with people who actively oppose us or make our lives miserable can be difficult, and it calls for a special measure of God's leadership if we are to respond with wisdom and care. Thus, the psalmist asks "Teach me your way, O LORD, and lead me on a level path" (v. 11).

Can you recall times when someone criticized your performance or opposed what you were doing? We can respond in ways that make the situation worse, or we can exhibit more positive behaviors that bring grace into the picture. The psalmist's practice of pausing to pray and seek God's leadership before going forward offers a word of wisdom for all.

Trusting God
(vv. 13-14)

Laments in the psalms often conclude with an expression of trust that God will respond positively, and Psalm 27 is no exception, as the poet averred: "I believe that I shall see the goodness of the LORD in the land of the living" (v. 13). In other words, the psalmist – whether king or commoner – expects to survive the crisis, remain "in the land of the living," and experience God's goodness again.

Some interpreters read v. 14 as a priestly oracle of assurance that responds to the postulant's prayer by counseling patience and trust. It is just as likely, however, that it could be the psalmist's own reflection. God had been present in the past (as expressed in vv. 1-6) and could be trusted to bless the psalmist again: he or she needed only to wait and trust in God's deliverance. The reminder to "be strong, and let your heart take courage" is reminiscent of Moses' charge to Joshua as he assumed leadership in Moses' place (Deut. 31:7, 23), a charge reiterated by Yahweh in a personal vision to Joshua (Josh. 1:6, 7, 9).

As Joshua trusted God and led Israel to many victories, so the psalmist sought to be strong and courageous as he maintained trust in God for help that was yet to come.

If we find that God seems far away in our own lives, perhaps this psalm may offer assurance and strength to us, too.

The Hardest Question
Is Psalm 27 one psalm or two?

A surface reading of Psalm 27 reveals what appears to be two psalms in one: the first six verses exhibit the qualities of a psalm of praise or trust, while vv. 7-14 have all the earmarks of a lament. Should we regard Psalm 27 as separate psalms by different authors, or from the same poet in very different situations?

It is not unusual for psalms to be combined or numbered differently. For example, Psalms 9 and 10 are separate in Hebrew, but one psalm in the Greek Septuagint (abbreviated as LXX). Likewise, Psalms 114 and 115 in the Hebrew text appear as Psalm 113 in the LXX, and thus in Catholic/Orthodox Bibles. But, Psalm 116 in Hebrew is divided into two psalms (114–115) in the LXX, and Psalm 147 appears as 146 and 147.

Psalm 27 is numbered as one psalm in both the Hebrew and Greek traditions, but should each part be read and interpreted separately, or did the final editor of Psalms intend for us to read them together?

On the basis of form alone, our inclination would be to identify two separate psalms. The first six verses comprise a psalm of trust, not unlike Psalm 23. It is a testimony of what God has done for the psalmist, and declaration of assurance that God will yet act on his or her behalf.

The second part of Psalm 27 is a classic lament. Psalms of lament typically begin with a cry for God to hear the petitioner's plea, usually in a time of distress or trouble when God seems far away. Laments plead with God for deliverance, and usually express trust that God will hear the prayer, frequently closing with words of praise or assurance in advance of it actually happening. All these characteristics are present in vv. 7-14.

It appears, then, that we have what were originally two psalms, but they must have been combined for a purpose. Some scholars surmise that the protagonist of the psalm is a king who initially praises God for past victories, but later pleads for deliverance in a more difficult time.

Whether we imagine a royal theme or not, the combination of two psalms, one of trust and one of lament, may also be seen as an intentional reminder that we all face ups and downs in life. There are times when we feel strong, close to God, and confident in our faith, as in vv. 1-6. There are other times when we struggle with various difficulties and feel far from God, as in vv. 7-14. In those times, we can look back to former experiences and trust that God's face will again look toward us with favor: we have only to wait for the LORD with strength and courage, trusting past experience for the promise of future deliverance.

Third Sunday after Epiphany

Third Reading
1 Corinthians 1:10-18

Perilous Polarities

Now I appeal to you, brothers and sisters, by the name of our Lord Jesus Christ, that all of you be in agreement and that there be no divisions among you, but that you be united in the same mind and the same purpose. (1 Cor. 1:10)

Have you ever ridden a "Tilt-a-whirl," "Octopus," or something similar at a traveling fair or an amusement park? The nausea-inducing rides consist of a series of arms, each with a seating compartment at the end. While the entire contraption goes round and round, the seating pods spin and the arms go up and down in a stomach-lurching orbit that threatens to launch partially digested funnel cakes, hot dogs, and turkey legs into the surrounding crowds.

Such ill-conceived contrivances may come to mind while contemplating today's text, in which Paul confronts a problem of division and dysfunction that was sickening the Corinthian congregation. **[A devilish design]** The competing factions – and there appear to have been several in Corinth – were not unlike the seating pods on that amusement ride: each one spinning on its own axis with little thought that all were connected to a central point.

One appeal
(vv. 10-12)

The carefully worded way Paul began his letter hinted that there was trouble in the air, and he wasted no time in confronting it. The church in Corinth, immature but proud, was riddled with dissension. The problem was so grave that, in one way or another, Paul's efforts to deal with it stretch from 1 Cor. 1:10 to 4:21.

Paul knew the danger that division can bring to a church, so he had already reminded the Corinthian believers that they all were called by God to live in *koinonia* (fellowship or communion) with Christ and other "saints" wherever the gospel was known.

> **A devilish design:** In preaching from 1 Corinthians, the early church father John Chrysostom (347–407) described the divisions at Corinth as being inspired by the devil.
>
> "The devil, seeing that a great city had accepted the truth and received the Word of God with great eagerness, set about dividing it. He knew that even the strongest kingdom, if divided against itself, would not stand. He had a choice weapon for doing this in the wealth and wisdom of the inhabitants, which made them exceedingly proud" (*Homilies on the Epistles of Paul to the Corinthians*, Proem, in Gerald Bray, ed., *1–2 Corinthians*, vol. 7 of ACCS NT, ed. Thomas C. Oden [InterVarsity Press, 1999], 2), cited by Scott Nash in *1 Corinthians*, Smyth & Helwys Bible Commentary [Smyth & Helwys, 2009], 67).

With v. 10, Paul spelled things out more clearly: "Now I appeal to you, brothers and sisters, that all of you be in agreement and that there be no divisions among you, but that you be united in the same mind and the same purpose."

Paul routinely addressed the Corinthians and other churches with the masculine term *adelphoi*, but he clearly was speaking to women in the church too. As a result, modern versions such as NRSV, NIV11, and NET expand the translation to include "brothers and sisters."

Paul knew that divisions existed. A visit from "Chloe's people" had filled him in on the fractured state of the church, where some claimed "I belong to Paul" (literally, "I am of Paul"), while others said "I am of Apollos" or "I am of Cephas." **[Chloe's people]**

The verse ends with "I am of Christ." Was there a fourth faction who claimed to be the true Christ party?

Chloe's people: Who was Chloe, and who were her people? The feminine form of the name tells us that Chloe was a woman, and the reference to "Chloe's people" gives the impression that she was a person of influence in the church. Chloe's ability to send the representatives suggests that she was a woman of means.

Beyond this, we can only speculate, for 1 Cor. 1:11 is the only place in scripture where she is mentioned. Chloe might have been one of several people in Corinth who hosted a house church in her home.

There are reasons to suspect that Chloe was a leader of one of the factions, perhaps the party of Paul, since her representatives had come to him. That effort makes it likely that she was deeply involved in the controversy and either seeking Paul's advice or appealing to him to exert his authority.

Or could the last statement be Paul's exasperated response: "I belong to Christ!"?

What were these divisions about? Scott Nash argues that disagreement over whether to accept Paul's authority was at the heart of the matter (*1 Corinthians*, Smyth & Helwys Bible Commentary [Smyth & Helwys, 2009], 24-29, 84-85). The city of Corinth, like other great cities of the time, would have had its share of homegrown or traveling sophists and rhetoricians who were known for their sparkling speech and clever arguments, and visitors such as Paul would have been measured against them.

Paul, by his own admission, was a steady worker and faithful witness, but not a polished speaker. In a later letter, Paul quoted his critics' judgment that "his letters are weighty and strong, but his bodily presence is weak, and his speech contemptible" (2 Cor. 10:10).

Apollos was known as "an eloquent man, well-versed in the scriptures" (Acts 18:24), so it is not surprising that some of the early Christians would prefer his leadership. Peter (Cephas) was not known for his scintillating speech, but he was regarded as chief among the apostles and perhaps favored by Jewish believers. Apollos spent some time in Corinth (Acts 19:1), but there is no other evidence that Peter had visited the city. We have no reason to suspect that either would have sought to cultivate a following in opposition to Paul.

It is possible that local church members skilled in public speech had developed their own followings and named their parties for one of the more famous leaders of the early church.

Scholars have long speculated what theological differences may have divided the Corinthians, but the dissension may have been as much about church politics and power as about theology.

Three questions
(v. 13)

Paul, despite his perceived shortcomings as a public speaker, was a master of rhetoric, and he understood the power of pointed, even sarcastic questions. In v. 13, he launched into three sharp queries: "Has Christ been divided? Was Paul crucified for you? Or were you baptized in the name of Paul?"

The first question exposes the absurdity of Christians choosing sides when all are called to follow the same Christ. We are human, however, and will have different understandings of what it means to follow Christ.

This has become increasingly apparent in the United States. Some believers insist that the only way to honor Christ is to regard the Bible as inerrant truth and interpret it literally – emphasizing proof texts that suit their conservative tastes and – often – a white nationalist political agenda.

Other believers take a more open view of scriptures and believe that Christ is best served when we adopt his approach of extending compassion to all people, with more emphasis on grace than law. They hold more progressive views on race, gender, sexuality, and social justice.

Those who lived through the controversy that wracked the Southern Baptist Convention in the 1980s and 90s know how ugly such conflict can be. While that conflict was couched in theological terms, politics and power were clearly at the heart of it.

Similar factions can develop within churches, even small ones. Can divorced-and-remarried persons serve as deacons? Can women be allowed to preach or called as pastors? Will the church welcome people who are gay or transgendered? Should worship follow a traditional model or a contemporary approach? Should the church buy a new van for mission trips and fellowship outings, or donate the money to direct mission support?

Division comes in many forms, and may arise for many reasons. When we frame our personal desires in theological language and use the Bible as a weapon against others, we find ourselves desperately in need of Paul's appeal to overcome divisions and "be united in the same mind and the same purpose" (v. 10b).

One answer
(vv. 14-18)

While Paul asked three questions, he addressed only the third one directly. The first two questions were primarily rhetorical, designed to show the foolishness of factionalism.

"Is Christ divided?" Of course not, though his followers might turn against each other because they hold to quite different images of Christ's life, work, and call.

"Was Paul crucified for you?" No one would have raised such a ridiculous question, but some may have shown more practical allegiance to Paul than to Christ, and such a query might shock them into considering where their deepest loyalty should lie.

The third question also had its absurd aspects: "Were you baptized in the name of Paul?" Paul knew that all members had been baptized in the name of Christ, even if some of them seemed to put more emphasis on the preacher than the savior.

Paul's comments about which persons he had baptized do not address the question directly, for they have to do with the act of baptism, not whether the new believers were baptized in Paul's name. Even so, Paul expressed some relief that he had baptized only a few of the Corinthian believers – not enough to create a viable faction.

Crispus, a former leader of the synagogue, along with a man named Gaius and family members of a certain Stephanas were the only people Paul could remember baptizing in Corinth. He did not want anyone claiming superiority because they had been baptized by the church's founder, and certainly not because they were baptized in his name (vv. 14-16). [**Effective baptism**]

Effective baptism: Paul's comments about baptism bring to mind a small branch on the Baptist tree known as "Landmark Baptists." Landmarkers believe that their sect can be traced all the way back to John the Baptist, and hold that baptism is not legitimate unless administered by a minister who is descended in a direct apostolic succession from him.

At all times, Paul sought to keep the spotlight on Christ. Jesus had not called him to baptize but to preach the gospel, and that "not with eloquent wisdom" such as the Corinthians loved, but with straightforward speech, "so that the cross might not be emptied of its power" (v. 17).

The phrase rendered as "eloquent wisdom" in the NRSV and "clever speech" in the NET is literally *sophía lógou*, "wisdom of words." Paul seemed to think the Corinthians had gone too far in attempting to make their church culturally appealing, or they were too influenced by those who emphasized style over substance, making impressive speeches that were not doctrinally sound.

Paul's goal was to see people come to trust in Christ, not because a slick-tongued evangelist had persuaded them to do so through an emotional appeal or because a skilled apologist had convinced them with a rational argument, but because they recognized the centrality of Christ's atoning death.

Paul wanted to maintain the priority of the message over the messenger, but some members of the church in Corinth had it the other way around: they were more loyal to a particular leader or a favored style or a theological position than they were to Christ.

Where does our loyalty lie? Have we ever found ourselves more concerned about a decision relative to the church building or the format of worship or the calling of a pastor than we were about serving Jesus? Can we rally around Christ as the unifying center that is stronger than our differences?

Those are not rhetorical questions.

The Hardest Question
What was behind the dissension at Corinth?

Scholars have long wondered if the factions Paul spoke of were based on theological differences, or whether they grew out of personal or political rivalries within the church. We have precious little evidence to go on: Paul's arguments against divisiveness in their ranks focus on the dangers inherent in some thinking their powers of speech or wisdom or spiritual unction made them superior to others. This suggests that old-fashioned competition for attention or power may have been at the root of the issue.

The possibility that theological differences divided the parties has led to considerable speculation, however, though the only real clues are found in the names Paul assigns to the factions: "I am of Paul." "I am of Apollos." "I am of Cephas." "I am of Christ."

Scholars generally picture the Paul group as being made up of loyal followers who held to his thorough-going insistence that salvation comes through faith and not works, that one pleases God by trusting Christ rather than by keeping the law. Paul's teachings were seen as liberating believers from Torah teachings such as kosher laws, and as promoting full fellowship with Gentile believers.

Peter, despite the experience of learning that God is not partial and seeing Gentile believers blessed by the Spirit in Acts 10, was known as a more traditional leader who continued to keep the Jewish law and maintained some separation between himself and Gentile believers (see Acts 15 and Galatians 2, where Paul confronted Peter directly).

Since Apollos was both Greek and known for his eloquence, some interpreters suspect that his group favored wisdom traditions and philosophical notions common among the Hellenistic Jews.

The Christ group (if Paul meant for it to be considered as a faction) is more of a puzzle. Some speculate that it may indicate believers who put more emphasis on spiritual gifts and were particularly proud of their ability to speak in tongues.

Evidence for any formal division along theological lines remains lacking. "Paul's major concern," Scott Nash argues, "seems to be not that they have adopted erroneous theologies but that they have allowed nontheological, worldly perspectives to shape their thinking and behavior" (*1 Corinthians*, Smyth & Helwys Bible Commentary [Smyth & Helwys, 2009], 85).

Third Sunday after Epiphany

Fourth Reading
Matthew 4:12-25

A Preacher Who Calls

And he said to them, "Follow me, and I will make you fish for people." (Matt. 4:19)

Life is all about beginnings. Each morning begins a new day. Each January begins a new year. Each step of schooling and every stage of life requires a new beginning: jobs, marriage, moves. Every task must be begun before it can be completed. Every obstacle introduces another challenge to be overcome.

Jesus' life was no different in this respect. The gospel of Matthew, which we follow in Year A of the lectionary, opens with a story of how Jesus' life began as an infant (chs. 1–2), then skips to his entry onto the public stage through baptism at the hands of John and public endorsement by the Spirit (ch. 3). Jesus' spiritual pilgrimage begins with the story of the temptation (4:1-11), and his active ministry begins with 4:12-25, our text for today.

The Revised Common Lectionary reading stops at v. 23, but the pericope continues through v. 25, so we will consider all of Matt. 4:12-25.

Jesus preaches
(vv. 12-17)

Matthew connects the beginning of Jesus' active ministry with a sharp break in John's: "Now when Jesus heard that John had been arrested, he withdrew to Galilee" (v. 12).

Matthew says nothing here about why John had been arrested, though a later story connects John's arrest with his public criticism of Herod Antipas for having married his brother Herod Phillip's wife, Herodias (14:3-4). This may or may not have been the same arrest: the Jewish authorities could have arrested him earlier for claiming publicly that Jesus was the son of God.

We have too little to go on, other than that John continued to have some disciples who remained with him.

> **Capernaum:** All four gospels locate Jesus in Capernaum at some point, but only Matthew says that he intentionally moved there, leaving his home in Nazareth, at the very beginning of his ministry. In Luke, Jesus is rejected in the synagogue at Nazareth before "he went down to Capernaum, a city in Galilee," in order to teach (Luke 4:31), apparently adopting it as a home base because Simon and Andrew had a home there.

The interesting thing to note is that Matthew portrays Jesus and John "hearing" about the other and responding through intermediaries, but not personally interacting.

Matthew's account does not suggest that Jesus returned to Galilee and settled in Capernaum out of fear that he might also be arrested, but rather describes the return as a fulfillment of prophecy. This is typical of Matthew's approach, the fifth of 10 times that he says Jesus did something as a fulfillment of prophecy. **[Capernaum]**

Nazareth was within the traditional tribal boundaries of Zebulon, and Capernaum was in the region designated for Naphtali. Perhaps this led Matthew to quote loosely from the Greek translation of Isa. 9:1-2, where the prophet had predicted that God would cause light to break upon the land of Zebulon and Naphtali, whose people had "walked in darkness."

Strangely, both Isa. 9:1 and Matthew's quotation in v. 15 describe the land of Zebulon and Naphtali as being "beyond" or "across" the Jordan, but they were both on the near side of the Jordan River. Elsewhere, "beyond the Jordan" (modern "Transjordan") routinely refers to the eastern side of the Jordan. Capernaum is located about three miles west of the river, but it was close to the Transjordan area, where Jesus also ministered.

Editor Matthew: Matthew's gospel draws heavily from the earlier gospel of Mark, which describes the beginning of Jesus' preaching ministry this way: "The time is fulfilled, and the kingdom of God has come near, repent and believe the good news."

Matthew's version is much shorter: "Repent, for the kingdom of heaven has come near" (v. 17). Perhaps it is because he included a specific prophecy that Matthew deleted "the time is fulfilled," though it is less clear why he did not include Jesus' call to "believe the good news." Perhaps he thought the good news was self-evident in the nearness of the kingdom.

Capernaum was located on the northwest edge of the Sea of Galilee (also called "Kinnereth" or "Gennesaret"). It was not a large town, but significant in part because a branch of the *Via Maris*, a major highway known as the "Way of the Sea," ran past it. Many Jews lived in the area, but a largely Gentile population also called it home.

Matthew, like others in the early church, saw Jesus' preaching as fulfilling the promise that light would dawn on those who had lived in darkness. "From that time Jesus began to proclaim 'Repent, for the kingdom of heaven has come near'" (v. 17). [**Editor Matthew**]

The call to "repent" (from the verb *metanoia*) is not an appeal to feel sorry for one's sins alone, but to turn away from a self-centered lifestyle and turn toward God. It reflects the meaning of the Hebrew word *shub*, commonly translated as "repent," that literally means "to turn around." The first step in adopting a "Jesus worldview" is to turn away from the world and turn toward Jesus.

Unlike Mark and Luke, Matthew uses "kingdom of heaven" rather than "kingdom of God," perhaps reflecting a growing desire among the Jews to show reverence for God's name by not pronouncing it.

But what is the "kingdom of heaven"? For many years, the Jews had hoped that God would break into history and set up an earthly kingdom. Prophets such as Isaiah and Micah had spoken of a day when all nations would come to Jerusalem to worship God and there would be peace on earth (Isa. 2:2-4, Mic. 4:1-4).

In Jesus' day, people were more likely to hope for a military messiah to arise, lead them to victory over the despised Romans, and reestablish an Israelite kingdom.

In the teaching of Jesus, the messianic age had come, but not as expected. Rather than restoring the Hebrew monarchy or setting up a new world order, Jesus introduced a radically different notion. The kingdom of God/heaven was not a particular place, but the spiritual realm in which God is king. The kingdom of God is the rule of God, the realm in which God operates. Think of it as the "-dom" (representing "domain" or "dominion") in "kingdom."

Jesus could say "the kingdom of God is at hand" because *he* was at hand. The rule of God was at work in his life and ministry. When Jesus called people to repent because the kingdom was near, he was calling them to live under God's rule and so bring the ethics of the kingdom to bear wherever they were.

Jesus calls
(vv. 18-22)

As Jesus began his active ministry, he did more than preach inspiring sermons to anonymous crowds: he also spoke to individuals, built relationships, and challenged a small group of people to follow him as disciples. The gospel writers agree that Andrew and Simon Peter were among the first disciples called, though John tells it differently. [**Who's on first?**]

Who's on first? Matthew 4:1-22 and Mark 1:16-20 tell essentially the same story: Jesus first saw Peter and Andrew casting their nets on the Sea of Galilee, called them, and they followed. He then repeated the process with James and John.

Luke's account (5:1-11) differs in that Jesus, pursued by a crowd, hopped into Simon's boat and asked him to shove it out into the water. After preaching from the floating pulpit, he told them where to cast their net to catch a great haul of fish, leading Peter to kneel in adoration. James and John, described as Simon's partners, were also amazed, and they joined Simon Peter in following Jesus. Though we may presume Andrew was present, he is not mentioned until 6:14.

John's version (1:35-42) says that Andrew and another unnamed person had become disciples of John the Baptist, who was preaching in Judea. Jesus met them there and invited them to stay with him. Andrew sought out his brother Simon and brought him to Jesus, who renamed him Cephas (Aramaic for Peter). The next day, Jesus found Philip, who introduced him to Nathanael (1:43-51). James and John do not enter the story until later.

As Mark and Matthew relate the story, Jesus was walking beside the Sea of Galilee when he saw Simon and Andrew, apparently within shouting distance of shore, casting their nets. The Greek word describes a small circular net, with weights around the outside. When thrown over a school of fish, one could pull a drawstring that would cinch the bottom and trap the fish. Modern fishermen use a similar net for bait casting. Peter and Andrew were probably after shoals of sardines that often came near shore.

With no prior recorded conversation, Jesus challenged the fishermen to leave their nets, follow him, and start fishing for people (vv. 16-17).

Further along the rocky shore, Jesus found James and John sitting in their boat and mending nets, which were often snagged and needed constant repair lest ripped places allow the fish an easy escape. Jesus called to them, presumably in a similar fashion.

In both cases, the story says, the men responded "*immediately,*" leaving their boats, nets, and family behind. What do we make of this? Mark tells the story as if the first disciples had never seen Jesus before, yet one simple command led them to leave their boats behind and follow him. Was Jesus' call so irresistible that a simple command on first sight was all it took to win their allegiance?

Let's examine the clues. In vv. 12-17, Matthew indicates that Jesus had already moved to Capernaum and started preaching. Capernaum was a small village, so it's unlikely that Jesus would have gone unnoticed, either there or in the surrounding area. We don't know how much time passed between Jesus' move to Capernaum, the beginning of his preaching ministry, and his call of these first disciples. Matthew is following Mark, who moved the story along at a rapid clip.

So, Matthew clearly implies that Simon, Andrew, James, and John would have seen and heard Jesus before, whether they had yet greeted him personally or not. They would have known about his preaching, which certainly included more than "Repent, for the kingdom of heaven is near." They may have been thinking already about how they might respond. Perhaps Jesus' visit to the lakeside and his personal challenge was all they needed to push them over the top.

Even so, the brevity with which Mark and Matthew tell the story emphasizes the power of Jesus' charismatic personality and the forcefulness of his call. Jesus called, and they responded – immediately.

And what did Jesus call them to do? To change their focus from catching fish to catching people. The metaphor is a little unwieldy, because when people who fish for a living make a catch, it's usually the end of the line for the fish. In Jesus' worldview, catching people meant living in a way that we draw others out of the world and into the kingdom, where the old life does end in a sense, but a new and better life begins.

As we wonder how well the first disciples knew Jesus, and what motivated them to leave their livelihoods behind and follow him as disciples, we can't help but ask ourselves what it takes to motivate us to follow Jesus and live as he called us to.

Why should any person give his or her first allegiance to God when the patterns and comforts of ordinary life are so familiar? What would attract us to a lifestyle of living and loving as Jesus taught us to do?

Would it take more knowledge about Jesus? A sense of desperation with no place left to turn, or a spiritual experience that we can't understand? In many cases, new followers are motivated by the example of a friend whose life seems so grounded and joyful that they want to be like him or her – and thus they are "caught" for the kingdom.

Jesus ministers
(vv. 23-25)

Matthew squeezes Jesus' early ministry and rapid rise in popularity into vv. 23-25. Jesus began to preach throughout Galilee, he said, teaching in the synagogues but more notably healing people of dread diseases and conditions: he ministered in both word and action. In this way, Jesus' reputation spread and "great crowds followed him from Galilee, the Decapolis, Jerusalem, Judea, and from beyond the Jordan." Though Jesus remained in Galilee, word about him spread and people flocked from all the surrounding areas as they came to learn about Jesus' worldview, grounded in the kingdom of God.

With these few verses, Matthew illustrates the spiritual hunger of the people, and Jesus' surprising manner of ministering to it.

How hungry are we, and how needy is our world? Are we ready to go fishing?

The Hardest Question

Why did Jesus begin his ministry in Galilee?

If Jesus wanted to make an immediate impact, one would think he'd choose to begin preaching in Jerusalem, or that he would take advantage of the crowds John had attracted to a wilderness area near the Jordan River, much closer to Jerusalem than Galilee. Why start in an out-of-the-way place such as Galilee?

In the time of Jesus, Galilee was a governmental district located north and west of the Sea of Galilee, stretching south to the Jezreel Valley, north to Lake Huleh, and west to the border with Phoenicia. Historically, its population was mainly non-Jewish, so much so that it was called "Galilee of the nations" (Isa. 9:1).

Today, the term is used more to describe a geographic region. "Upper Galilee" refers generally to the area north of the Sea of Galilee, while "Lower Galilee" refers to the area west of the Sea of Galilee and south to the Jezreel Valley.

When the Jewish Hasmonean king Aristobulus conquered the area around 104 BCE, he sought to force Gentile residents to convert to Judaism or leave the area. By the first century CE, however, the Romans had long been in control and Galilee included healthy groups of both Jews and Gentiles, with individual towns being predominantly Jewish or Roman. Jesus' home village of Nazareth was in Galilee, as was Capernaum, which Mark identifies as the home of Peter and Andrew.

Jews from Galilee apparently spoke with distinctive accents (Matt. 26:23), and some belonged to a movement of anti-Roman activists known as the Zealots (one of Jesus' disciples was known as "Simon the Zealot").

So, why would Jesus begin his work in Galilee? While no one can claim to know the mind of Christ, several factors may have entered his thinking. First, Galilee was familiar to Jesus; it was where he grew up, where his family and friends lived.

Second, the anti-Roman activism in Galilee may suggest a general unrest with the status quo that could have made its population ripe for a message that was radically new. And, although Jesus made a point of saying he had come first to the Jews, he knew that many Gentiles would hear his message, too.

Third, Galilee was located at a distance from Jerusalem, where the Jewish authorities would certainly be opposed to Jesus' message. By beginning his work in the backwater towns of Galilee, Jesus had a better chance of building a strong following before the authorities sought to silence or discredit him. Though John's gospel says he made brief visits to Jerusalem, the other gospels have him remain outside of Jerusalem until Palm Sunday. Thus, the gospels pay special attention to the time when Jesus "set his face to go to Jerusalem" (Luke 9:51), because it would mean the end of his earthly ministry.

Fourth Sunday after Epiphany
First Reading
Micah 6:1-8

The Bottom Line

He has told you, O mortal, what is good; and what does the LORD require of you but to do justice,
and to love kindness, and to walk humbly with your God? (Mic. 6:8)

By the fourth Sunday of Epiphany, New Year's resolutions may already have gone by the wayside, but there's still time to think about how we plan to carry out our lives during the coming year. What do we want to do, and what do others expect of us? What does our family expect? What's expected in our job, or in our volunteer positions? What does our community or our country expect? More importantly, what does God expect of us?

> **Covenant lawsuits:** Micah's portrayal of a lawsuit (Hebrew *rîb*) between God and Israel is often called a "covenant lawsuit" because the law it was based upon – and which Israel had violated – was the covenant agreement between Yahweh and Israel, first sealed at Sinai and renewed a number of times afterward.
>
> Other Old Testament texts that portray similar lawsuits can be found in Psalm 50; Isa. 1:2-3, 3:13-15; and Jer. 2:4-37.

A challenging lawsuit
(vv. 1-5)

Fortunately, the Bible offers a very good answer. It is found in the writings of the prophet Micah, who often pointed out how Israel had fallen short of God's expectations for them.

Micah lived and worked in and around Jerusalem during precisely the same period as Isaiah, the latter part of the eighth century BCE. He hailed from Moresheth, a village near the city of Gath, in an area of fair and fertile hills about 20 miles southwest of Jerusalem.

Micah appears to have belonged to the proletarian class. He had a keen social conscience and was a champion of the peasantry. He promoted ethical living and forcefully condemned the injustice, greed, and decadence of the controlling aristocracy who lived in the cities.

He was probably born about 760 BCE: at least one of his oracles predates the fall of Samaria in 722, and other oracles seem to be clustered around times of Assyrian aggression in 711 (Sargon II) and 701 (Sennacherib). Micah prophesied the destruction of Jerusalem, which came under siege in 701 but did not fall for another 125 years.

Micah's name is probably a contraction of *micaiyah*, which would mean "Who is like Yahweh?" Micah was a gifted prophet, and apparently had some influence, at least on Hezekiah. We read about this in Jer. 26:18-19, which quotes Micah 3:12 – the only time in the Old Testament where a prophet is named and quoted verbatim.

In a speech that opens ch. 6, Micah portrayed a dramatic scene in which God called Israel to court with the mountains and hills, the "enduring foundations of the earth," as both witnesses and jury (vv. 1-2). **[Covenant lawsuits]**

Acting as God's prosecuting attorney, Micah asked "O my people, what have I done to you? In what have I wearied you? Answer me!" (v. 3). Micah began by asking why the people would complain against God. Were they tired of waiting for an easier life when their present troubles were their own fault? Was God not living up to their expectations of a carefree life?

Like other prophets, Micah pointed to the many ways in which Yahweh had been faithful to Israel: God had brought the people up from Egypt, providing Moses as their leader, Aaron as their priest, and Miriam as a prophet (v. 4). When King Balak of Moab paid the pagan shaman Balaam to pronounce a curse on Israel, Yahweh forced him to speak only good of the people's future (v. 5a). When the people were finally ready to enter the Promised Land, God led them from Shittim, their last camp east of the Jordan, to Gilgal, their first camp in Canaan (v. 5b), crossing the river on dry land. Had the people forgotten these things?

A poor defense
(vv. 6-7)

Micah believed the people had failed to appreciate God's blessings and had ignored God's guidance. He perceived that they had substituted religion for righteousness. They understood rituals, but not respect. They were quite good at religion: they worshiped at the temple, sacrificed animals, and paid requisite tithes, but the way they lived was a different matter.

Micah saw through the trappings of Israel's religious practices to recognize that the people had reduced their religion to a system of bribing God with prayers and sacrifices in hopes that Yahweh would adopt a positive attitude toward them, but it wasn't God's attitude that needed changing. It was theirs.

The people's only defense, which Micah quoted sarcastically in vv. 6-7, was locked into the categories of ritual and sacrifice. "What do you expect of us?" he portrayed them as asking. "How do you want us to approach you? With whole burnt offerings? With year-old calves? With thousands of rams, or tens of thousands of rivers of oil? Shall we sacrifice our firstborn children as payment of our transgressions?" (vv. 6-7).

Whole burnt offerings, the '*ōlâ* or "holocaust" sacrifice, called for an entire animal, usually a young sheep or goat, to be burned on the altar. These were offered less often than *shelamîm* offerings, in which God was offered the blood and visceral fat, while worshipers and the priests cooked and ate the meat. Did God want a higher percentage of whole burnt offerings, or for more of them to be year-old calves, which were more valuable than younger animals?

With increasing sarcasm, Micah imagined them upping the ante. Does Yahweh want "thousands" of rams? "Ten thousand rivers" of valuable olive oil? Would God

never be pleased? Should they go the ultimate distance and sacrifice their first-born children to atone for their sins?

The answer, or course, was "No" on all counts. Child sacrifice was expressly forbidden by the law (Lev. 18:21, 20:2-5; Deut. 18:10), and the prophets strongly condemned it (Jer. 7:31, 19:5; Ezek. 16:20-21, 20:26; Isa. 57:5).

Micah understood that God was not interested in more ritual sacrifices or more religious acts. God wanted Israel to be righteous, not just religious, and that desire has not changed. Believers today are not called to religion so much as to a right relationship with God and others. As Ralph L. Smith put it, "So when we come before God we must remember that it is not so much what is in our hands but what is in our hearts that finds expression in our conduct that is important" (*Micah–Malachi*, vol. 32, Word Biblical Commentary [Zondervan, 1984], 51).

What God expects
(v. 8)

And so, in God's behalf, Micah offered a remarkable response that countless believers have memorized as a guideline for life: "He has told you, O mortal, what is good; and what does the LORD require of you but to do justice, and to love kindness, and to walk humbly with your God" (6:8).

In this charge Micah laid out the bottom line of God's expectations for all people. Most translations say "He has told you, O man, what is good …," but the word translated as "man" is '*adam*, the Hebrew word for humankind. In context, Micah was talking to Israel – both men and women – but God's purpose was for the people of the covenant to become witnesses and examples for all nations to follow.

This is what God expects of all mortals. We live in a world where people practice prejudice, love selfishness, and walk arrogantly as their own gods, but what God expects is that we do justice, love kindness, and walk humbly before God.

Micah did not claim that this was any new revelation. "He has (already) told you," he said. The teaching of Moses, the Ten Commandments, and the proclamation of other prophets had often declared the kind of attitudes and actions that God expects. **[Do justice]**

What does it mean to "do justice"? Micah used the word *mishpat*, a term that could describe a legal decision

Do justice: When I was a boy, students from all 12 grades rode the school bus together. In our county, we had two schools. One was for the white children, and one was for the black children, and both of them served all 12 grades on single campuses.

A boy several years older than me was named Jimmy Justice. I rarely had the nerve to talk to older students, but when Jimmy was about to graduate, I saw him passing as the buses rolled out, and I yelled out the window, "Do justice, Jimmy!"

As I spoke those words to a boy named Justice, it never occurred to me that we were both willing participants in a school system that was inherently unjust, because it treated people of one race as more precious and privileged than people of another race. I was so much a part of the culture in which I lived that I did not question the inherent injustice of it. Only later would I be confronted with my homegrown prejudices, and to appreciate the importance of basic human rights for all people. I suspect others could share similar stories.

or judgment, but more often referred to actions that are right and just for all people. Both history books and daily newspapers are replete with the terrible results of what happens when people do not treat others justly. When we label others with pejorative nicknames or lump them into a less favored category, they cease to be real people in our eyes. Because we don't see them as deserving of the same respect we receive, it's much easier to abuse them.

That's how the early American South justified slavery, how Hitler justified the gas chambers, and how militant religious extremists justify the mass murder of innocent civilians. That's how young men who think of themselves as upstanding citizens can justify terrorizing other young men because they are gay, or how some politicians can feign piety only to gain power.

Amos, Micah's contemporary, also upheld the virtue of justice. In words more familiar to us from a speech by Martin Luther King than from Amos, he also called on Israel to stop putting their trust in elaborate religious rituals. Instead, he said, "let justice roll down like waters, and righteousness as an ever-flowing stream" (Amos 5:24).

Doing justice begins with respect for the humanity and basic rights of all people – and it includes coming to the aid of those who are victims of injustice and cannot help themselves. King once asked: "Life's most persistent question is, 'What are you doing for others?'" And he observed that "The ultimate tragedy is not the oppression and cruelty by the bad people, but the silence over that by the good people."

It is so easy for custom and culture to blind us to injustice. Popular "reality" television competitions depict settings in which lying, cheating, backstabbing, and betrayal are all okay because "that's how you play the game." But life is not just a game, and others do matter.

Justice begins with respect for others, including those who look different, those who talk different, and even those who have different ideas. As King famously observed, "Injustice anywhere is a threat to justice everywhere."

What is our motivation for practicing genuine justice? Are we to go out on a limb and stand up for others just because God said so? Are principles and ideals of justice enough?

Of course not. Micah's audience had the law. They had a very clear set of moral and ethical codes to live by, but they weren't following them. That's because real justice cannot be motivated by fear of breaking the law alone. Real justice starts in the heart. It not only respects other people, but also loves them and wants what is best for them.

That's why Micah goes on to say "to do justice, *and to love kindness.*" That latter phrase can be translated in different ways. The familiar KJV and the NIV11 say "to love mercy." The NASB20 and NRSV have "to love kindness." The NET says "to be faithful." All of these elements are important, and it is this kind of faithful, steadfast love that motivates real justice. **[A course in kindness]**

Justice and mercy grow directly from a daily walk with God. Micah reminds us that we are called not only to walk with God, but also to walk humbly, modestly, and attentively.

So many problems in our world could be overcome if more of us could learn the art of humility. Any time people are dead certain that they have all the answers, one can be dead certain that strife will follow.

When religious leaders of any persuasion think they have a handle on all truth, or when political leaders think their way is the only way, or when husbands and wives are unwilling to compromise, there *will* be strife. There *will* be hurt. There *will* be pain.

A course in kindness: If anyone needs a remedial course in how to "love kindness," I suggest finding online videos of *Mister Rogers' Neighborhood*.

Fred Rogers was the kindest person I have ever met. In 1994, my young daughter Bethany was killed in a wreck caused by a drunken driver. While at home recovering from my own injuries, I wrote Mister Rogers a letter and thanked him for being a part of Bethany's neighborhood, for making her feel special every day.

After receiving the letter, Fred took the time to call and reach out, beginning a meaningful friendship that lasted until his untimely death in 2003.

I once visited Fred in his office above the PBS studio in Pittsburgh where *Mister Rogers' Neighborhood* was filmed. His office was tiny: no desk, just piles of trolleys and pictures to autograph for children, books and scripts, writing materials, and an eclectic collection of pictures and quotations on the wall. On one was a Hebrew verse about love, and a plaque with the Greek word for grace. Another wall sported a large piece of Chinese calligraphy that he translated as a traditional proverb: "If you want to see yourself clearly, don't look in muddy water."

One of Fred's greatest gifts was his ability to act as an undistorted mirror – to reflect back to people their inherent, essential worth and lovableness. I learned from Mister Rogers that when you show respect, it helps others feel worthy of respect. When you show love, they feel lovable. When you act as if they are special, they feel special.

That's the best picture I know of what it means to "love kindness." We will make our families, our neighborhoods and our world a better place if we work at becoming a person who is steadfast and loving.

Unless we are willing to admit that we might be wrong about something, or that the reality of a situation might be bigger than we yet comprehend, there is no room for change or growth in our own life, or in our relationships with others, or even in our relationship with God.

We can't know all the answers *and* walk humbly with God at the same time. God is far beyond our comprehension, bigger than what is revealed in the Bible, surpassing our imagination. There is much God wants to teach us, but we cannot learn if we are not teachable, and we are not teachable if we do not have some humility about us.

We may wonder about many things, but we don't have to wonder what God expects of us. We are called to *do justice*, to *love kindness*, to *walk humbly* with our God. If we can do that, we can be confident that our commu-

nities, our nation, our world will all be better for it – and that would be a very good thing.

The Hardest Question
Is it mercy, or love?

As noted earlier, the second element in God's expectations is often translated differently. The familiar KJV and the NIV11 say "to love mercy." The NASB20 and NRSV have "to love kindness." The NET says "to be faithful." What are they translating? The Hebrew has "and to love *chesed*." The word can be translated as "mercy" or as "kindness," but is more than both. Some have tried to capture it with "lovingkindness." Often it conveys the idea of loyalty or faithfulness. Perhaps the best translation is "steadfast love."

Chesed is the quintessential attitude of God toward God's people, used often in the Hebrew Bible. Think of Psalm 118, where every verse is punctuated with the phrase "His steadfast love endures forever." That's the word *chesed*.

Consider the story of when Moses on the mountain asked to see God. Yahweh passed by, the text says, and proclaimed a self-revelation of divine character: "Yahweh, Yahweh, a God merciful and gracious, slow to anger, and abounding in steadfast love and faithfulness …" (Exod. 34:6). In that text, "steadfast love" translates the word *chesed*.

Chesed is the closest Old Testament equivalent of the New Testament word *agapē*, which describes the kind of steadfast and self-sacrificing love that Jesus showed for all people, and that Jesus called his followers to show to others.

Remember that Micah enjoined his hearers to "love" this practice of *chesed*.

More than once, Jesus taught that the sum of God's commands is to love God and love others. In John 13:34-35, he said "I give you a new commandment, that you love one another. Just as I have loved you, you also should love one another. By this everyone will know that you are my disciples, if you have love for one another."

To love mercy, to love kindness, to show steadfast love, is to love as Jesus loved. If we are to be the people God has called us to be and that the world so desperately needs us to be, we will do justice precisely because we share that steadfast, merciful love. We know what it means to receive mercy, and out of gratitude we learn to show mercy as we walk humbly before God.

Fourth Sunday after Epiphany

Second Reading
Psalm 15*

What God Expects

O LORD, who may abide in your tent? Who may dwell on your holy hill? (Ps. 15:1)

Imagine standing in attendance for worship before the temple of Yahweh in Jerusalem. You have traveled far over the course of many days to reach this holy spot, a place of mystery and majesty, a place that is said to be the very house of God. Together with other pilgrims, you stand shoulder to shoulder on the stone pavement outside the temple, anxiously waiting for the priests to arrive and for the worship service to begin.

Perhaps you have come with questions about God, and wonder if you are indeed worthy to come into such a sacred space. You secretly ponder whether you might dare to think that the Lord himself is present in your own heart and life.

A quick hush sweeps across the crowd as a man clad in priestly regalia finally enters and mounts a platform. Surprisingly, he gives voice to your own question: "O LORD! Who may abide in your tent? Who may dwell on your holy hill?" (v. 1). [**Divine expectations**]

As you wonder if there is an appropriate congregational response that you don't know, a cultic prophet steps up and gives the answer: "Those who walk blamelessly, and do what is right, and speak the truth from their heart; who do not slander with their tongue, and do no evil to their friends, nor take up a reproach against their neighbors; in whose eyes the wicked are despised, but who honor those who fear the LORD; who stand by their oath even to their hurt; who do not lend money at interest, and do not take a bribe against the innocent. Those who do these things shall never be moved" (vv. 2-5).

Questions and answers

The psalms of the Bible were the hymns, prayers, and liturgical readings of Israel. The scenario suggested above is one possible way in which this psalm might have been used in worship. The text poses an age-old question, one that every person who is aware of God must ask: "How can I experience God's presence in my life?"

The first verse poses the query in two different but related ways. "Who may abide in your tent? Who may dwell on your holy hill?" The Hebrew word translated "abide" (more literally, "sojourn") means "to keep company with," "to travel with," or "to share life with." It was used to describe nomadic clan members who journeyed, worked, and lived together.

The word used for "tent" could refer to the common tents in which nomadic peoples lived, but it could also describe the portable tent that housed the Ark of the Covenant and was thought to be the epicenter of Yahweh's presence on earth. There were other, more technical words to describe the tabernacle, but scripture often refers to it as "the tent of meeting," "the tent of Yahweh" (1 Kgs. 2:28), the "house of the tent" (1 Chron. 9:23), or simply "the tent." The Hebrews believed that God's presence literally

---

Divine expectations: The theme of divine expectations is prominent in both Old Testament texts for the fourth Sunday after Epiphany in Year A. The first reading, from Mic. 6:1-8, asks "What does the Lord expect of you?" The second, Psalm 15, begins with the question of who may abide in God's presence – of what God expects.

Psalm 15 also appears as an alternate second reading for Proper 17 in Year B and Proper 11 in Year C.

Tents: Traditions vary concerning the wilderness "tent of meeting." Most often, it seems to be synonymous with the tabernacle where the Ark was kept and sacrifices were offered, located in the center of the tribal encampments (Exod. 27:21; 28:43; 29:4, 10, 30; and many more). Another tradition, however, describes it as a separate tent that Moses pitched outside of the camp and repaired to when he wanted to commune with God (Exod. 33:7-11).

dwelt in the tabernacle. To sojourn in the Lord's tent was to experience the Lord's presence. [**Tents**]

"Who may dwell on your holy hill?" repeats the thought. The verb we translate as "dwell" (*shakan*) became, in participle form, the primary technical word for God's dwelling place (*mishkan*), the tabernacle. The inclusion of "your holy hill" speaks to a time when the tabernacle had come to rest in Jerusalem, on Zion, God's "holy hill."

Do the right thing
(vv. 2a, 4a)

The question, then, is "Who is worthy to brave the awesome holiness of God's presence?" Despite its inclusion in Israel's book of temple liturgy, the answer is not ritualistic or even particularly religious. Rather, the requirements are ethical. It is the kind of message we expect to hear from the eighth-century prophets, who challenged Israel to avoid trusting empty rituals and to practice right living, or from the "wisdom school" of ancient Israel, which emphasized the need for obedience and doing good.

The response (vv. 2-5a) is cast in the form of good Hebrew poetry, which is characterized by a repetition of thoughts – a rhythm not of sound, but of sense. The punctuation preserved in the Masoretic text (the basis of our current Hebrew editions of the Old Testament) divides the response into five sections, with the first two consisting of three lines each.

This form is followed by most modern translations, but I would argue that the text should be divided more naturally into six couplets, arranged in careful fashion so that the second three couplets mirror and amplify the thought of the first three. That is, the fourth couplet is related to the first, the fifth to the second, and the sixth to the third.

The first couplet insists that the people who dwell in God's presence are "those who walk blamelessly, and do what is right" (v. 2a). The psalmist had no illusions of perfection. To walk blamelessly and do right is to orient oneself toward right living because it is in one's nature as a child of God to do so.

One who does right, even in the Old Testament milieu, recognizes that walking rightly before God is not a performance of duty, but the living out of a relationship of grace. It is not so much a requirement to come into God's presence, but a result of knowing God's spirit.

This first characteristic is related to the fourth: "in whose eyes the wicked are despised, but who honor those who fear the LORD" (v. 4a). Because of their love for God, those who "dwell on his holy hill" not only seek personal righteousness, but also honor this quality in others. The verse does not encourage the faithful to act hatefully toward those who behave wickedly, but to give praise where it is due, to those who live respectfully before Yahweh.

The importance of this verse becomes evident for contemporary life when we consider who is truly honored in American society. Some of the high-profile people who garner the greatest acclaim exhibit the most immoral or corrupt lifestyles, and yet they have millions of fans while sacrificial servants go unsung and unappreciated.

Say the right thing
(vv. 2b-3a, 4b)

Right action is reflected in right speaking. Those who know God's presence "speak the truth from their heart," and "do not slander with their tongue" (v. 2b-3). Speaking the truth is a primary quality of "blameless" living. The scriptures teach that we worship a God of truth (Ps. 119:160; John 1:14, 14:6), while lies and deceit have a more diabolical source (Heb. 6:18, John 8:44).

The one who knows God's presence speaks truth not from fear, but because it is in her nature: it comes "from the heart." Such persons speak truthfully because they are truthful people. They do not "wander about on their tongue" (literally), speaking untrustworthy or slanderous words.

The second requirement is related to the fifth: "who stand by their oath even to their hurt" (v. 4b). Here we have a picture of someone who has sworn to do something, and later discovers that it will be to their disadvantage to follow through. Yet, because she is the kind of person who stands by her word, she keeps her promise.

We live in the era of "alternate truth," conspiracy mongering, and "the Big Lie." Some individuals subscribe to the belief that if you tell a lie often enough, people will believe it. Sadly, many do. This represents the opposite of the psalm's call to be people who "speak the truth from their heart" – not from conniving corners of their brains.

Avoid the right things
(vv. 3b, 5a)

The third and sixth responses have to do with personal relationships. Those who dwell in God's presence "do no evil to their friends, nor take up a reproach against their neighbors" (v. 3b). They "do not lend money at interest, and do not take a bribe against the innocent" (v. 5a).

Like the Ten Commandments, these four phrases use negative imagery to promote positive behavior. "Do no evil" can encompass any type of harmful behavior to another, even as "takes up no reproach" (NIV11 "casts no slur") covers a wide range of injurious language. The meaning of these commands is obvious.

Godly persons avoid both evil actions and harmful words toward their friends and neighbors. The word translated "friend" usually implies a close relationship, but it can also be used in the sense of "fellow citizen" or any others with whom we have some reciprocal relationship. It is the same word used in Lev. 19:18 and later quoted by Jesus: "you shall love your neighbor as yourself."

The word rendered as "neighbor" literally means "one who is near." It can refer to a close kinsman, someone living close by, or someone who happens to be near at the moment. Both words, then, suggest that this command is for all persons. Those who know God's presence treat family, friends, and persons on the street with the same care: they do no harm, either to their persons or their reputations.

The last couplet gives two specific examples of such harmful behavior. "Do not lend money at interest" is not a blanket scriptural injunction against bankers or investors, but is an appeal for persons not to exploit one another, especially the poor, lending money at exorbitant interest. Today's "payday lenders" and other predatory loan sharks offer the perfect image of what the psalmist condemned.

This is an old problem. The Nuzi tablets from ancient Iraq, among other cuneiform documents, show that interest rates of 33-50 percent were not uncommon in the ancient Near East.

In Israel, wealthy landowners commonly charged high interest on loans to destitute neighbors. When the borrowers were unable to pay, their homes and lands would be confiscated. Sometimes, the poor themselves were sold into slavery to pay their debts. The prophets routinely and roundly condemned such practices (e.g., Mic. 2:1-2, Isa. 5:8).

Few of us are involved in interest-gouging, but that does not absolve us of a concern for social justice. There are many ways of exploiting the poor. Migrant workers and minimum wage earners often fall prey to unscrupulous employers who take advantage of their need. Those who profit from the system – including any of us who enjoy lower prices enabled by poverty-level wages – must confess complicity in wrongdoing.

Those who dwell in God's presence know God's heart, and God's heart bleeds compassion for the poor, the disadvantaged, the outcasts of society. Jesus' teaching about the judgment in Matt. 25:31-46 makes it clear that this Old Testament idea lives on. Those who inherit the kingdom and are welcomed by the Father are those who showed kindness to "the least of these my brethren."

The psalmist concludes with a single thought that returns to the opening question: those who live out such compassionate lives because of their devotion to God will be assured of their place in God's tent, on the Lord's holy hill. They will "never be moved" (NRSV) from their place in God's presence; they will "never be shaken" (NJPS) from their faith. So may it be.

The Hardest Question
Are we complicit in the exploitation of the poor?

Unconscious complicity is a hard thing to think about, so we usually don't. We don't like to consider ways in which we may have profited – and continue to benefit – from the oppression of others.

Consider the antebellum mansions found in many southern towns, often with names such as the "Historic (family name) House." A sign may credit the original owners with contributions to the town, land for a park, the building of churches, or other charitable efforts. Local schools may be named for them. Overlooked, however, is the fact that the benefactors' wealth may have been gained largely through slave labor, which involved robbing human beings of their freedom, buying and selling them like cattle, and forcing them into a life of hard labor and poverty.

Current generations may continue to benefit from the economic development or donations made in those past eras without ever thinking about how many people suffered to make it possible.

In a broader sense, even after slavery was officially abolished, white families through the years have benefited from the privileges of being white and having greater financial or political resources. Discriminatory laws and practices have led to generational divides between those born with and without such privilege, and promoters of white nationalism desperately seek to maintain their positions of power.

Similar exploitation continues. Untold millions of people born into poverty have little chance of escaping because economic systems are designed to benefit the wealthy on the backs of the poor. Poorly educated or less privileged people stuck in minimum wage jobs find it extremely difficult to get ahead. They are much less likely to ever own a home or put away savings for a comfortable retirement. Meanwhile, those of us who are better off benefit from cheap fast food and ride the escalating value of homes we were able to purchase.

We often don't stop to think that the clothes we wear and even many of the technological gadgets we use were manufactured by people in third-world countries who are paid a mere pittance. The meat we eat may have been slaughtered by packing house workers who routinely suffer job-related injuries brought on by demands for greater speed. Rare metals in our computers or batteries may have been mined by poorly paid workers in dangerous conditions.

Human nature being what it is, it's unlikely that endemic systems of oppression will change any time soon. We may not be able to find a grocery store or big-box retailer that doesn't carry goods made in exploitive ways. We cannot easily escape the privilege that gives some of us a built-in advantage in life. But we can seek to be more conscious of ways in which others suffer for our benefit, do what we can to treat others justly, and look for ways to give back to communities that historically have been oppressed.

It's complicated, but it's also important if we truly care about issues of justice, if we truly want to be among those who experience and share the presence of God.

Fourth Sunday after Epiphany

Third Reading
1 Corinthians 1:18-31*

Foolhardy Wisdom

For God's foolishness is wiser than human wisdom, and God's weakness is stronger than human strength. (1 Cor. 1:25)

Have you ever learned something new or grasped a novel insight that seemed to turn your way of thinking about something upside down?

Perhaps you've known a person whose insecurities seemed ridiculous – until you discovered that she had been abandoned as a child and grew up in a string of foster families. Then you understood.

Or maybe you took a college or seminary course in Old or New Testament that completely changed the way you look at the Bible.

In 1 Cor. 1:18-31, Paul's argument was designed to convince the Christians in Corinth that their way of thinking – their culture's understanding of wisdom – needed a global shift. His goal was to turn their world upside down.

Corinth was a cosmopolitan center where rich and poor alike admired public speakers who could impress hearers with eloquent displays of wisdom. Notable Greek philosophers, Jewish scholars, and professional rhetoricians could attract the same kind of acclaim as modern-day movie stars or pop idols, even without the benefit of celebrity magazines and Twitter accounts.

The church in Corinth was beset by conflict in several areas. Paul's letter alluded to the conflict in vv. 1-17 and addressed specific issues beginning in ch. 3. In the meantime, the apostle sought to lay a theological foundation as a basis for later arguments. Most of the conflicts related to power struggles in which various groups considered themselves superior to others, or in possession of deeper knowledge.

Thus, Paul found it needful to contrast the potentially divisive wisdom of the world with the powerfully transforming word of the cross.

The power of the cross
(vv. 18-19)

Paul confessed that the whole notion of the cross sounds crazy. Would anyone be so insane as to invent a religion whose messiah was humiliated through a public crucifixion? That sounds like stupidity on steroids. But the wisdom of the world fails to comprehend the surprising wisdom of God.

"For the message about the cross is foolishness to those who are perishing, but to us who are being saved it is the power of God," Paul said (v. 18).

The cross divides the world's population into two groups, the apostle insisted: those who are perishing and those who are being saved. That's powerful.

Note that Paul spoke of this in the present tense, which in Greek implies continuation. "Those who are perishing" does not imply immediate death, but does describe those who follow a path that leads to death.

To those who are spiritually dying, the gospel of the cross sounds like foolishness (*mōria*, the root of the English word "moron"). To the human mind, the thought of a god submitting to the humiliation of a public execution makes no sense: it's moronic. Rational arguments such as those taught by Greek philosophers seem much more reasonable.

But God's wisdom has a way of turning things upside down. Paul drew on Isa. 29:14b to reinforce his

---

*This text is also used for the third Sunday of Lent in Year B.

More context: If we look beyond Paul's brief quotation to its surrounding context, we can gain a better understanding of why Paul chose to cite this text. Consider all of Isa. 9:13-14: "The Lord said: Because these people draw near with their mouths and honor me with their lips while their hearts are far from me, and their worship of me is a human commandment learned by rote; so I will again do amazing things with this people, shocking and amazing. The wisdom of their wise shall perish, and the discernment of the discerning shall be hidden."

The text is part of a judgment oracle against the leaders of Judah, who talked a good game about worshiping God, but didn't put it into action. When the country was threatened by Assyria, they chose the rational route of seeking security through political alliances rather than trusting God, as Isaiah advised.

As Richard Hays puts it, "Isaiah's point is that God-talk is cheap and that God's action will shut the mouths of the wise talkers.... The Corinthians, with their prized speech gifts, make a show of possessing wisdom and honoring God with their lips, but their fractious behavior shows that in fact their hearts are far from God. Thus, like Judah in Isaiah's oracle, they stand under the sentence of divine judgment which will nullify their professed wisdom and unmask their professed piety as a sham" (*First Corinthians*, Interpretation [John Knox Press, 1997], 29).

contention: "I will destroy the wisdom of the wise, and the discernment of the discerning I will thwart" (v. 19). [More context]

In contrast to "those who are perishing," Paul spoke of "those who are being saved," who find in the cross the power of God. "Those who are being saved" are on the pathway of life, with eternity as their ultimate destination.

The life of faith is empowered by Christ's self-sacrificing love at work in the believer. The power of the cross is the forgiveness of God, transforming the lives of those who put their trust in Christ.

The wisdom of the world
(vv. 20-25)

Paul's argument points to three models of earthly wisdom: wise philosophers, Torah experts, and skilled orators.

To people like these, the gospel of the cross appeared as foolishness: it made no sense for a deity to save humans through self-sacrifice.

That's why Paul insisted that God's wisdom is of an entirely different nature than earthly wisdom. What seems foolish to humans makes perfect sense to God, even a divine willingness to be stripped, beaten, and nailed to a cross for the sake of humans (v. 23).

Nothing could seem more ridiculous to those who look for salvation in a powerful leader, a surpassing philosophy, or a new technology, but the salvation of God does not come through intellectual arguments any more than through keeping the law. Salvation comes through faith as "the called" – those who respond to God's call by trusting Christ – discover that Christ is indeed "the power of God and the wisdom of God" (v. 24).

Believers learn that God's gift of life is not gained as a result of human wisdom. Rather, *true* wisdom comes through true surrender to God's way of thinking. Paul's readers, like most of us, lived in a sophisticated society that found pride in self-reliance and continual achievements. Still, he said "God's foolishness is wiser than human wisdom, and God's weakness is stronger than human strength" (v. 25).

When we base our evaluation on wisdom that makes sense in human categories, it is not surprising that the

A new lens: In discussing Paul's emphasis on the cross as it relates to human ideas about wisdom and foolishness, Scott Nash has written that "The problem lies in perception. Part of the barrier to clear perception lies with the tunnel vision of the viewers, since their seeing has been shaped by the world. But part of the astigmatism comes from the lens needed to correct their vision: the cross. This lens blocks the vision of those who cannot see beyond it. It does not grant light for seeing in this world (*aiōn*) because it refracts a light from another world (*aiōn*), the 'age' to come that has dawned in the cross of Christ.

"Paul's apocalyptic viewpoint is evident here. The cross marks the inauguration of a new age, but unless one is living in that new age one's vision is still controlled by the old age. From the vantage point of the new age, the foolishness of this age's wisdom is apparent. To get to that vantage point, one's old lens must be shattered by the shocking impact of the spectacle of the cross. This occurs in the encounter with the proclaimed word of the cross, a message so characteristically foolish in the view of worldly wisdom that it calls into question the presuppositions of that wisdom" (*1 Corinthians*, Smyth & Helwys Bible Commentary [Smyth & Helwys, 2009], 90).

gospel message seems strange: it's not rational. Those who open their minds to God's way of thinking have to stretch beyond human logic, but in doing so may come to appreciate a deeper and broader wisdom. [A new lens]

The pride of the church and the work of Christ
(vv. 26-31)

Human nature loves to brag, and various factions of the church at Corinth boasted that their way of understanding and expressing faith was superior to the way others worshiped. Paul insisted that human pride and humble acceptance of Christ's saving work cannot coexist, and he sought to drive the point home in vv. 26-31. After speaking about society in general, Paul turned his attention to the church.

The church in Corinth had some influential members, including Crispus, the former leader of the synagogue (Acts 18:8); Gaius, whose home was large enough to host the church; and Erastus, who was city treasurer (Rom. 16:23). It's likely that most members did not belong to the intelligentsia, the power brokers, or the cultural elite of Corinthian society (v. 26). Still, Paul believed God could use their very weakness to impress the strong, even as the foolishness of the gospel was destined to challenge the wise (v. 27).

To the world, lowly people and crazy ideas may seem unimportant, but from the perspective of eternity, it is the proud who will become nothing (v. 28). Paul insisted that this paradox is not only intentional, but also necessary. As long as salvation is attainable by human means, however strict the requirements, God falls out of the equation and human pride reigns supreme.

But salvation is a gift of God, not the reward of good or wise or powerful works. No one can boast about having achieved salvation when he or she knows that God alone is the source of life (v. 29).

The issue of boasting is a recurring theme in the Corinthian correspondence, and the frequency with which Paul addresses it betrays the danger it poses. Self-assured boasting cannot coexist with trusting faith.

The ultimate source of the believer's life is not found in philosophy or science or even the Higgs boson, inappropriately tagged as "the God particle." Abundant life, ultimate life is found in Christ Jesus, "who became for us wisdom

from God, and righteousness and sanctification and redemption" (v. 30).

Notice the fourfold description of Christ's work packed into this verse. To say that Christ is our *wisdom* is not just to identify Jesus with the personified wisdom of the Wisdom literature in the Old Testament and the rabbinic traditions, but to say that Jesus is the final source of our knowledge of God.

To say that Christ is our *righteousness* means that Christ is the one who puts us right with God. We are incapable of achieving that status by our own merit, but through our acceptance of Christ's work on our behalf, we can enter a right relationship with God (Rom. 8:33).

Those who are put right with God begin the lifelong challenge of growing in holiness, but such growth is also a work of Christ in us, so Paul could say he is our *sanctification*. In Christ we are set apart to live for God and give our time and our money in sharing God's love, even when it seems like foolishness to the world.

Finally, Christ is our *redemption*. The word Paul used denoted the ransom price paid to set someone free from slavery or imprisonment. We do not have to subscribe to an elaborate "ransom theory" of the atonement to appreciate Paul's imagery. Knowing what it is like to live in bondage to sin and the fear of death, we rejoice in the great Christian hope – the promise that Christ's atoning life, death, and resurrection have set us free to live an abundant and eternal life within the care of Almighty God.

Paul concluded his argument with another reference to scripture, a loose and abbreviated quotation from Jer. 9:23-24. [Boasting in God] If there is any boasting to be done, we should boast in what God has done, not in our own accomplishments. Paul expressed this same thought even more eloquently in Gal. 6:14: "May I never boast of

> **Boasting in God:** Paul's citation from Jeremiah is a small part of this larger text: "Thus says the LORD: Do not let the wise boast in their wisdom, do not let the mighty boast in their might, do not let the wealthy boast in their wealth; but let those who boast boast in this, that they understand and know me, that I am the LORD; I act with steadfast love, justice, and righteousness in the earth, for in these things I delight, says the LORD" (Jer. 9:23-24).

anything except the cross of our Lord Jesus Christ, by which the world has been crucified to me, and I to the world."

The Hardest Question
Who were the "wise" of whom Paul spoke?

Paul addressed three categories of notably wise people in Corinth: philosophers (mostly in the Greek tradition), scribes (experts in the Jewish law), and popular rhetoricians who gained acclaim through public speeches (not unlike today's syndicated columnists or news commentators). All of them were off base when it came to understanding what God was up to, Paul said.

Greek sages expected no divine intervention, but sought the meaning of life through rational philosophies that promised peace within persons and between nations. They were much like many modern persons who harbor hopes that the scientific and technological achievements of our own age may lead to a new utopia, despite evidence that technological advances can also lead to greater potential for violence and harm.

Experts in the Jewish scriptures may have expected a messiah, but only one whose power was undeniable, a champion who would reunite Israel under a rejuvenated Davidic throne and lead the nation to new heights of glory. For them, a crucified messiah was a contradiction in terms, for the Old Testament pronounced a curse on anyone hanged on a tree (Deut. 21:23, cf. Gal. 3:13).

In Greek culture, public figures who argued with rhetorical eloquence on issues of the day received great acclaim. Their debating style was grounded on logical arguments that reached rational conclusions and wowed their listeners with convincing rhetoric.

While all three categories of "wise men" could impress their listeners, Paul insisted that their dependence on human reasoning rendered them blind to the deepest truth of the gospel.

A crucified savior may not make any sense to human ears, but as Paul insisted, even the foolishness of God far surpasses the best of human wisdom.

Fourth Sunday after Epiphany

Fourth Reading
Matthew 5:3-12*

Teaching Upside Down

Blessed are the poor in spirit, for theirs is the kingdom of heaven. (Matt. 5:3)

On the side of a hill, the Lord Jesus sat down, and he began to teach – and multitudes of people gathered round to hear what he had to say.

Have you ever wondered, had you been around in those days, if you would have been among those who came to hear what became the immortal "Sermon on the Mount," which began with the curious "Beatitudes," our text for the day?

It's likely that the material in Matthew 5–7 preserves a collection of Jesus' teachings rather than the text of a single sermon, but it is designed to illustrate the content, character, and popularity of Jesus' teaching.

We wonder how Jesus became so popular, and so quickly. Biblical narratives are often compressed, and Matthew squeezed Jesus' rapid rise in popularity into three verses (4:23-25). Jesus preached throughout Galilee, Matthew said, teaching in the synagogues but more notably healing people of various diseases and conditions. As Jesus' reputation spread, "great crowds followed him from Galilee, the Decapolis, Jerusalem, Judea, and from beyond the Jordan." Though Jesus remained in Galilee, people flocked from all the surrounding areas.

Jesus yearned for people to look beyond miracles and healings and begin to understand the true demands of the gospel. So, on the side of a hill, the Lord Jesus sat down, and he began to teach the multitudes who were just beginning to understand who he was – and he turned their world upside down.

If we listen, he may upend our worlds, too.

Humble blessings
(vv. 3-5)

"Blessed are the poor in spirit," Jesus began, "for theirs is the kingdom of heaven" (v. 3). "Blessed" translates the Greek *makarios*, which can also mean "happy." That must have confused people who never thought of putting "poor" and "blessed" in the same sentence.

Jesus' message began with the unavoidable truth that the first step in spiritual growth is to recognize our spiritual poverty. A sense of poverty motivates us to work at improving our situation. We all have a problem with spiritual poverty, and we try to fill that emptiness in a variety of ways, many of them harmful to our health, our relationships, and our spirit. **[Spiritual poverty]**

Those who would escape spiritual poverty learn to trust in God's sustaining grace. Long-time believers learn that times of spiritual growth often begin with times of spiritual brokenness.

As if that were not enough, Jesus went on: "Blessed are those who mourn, for they will be comforted" (v. 4).

Spiritual poverty: Perhaps you are familiar with 12-step programs for addictions to alcohol or some other drug, or even to addictive habits such as gambling. The programs commonly teach that the first step in recovery is to admit the problem, to stand before the group and say "My name is Fred (or Sue, or Bartholomew), and I am an alcoholic/ a drug addict/a sex addict/a gambling addict/etc."

We can't deal with our emptiness until we recognize and confess the unhelpful ways that we have tried to fill it, and the deep need we have for divine help.

---

*This text is also used for All Saints Day in Year A.

Those who mourn the loss or rejection of a loved one know what it is like to feel the emptiness that follows. Where's the comfort in that?

Deep mourning – especially mourning for a death that seems out of time and out of God's plan – may naturally lead one to question his or her faith. As a result, some people depart from faith, feeling somehow betrayed that God had let them down, even though God has not promised perfect protection to those who follow. Others, however, find the brokenness of mourning to be the first steps of a new, deeper, more profound faith, a faith that does not depend on happy circumstances, but rests in the presence of Christ's Spirit.

Putting our trust in Christ requires humility, acknowledging that we need something beyond ourselves. "Blessed are the meek," Jesus went on, "for they shall inherit the earth" (v. 5).

Some of those present might have recalled the claim in Ps. 37:11 that "the meek will inherit the land, and will enjoy great peace." The word Jesus used may have carried less baggage than our word "meek," which may lead us to think "weak," "timid," "cowardly."

That is not what Jesus had in mind. Jesus could speak of himself as "meek" (Matt. 11:29), but he was no coward. "Meekness" does not suggest fears of worthlessness, but humility. We may have strong self-esteem, but be humble enough to look past ourselves and learn to love both God and others. God has a world full of blessings for those whose confidence is expressed in kindness.

The first three "beatitudes" share similar themes of poverty. The next sequence moves toward the theme of hunger.

Hungry blessings
(vv. 6-9)

Jesus could see the hunger in the eyes of those who gathered around, hunger for so many different things. He focused on the most important: "Blessed are those who hunger and thirst for righteousness, for they will be filled" (v. 6).

People who grow spiritually do so because they want to. They have a deep hunger to know God's way, a continual thirst to experience God's presence, and a willingness to do something about it.

> **Come and eat:** Isaiah of the exile wasn't talking about Bible study when he offered God's great invitation, "Come, all you who are thirsty, come to the waters; and you who have no money, come, buy and eat! Come, buy wine and milk without money and without cost. Why spend money on what is not bread, and your labor on what does not satisfy? Listen, listen to me, and eat what is good, and your soul will delight in the richest of fare" (55:1-2). He was, however, talking about listening to God, and the best way we can do that today is through Bible study, prayer, and worship.

One way to feed spiritual hunger and thirst is through prayer and meditation. A psalmist prayed: "As a deer pants for the waterbrooks, so my soul pants for thee" (Ps. 42:1). If we are thirsty, we look for water. If we want to experience the presence of God, we take time out, go inside our hearts, and discover that God is already looking for us.

We may also feed our spiritual hunger and thirst through Bible study. As we read the gift of scripture, we find much that puzzles us, and much that rewards. Working through the difficult passages in addition to the obvious ones helps us to develop our ability to study and learn and grow. **[Come and eat]**

We may also feed that hunger and thirst through worship. It is no accident that Jesus instructed his followers to remember him as a community of believers, eating bread and drinking wine in a spirit of communion. In worship – opening our hearts to God – we can find food for our hungry souls.

Those who hunger for the righteousness of God will grow in their experience of God's presence, but they will also develop a greater desire to serve God. Jesus mentioned three specific kinds of action:

"Blessed are the merciful," Jesus said first, "for they will obtain mercy" (v. 7). When Jesus taught his followers to pray, he made it clear that those who desire forgiveness must also be willing to forgive others (Matt. 6:12, 14-15). One cannot carry grudges and grow spiritually.

Those who are hungry for righteousness also hunger to do what is right. "Blessed are the pure in heart," Jesus added, "for they shall see God" (v. 8). When we experience God's gracious forgiveness, and we understand something of God's sacrifice in bringing about our forgiveness, we also experience a desire to be more like Jesus. We do not want to cause God any further hurt, or to experience the pain of our own shame.

Few things are more painful than the inner, certain knowledge that we are hypocrites. We have ways to mask that pain so that we do not feel it so much, but those who are sensitive to it have a great hunger to be pure in heart, not only toward God, but also for good.

The hunger for righteousness also motivates a hunger for peace. "Blessed are the peacemakers, for they will be called the sons of God," Jesus said (v. 9). He did not say "Blessed are the peaceful," which we might be happier to hear, but "Blessed are the peace*makers*." Making peace can be hard work, and is not always peaceful or even appreciated, but it is needed.

Is anything more needed in our country, or in our world, than peace? Only when we can relate to one another with peace rather than hostility and division can we begin to tackle the many other issues that face us.

Peacemakers are not passive people who simply avoid stirring the waters, but persons who are willing to go out on a limb to bring others together. Peacemakers give themselves to helping others find peace with God, peace at home, peace in their workplace, peace in their world. No one else gives more evidence through their lives that they are truly the children of God.

Hard blessings
(vv. 10-12)

Jesus' hearers must have thought he had gone off the deep end when he concluded his series of blessings with "Blessed are those who are persecuted because of righteousness, for theirs is the kingdom of heaven" (v. 10; vv. 11-12 repeat the same thought).

The eager listeners who covered the mountain's slope may have listened keenly to Jesus' insistence that the only ones who grow spiritually are those who are hungry enough to do something about it. They may have been less apt to pay attention when Jesus went on to insist that deep spiritual blessedness comes through the experience of hard times.

This was not a new thought entirely, for Jesus had already talked about poverty and mourning as the seedbeds of spiritual growth. He moved on to the kind of hard times that result from persecution.

> **Persecution, sort of:** We don't really comprehend "persecution," but we do understand rejection, a milder form of it. If we are serious about our faith, we may at times face exclusion from some circles, and that hurts. Sometimes it hurts so much that we may be tempted to abandon our faith in God to be accepted by people. But there is another option: We can carry our suffering to the one who has already taken our pain upon his own shoulders. We can entrust our lives to the Lord of life. We can plant our feet ever deeper into the soil of faith, and experience new growth in the midst of adversity.

Some American Christians cry "persecution" when they don't get special privileges, but none of us have tasted the first measure of what the Christians in first-century Rome endured. We've never felt what the Jews in Europe encountered under Hitler's regime. We don't know what it's like to be a Palestinian living under Israeli occupation.

If we did, it is likely that we probably would know a deeper measure of faith than we have now. If you want to strengthen someone's faith, just try and force them to give it up. [**Persecution, sort of**]

On the side of a hill the Lord Jesus sat down, and he began to teach.

He taught about … humility, hunger, hard times. To human ears, those ingredients may sound like a recipe for misery, but Jesus considered them building blocks of the abundant life, of what it means to be spiritual. They are reminders of what it means to be serious about our faith, what it means to grow in grace.

Perhaps, more often we should wish each other the humility and poverty of spirit to understand our need for Christ. We could wish that each other might have a hunger for righteousness, for mercy, for purity, for peace. We might even wish each other hard times, if that is what it takes, to deepen our faith and quicken our growth in the spirit of Christ. Would we welcome such blessings as Jesus gave?

The Hardest Question
Where's the comfort in mourning?

One of the hardest Beatitudes to get a handle on is the second one: "Blessed are those who mourn, for they shall be comforted." Somehow, those words don't seem to go together, but they were an integral part of the mission statement from Isaiah that Jesus adopted and announced in his home synagogue (Isa. 61:1-3, Luke 4:16-21):

> The Spirit of the Sovereign Lord is upon me, because the Lord has anointed me to preach good news to the poor. He has sent me to bind up the broken hearted, to proclaim liberty to the captives and release from darkness to the prisoners, to proclaim the year of the Lord's favor and the day of vengeance of our God, and to comfort all who mourn, and provide for those who grieve in Zion – to bestow on them a crown of beauty instead of ashes, the oil of gladness instead of mourning, and a garment of praise instead of despair.

Bringing comfort to the bereaved was at the heart of Jesus' personal mission in life, and so it is no accident that when he explained his view of the kingdom into the short speech we remember as the "Beatitudes," he included this word: "Blessed are those who mourn, for they shall be comforted."

Some interpreters would add to what Jesus says and assume that he means "blessed are those who mourn for their sins." It is true that those who grieve over their sins and seek forgiveness will also find comfort. But, in this text, Jesus says nothing about sins. In the text from Isaiah, there is nothing about sins. It is about mourning and grief and pain because of loss – and yet, the hope of comfort.

It helps to realize that when we mourn for someone or something we have lost, we would not be mourning at all if we had not been blessed already. The grief we feel in loss is the flip side of the blessing we knew before.

But how can following Jesus' way bring comfort from mourning? In one sense, we can say that as long as we hold dear those special memories of the way our loved ones have blessed us, that sense of blessedness will live on. The grief itself is a blessing. Furthermore, Jesus was insisting that those who trust in him can find joy and blessing even in their sorrow.

Because of our Christian hope, we believe that our loved ones in the Lord are not lost forever. When we mourn for them, remember them, cry over our sweet memories of them, that great depth of feeling is not only a tie to the past, but also a foretaste of the future, when we are reunited in God's eternal kingdom.

We know that some people struggle to get past their grief. They may spend the rest of their days in mourning, identifying as victims. Their refusal to move on through the stages of grief and find healing leads to the shortening of their own life.

We need more than grief – we need relief! And here is where that wonderful promise comes in. Jesus offers comfort. He offers healing. He offers hope. To use the psalmist's words, "He restoreth my soul."

God may work through the love of friends and family. God may work through counselors or pastors. God may work through insights we gain from scripture or in other ways. God also brings comfort through his own mysterious and mystical and utterly wonderful presence. "I will not leave you comfortless," Jesus said, "I will come to you" (John 14:18).

The Holy Spirit has not gone away, but is still at work in our midst.

In God's people, in God's presence, in God's promise, we find comfort. "Blessed are those who mourn, for they shall be comforted."

Fifth Sunday after Epiphany
First Reading
Isaiah 58*

Justice's Reward

… if you offer your food to the hungry and satisfy the needs of the afflicted,
then your light shall rise in the darkness and your gloom be like the noonday. (Isa. 58:10)

What comes to mind when you hear the word "justice"? Often we think mainly of the court system, and whether justice is being done when cases are decided. Did the accused really do it? If so, is the punishment he or she receives commensurate with the crime?

But justice is a far broader subject than case law and "the justice system." It is entirely possible for an individual to live within the law, yet practice injustice. It is possible, indeed, for an entire society to be riddled with policies that are inherently unjust. [**Justice**]

What would you identify as justice issues in our society? Christian believers of good will may disagree on specific positions, but we should agree that those who follow God are called to work for justice that respects the dignity and rights of all.

Futile fasting
(vv. 1-5)

Today's text comes from the closing section of Isaiah, a part of the book that many scholars refer to as "Third Isaiah" (chs. 56–66), because it appears to be set in Jerusalem after the return from exile, more than 150 years after the ministry of Isaiah of Jerusalem.

The latter prophet, however, was well schooled in the teachings of the original Isaiah, and he was in touch with the same God. When he saw similar conditions and behaviors, he responded in similar ways.

> **Justice:** "Legal" does not necessarily equal "just." Recall that America once condoned slavery. It was legal, but unjust. Prior to the Civil Rights Movement gaining traction in the 1950s and 60s, segregation was also acceptable by law. It was legal, but unjust.
>
> Other issues continue to raise questions about justice, for example: immigration policies, especially as they relate to people who were brought to America as children; a tax and financial system that favors the rich, whose wealth steadily increases while poor and middle-class incomes remain static or fall; marriage and property laws that once recognized heterosexual partners but denied basic rights to same-sex couples; prison convictions and sentences that follow racial lines.
>
> Are these justice issues? Not everyone will agree on every position, but questions of justice abound. Should Christians be concerned about them?

The setting of today's text is the city of Jerusalem, possibly 50 years or more after the ending of the exile, at some point after the temple had been rebuilt and Jewish religious rituals restored.

It was also, unfortunately, a time when the families who had returned from Babylon with considerable wealth had been able to consolidate their positions and expand their holdings by taking advantage of their poorer Hebrew neighbors. [**When was it?**]

The first five verses are a series of charges and questions. Some scholars imagine an elaborate drama playing out with as many as five speakers, but it is also

---

Related and overlapping readings from this text are used at different times. Isaiah 58:12 is a text for Ash Wednesday in Years A, B, and C. Isaiah 58:9b-12 is used for Proper 16 in Year C. This study will cover the full chapter 58.

possible to imagine that the prophet is speaking throughout, quoting both the God who called him to prophesy and the people who claimed to have believed they were living righteously.

The text begins with what the prophet describes as a divine cry: "Shout out, do not hold back! Lift up your voice like a trumpet! Announce to my people their rebellion, to the house of Jacob their sins" (v. 1).

Particular sins are presented, but through sharp sarcasm. Yahweh declares that Israel's people "seek me and delight to know my ways, *as if* they were a nation that practiced righteousness and did not forsake the ordinance of their God …" (v. 2).

The people act as if they really want to know God, as if they delight in God's presence – but they claim that God has ignored them: "Why do we fast, but you do not see? Why humble ourselves, but you do not notice?" (v. 3a).

Fasting originated in Israel as a means of expressing grief: in times of sorrow – including penitence – people might rip their garments or put on sackcloth, sprinkle ashes on their heads, and go without food for a period of time. Over time, however, fasting became a ritualized religious observance that could display outward piety without inner conviction.

Although many other circumstances were different, the attitude of many post-exilic Hebrews in the mid-fifth century was not very different from that of their pre-exilic ancestors, about 200 years before (cp. the charges here with those in Isa. 1:11-17, from the eighth century).

Yahweh's charge was that the people fasted to serve their own interests rather than to honor God. They were satisfied with an outward show of righteousness that didn't really cost them anything more than a missed meal or two that could be made up with later feasting.

The problem was that their pious fasting was not accompanied by righteous living. While patting themselves on the back for their ritual performance, some were simultaneously oppressing people who worked for them and quarreling with each other, even to the extent of physical violence (v. 3b-4a).

That kind of fasting would win them no points with God, who took no delight in watching people bowing in worship while pressing the faces of the poor into the dirt (v. 5).

Does any of this connect with us? Few of us fast for religious reasons, but do we not have a similar tendency to practice aspects of religion that we like or that flatter our reputation, while ignoring the hard work of seeking justice for the oppressed and loving our neighbors as we love ourselves?

We may choose a worship service that suits our sensibilities and doesn't go on too long, for example, and contribute just enough to be respectable without making a sacrifice. Do we ever take time to examine our true motives in worship? [**Fasting**]

Faithful fasting
(vv. 6-7)

The prophet declared in no uncertain terms that God would not endorse hollow fasting. Rather, God desired to see justice unleashed and the oppressed go free, to see the hungry fed and the homeless housed, to see the naked clothed and family ties acknowledged (vv. 6-7).

Wealthy Hebrews had ways of putting poor people under financial pressure, loaning them money, and with the help of corrupt officials, seizing their land or even forcing them into indentured servitude when they could not pay their debts (Neh. 5:4-5).

Under the postexilic governor Nehemiah's administration, the problem reached such proportions that Nehemiah demanded an end to loans at excessive interest and declared an unscheduled Jubilee, ordering that fields and homes should be returned to those who had lost them to unjust debt practices (Neh. 5:7-12).

Predatory lending practices remain all too common in our own culture, despite the efforts of many states to outlaw them. God's desire is that God's people work toward a system in which all people have equal opportunities, in which the deck is not stacked against those who are poor, young, old, or have minority status.

Every yoke that binds people – every practice that restricts or denies persons the dignity and rights that every human should enjoy – every bond should be broken, God declared: that is the fast God desires.

From fasting to feasting
(vv. 8-14)

This is how the world sees God at work in the lives of God's people. The worship God wants is found in a caring humility that leads one to work for the good of others.

If the people would live in accord with that challenge, their witness would be like dawn's light breaking out over the world, spreading healing and hope through the land (v. 8). Then they could call on God and expect a more sympathetic ear: "you shall cry for help, and he will say 'Here I am'" (v. 9a).

Notice the conditional character of vv. 9b-10: *if* the people would remove the yoke of oppression, stop pointing fingers and speaking evil … *if* they would share their food with the hungry and help the afflicted, *then* their light would shine as a testimony of true righteousness, even amid the darkest of days.

The prophet believed that caring for others would open the door to care from God (vv. 11-12). In a land constantly threatened by drought, God's people could become "like a watered garden, like a spring of water, whose waters never fail" (v. 11).

Ancient ruins – probably a reference to parts of Jerusalem that had been destroyed but never rebuilt – would be reconstructed as a home for many generations of the faithful, and those responsible for such blessed work would be remembered as the "repairer of the breach" and "the restorer of streets to live in" (v. 12).

With vv. 13-14, the prophet returned to the theme of conditions and promises, this time with respect to sabbath keeping. [**A sabbath day's journey**] The sabbath should be used to honor God and not just for "serving your own interests or pursuing your own affairs" (v. 13), he said. This was an issue in Nehemiah's day as he locked the gates and sought to enforce a ban on merchants doing business on the sabbath (Neh. 13:15-22).

Isaiah promised that those who practice sabbath properly would bring delight to Yahweh, who would grant them the blessings of food, clothing, and presence that God had promised to Jacob (Gen. 28:10-21).

> **A sabbath day's journey:** The NRSV's "refrain from trampling the Sabbath" is an attempt at making sense of a difficult text. It literally means "if you turn from the Sabbath your feet," and may refer to the developing notion that one should limit the amount of walking done on the Sabbath. By the first century, the length of an allowable "Sabbath day's journey" was codified as 2,000 cubits, or just over half a mile.

Christian readers must be careful in interpreting passages such as this. We no longer live under a conditional covenant in which success or failure is believed to be directly commensurate with obedience to God.

We cannot claim, based on this passage, that if we practice ethical living and proper worship, we will be repaid with material blessings. We can, however, be assured that such behavior will shine as a helpful beacon in the midst of a land darkened by greed that is sometimes masked behind self-righteousness.

And we must ask – this passage demands that we ask – what sort of motives we have in worship. Are we seeking only those aspects of religious practice that please us, or "fasting" in the way that pleases God: through ethical living that shows care for the poor, hungry, homeless, and oppressed?

It's a question worthy of our deep and careful thought.

The Hardest Question
What about *my* worship?

The hardest question relative to today's text may be in applying it to our own situations. Let's face it: few of us fast, at least for religious reasons. We may give up chocolate for Lent or adopt a diet that includes intermittent fasting, but it's not common for modern Christians to fast as a means of expressing devotion to God. If we do fast, it's often connected with seeking something from God.

Notice how similar this passage is to other texts in which the basic message is that true religion is not demonstrated through fasting or sacrifices or public prayers, but through ethical and caring living. Consider these examples:

And Samuel said, "Has the LORD as great delight in burnt offerings and sacrifices, as in obeying the voice of the LORD? Surely, to obey is better than sacrifice, and to heed than the fat of rams." (1 Sam. 15:22)

With what shall I come before the LORD, and bow myself before God on high? Shall I come before him with burnt offerings, with calves a year old? Will the LORD be pleased with thousands of rams, with ten thousands of rivers of oil? Shall I give my firstborn for my transgression, the fruit of my body for the sin of my soul? He has told you, O mortal, what is good; and what does the LORD require of you but to do justice, and to love kindness, and to walk humbly with your God? (Mic. 6:6-8)

Religion that is pure and undefiled before God, the Father, is this: to care for orphans and widows in their distress, and to keep oneself unstained by the world. (Jas. 1:27)

Texts such as Zech. 7:4-10 and Matt. 25:37-45 have a similar theme. If we are unlikely to fast regularly, or to offer sacrifices on the altar, can you think of other religious practices we may keep, but that may be meaningless in God's sight if they are not accompanied by just living?

On the other hand, if we have never forced someone into virtual bondage, of what injustices might we be guilty? Have we benefited from the exploitation of others, but have never given back? Have we been aware of needs and yet failed to help the hungry or homeless, the sick or struggling? What attitudes have we held toward people of minority races or ethnicities or social backgrounds or gender identities?

Consider taking the time to paraphrase Isa. 58:6 by filling the blanks with worship practices or justice issues that you believe God might hope to see in you: "Is not this the _____ that I choose: to _____, to _____, and to _____?"

Fifth Sunday after Epiphany

Second Reading
Psalm 112*

Promises, Promises

They have distributed freely, they have given to the poor; their righteousness endures forever; their horn is exalted in honor. (Ps. 112:9)

Psalm 112 promises positions of power, an abundance of wealth, and lasting security to those who keep God's commands. If only it always worked out that way…

Today's psalm text continues the theme of the first reading from Isaiah 58, drawing a direct connection between pious living and bounteous rewards. Prosperity preachers love texts such as this one, assuring their congregations in person or on television that God has promised untold material blessings for those who are faithful.

The promises grow from the covenant theology of Deuteronomy that pervades most of the Old Testament. In no uncertain terms, the covenant between Yahweh and Israel promised a life of blessings for those who proved faithful, and threatened doom and gloom for those who did not.

A classic formulation of the arrangement is found in Deut. 30:15-18: "See, I have set before you today life and prosperity, death and adversity. If you obey the commandments of the LORD your God that I am commanding you today, by loving the LORD your God, walking in his ways, and observing his commandments, decrees, and ordinances, then you shall live and become numerous, and the LORD your God will bless you in the land that you are entering to possess. But if your heart turns away and you do not hear, but are led astray to bow down to other gods and serve them, I declare to you today that you shall perish; you shall not live long in the land that you are crossing the Jordan to enter and possess."

> **Spelling it out:** Consider how specific the Deuteronomist was in his promises: "All these blessings shall come upon you and overtake you, if you obey the LORD your God: Blessed shall you be in the city, and blessed shall you be in the field. Blessed shall be the fruit of your womb, the fruit of your ground, and the fruit of your livestock, both the increase of your cattle and the issue of your flock. Blessed shall be your basket and your kneading bowl. Blessed shall you be when you come in, and blessed shall you be when you go out. The LORD will cause your enemies who rise against you to be defeated before you; they shall come out against you one way, and flee before you seven ways. The LORD will command the blessing upon you in your barns, and in all that you undertake; he will bless you in the land that the LORD your God is giving you" (Deut. 28:2-8).
>
> In vv. 16 and following, the blessings are reversed and the disobedient are promised curses instead – and in more graphic detail than the blessings. The Deuteronomist, writing in Moses' name sometime in the late seventh century, pulled out all the stops in calling the recalcitrant people back to faithfulness in Yahweh.

Deuteronomy 28 spells it out in greater detail, with extra emphasis on curses for disobedience. The first 14 verses promise specific blessings if the people remain faithful: abundant crops, many children, success in battle. More than three times the effort is devoted to those who turn to other gods, though: vv. 15-69 elaborate detailed misfortunes and curses that would fall on them. [**Spelling it out**]

Texts such as these were directed primarily at the nation, but they applied equally to individuals. David, as a prime example, succeeded at every turn so long as he remained faithful and sought Yahweh's guidance (1 Samuel 16–2 Samuel 10), but after he used his position of power to take advantage of Bathsheba and then arranged for her husband Uriah to be killed when she became pregnant (2 Samuel 11), it was all downhill for David. His son by Bathsheba died in childhood. His oldest son Amnon raped his half-sister, Tamar. Tamar's full brother Absalom murdered Amnon, and later Absalom led a military coup against his father. The coup failed and the beloved Absalom was killed, leaving David distraught and much diminished as a king (2 Samuel 12–20).

Israel's sages taught a similar theology of retribution, though it was not based on the covenant, but on the belief that God had established a divine order in the universe. Those who lived wisely in accord with that order prospered, while foolish people who followed their own way suffered. Evidence of this is seen in wisdom psalms, such as Psalm 1, and the collection of adages and observations that make up the book of Proverbs.

Even Old Testament observers knew that the formula was too simple. Everyone knew of righteous people who suffered for no apparent reason, and greedy or malicious people who enjoyed prosperous lives. Thus the Hebrew Bible contains the hard questioning of Job and the sharp cynicism of Ecclesiastes, who called everything into question.

The tit-for-tat theology of the Deuteronomist persisted into New Testament times, when it remained a popular belief that everyone got what they deserved. This is why, when people told Jesus about a group of Galileans who had been executed by soldiers inside the temple, his first question was "Do you think that because these Galileans suffered in this way, they were worse sinners than all other Galileans?" (Luke 13:1-2).

Jesus refused to connect righteous behavior with material blessings. Indeed, he insisted that his followers should be prepared to face hardship and suffering: "I have told you these things so that in me you may have peace. In the world you have trouble and suffering, but take courage – I have conquered the world" (John 16:33). Jesus sent his disciples on mission with no extra food or clothing (Luke 10:4), and he insisted that those who came after him should also be willing to bear a cross (Luke 14:27).

The Apostle Paul often acknowledged the reality of suffering, and he gloried in the way suffering leads to perseverance (Rom. 5:3), considering present sufferings to be of little account compared to what he believed lay in store for believers (Rom. 8:18).

We could cite other examples, but the point is this: while the ancient Hebrews believed that blessings automatically followed obedience, that was understood as a covenant arrangement between God and Israel. Modern Christians misinterpret the Bible if we read texts such as today's psalm to suggest a direct connection between righteousness and rewards.

Given that lengthy proviso, let's imagine how an ancient Hebrew would have heard Psalm 112.

A confident future
(vv. 1-3)

The psalm begins with a call to praise Yahweh and the affirmation "Happy are those who fear the LORD, who greatly delight in his commandments" (v. 1). "The fear of the LORD is the beginning of wisdom," said one of the sages behind the book of Proverbs (1:7, 9:10), and also the author of Ps. 111:10, the last words prior to today's text.

To fear the Lord was to respect God's sovereignty and obey God's teachings. Those who did so were promised long life by the Deuteronomist. Hence, the psalmist was confident that "Their descendants will be mighty in the land; the generation of the upright will be blessed" (v. 2). But there is more to a successful life than length of days. The author went on to claim: "Wealth and riches are in their houses, and their righteousness endures forever" (v. 3).

Had this been the psalmist's personal experience, or did he mainly enjoy the exercise of putting the traditional theology into poetry? We cannot know.

A righteous present
(vv. 4-6)

The following three verses flesh out behaviors characteristic of the faithful: "They rise in the darkness as a light for the upright; they are gracious, merciful, and righteous" (v. 4). True God-fearers were shining examples to others. They showed grace to those who wronged them, and mercy to those who were in their debt.

> **Sheol:** Through most of the Old Testament period, Hebrew people had no concept of heaven as a place of eternal reward, and hell as a place of punishment. They believed that all people went into a netherworld known as Sheol, which was depicted as being somewhere in the earth's depths (Job 11:8, Prov. 15:24, Ezek. 31:15-18). It could also be called "the pit," as in Job (33:18, 22, 24, 28, 30) and in the Psalms (88:4, 6; 103:4; 143:7). Proverbs 1:12 combines the two, as does Isa. in 45:15: "But you are brought down to Sheol, to the depths of the pit."
>
> Ezekiel offered a description in this warning against the city of Tyre: "then I will thrust you down with those who descent into the Pit, to the people of long ago, and I will make you live in the world below, among primeval ruins, with those who go down to the Pit, so that you will not be inhabited or have a place in the land of the living" (Ezek. 26:20).
>
> Sheol was thought of as a gloomy and decaying abode. Isaiah 14:11 imagined its residents lying on beds of maggots, with worms for their covering.
>
> Yet, stories such as Saul's request for a necromancer to call up Samuel from Sheol suggest that it could be thought of as a place of rest from which Samuel did not want to be disturbed (1 Sam. 28:15).
>
> In his misery, Job thought of Sheol as a place of equanimity. If only he could have died at birth, he said, "Now I would be lying down and quiet; I would be asleep; then I would be at rest with kings and counselors of the earth who rebuild ruins for themselves, or with princes who have gold, who fill their houses with silver" (Job 3:13-15).

The righteous practiced generosity in lending to others and conducting their business "with justice," suggesting that they did not take advantage of the poor. They did not force debtors to give up their ancestral land or sell their children into indentured slavery when they were behind on their payments (v. 5).

Their just dealings would cement their place in the community and in its memory: "For the righteous will never be moved; they will be remembered forever" (v. 6).

Until late in the postexilic period, the Hebrews did not expect much of an afterlife. They believed that everyone went to Sheol, a shadowy underground place where good and evil, rich and poor entered an uncertain existence still vaguely bound to their earthly remains. **[Sheol]**

Confident living
(vv. 7-10)

As Israel was promised victory over its enemies, so the psalmist saw the righteous as fully confident, fearing none but God: "They are not afraid of evil tidings; their hearts are firm, secure in the LORD" (v. 7). The next verse speaks of steady assurance that "in the end," the just "will look in triumph on their foes" (v. 8).

This does suggest potential times of difficulty, for the presence of enemies clearly implies conflict or struggle. Such things do not faze the faithful, however.

The psalm draws to a close with another reminder that obedience and fortune are linked: "They have distrib-

uted freely, they have given to the poor; their righteousness endures forever; their horn is exalted in honor" (v. 9).

The final verse may have been original, or possibly added later. It reflects the same idea, but from the opposite point of view: "The wicked see it and are angry; they gnash their teeth and melt away; the desire of the wicked comes to nothing" (v. 10).

The author imagines a frustrated person who thinks that his chicanery, manipulation, or oppression of others will be profitable, only to learn that it is the just and generous who prosper. Surely frustration would result.

Can we learn something from this psalm? While acknowledging that it was written to people who lived in a different time and under a different covenant, we can also take comfort from the psalmist's assurance that God is at work in the world, and that God pays attention to how we behave.

We may not expect God to reward us with riches for every act of charity, but we can trust that God is pleased when we choose to live as Jesus lived, when we choose to work for justice, demonstrate grace, and practice generosity toward others.

One option for interpretation is to shift the promised rewards from this life to the next, as Paul did in saying that he counted earthly suffering as nothing compared to "the glory about to be revealed to us" (Rom. 8:18).

Like many other early Christians, Paul expected Christ to return in glory, and to do so soon. Earthly riches could not compare with the future he anticipated for those who followed faithfully.

We are less likely to anticipate the kind of heavenly interjection that enlivened Paul's hopes, and we may not gain wealth in proportion to our beneficence, but we too may be confident that the justice, grace, and generosity the psalmist praised will certainly honor Jesus and make our world a better place.

The Hardest Question
How is one's "horn" exalted in honor?

Verse 9 of the text speaks of generous and obedient people by saying "their righteousness endures forever; their horn is exalted in honor." What does that mean?

The metaphor of a "horn" could suggest honor or dignity: but why?

Peoples of the ancient Near East, having observed powerful horned animals, typically saw horns as a sign of power. Mesopotamian gods were routinely portrayed with horns curled around their heads like a crown, and kings who claimed to be divine likewise included horns on commissioned images of themselves.

The Israelites used animal horns as containers for liquids such as anointing oil, and they punctured the small end of horns to make the trumpet-like *shofar*, used for signaling, in war, or in temple worship.

Sacrificial altars typically bore symbolic horns at each corner as prominent features to which blood was applied during ceremonies (Exod. 27:2, 29:12, and others). Accused persons seeking asylum could take hold of the horns of the altar (1 Kgs. 1:50, 2:28). Amos spoke of the horns of the altar at Bethel being cut off as a punishment for Israel's sin (Amos 3:14).

Metaphorically, horns spoke of a king or country's power, strong in victory (1 Kgs. 22:11) or broken in defeat (Jer. 48:25). Ephraim and Manasseh were described as having "horns like the horns of a wild ox" as a symbol of their might (Deut. 33:17). Hannah's song of praise says Yahweh will give strength to the king and "exalt the horn" (NRSV "power") of the anointed (2 Sam. 2:10). A similar metaphor is found in Ps. 89:17: "For you are the glory of their strength, by your favor our horn is exalted." The same psalm says that God's steadfast love and faithfulness will bless the king, so that "in my name his horn shall be exalted" (Ps. 89:24).

Psalm 75 warns against promoting one's own "horn," an image of excessive pride (Ps. 75:5), leaving such exaltation to God: "All the horns of the wicked I will cut off, but the horns of the righteous shall be exalted." Similar themes are present in Ps. 92:10 and 112:9, today's text. To "exalt the horn" is a metaphorical way of expressing honor toward the faithful.

Fifth Sunday after Epiphany

Third Reading
1 Corinthians 2

Spiritual Secrets

For I decided to know nothing among you except Jesus Christ, and him crucified. (1 Cor. 2:2)

Have you ever participated in a formal debate? Good debaters are skilled in marshaling rhetorical devices and rational arguments to make their case. By appealing both to the emotions and the intellect, a skillful orator can take even a ridiculous proposition and convince many people it is true.

While the Christians Paul addressed in Corinth were accustomed to oral debates in the public square, the "debates" we are familiar with today are more typically one-sided exhibitions played out in opinion columns, blogs, and video clips – which can also make persuasive arguments for false claims.

Consider the hundreds of political ads that jam the airways each election season. They are frequently based on complete lies, half-truths, or misleading accusations, yet many voters find them convincing – especially if the candidates' claims match their own biases or preferences. It's enough to make a thinking person gag, but also an effective reminder of the power of compelling rhetoric.

The testimony of God
(vv. 1-5)

Paul's letter to the Corinthians was designed, in large part, to counter conflict that arose from overconfident people pushing competing agendas.

Having argued in the previous chapter that human and divine wisdom exist on entirely different levels, Paul insisted that his message to the Corinthians was not based on human oratory, but on Christ alone. "I did not come proclaiming the mystery (or 'testimony') of God to you in lofty words or wisdom," he said (v. 1).

Manuscript evidence for v. 1 is divided: some ancient sources speak of the "mystery" of God (*mustērion*), and others have "testimony" (*marturion*) (see also 1:17). A good case can be made for either being the original reading.

The Corinthians were accustomed to hearing Greek orators or philosophers speak with impressive force, but Paul refused to be judged by style, polish, or rhetoric alone. He knew that the gospel of Christ does not make sense by human categories of logic, in which the concept of a crucified God seems like so much foolishness (1:18).

We have evidence for this. Sometime in the early history of the church, someone who thought the faith was foolish ridiculed a Christian believer by scratching a graffito into a plaster wall near Palatine Hill in Rome. The drawing portrayed a donkey-headed man on a cross, and another man looking up in worship. A crude inscription labels it "Alexamenos and his god." **[Foolishness?]**

Paul recognized that the concept of a crucified savior would seem laughable to the world (1:18-25), but he remained determined "… to know nothing among you except Jesus Christ, and him crucified" (v. 2). His testimony about Christ was not proclaimed in the elegant speech of a professional orator, but in the wondrous amazement of a sinner who had been saved by grace and who could speak of it only "… in weakness and in fear and in much trembling" (v. 3).

Paul understood that rational arguments for the gospel would be largely ineffective, and any results produced by them would probably be short-lived. He was more concerned that people appreciate the power of God than simply gain knowledge about God. Thus, he said, "My speech and my proclamation were not with plausible

Foolishness? The graffito referenced in the lesson can be found here, both as a line drawing (http://upload.wiki media.org/wikipedia/commons/a/a9/AlexGraffito.svg) and from the original (http://en.wikipedia.org/wiki/File:-Alexorig.jpg). The date is uncertain, with estimates ranging from the first to the third centuries CE.

words of wisdom, but with a demonstration of the Spirit and of power, so that your faith might rest not on human wisdom but on the power of God" (vv. 4-5).

What convincing "demonstration of the Spirit and of power" did Paul have in mind? Perhaps his preaching had been accompanied by an outpouring of the Spirit that manifested itself in a variety of ways, including miracles of healing, speaking in tongues, and other spiritual gifts. Unfortunately, the Corinthians had managed to turn those gifts into a source of conflict, too (see chs. 12–14).

Paul would also have credited the Spirit with the outbreak of faith among the Corinthians. The growth of the church, like the salvation of the sinner, is the work of God, the fruit of God's empowering Spirit. [**A section marker?**]

The mystery of God
(vv. 6-13)

With v. 6, Paul shifted gears, but his precise intent is unclear, and interpreters have struggled mightily with understanding 2:6-16. A surface reading suggests that Paul turned to the subject of Christian maturity, promising that he did in fact have additional mysteries to share with those who were spiritually mature.

That would contradict everything Paul had said in 1:18–2:5, however, for there he insisted that believers have no need of esoteric mysteries.

For this reason, it may be best to read these verses as irony or sarcasm in which Paul was saying something to the effect of, "You want mystery? I'll give you mystery!" He had already insisted that God's secret is subsumed in the cross of Christ, and that was all the mystery anyone needed.

Whether Paul turned to irony or simply adopted his opponents' terminology to bolster his own case, he may have been responding to criticism that his version of the gospel was too simplistic – that he had not revealed to the church the real mysteries of Christ that others claimed to know.

The criticism could have been fueled by the popularity of Jewish apocalypticism, which looked to ancient prophecies for secret revelations of a new age, or of mystery religions that initiated members through clandestine ceremonies and mystic rituals.

Other critics may have promoted an incipient heresy we know as Gnosticism, which claimed that persons could ascend to higher spiritual realms by attaining secret knowledge (*gnosis*).

It is also possible that some Corinthians had been more impressed with the teaching of Peter and Apollos (see 1:12, 3:4) than with Paul's straightforward version of the gospel.

What did Paul mean by "Yet among the mature we do speak wisdom, though it is not a wisdom of this age or the rulers of this age, who are doomed to perish" (v. 6)?

Some Corinthians evidently considered themselves to be more mature than others, but Paul saw immaturity on every hand. Perhaps we should understand his use of

A section marker? Some scholars note that Paul's statement in 2:5, "so that your faith might rest not on human wisdom but on the power of God," forms an inclusio with his earlier assertion in 1:18: "For the message about the cross is foolishness to those who are perishing, but to us who are being saved it is the power of God."

The twin references can be seen as bookends marking the extent of Paul's argument that salvation comes through the power of God rather than human wisdom. With 2:6, he moves to a different subject, discussing the movement toward Christian maturity.

"mature" to be in quotation marks, a sarcastic setup before calling them spiritual babies (3:1).

Whether we read his tone as ironic or not, Paul insisted that the "wisdom of this age," the human attempt to make sense out of life, would have no future.

"This age" is a reminder that Paul saw salvation in eschatological terms. He saw Christ's crucifixion as introducing a new epoch. Those who still belonged to "this age," whether wise or powerful, were bound to perish. Those who trusted Christ, however, belonged to the new and eternal era.

Paul contended that the "secret and hidden" wisdom that God "decreed before the ages" (v. 7) was not arcane knowledge revealed to a few: it was the straightforward gospel of Christ as the fulfillment of God's purpose to bring salvation to the world.

This hidden purpose of God had been revealed in Christ, Paul said, but "the rulers of this age" did not understand God's plan, or else they would not have crucified Christ (v. 8). **[Rulers of this age]** There could be no greater truth or deeper secret than this, Paul argued – no more important bit of knowledge than the revelation that Christ died to redeem the world. The Corinthians would do well to grasp this truth more completely before demanding deeper knowledge.

Understanding v. 9 is problematic. Paul introduced an Old Testament quotation in his typical manner ("as it is written …"). However, the quotation itself – "What no eye has seen, nor ear heard, nor the human heart conceived, what God has prepared for those who love him" – does not appear in the Old Testament. It is likely that Paul was freely adapting Isa. 64:4: "From ages past no one has heard, no ear has perceived, no eye has seen any God beside you, who works for those who wait for him."

If this was the text Paul had in mind, we should not overlook his substitution of the word "love" for "wait." God's eternal gift is not for those who gain wisdom or speak with eloquence, but for those who love God. And those

> **Rulers of this age:** Some interpreters regard the "rulers of this age" (*archontōn*) as a reference to spiritual powers or demons, but Paul's argument that they crucified Christ out of ignorance seems to make it clear that he had earthly rulers in mind.

> **Mind, or spirit?** In v. 16 Paul quoted from Isa. 40:13: "For who has known the mind of the Lord, so as to advise him?" In doing so, he changed Isaiah's "spirit of the Lord" to "mind of the Lord," expressing his belief that one who truly knows God can know the mind of Christ.

who understand God best are not those who learn from human teachers, but from God's indwelling Spirit (v. 10). Just as we know ourselves better than anyone else when we're in touch with our own spirit, so no one fully understands God except God's own Spirit (v. 11).

It is the Spirit of God, not of the world, that introduces us to the deeper mysteries of the faith and to the reality of our spiritual gifts (v. 12), Paul said. Appreciating the deeper things of God is not a matter of deep knowledge, but of deep faith and openness to God's Spirit. Spiritual things cannot be communicated in logical categories, but in a common ground of experience known to those who experience God's Spirit (v. 13).

Self-directed people (*psuchikos*) can neither understand nor receive the gifts of God's Spirit, Paul said, because they are not in touch with the Spirit. A radio cannot receive an FM signal if the dial is set to AM. If we are unwilling to tune our hearts to the signals of the Spirit, all we hear is static (v. 14).

On the other hand, those who are spiritual (*pneumatikos*) know the presence of God, and they know what God has revealed to them, which is not subject to the judgment of others (v. 15).

How do we determine if someone's teaching is true? Who truly knows the mind of the Lord (v. 16)? The testing stone, Paul said, is Christ, and he claimed boldly that "We have the mind of Christ." **[Mind or spirit?]**

That, Paul might say, is real wisdom.

The Hardest Question
How should we interpret the style of 1 Cor. 2:5-16?

Richard Hays argues forcefully for an ironic reading of Paul's rhetoric in this text. Hayes notes that irony – saying one thing while meaning another – is a powerful but dangerous rhetorical device, as it relies on the reader to pick up cues that the passage should be read tongue-in-cheek rather than literally.

As an example, consider the way we may respond to a question by saying "Yeah, right," when what we mean is "Absolutely not!"

It could be even more dangerous to read the text straight, however. Literal readers could use the passage "as a classic proof-text for Gnostics, elitists, and enthusiasts who want to assert their possession of a spiritual insight exalted above that of their fellow Christians" (Hays, *1 Corinthians*, Interpretation [John Knox Press, 1997], 40).

Hays offers five reasons why the passage should be read as irony:

1. "Paul has already explicitly and unambiguously defined the content of true wisdom" as Christ crucified, Hays writes, as "Christ the power of God and the wisdom of God" (1:22-24). The wisdom of God, which far surpasses human wisdom, is the cross: no further secrets are needed.

2. "Therefore, the discourse in 2:2-16 has to be read as ironic," Hays argues; otherwise, Paul would have undermined his own arguments in 1:18–2:5. Paul uses ironic reversals in other places, and appears to be doing so here.

3. The categories Paul uses to explain God's wisdom "are not philosophical but apocalyptic in character" and based on God's revelation "rather than on human capacities for knowing."

4. The distinctions in the passage are not between mature and immature Christians, but between Christians (who have entered the new age) and non-Christians (who remain in the old age).

5. The meaning of spiritual maturity is defined in 3:1-4, but with an ironic twist: "those who are mature act in love rather than in jealousy and quarreling. Authentic wisdom is thus characterized by unity and humility rather than by special knowledge and rhetorical skill." (Hays, 40-41)

Keeping these things in mind, it appears likely that Paul intended for the passage to be understood ironically, rather than as an assertion that he did in fact have deeper mysteries to reveal.

Fifth Sunday after Epiphany
Fourth Reading
Matthew 5:13-20

Salt, Light, and Law

Do not think that I have come to abolish the law or the prophets; I have come not to abolish but to fulfill. (Matt. 5:17)

Have you ever had your worldview challenged? From childhood, we develop an embedded understanding of how things are. Our cultural biases, levels of aspiration, and general attitudes toward life are formed early and stay late – unless further experiences lead us to reevaluate. That may happen when we move to a different location, go off to college, enter the armed forces, spend time in a different culture, or come face to face with heartache or tragedy. Such things can shift our way of seeing the world.

With his "beatitudes," Jesus turned traditional ways of thinking upside down by ascribing blessedness to unlikely people. Who would think being poor, grieving, or meek could merit the term "blessed," which can also be translated as "happy"?

Teachings that follow the beatitudes also put an interesting twist on common conceptions of righteousness. Jesus knew these would put him at odds with the religious authorities and with the common religious thought of the day, but he had come to teach a new way of righteousness.

His teachings were not out of touch with the typical tenets of Judaism, but designed to go "higher and deeper" into a new way of life. **[Jesus as teacher and sage]**

On being salty
(5:13)

In modern English, "salty" is not a compliment, but suggests coarse or vulgar behavior. Salty language is inappropriate for delicate ears. Jesus used the metaphor in a much more positive way, challenging his followers to remain faithful and make the world a better place. "You are the salt of the earth," he said (v. 13a). Salt can be used both to flavor food and to preserve it. In the ancient world, where refrigeration was non-existent, salt was so highly valued that compensation for Roman soldiers included an allowance for salt: both "salt" and "salary" are derived from *sal*, the Latin word for salt.

Egyptian, Greek, and Roman physicians used salt as a disinfectant or in healing ointments and poultices. Hebrew midwives or mothers rubbed newborn babies with salt (Ezek. 16:4), possibly to ward off infection and also to symbolize a wish that the child would live a life of integrity. For the Israelites, salt was a symbol of faithfulness and probity: they were to include salt in their sacrifices and offerings as a "covenant of salt" that called for faithful living (Lev. 2:13, Num. 18:19, 2 Chron. 13:5).

Jesus used the metaphor to challenge his followers to add a lasting and flavorful quality to their communities and the world. As they exhibited the love and character of Christ, they would make life better for all. **[Salt and wisdom]**

What did Jesus mean by the additional phrase, "but if salt has lost its taste, how can its saltiness be restored?"

Jesus as teacher and sage: Matthew's gospel, more than the others, portrays Jesus as a teacher and his disciples as learners. The Greek word *mathētēs*, translated as "disciple," literally means "learner." It occurs 73 times in Matthew, compared to 46 times in Mark and 37 times in Luke. Though Jesus' disciples referred to him as Lord, when others approached Jesus, they typically called him "rabbi" or "teacher." As we read and interpret Matthew's gospel, it is helpful for us to consider Jesus' teachings as those of a wise sage explaining how things are—and how they should be—to his students. (For more on the sapiential character of the First Gospel, see Ben Witherington III, *Matthew*, Smyth & Helwys Bible Commentary [Smyth & Helwys, 2006], 16-21.)

> **Salt and wisdom:** The verb Jesus used for salt "losing its savor" literally meant "to grow foolish." One who had surrendered his wisdom for foolishness was like salt that had lost its potency. If Jesus taught in Aramaic, as we suppose, he may have used intentional wordplay: the Aramaic word for salt is *tabel*, while the similar word *tapel* means "foolish."

Today we can buy salt – cheaply – that is pure sodium chloride, often with a bit of iodine added to ward off thyroid problems.

In our experience, when salt dissolves, it disappears entirely. In first-century Palestine, however, salt commonly sold on the street may have come from evaporation pools on the Mediterranean coast, or from the Dead Sea, which has a salt content seven times more concentrated than ocean water. Less than half of the salt content in Dead Sea water is sodium chloride, however. Whether collected from aggregates on the shore or evaporated from the water, salt was typically mixed with sand or tiny grains of gypsum. The impurities had the same appearance as salt, but did not dissolve or add flavor. Once the salt was dissolved, there might be a residue that had the appearance of salt, but it was not salt, and it was good for nothing other than to be thrown out.

Jesus was all too familiar with people whose faith was all show and no substance. He challenged his followers to be salt, not sand; to live out a faith that was genuine.

On being light
(vv. 14-16)

Believers are to be not only authentic, but also visible. "You are the light of the world," Jesus said. "No one after lighting a lamp puts it under a bushel basket, but on the lampstand, and it gives light to all in the house" (v. 14a, 15). Jesus' point was clear: there is no purpose in lighting a lamp if it's not going to be seen or provide illumination for a useful space.

Jesus lived long before the advent of electricity or even gas lamps. After dark, people lit their homes with small lamps that burned olive oil. The lamps were typically the size of a person's palm, so they could be carried easily from place to place and set on a table or into a niche in the wall.

> **Salt and light:** Matthew was not alone in reporting Jesus' use of salt and light as metaphors for faithful living. See also Mark 4:21, 9:50 and Luke 8:16, 11:33, 14:34. Note that the different evangelists set these comments at different places in Jesus' ministry.

Oil was expensive and not to be wasted: no one would think of lighting a lamp and then hiding it.

John's gospel cites Jesus as saying, "As long as I am in the world, I am the light of the world" (John 9:5), but Jesus knew that he would not always be physically present. His light would need to shine on through his followers. That's why he went on to say "*You* are the light of the world." As the lights of a hilltop city make it clearly visible to anyone who can see, so his followers were to shine as beacons of goodness, grace, and hope. In case they had failed to understand, Jesus charged them: "Let your light shine before others, so that they may see your good works and give glory to your Father in heaven" (v. 16).

Jesus' hearers may have known of the Essenes, a Jewish sect whose members chose to live in isolation so they could better follow strict guidelines of purity. They sought to be righteous, but remained apart from others, keeping their light to themselves. Jesus wanted his disciples' faithful living to benefit others: they were the light of the *world*.

Modern believers who would hear Jesus today might benefit from asking if our light shines only within the bushel basket of our church building, or whether we exhibit it daily. Others cannot see or experience the light of Christ within us and be inspired to turn toward God if believers do not carry their light – and their good works – into the world. [**Salt and light**]

Jesus and the law
(5:17-20)

Jesus' teaching often seemed at odds with the traditional laws of Judaism and rabbinic interpretations of the Pentateuch. Some might have responded by thinking that Jesus had come to abolish the law, but that was not the case. Jesus wanted his hearers to understand that his work did not dismiss the law, but fulfilled it (v. 17).

Jesus' statement that "not one letter or one stroke of a letter" (v. 18) would pass away does not imply that his followers should slavishly follow every aspect of the Old Testament law, however: in the following verses, Jesus directly challenged some of those very tenets. It may seem counterintuitive, but the true fulfillment of the law might involve moving past some less important or culturally conditioned aspects of the law. Otherwise, Christians would still be commanded to eat kosher and offer animal sacrifices for *yom kippur*, and the Apostle Paul would be spinning in his grave.

To fulfill the law is to understand and live out God's purpose in giving the law. The late Malcolm Tolbert explained it this way: "God's purpose, as revealed in the Bible, is to create a people who will love and serve him and one another. This purpose was behind God's dealing with Israel, including his giving of the law, and it was brought to fruition in the life of Jesus the Messiah. In this way the law, seen in its totality, is fulfilled" (*Good News from Matthew* [Broadman Press: 1975], 43).

To fulfill the law is to be neither loose nor legalistic with its teachings, but to seek its true meaning through what God has done in Christ. Luke quoted Jesus as agreeing with an expert in the Jewish law that the essence of the law was to love God with all one's being, and to love others as oneself (Luke 10:25-28).

People of Jesus' day regarded the scribes and Pharisees, who sought to fulfill every requirement of the law, as being especially righteous – to the extent that they would tithe portions of seasoning herbs grown in their gardens. Later, Jesus charged them with hypocrisy: "For you tithe mint, dill, and cumin, and have neglected the weightier matters of the law: justice and mercy and faith" (Matt. 23:23).

Jesus told his followers that their righteousness must exceed that of the scribes and Pharisees, but how could one go beyond the legendary righteousness of Judaism's religious all-stars? To illustrate his meaning, Jesus spun out a series of illustrations of how the law had been interpreted in the past, and how the fulfillment of the law through his teaching and work might be different (5:21-48).

Jesus' teaching gives modern believers much to think about. Are we bright and salty Christians who enlighten and season the world around us, making it a better place, or do we compartmentalize our piety for Sundays alone? What are some practical ways in which we can be salt and light to the people in our lives during this coming week?

The world is waiting.

The Hardest Question
Was Jesus inconsistent in his comments about the law?

What Jesus has to say about the law in vv. 17-20 can appear confusing. On the one hand, he said "Do not think that I have come to abolish the law or the prophets; I have come not to abolish but to fulfill." He went on to say, with some emphasis, "For truly I tell you, until heaven and earth pass away, not one letter, not one stroke of a letter, will pass from the law until all is accomplished" (vv. 17-18). The familiar "not one jot or one tittle" of the KJV is a direct translation that makes the statement even more emphatic.

"Jot" translates "*iota*," the smallest Greek letter, equivalent in some ways to the small Hebrew letter *yod*, which resembles an apostrophe. The word "tittle" refers to tiny strokes that distinguish two similar letters. In the Hebrew script current in Jesus' day, for example, the letters *daleth* and *resh* are very similar, with the exception that the upper line of the *daleth* extends a bit beyond the edge, like a small horn. That's a tittle. After declaring that jots and tittles would not pass away, Jesus went on to say that those who break even the least commandment, or who taught others to do so, would be counted least in the kingdom of heaven (v. 19).

In short order, however, Jesus began a series of six teachings in which he challenged traditional Jewish understandings of the law, giving them new interpretations (vv. 21-48). In his ministry, Jesus showed little concern for Jewish purity rituals or Sabbath rules that were based on current interpretations of the law. How, then, could he say that not one letter of the law would pass away until all was fulfilled? How could Jesus take such liberties with the law while not invalidating it?

We note, first of all, that Jesus is talking about more than the law. "Do not think that I have come to abolish the law or the prophets," he said. "I have come not to abolish, but to fulfill." Jesus came to fulfill both the law and the prophets – to bring both the guiding law and the hoped-for promises of Israel to the end that God intended. In some cases, that meant a radical revisioning of God's purpose in establishing a law, or speaking through a prophet. The advent of Jesus brought the world to a new place, a new eschatological reality pointing toward ultimate fulfillment when God brings all things to an end and creates a new heaven and a new earth. At that time, there would be no need for the old laws and prophecies.

In the meantime, it was important for people to understand God's desired purpose in giving the law or speaking through the prophets. In the new reality introduced by Jesus, some aspects of the law were no longer needed (animal sacrifice, for example), while other laws needed to be understood within a broader application. For Jews who chose to continue living under the law, Jesus insisted that they must observe it all. Those who followed Jesus into the life of the kingdom might no longer need to follow every ritual demand, but they would learn that the call to love as Jesus loved could be even more demanding.

Sixth Sunday after Epiphany
& Season after Pentecost: Proper 1

First Reading
Deuteronomy 30:15-20

[This text is also read for Proper 18 in Year C.]

Choose Rightly!

Choose life so that you and your descendants may live, loving the LORD your God, obeying him, and holding fast to him … (Deut. 30:19b-20a)

Second Reading
Psalm 119:1-8

[This text is also read on Proper 26 in Year B.]

Law Lovers

Happy are those whose way is blameless, who walk in the law of the LORD. (Ps. 119:1)

Third Reading
1 Corinthians 3:1-9

Growing Children

For as long as there is jealousy and quarreling among you, are you not of the flesh, and behaving according to human inclinations? (1 Cor. 3:3)

Fourth Reading
Matthew 5:21-37

Then, and Now

So when you are offering your gift at the altar, if you remember that your brother or sister has something against you, leave your gift there before the altar and go; first be reconciled to your brother or sister, and then come and offer your gift. (Matt. 5:23-24)

---

*Note: lessons for the Sixth–Ninth Sundays after Epiphany use the same texts as Propers 1–4 in the Season after Pentecost. The lessons appear in Volume 3A of this commentary. Titles and text are listed for reference.

Seventh Sunday after Epiphany
& Season after Pentecost: Proper 2

First Reading
Leviticus 19:1-18 (RCL 19:1-2, 9-18)

[This text is also read for Proper 25 in Year A.]

Being Holy

*You shall not take vengeance or bear a grudge against any of your people,
but you shall love your neighbor as yourself: I am the LORD. (Lev. 19:18)*

Second Reading
Psalm 119:33-40

[This text is also read for Proper 18 of Year A.]

Teach Me, Lord

Give me understanding, that I may keep your law and observe it with my whole heart. (Ps. 119:33)

Third Reading
1 Corinthians 3:10-23 (RCL 3:10-11, 16-23)

Quality Construction

For you belong to Christ, and Christ belongs to God. (1 Cor. 3:23)

Fourth Reading
Matthew 5:38-48

Seriously?

Be perfect, therefore, as your heavenly Father is perfect. (Matt. 5:48)

Eighth Sunday after Epiphany & Season after Pentecost: Proper 3

First Reading
Isaiah 49:8-16a
Show Yourselves!

Sing for joy, O heavens, and exult, O earth; break forth, O mountains, into singing!
For the LORD has comforted his people, and will have compassion on his suffering ones. (Isa. 49:13)

Second Reading
Psalm 131
Humility and Hope

O Israel, hope in the LORD from this time on and forevermore. (Ps. 131:3)

Third Reading
1 Corinthians 4:1-5
A Very Small Thing

Therefore do not pronounce judgment before the time, before the Lord comes, who will bring to light the things now hidden in darkness and will disclose the purposes of the heart. Then each one will receive commendation from God. (1 Cor. 4:5)

Fourth Reading
Matthew 6:24-34
What, Me Worry?

Therefore I tell you, do not worry about your life, what you will eat or what you will drink, or about your body, what you will wear. Is not life more than food, and the body more than clothing? (Matt. 6:25)

Ninth Sunday after Epiphany
& Season after Pentecost: Proper 4

First Reading
Genesis 6:1–8:19 (RCL 6:9-22, 7:24, 8:14-19)
A Flood of Trouble

The LORD saw that the wickedness of humankind was great in the earth, and that every inclination of the thoughts of their hearts was only evil continually. (Gen. 6:5)

Optional First Reading
Deuteronomy 11:18-28 (RCL 11:18-21, 26-28)
A Call to Remember

You shall put these words of mine in your heart and soul, and you shall bind them as a sign on your hand, and fix them as an emblem on your forehead. (Deut. 11:18)

Second Reading
Psalm 46

[This text is also read for Proper 29 in Year C.]

When All Else Fails

Be still, and know that I am God! I am exalted among the nations, I am exalted in the earth. (Ps. 46:10)

Optional Second Reading
Psalm 31:1-5, 19-24

[Psalm 31:1-5, 5-15 is also read on the Fifth Sunday of Easter in Year A and for the Sixth Sunday of Lent, Liturgy of the Palms in Years A, B, and C. Psalm 31:9-16 is read for the Liturgy of the Passion in Years A, B, and C. A commentary on Psalm 31:1-24 appears in Volume 2A of this resource, under the Sixth Sunday of Lent, Liturgy of the Passion.]

Refuge and Redemption

Be gracious to me, O LORD, for I am in distress; my eye wastes away from grief, my soul and body also. (Ps. 31:9)

Third Reading
Romans 1:16-17, 3:22b-31 (RCL 1:16-17, 3:22b-28 [29-31])
Hope for the Guilty

… all have sinned and fall short of the glory of God. (Rom. 3:23)

Fourth Reading
Matthew 7:21-29
Firm Foundations

Everyone then who hears these words of mine and acts on them will be like a wise man who built his house on rock. (Matt. 7:24)

Transfiguration Sunday*
First Reading
Exodus 24:12-18

Clouds of Fire

Now the appearance of the glory of the LORD was like a devouring fire on the top of the mountain in the sight of the people of Israel. (Exod. 24:17)

A first glance at today's reading might lead us to wonder what modern believers could possibly garner from an old story about Moses meeting God on Mount Sinai, an activity we are unlikely to repeat. It's not even something we can attempt, given that we don't know where Mount Sinai is located.

We read the text on Transfiguration Sunday because it describes a time when Moses met God in a cloud on a mountain, a story that foreshadows the day when Jesus took Peter, James, and John to a mountain, where they were engulfed in a cloud and granted a vision of Jesus in a shining, glorified body – and the company of Moses and Elijah.

As we consider the Exodus account, we may notice other similarities between the two stories.

Not the first time

The Sinai narratives are composed of multiple stories that have been stitched together, although not always evenly. Moses makes several excursions to the mountain, but the number of trips up and down don't always match.

When we come to Exodus 24, Moses has already been to the mountain more than once. Soon after arriving at Sinai, according to 19:3, "Moses went up to God," and Yahweh instructed him to offer a covenant relationship to the Israelites, saying "Thus you shall say to the house of Jacob, and tell the Israelites: You have seen what I did to the Egyptians, and how I bore you on eagles' wings and

brought you to myself. Now therefore, if you obey my voice and keep my covenant, you shall be my treasured possession out of all the peoples. Indeed, the whole earth is mine, but you shall be for me a priestly kingdom and a holy nation. These are the words that you shall speak to the Israelites" (19:4-6).

After consecrating the people, Moses announced that Yahweh would descend upon the mountain "in the sight of all the people" (19:11) and warned them to stay back. Three days later "there was thunder and lightning, as well as a thick cloud on the mountain, and a blast of a trumpet so loud that all the people who were in the camp trembled," then "Moses brought the people out of the camp to meet God" (19:16-17).

Can you imagine?

After more smoke, fire, and earth shaking, according to the story, Yahweh descended to the mountain and called Moses to come up, then instructed him to go back down and warn the people again to stay away from the mountain. Then, as the story goes, God spoke the Ten Commandments aloud (20:1-17), though it appears the people witnessed only thunder and lightning, the sound of a trumpet, and the mountain smoking (20:18). Frightened, they pleaded with Moses to handle all future communications with God: "but do not let God speak to us, or we will die" (20:19).

Moses then returned to "the thick darkness where God was" (20:21). The narrative appears confusing at this

Transfiguration Sunday can be anywhere from the fourth to tenth Sunday after Epiphany, depending on the date of Easter, which determines the date of Ash Wednesday and the beginning of Lent.

point due to the editorial insertion of a collection of laws often called the "Book of the Covenant," written much later but inserted in 20:22–23:33 to assert Mosaic authority. After the lengthy interruption, the narrative resumes with Yahweh instructing Moses to bring three close associates and 70 elders of Israel with him to the mountain. They were to worship at a distance while Moses alone approached Yahweh's presence (24:1-3).

Before the ascent, however, Moses led the people in a formal covenant ceremony, explaining what God expected, and the people responded affirmatively: "All the words that Yahweh has spoken we will do" (v. 3).

Moses then wrote down "all the words of Yahweh," presumably relative to the Book of the Covenant, the text says (v. 4a).

Starting early the next morning, Moses built an altar at the foot of the mountain, set up 12 standing stones for the 12 tribes of Israel, and sacrificed oxen (vv. 4b-6). **[Standing stones]**

Moses then read all the words he had previously pronounced and then written down the day before, and again the people indicated their agreement to the covenant conditions (v. 7). Moses "sealed the deal" by sprinkling blood from the sacrifices over the people as a symbol of their acceptance of the covenant (v. 8).

Standing stones: Upright stones called *massebôt* were commonly erected at sacred places in the ancient Near East. Cultic sites associated with Canaanite worship often included such monuments – generally unworked stones, oblong and roughly flat in shape, and two to four feet in length. The base of the stones would be sunk in the ground just enough for the remainder to stand upright. Excavations at Hazor and Dan, among other places, have uncovered examples that visitors can still see.

Despite a divine order to break the *massebôt* dedicated to other gods into pieces (Exod. 23:24), Hebrews often used standing stones as reminders of a sacred encounter. Jacob erected one after his vision at Bethel (Gen. 28:10-22). Two different stories relate to Joshua setting up 12 stones at Gilgal to recall Israel's crossing of the Jordan (Josh. 4:1-9). Samuel erected a memorial stone and called it "Ebenezer" (stone of help) after the Israelites defeated the Philistines in battle (1 Sam. 7:7-12)–the meaning behind the phrase "here I raise mine Ebenezer" in the familiar hymn, "Come Thou Fount of Every Blessing."

Exceptions : Moses and the elders of Israel were not the only people to survive a visionary encounter with God. Jacob boasted that he had seen God but did not die, naming the site of his memorable wrestling match "Peniel," meaning "face of God" (Gen. 32:30). Gideon later feared death when the "angel of Yahweh" appeared to him, but was assured that he would not die (Judg. 6:22-23).

Afterward, Moses led Aaron, Nadab, Abihu, and 70 elders of Israel up the mountain, where "they saw the God of Israel. Under his feet there was something like a pavement of clear sapphire stone, like the very heaven for clearness" – perhaps a suggestion that the visual manifestation of God was suspended in mid-air (vv. 9-10).

Despite other traditions that claimed anyone who saw God would die (Exod. 33:20) and the people's expressed fear of death if God spoke to them directly (Exod. 20:19), the account insists that "God did not lay his hand on the chief men of the people of Israel; also they beheld God, and they ate and drank" (v. 11). **[Exceptions]** The sacred meal, reportedly held in God's very presence, reflected a common way to affirm covenant agreements (Gen. 26:28-30, Deut. 27:1-8).

Back to the mountain
(vv. 12-18)

This brings us to the day's text, in which Moses was again called up the mountain to meet with God, this time to receive the commands on stone tablets written by God. The sudden appearance of Joshua (who had not been mentioned previously) betrays seams in the text, which is mainly from the Priestly and Elohistic traditions.

The first and second halves of the chapter (vv. 1-11 and 12-18) echo each other. Both begin with Moses being called to come up the mountain, and both describe Moses moving up the mountain and drawing nearer to God. Although Joshua is said to have gone part of the way with Moses, all four uses of the verb meaning "to come/go up" (vv. 12, 13, 15, and 18) are associated with Moses.

Some writers see Moses' progressive isolation and ascent as a process of sanctification, setting him apart for special service as the primary link between God and the people.

One would expect the story to move apace, but a call to "wait" slows the narrative and adds tension. Moses instructed the elders (who have reappeared) to wait for his return (v. 14), and when he arrived atop the mountain, he also had to wait for a surprising six days. "The cloud covered the mountain" (v. 15), and "the glory of the LORD settled on Mount Sinai, and the cloud covered it for six days" before God spoke (v. 16).

Despite the cloud, "the appearance of the glory of the LORD was like a devouring fire on the top of the mountain in the sight of the people of Israel" (v. 17) – but they were in for more waiting: Moses remained on the mountain for 40 days.

What comes next is another reminder that Exodus has been edited from disparate sources: the section began with an instruction for Moses to come up and receive "the tablets of stone, with the law and the commandment, which I have written for their instruction," presumably an engraved copy of the Ten Commandments.

The two tablets are not mentioned again until 31:18, however: "When God finished speaking with Moses on Mount Sinai, he gave him the two tablets of the covenant, tablets of stone, written with the finger of God."

In between are seven long chapters (25–31) describing the intricate rules and regulations for building the tabernacle and the Ark of the Covenant, and for setting up the system of priests and Levites and sacrifices and ceremonies that would characterize Israel's worship. The same material is repeated almost verbatim in chapters 35–40, which relate how Moses carried out the instructions.

What do we make of this story now? In one sense, we can see the revelation of God to Moses in Exodus 24 as a foreshadowing of the revelation of Christ to the world, particularly as seen in his transfiguration. As Moses took three close companions along with others who remained at a distance, Jesus took three of his disciples to a mountain while leaving the others at a distance.

As a cloud representing the presence of God descended upon Sinai, so Matthew's transfiguration story speaks of a cloud surrounding Jesus and his disciples on the mountain (Matt. 17:5). As God appeared to Moses and Israel in "a devouring fire," when Jesus was transfigured "his face shone like the sun, and his clothes became dazzling white" (Matt. 17:2).

Moses met God on a high mountain that stood tall above a level plain, and his ascendant experience is related

---

Mountains: Judy Fentriss-Williams notes: "In the ancient Near East, the mountain is considered a pillar of the earth, holding the sky in place. With its head reaching toward the heavens, the mountain or high place is the bridge between earth, the realm of humans, and the heavens, the realm of the gods. As such, a mountain is the place for divine encounter" (*Feasting on the Word, Year A*, ed. David L. Bartlett and Barbara Brown Taylor, vol. 1 of Accordance electronic ed. [Westminster John Knox Press, 2010], para. 5341).

---

amid the expanses of legal requirements and tabernacle building. His story could remind us that life and ministry often consist mainly of the mundane, but not without the possibility of peak experiences. **[Mountains]**

Moses' encounter with Yahweh on Sinai made it clear to Israel that God had plans for the people, which they could learn by listening to Moses. The disciples' vision of Jesus being transfigured concluded with a voice from the cloud saying "This is my Son, the Beloved; listen to him!" (Mark 9:7).

Transfiguration Sunday is the last Sunday after Epiphany and before Ash Wednesday. As Moses was said to have spent 40 days on the mountain learning from God, so the period of Lent calls us to 40 days of introspection and listening for God's voice.

On Transfiguration Sunday or any other day, we can't expect to see a flaming vision of God's presence, but we can be confident that God still desires to speak, if only we will listen.

The Hardest Question
Where was Mount Sinai?

The short answer to the question is, "We don't know." One reason we don't know is that the Hebrews never treated it as a place of pilgrimage. This is surprising, given the importance of Sinai in relation to the traditions of law giving and covenant making that reportedly occurred there.

It's likely that later Hebrews didn't know the location, either. Documents related to the Exodus from Egypt, the sojourn at Sinai, and the wilderness wandering were not written until hundreds of years later, when an alphabetic script had developed as an adaptation of Egyptian hieroglyphics and adopted for writing Hebrew. By that time, the writers were repeating ancient traditions but had no personal knowledge of the specific locations.

The varied sources don't even agree on the mountain's name: the Yahwistic and Priestly sources commonly call it Sinai, while the Elohistic tradition and the Deuteronomist characteristically call it Mount Horeb.

Despite its reputation as the place where Moses met God, the Hebrews paid little attention to Sinai in later years. After the writing of Deuteronomy and the centralization of worship in Jerusalem, Mount Zion became the locus of pilgrimage and prayer.

This has led some writers, such as Benjamin Sommer, to suggest that Sinai was more of a religious idea than a geographical place in Israel's memory ("Sinai," from the Society of Biblical Literature Bible Odyssey website, https://www.bibleodyssey.org:443/places/main-articles/sinai).

Many have speculated about the location, however. The most popular view goes back to an early church tradition that deemed an imposing mountain called Jebel Musa in the southern Sinai Peninsula as the site of Sinai (*Jebel Musa* is Arabic for "the mountain of Moses"). The tradition goes back to the mid-fourth century CE. The Monastery of St. Catherine was built on a high shoulder of the mountain in the sixth century. While the monastery sits at just over 5,000 feet, the mountain rises to 7,498 feet.

The monastery is known for its massive collection of manuscripts, second only to the Vatican. A German scholar named Count Friedrich von Tischendorf discovered one of the earliest manuscripts of the Bible there, dating to the fourth century CE. He named it Codex Sinaiticus.

In modern times, Jebel Musa has become a tourist attraction, with hikers departing from the monastery at 2:00 a.m. to climb the mountain and watch the sunrise from the top.

The earliest Jewish traditions, however, locate the mountain just east of the Sinai in what is now northwest Arabia, in the area known in Exodus as Midian – where Moses lived for many years with his wife, Zipporah, and her father, Jethro. Exodus 3 says that Moses was pasturing his father-in-law's sheep when he met God in a burning bush on the same mountain where he would later receive the law. A tall mountain in that region known as Jebel al-Lawz has often been associated with Sinai.

Other sites have been proposed, including Har Karkom, located in the northern Sinai Peninsula, not far from the oasis of Kadesh Barnea, where the Israelites reportedly camped for some time. The remains of a Bronze Age sanctuary and rare examples of rock art are found there.

It is unlikely that we will ever know the location of Sinai for sure, and that is just as well. As Sommers noted, it is the idea that matters most.

Transfiguration Sunday
Second Reading
Psalm 2

More Than Meets the Eye

I will tell of the decree of the LORD: He said to me, "You are my son; today I have begotten you." (Ps. 2:7)

We often find ourselves caught between the ideal and the real. We have an idea of what an ideal life would be like, or of what – ideally – we would like to do and be. Yet, we're also confronted by a daily reality that might be very different.

When election season rolls around, for example, we vote for candidates in hopes that they will uphold our social or economic or moral ideals. Sadly, the victors may go to Washington or their state legislatures, only to discover that their ideals – and ours – soon run aground on the rocky shore of partisan politics.

The real and the ideal are often quite different.

Psalm 2 describes the coronation of a new king over Israel. It speaks in ideal terms, as if all the surrounding nations should recognize both God and God's king as their leader, even though the real situation in life was usually quite different.

Psalm 2 is an appropriate text for Transfiguration Sunday because it speaks of a metaphorical transformation in the life of a new king over Israel. On his coronation day, the new king was thought to enter a special relationship with God as God's "son," through whom the Davidic covenant would be fulfilled: God would act toward Israel (symbolized by the king) as a father, blessing or punishing as needed. [**Coronation psalms**]

Israel – again symbolized by the king – was called to renew its commitment to the covenant with God. New Testament writers saw the psalmist's metaphor of divine sonship as a prophecy to be fulfilled in Jesus. In the transfiguration of Jesus as told in the gospels, Jesus was revealed to the disciples as the true Son of God. The words "This is

> **Coronation psalms:** Psalm 2 is one of about 13 psalms that are often called "Royal Psalms," or "Royal Davidic Psalms," because they have to do with the kings of Israel. This psalm is one of several that may have been used as "Coronation Psalms" to celebrate a new king's enthronement.

my Son" (Matt. 17:5) may have intentionally reflected Ps. 2:7: "You are my son; today I have begotten you."

At first, the text may seem totally unrelated to our present situation, but if we stick with it, it will challenge us to examine our own relationship with God, and ask to what extent it is real, or if it remains an ideal.

The opposition plots
(vv. 1-3)

Psalm 2 was almost certainly written to celebrate the accession of a new king. It was intended for two audiences: foreign kings who were almost certainly not present, and representatives from the people of Israel who were.

In antiquity, where newscasts were unknown and spy networks were limited, a new king was largely an unknown quantity. For nations that had been obliged to pay tribute as vassals to a stronger kingdom, a transition in leadership was often seen as an opportunity to rebel against the new order and regain full independence.

Israel was rarely in a position to hold sway over surrounding nations, with the possible exceptions being the early reigns of David and Solomon. The united monarchy divided after Solomon, splitting into the smaller kingdoms of Israel (in the north) and Judah (in the south).

For most of their existence, Israel and Judah were more likely to be the vassals than the overlords, subject at various times to the superpowers of Egypt, Assyria, or Babylon, or even to smaller kingdoms such as neighboring Syria.

Whether the nation was weak or strong, however, the coronation of a new king would have involved considerable pomp and propaganda as officials hyped the new king's prospects in hopes of impressing both domestic and foreign audiences.

This was especially the case in the southern kingdom, where the line of David was maintained, and each king was thought to inherit the promises of a lasting kingdom that God had made to David. It is most likely, then, that Psalm 2 would have been preserved and used in Judah.

The psalm may have originated as early as Solomon's accession, for the style and vocabulary of the Hebrew text appears to be quite old, perhaps as early as the 10th century BCE, when Solomon ruled. The psalm could have been used at any point in the monarchy's history, however: we need not try to associate it with a particular king.

The text begins with the worship leader (or possibly the new king) imagining what plots other nations might be hatching due to the transition, anticipating a time of weakness. Opposition to Israel's king, however, was also perceived as a challenge to Israel's God: when "the rulers take counsel together," it is "against the LORD and his anointed" (v. 2b). [Who's speaking when?]

Who's speaking when? One person, such as the king, could have recited Psalm 2 while quoting the words of others, but we can imagine that multiple speakers could have performed it during the coronation service as follows:

• A worship leader or possibly the king imagines that other nations are considering rebellion (vv. 1-2).
• The foreign leaders (or someone quoting them) express their rebellious plans (v. 3).
• The worship leader or king imagines God' derisive reaction (vv. 4-5).
• Someone speaking for God declares that God has installed a new king (v. 6).
• The new king announces that God has "begotten" him as God's "son" and empowered him to rule (vv. 7-9).
• The king or worship leader addresses the rulers of other nations, warning them to honor God's chosen king (and hence, God) or face severe judgment (vv. 10-12).

The rulers' desire to "burst their bonds asunder and cast their cords from us" portrays them as leaders of vassal states who devise plans to revolt and regain their freedom from Israel before the new king could establish strong control over his army.

For the psalmist, to rebel against God's people was to rebel against God, and that was serious business.

God responds
(vv. 4-9)

The psalm portrays God as responding to the antagonism of upstart kingdoms with divine sneers, jeers, and such fury that the nations would tremble in terror as God declared: "I have set my king on Zion, my holy hill." Though most translations obscure it, the Hebrew text is particularly emphatic in v. 6, using both a personal pronoun and a first-person verb. The structure could be translated something akin to "I myself have set my king on Zion ..."

The new king did not take the throne simply because he was next in line, the psalm insists, but because God had chosen him.

The new king agreed: with vv. 7-9, he dares to claim that God had personally spoken to him, effectively adopting him as a son through whom God would relate to Israel.

This notion may sound strange to us, but Israel's theology of kingship could imagine a special covenant relationship between God and king, one so close that it could be described in filial terms.

Thus, the king could claim that God had said "You are my son; today I have begotten you" (v. 7a). In a sense, the king was thought to be "born again" into a new relationship with God. This did not make the king himself divine, as the peoples of Egypt and Mesopotamia pretended their potentates to be. Rather, it made him a symbolic "son of God," representing Israel as the children of God.

As the ceremony unfolded, it is likely that a written document (or decree) would have been fashioned and given to each king, emblematic of his legitimacy as the new ruler. When the king said "I will tell of the decree of the LORD," he may have been referring to this.

The document would serve as a formal declaration of the king's right to rule and as a renewal of the covenant

> **The king's decree:** The words translated as "covenant" or "decree" in 2 Kgs. 11:12 and Ps. 2:7 are different, but they may refer to the same idea. In 2 Kings, the decree is called an *'ēdut*, a word that can mean "testimony," "law," or "decree." The NRSV translates it as "covenant," based on its presumed content. The word in Ps. 2:7 is *choq*, which means "statute," "law," or "decree." It is derived from a verbal root that means "to engrave," which may suggest that the king was holding a written decree legitimating his kingship.

between God and Israel. When young Jehoash was made king of Judah, for example, the high priest Jehoiada "put the crown on him, and gave him the covenant" (or "decree," 2 Kgs. 11:12). [**The king's decree**]

The Hebrews believed that God had established an eternal covenant with David and his descendants, promising to bless Israel's kings as they proved obedient, but to punish them when they turned away (2 Sam. 7:8-17). That covenant, declared by the prophet Nathan, included the concept echoed in Ps. 2:7: "I will be a father to him, and he shall be a son to me" (2 Sam. 7:14a).

The Davidic covenant included a promise that God would plant Israel firmly in the land "so that they may live in their own place, and be disturbed no more; and evildoers shall afflict them no more, as formerly, from the time that I appointed judges over my people Israel; and I will give you rest from all your enemies" (2 Sam. 7:10b-11).

That promise is reflected in vv. 8-9, in which the king claims that God has promised him power to defeat all enemies with "a rod of iron" – perhaps a reference to his scepter – breaking and smashing them like clay pots.

The images of violence may appear troubling, but they were part and parcel of the rhetoric of kingship, formal declarations of bravado designed to inspire confidence among the king's subjects and to instill fear into his enemies.

Word of caution
(vv. 10-12)

The psalm closes with a warning to other rulers that they should honor Israel's new king, and in so doing they would honor Israel's God, Yahweh.

Whether we should regard the speaker in these verses as the king or the psalmist/narrator is unclear. The text is uncertain and the passage is very difficult to translate, but the message seems plain enough: those who are wise will "Serve the LORD with fear" and do obeisance to the king lest Yahweh grow angry and wreak destruction upon them.

In contrast, the psalm concludes, those who seek refuge in God – in part by honoring God's chosen king – will find happiness and blessing.

Enough with ancient kingship: at some point, we must ask ourselves "So what?" We don't live in ancient Israel, and we don't have a king, and don't want one. What could this 3,000-year-old coronation hymn possibly say to us?

Let's consider two things. First, we note that the psalm, though originally written to celebrate the accession of Hebrew monarchs, came to be seen by the early church as a foreshadowing of Jesus' incarnation as God's son. Israel's rulers never lived up to their potential, and the editorial judgments rendered by the author of 2 Kings are routinely negative: only Josiah and Hezekiah followed Yahweh closely enough to escape charges of being evil kings.

God's promise to the king in Psalm 2 was little more than an ideal hope in Israel's past, but early Christians believed it had been finally fulfilled in Jesus, the only one of whom it could truly be said "You are my Son, today I have begotten you" (see Acts 13:33; Heb. 1:5, 5:5, where Ps. 2:7 is quoted).

Secondly, as residents of Israel and surrounding nations were urged to serve God by serving God's appointed king, so we serve God best when we follow the teachings of Jesus, who spent much of his ministry proclaiming the kingdom of God.

Trusting Christ is a transformational event. As the kings of Israel were symbolically "begotten" as sons of God on the day of their accession, so Jesus challenged people to be "born again" by putting their trust in God and living as the children of God.

The psalm challenges us to ask how faithfully we are living out that charge.

Is our faith more than an ideal, or do our daily actions show it to be real?

The Hardest Question
How did Psalm 2 come to be considered a messianic psalm?

As indicated previously, Psalm 2 appears to have been written for use at the coronation of a king in the life of ancient Israel. It was not designed or intended as a prophecy. How then did it come to be regarded as a messianic psalm par excellence?

From the time that Israel adopted the model of a monarchy, it was understood that the king ruled in God's behalf, and Israel was to be a model of the kingdom of God on earth. This is reflected in Psalm 2. As Peter C. Craigie has put it: "The Lord, the Enthroned One (v. 4), was the universal king, but his earthly representative was his 'son,' the Davidic king. Because God is a universal God, the earthly king's jurisdiction is also presented in world-wide terms (2:8-9), though with respect to the Davidic kings, the world-wide authority always remained an ideal rather than a reality" (*Psalms 1–50*, vol. 19, Word Biblical Commentary [Word Books, 1983], 68).

After the kingdom of Judah was conquered by the Babylonians in 587/86 BCE, the Davidic kingdom ceased to exist as a political entity, and any hopes of Israel ruling the world were dashed. This forced Israel's theologians to reframe their understanding of the Davidic covenant.

Over time, various views emerged. Since the Davidic covenant was thought to be eternal, any future hopes would have to include a descendant of David in some sort of royal role.

Israel's kings were anointed with oil as the designated monarch (1 Sam. 10:1, 16:13; 2 Sam. 2:4, 5:3), and the term "anointed one" (*mashiach*, which became the English "messiah") came to be used in a hopeful sense with reference to a future descendant of David who would establish a new kingdom of Israel.

There was still some hope of this in Jesus' day, as groups such as the Zealots longed for a leader to spark a rebellion against Rome. From the beginning of his ministry, Jesus talked about the kingdom of God (Mark 1:14-15) as the central focus of his preaching.

Many had hopes that Jesus, who displayed miraculous powers, would be the one to restore a physical kingdom, but when it became clear that Jesus had a more spiritual reality in mind, the understanding of "messiah" began to shift.

After Jesus' crucifixion and resurrection, early believers began to think of him as the anointed one, the ultimate son of David – and son of God – who was lord of a universal kingdom that would one day be fulfilled in both a physical and a spiritual sense.

The language of Psalm 2, with its emphasis on the king as the son of God, was adopted as a foreshadowing of his messianic role. This could hardly be clearer than in Paul's argument for Jesus as the fulfillment of Israel's messianic hopes in Acts 13. "And we bring you the good news that what God promised to our ancestors he has fulfilled for us, their children, by raising Jesus; as also it is written in the second Psalm, 'You are my Son; today I have begotten you'" (Acts 13:32-33, see also Rom. 1:4).

The church's emerging theologians saw Herod, Pilate, the Romans, and even Hebrew opponents as equivalent to the kings who conspired against the king in Ps. 2:1-3. Jesus had overcome them, not in the violent manner of Ps. 2:9-11, but through his resurrection and victory over death. The citations argue for the divinity of Christ but quote Psalm 2, "You are my Son; today I have begotten you."

While speaking of Christ as the true king of all, however, early Christians recognized that there was no earthly counterpart. This led to a new understanding of apocalyptic and eschatological texts from Daniel and Ezekiel, with Jesus as the one who exercises ultimate dominion over heaven and earth alike. Imagery drawn from Psalm 2 is evident in Rev. 1:5, 2:27, 6:17, 12:5, and others.

Biblical interpreters refer to the developing interpretation as *sensus plenior* or "the full sense," ascribing significance to a text that goes beyond what the original writer intended. While some modern interpreters carry this too far by finding symbolism and typological references to Christ in every corner of the Hebrew Bible, the flowering of Psalm 2 as a messianic text provides an example of when such interpretation is appropriate.

Transfiguration Sunday

Alternate Second Reading
Psalm 99*

Who Needs a King?

Mighty King, lover of justice, you have established equity; you have executed justice and righteousness in Jacob. (Ps. 99:4)

The book of Psalms consistently ranks as the most-read book in the Bible, but some psalms are easier to love than others. We like warm and fuzzy psalms such as Psalm 23 and others that offer comfort or assurance. We like wisdom psalms on the order of Psalm 1 that offer sage advice for the faithful life. We like celebratory hymns in the vein of Psalm 100 that exalt God as Lord of all.

Other psalms don't connect as well: imprecatory psalms such as Psalms 69 and 109 may offend us, while royal psalms like Psalms 2 and 18 may seem alien to us. Today's text, an alternate reading for Transfiguration Sunday, praises God as a just king who has revealed Godself in manifold ways.

At the close of the Epiphany season, another reminder of God's self-revelation is appropriate. If we look hard enough, we may find ways to convert the psalm's archaic imagery into a meaningful message for our own time.

A God who reigns
(vv. 1-3)

When we think about God, various images arise. "Heavenly Father" may come to mind, or terms such as "Master" and "Lord." We may be less likely to think of the word "King." We don't live under a king, but it was typical for ancient folk who lived in monarchies to use royal terminology when thinking of God.

Today's text is the last of a group of six psalms (47, 93, 96–99) that focus on God's kingship over the earth, the universe, and all peoples, not just over Israel. The psalms

> **Facets:** In speaking of the six psalms that celebrate the single theme of God's kingship, John Durham wrote: "But despite this similarity, each of the poems of God's kingship has its own emphasis. They are like facets of a unique diamond, each flashing the same fire in its own distinct hue" ("Psalms," in *The Broadman Bible Commentary*, vol. 4 [Broadman Press, 1971], 371).

would originally have been sung in worship at the temple in Jerusalem, and all of them include the happy affirmation "Yahweh reigns!" **[Facets]**

While all six psalms recognize God's universal sovereignty, each has a different emphasis: Psalm 47 celebrates God as the king of all the earth, Psalm 93 praises God's kingship over chaos, and Psalm 96 points to God as the ruler of all peoples. The manifestation of God's dominion through earth-shaking theophanies is at the heart of Psalm 97, while Psalm 98 speaks of God's manifestation in deliverance.

Psalm 99, our text for today, commemorates various ways in which God's holiness is revealed through a threefold declaration of divine holiness in vv. 3, 5, and 9. The first section leaves no doubt as to the subject of the psalm: it opens with the stirring shout "The LORD is king," or more literally, "Yahweh reigns!"

God reigns, the psalmist claimed, with such power and magnificence that all peoples should tremble and the earth should quake at the very thought of Yahweh's presence "enthroned upon the cherubim" (v. 1). The reference is to the "Holy of Holies," where the Hebrews imagined God sat upon an invisible throne above the twin

---

*This text is also used for Transfiguration Sunday in Year C.

> **Atop the cherubim:** While the Hebrews typically thought of Yahweh as being enthroned above the cherubim in the temple, they recognized that God could hardly rule the world if limited to that place. In Israel's imagination, cherubim often remained in God's company, however. Ezekiel's vision of Ezek. 1:22-28 suggests that a group of four winged cherubim surrounded God's throne, carrying it through the air as a sort of flying vehicle.

cherubim atop the Ark of the Covenant (Exod. 25:22, 1 Sam. 4:4, 2 Kgs. 19:15). **[Atop the cherubim]**

The temple was in Jerusalem, alternately known as "Zion." Thus the psalmist declared "The LORD is great in Zion," where "he is exalted over all the peoples" (v. 2). This led into a call for all to render praise to God's "great and awesome" name, for "Holy is he!" (v. 3).

What comes to mind when we think of the word "holy"? Typical answers might include piety, purity, an absence of sin, or a life of total devotion to God. The Hebrew concept of holiness was not so much one of purity or sinlessness, however, as it was of separateness or distinctiveness. For Israel to be holy was primarily to be "set apart" as God's special people. The Hebrews considered God to be beyond sin, of course, but the prime significance of "holiness" is that Yahweh was unique, apart from all others, not just at the top of the created order but above it and responsible for it.

A God of justice
(vv. 4-5)

Israel's holy God could be praised for many reasons. What comes first to the psalmist's mind is that God's power is expressed in justice and equity for God's people. The first few words of v. 4 are difficult to translate, but clearly speak of justice. A literal reading would be "and strength, a king, justice he loves." Changing a single vowel – remembering that vowels were not part of the original text – would turn "strength" into the adjective "strong," an option chosen by most translators. The NRSV renders it "Mighty King, lover of justice," while NET has "The king is strong; he loves justice."

In either case, the meaning is clear: the psalmist hails God as one who not only loves justice, but who also has established it: "you have executed justice and righteous-

> **Social justice:** Old Testament texts calling for just care of widows, orphans, and immigrants can be found in Exod. 22:22; Deut. 10:18; 14:29; 16:11, 14; 24:17-21; 26:12-13; and 27:19, among others.

ness in Jacob" (v. 4b). Jacob was often used as a synonym for Israel. He was remembered as the father of 12 sons who gave rise to the 12 tribes of Israel, and indeed, his name had been changed to "Israel" (Gen. 32:28).

Although Jacob clearly represents Israel, the psalmist's use of the name is a bit surprising in this context, for Jacob was known as a conniving cheat who fast-talked his brother into surrendering his birthright (Gen. 25:29-33), and who later deceived his father Isaac into giving him the blessing that was due to his firstborn brother (Genesis 27). Some model of justice! That God could use such fallible people to establish a nation founded on principles of equity and justice for all people – including the widows, orphans, and immigrants who lived on the margins – is worthy of considerable praise. **[Social justice]**

As in the first stanza, the psalmist turned from his own praise of God to calling on others to join in the hallelujahs: "Extol the LORD our God; worship at his footstool." Worshiping at God's "footstool" is yet another reference to God's imagined enthronement above the Ark of the Covenant in the Holy of Holies – an apt image for the closing cry in v. 5: "Holy is he!"

A God who relates
(vv. 6-9)

Having praised God's power and justice, the poet reminded worshipers of how long God's blessings had been evident, citing the divinely inspired leadership of Moses and Aaron as an example. Even though Aaron was known as the first priest and Moses as the lawgiver, Moses also exercised the priestly functions of interceding with God on behalf of the people, which seems to be the psalmist's concern. Samuel, a priest who also acted as the last of the judges, is also remembered. "They cried to the LORD, and he answered them" (v. 6).

We might expect the cry and response to be for deliverance or vindication for Israel, but the psalmist recalled something more basic: "He spoke to them in the pillar of cloud; they kept his decrees, and the statutes that he gave them" (v. 7). This is the root of the justice the psalmist had mentioned in v. 4 and the holiness he called to mind throughout: God's gift to Israel of the law. God did not impose justice in the sense of forcing people to do what is right: that would violate human freedom. Rather, in the Torah God gave to Israel the basis for a society built on justice and equity. The people did not always obey the commandments, as the Hebrews' narrative theologians and prophets often reminded them, but the gift of a just system was in place.

Moses, Aaron, and Samuel are named as examples of the type of life God's people should live. They were not perfect, and their faults are chronicled along with their victories. Yet, their lives were characterized by faithfulness, and when they fell short, they turned to Yahweh for forgiveness. God answered them, the poet declared: "you were a forgiving God to them." Yet, God also disciplined them when they sinned, as "an avenger of their wrongdoings" (v. 8).

The psalmist concluded the third section as he did the first two, by calling on the Israelites to praise their holy God: "Extol the LORD our God, and worship at his holy mountain" (v. 9a). The holy mountain does not refer to Sinai, but to Jerusalem, often called Mount Zion. As he had closed the two previous stanzas, so the psalmist ends the psalm with a call to remember God's unique nature: "for the LORD our God is holy."

So much and so good for Israel, but what might this text say to contemporary Christians whose relationship with God is not based on obedience to the covenant law given to Israel? First, we should acknowledge our debt to the law: the moral principles found in the Ten Commandments and further elaborated in directives to love one's neighbor and care for the marginalized are at the heart of our modern understanding of personal morality and social justice.

Second, we who come to God through Christ may recall that Jesus demonstrated a constant concern for justice. Luke suggests that Jesus adopted as his mission statement a text from Isa. 61:1-2 that spoke of justice for the oppressed and comfort for the brokenhearted (Luke 4:18). In his ministry on earth, Jesus healed the sick, showed special care for the poor, and taught his disciples to love God and to love others as they loved themselves (Luke 10:27). "I give you a new commandment," Jesus said, "that you love one another. Just as I have loved you, you also should love one another" (John 13:34).

As the psalmist praised Yahweh as the king of all, Jesus inaugurated the kingdom of God – or rule of God – in which God's people are called to practice love for God and justice for all. Like Israel, we may also fall short of our calling, but our failure does not diminish the praise due to the powerful, just, and holy God who is king of all.

The Hardest Question
In what way was God an "avenger" to Moses, Aaron, and Samuel?

In v. 8, the psalmist says that God was forgiving in response to the prayers of Moses, Aaron, and Samuel, but was also "an avenger of their wrongdoings." What does that mean?

The NRSV translation (above) follows a traditional interpretation that the psalmist believed God was forgiving toward Moses, Aaron, and Samuel, but also punished them for their sins when they fell short of divine expectations.

Some scholars follow another option, assuming that the avenging reference is directed toward those who had turned against Israel's leaders, so that God took vengeance on those who attacked or opposed them. When Korah gathered followers and challenged Moses and Aaron's leadership during the wilderness wandering, for example, both the rebels and their households met the ugly fate of being swallowed up by the earth (Numbers 16).

Other interpreters choose yet a third option. A small change in the vowel pointing to the word that means "an avenger" could change it to a rare participial form of another word that means "to purify." If that were the correct reading, it could mean "one who purified them from their wrongdoings."

If we assume the traditional interpretation is correct, what wrongdoings and punishments did the psalmist have in mind? We don't normally think of Moses, Aaron, or Samuel as bad examples, but they also had shortcomings. Aaron, we recall, gave in to the demands of the people in constructing a golden calf while Moses was away for 40 days, receiving the law (Exodus 32). Surprisingly, Aaron survived that incident unscathed. Years later, however, both Moses and Aaron were complicit in failing to follow God's explicit instructions when calling forth water from a rock, and as a result were not allowed to enter the promised land (Num. 20:1-13).

Samuel's sin and punishment are not spelled out as clearly, but they are implicit in his failure to rein in his two corrupt sons, whom he had appointed as judges (1 Sam. 8:1-3). Immediately after describing how Samuel's sons "took bribes and perverted justice," the narrator tells the story of how the elders of Israel rejected Samuel's leadership, demanding a king instead (1 Sam. 8:4-22). Told by God to give the people what they wanted, Samuel appeared to have few happy days from that point on.

Third Reading
2 Peter 1:16-21

A Message That Glows

For he received honor and glory from God the Father when that voice was conveyed to him by the Majestic Glory, saying, "This is my Son, my Beloved, with whom I am well pleased." (2 Pet. 1:17)

Every person's life is marked by milestone events. Some are mostly positive: graduations, weddings, or the birth of children. Others have a negative cast: the accident, the downsizing, the death of a loved one. Whether positive or negative, milestone events have the power to shape or influence our lives from that point on.

Jesus' life was also marked by milestone events: his baptism, for example, when he heard a voice saying "You are my Son, the Beloved; with you I am well pleased" (Luke 3:22).

Perhaps the most memorable event, at least to his disciples, was the evening when Jesus led Peter, James, and John up a dark mountainside and was transfigured before their eyes, taking on a bright appearance that might have mirrored his heavenly form. Surrounded by a cloud, flanked by shining apparitions of Moses and Elijah, Jesus again heard a heavenly voice affirm him while challenging the disciples: "This is my Son, the Beloved; with him I am well pleased; listen to him!" (Matt. 17:5).

The story of the Transfiguration was told and retold, often with different details, as evidenced by the gospel accounts of Mark 9:2-8, Matt. 17:1-8, and Luke 9:28-36. The story is also reflected in today's epistle text for Transfiguration Day, from the little book of 2 Peter.

An eyewitness account
(vv. 16-18)

The letter of 2 Peter is rarely considered a favorite text among mainstream Christians, though believers who are big on judgment and hell and trying to prove inerrancy often quote it. The author was almost certainly not Simon Peter, though the first verse claims it to be so. Like many other writings of the period, it was written long after the apostle's death, possibly by a disciple or admirer of Peter, taking on the apostle's persona to add authority to his words.

The author does not identify his audience, so we cannot know whether it was directed toward readers in Rome, in Asia Minor, or elsewhere. What seems clear is that some readers had been influenced by Epicurean philosophy, which taught that the greatest good was to seek a life of modest pleasure and an absence of worry. Epicureans urged others not to fear gods, death, or the prospect of judgment after death, for such concerns added stress to life.

As a result, Epicureans scoffed at the notion of the Parousia or "Appearing," the return of Christ in judgment.

---

2 Peter as a "testament": Scholars have categorized 2 Peter largely as a "testament," a popular genre during the first century. Richard F. Wilson, in the Smyth & Helwys Bible Commentary on 2 Peter, explains:

The "testament" genre is most common in the pseudepigraphical literature of Hellenistic Judaism, and also appears to have some relationship to the "farewell speech" found in several New Testament works, such as John 15–17, Acts 20:17-38, and, perhaps, Philippians 1:12-30. Testaments and farewell speeches share three common features: an announcement of the impending death of the supposed author, a series of reminders of his legacy as a teacher or prophet, and warnings about false prophets or teachers who will threaten the memory of the teacher and his teachings. (*1&2 Peter, Jude* [Smyth & Helwys, 2010], 309-10)

They argued that people should live a balanced life each day without worrying about future punishments or rewards, for death would mean only dissolution.

The letter of 2 Peter is concerned mainly with defending the belief that Christ would return to judge, providing adequate motivation for Christians to live just and moral lives.

The author wasted little time in getting to his main point. After the accustomed greetings and a short homily about the demands of the Christian life (1:1-11), he portrayed himself as Peter, soon to die and determined to pass on his last testament to the people. [2 Peter as a "testament"] Presenting a defense of the Parousia as the primary concern of the beloved Peter's dying words would have added authority and force to the author's message.

The author of 2 Peter and his readers both knew the letters of Paul, and were probably communicating 30–40 years after both Paul and Peter had died – another full generation – so it is not surprising that some Christ followers had begun to doubt whether Jesus would return at all.

Epicureans considered all stories of the gods or the afterlife to be human inventions, which they called myths, so it is likely that Peter was responding directly to those influenced by them when he wrote "For we did not follow cleverly devised myths when we made known to you the power and coming of our Lord Jesus Christ, but we had been eyewitnesses of his majesty" (v. 16). [Myths]

The resurrection and return of Jesus were no made-up stories, the author insisted. Rather, in the persona of Peter, he claimed to have been an eyewitness of Jesus' power and majesty and message that he would come again.

To support this view, the author calls on Peter's presence at the transfiguration of Jesus, though his account is quite different from the gospels. He does not mention Moses and Elijah being present, or the surrounding cloud. He speaks of God's voice as coming from "the Majestic Glory," and the message does not match any of the gospels, though Matthew's version (cited above) is close.

The gospel writers saw the Transfiguration as a second divine affirmation of Jesus as the Messiah: at both his baptism and his transfiguration, a heavenly voice declared "This is my Son, the Beloved."

The author of 2 Peter goes further, interpreting the Transfiguration as a prophetic confirmation of Christ's

> **Myths:** The word "myth," in English, can be understood in a variety of ways. Some writers use the word "myth" to describe any story involving gods, with no judgment as to whether the story is true or false. Others use the word to describe a story that seems to take place outside of the time and space we know. Still others use it to describe a literary genre of stories related to the origins of things, and to relationships between gods and humans. In this sense, the word has neutral or positive connotations.
>
> In the New Testament, the word "myth" seems always to be understood in a negative sense, as a story that is not true. This is the case in 1 Tim. 1:4, 4:7; 2 Tim. 4:4; Titus 1:14; and 2 Pet. 1:16, all of which use the term negatively.

parousia: "For he received honor and glory from God the Father when that voice was conveyed to him by the Majestic Glory, saying, 'This is my Son, my Beloved, with whom I am well pleased.' We ourselves heard this voice come from heaven, while we were with him on the holy mountain" (vv. 17-18).

A prophetic account
(vv. 19-21)

Having cited apostolic authority as a witness to the Transfiguration and a defense of the belief in Christ's return, the author then turned to prophecy as a second defense. Some believers would have come to doubt the Old Testament prophesies of a day when God would come in glory to judge the world and set up an eternal kingdom.

The author of 2 Peter, however, saw the Transfiguration as a confirmation of prophecy's trustworthiness: "So we have the prophetic message more fully confirmed" (v. 19a).

With both prophecy and the Transfiguration standing as evidence that Christ would return as judge, the author added "You will do well to be attentive to this as to a lamp shining in a dark place, until the day dawns and the morning star rises in your hearts" (v. 19b).

What prophecies did the author have in mind? We can only presume that his readers knew, and they had probably discussed them before. It is likely that texts such as Psalm 2 – quoted at both Jesus' baptism and transfiguration – would have been part of the discussion. Likewise, Dan. 7:13-14, which spoke of the coming of a "son of man," was popularly considered a prophecy of Jesus.

The writer's statement in v. 20 suggests that critics had accused him of wrongly interpreting scripture, so he responded that no interpretation was necessary: one only had to read the words given by God to the prophets, for "no prophecy of scripture is a matter of one's own interpretation, because no prophecy ever came by human will, but men and women moved by the Holy Spirit spoke from God" (vv. 20-21).

While fundamentalist Christians often cite this verse to support their belief in a "verbal, plenary, inerrant inspiration of scripture," this was clearly not the author's intent. His concern was to defend prophecy as a trustworthy source of information for guiding the Christian in daily living, not to expound upon a modern debate about the inspiration of scripture.

The author went on in the first three verses of ch. 2 to warn against false prophets, noting that they existed in the Old Testament world and in the present, leading people to "follow their licentious ways" and seeking to "exploit you with deceptive words" (2:1-3). He devoted the rest of that chapter to expounding upon various punishments and condemnations rendered to those who proved to be false.

A passionate teaching

Why was defending the *parousia* so important to the author? It was because he saw belief in the return of Jesus and the certainty of judgment as a powerful motivator for Christians to remain faithful in difficult or tempting times. [**Great expectations**]

In ch. 3 he warned against scoffers who would lead others to doubt Christ's return and thus face the dissolution of the present world unprepared (3:1-10). In the light of Christ's sure return and judgment, however, he asked "what sort of persons ought you to be in leading lives of holiness and godliness?" (3:11).

Any delay in Christ's return should be seen as a sign of God's patience, he said, allowing more people to be saved (3:15). The letter concludes with a challenge for believers to acknowledge the warning of future judgment and avoid error, choosing instead to "grow in the grace and knowledge of our Lord and Savior Jesus Christ" (3:18).

Readers of 2 Peter today have lived for many more years with no sign of Christ's predicted return. Whether

---

Great expectations: As background to today's text, it's helpful to know that many early Christians fully expected Jesus to return in their lifetimes, and with good reason.

The gospels claim that when Jesus sent the Twelve to preach among the Jews, he said "truly I tell you, you will not have gone through all the towns of Israel before the Son of Man comes." In Matt. 16:28 (Mark 9:1), he reportedly said "Truly I tell you, there are some standing here who will not taste death before they see the Son of Man coming in his kingdom." After an unusual apocalyptic teaching, the gospels record Jesus as saying "Truly I tell you, this generation will not pass away until all these things have taken place" (Matt. 24:34; Mark 13:30, 21:32). These sayings are qualified somewhat by Jesus' insistence that he did not know when the kingdom would come (Mark 13:32).

Paul apparently expected Christ to return within his lifetime or that of his readers, explaining to the Thessalonians that believers who had died would be raised first, then living believers would be "caught up" in the air to meet Jesus (1 Thess. 4:15-17). Like Jesus, however, Paul warned that no one could know the exact hour of Jesus' return: the Day of the Lord would arrive "like a thief in the night" (1 Thess. 5:1-3).

---

we anticipate the same sort of future scenario or not, our calling is the same. The author of 2 Peter used the fear of future judgment to motivate present behavior. But should we need the threat of punishment as an incentive to love others as Christ taught us, behaving as good and generous and kind people who try to make the world a better place?

If we can focus on following what Jesus taught in his first coming, we needn't worry about the second, and we'll undergo a transfiguration of our own.

The Hardest Question
Why do scholars think the Apostle Peter did not write 2 Peter?

Few contemporary scholars believe Simon Peter, one of the first disciples called by Jesus, could have written the book that bears his name. Several lines of evidence point to this conclusion.

First, we know that it was common during the first and second centuries for pseudonymous authors to write letters or treatises claiming to have been written by well-known biblical characters, and this was an accepted practice.

Many examples of New Testament pseudepigrapha are known, most of which were not accepted as scripture. Peter was an especially attractive apostle for such purposes, and several pseudepigrapha claim Petrine authorship. These include documents called "The Gospel of Peter," "The Acts of Peter," "The Acts of Peter and the Twelve Apostles," "The Epistle of Peter to Philip," "The Apocalypse of Peter," and "The Coptic Apocalypse of Peter."

Several letters included in the New Testament claim to have been written by someone other than the actual author. Many scholars doubt that the letters to Timothy and Titus were written by Paul, for example, or that either 1 or 2 Peter came from the crusty fisherman's hand.

Pseudonymous authors often went to some lengths to pose as their famous counterpart, and 2 Peter is no exception. The writer claims to be "Simeon Peter," but uses an alternate spelling of "Simon." He also speaks of his impending death (1:14), claims to have been an eye-witness to the Transfiguration (1:16-18), and refers to an earlier letter (3:1), which may be attempts to make the letter sound more authentic.

At the same time, the author betrays his later context in several ways. He is writing primarily to defend the belief that Christ would return, which many had begun to doubt or to outright deny. In 3:4, he quotes opponents as saying: "ever since our ancestors died, all things continue as they were from the beginning of creation." This appears to be a reference to the generation of the apostles who first predicted that Christ would return.

Similarly, in 3:15-17 he mentions the letters of "our beloved brother Paul," making reference to a collection of Pauline letters that may already have been considered equivalent to other scriptures. The traditionally accepted date for Paul's death is around 62 CE, and it's likely that Peter died about two years later. It is highly unlikely that Paul's letters could have been collected and already considered to be scripture in that short period of time: 2 Peter was probably written considerably later.

The letter of 2 Peter is also highly dependent on the little book of Jude, a late first-century text that draws on non-biblical apocalyptic works such as "1 Enoch" and "The Testament of Moses." Much of 2 Peter 2:1–3:3 shows strong similarities to Jude vv. 4-18.

These considerations, along with elements of literary style and theological emphasis, make it extremely unlikely that 2 Peter could have been written by the apostle. Rather, it appears to have originated in the late first or early second century, long after Peter's death.

Transfiguration Sunday

Fourth Reading
Matthew 17:1-8

Keeping Secrets

While he was still speaking, suddenly a bright cloud overshadowed them, and from the cloud a voice said, "This is my Son, the Beloved; with him I am well pleased; listen to him!" (Matt. 17:5)

Superheroes are ubiquitous these days: blockbuster movies, TV series, comic books, and children's cartoons regularly feature drab "normal" characters who can quickly transform themselves into tights-wearing superheroes at a moment's notice. It's all fantasy, but one that people have enjoyed since "Superman" comics first appeared in 1930.

Our text for today describes the one man in history whose transformation was not just super, but supernatural. What's more, those who choose to follow Jesus can be transformed, too.

A special appearance
(vv. 1-2)

We often refer to this memorable story as the "Transfiguration of Christ." The word "transfiguration" derives from Jerome's fourth-century translation of the Bible into Latin, where he rendered the Greek word *metamorphōthē* with *transfigurato*. In other texts, the same word is translated as "transformed," or "changed," as in Rom. 12:2 and 2 Cor. 3:18.

Matthew's account is set near the end of Jesus' ministry, as he prepared to make his final journey to Jerusalem. As if seeking to renew his strength for the journey – and to give instruction to his closest followers – Jesus led his 12 disciples northward in Galilee to the territory near the city of Caesarea-Philippi, and they rested there near the foot of snow-capped Mt. Hermon in a beautiful and fertile area. Nearby was a temple dedicated to the worship of the Roman emperor, and not far away was an area devoted to

> **Three versions:** All three synoptic gospels contain stories of the Transfiguration (Matt. 17:1-9, Mark 9:2-10, Luke 9:28-37), each with distinctive characteristics. Matthew says that "his face shone like the sun, and his clothes became dazzling white" (Matt. 17:2). Mark mentions only Jesus' clothes, which "became dazzling white, as no one on earth can bleach them" (Mark 9:3). Luke also speaks of dazzling white clothes, and says "the appearance of his face changed" (Luke 9:29). All three accounts say the three disciples were terrified, but Matthew is the only gospel to include Christ's comforting words and touch (17:6-7).
>
> Mark speaks of Elijah and Moses appearing with Jesus, while the other two synoptics list Moses first. Perhaps Mark's prophetic interest was paramount, while Matthew and Luke followed the chronological appearance and relative importance of the two by putting Moses before Elijah. Mark is also more likely to point out the disciples' foolishness or failures.
>
> Luke (9:28-36) tells the longest story, and his version alone preserves the tradition that the disciples were so sleepy that they could barely hold their eyes open when Jesus' transformation took place (9:32). This gives more of a dreamlike quality to the disciples' experience, emphasizing its visionary nature. Luke is also the only gospel to divulge the contents of Jesus' conversation with Moses and Elijah: he says they were talking about Jesus' imminent "departure" (literally, his "exodus") from Jerusalem – a departure that would come by way of the crucifixion (9:31).

the nature god Pan. Jesus was about to show them who truly deserved their worship.

Three men among the 12 were closer to Jesus than the others (cp. Matt. 26:37; Mark 5:37, 13:3). [**Three versions**] Perhaps Jesus depended on them to learn some lessons first, and then explain them to the other disciples.

So it was that he took Peter, James, and John with him as they climbed the mountain in search of an isolated spot for a time of prayer.

As they prayed, something totally unexpected happened. Jesus' appearance was suddenly – and radically – changed. Matthew and Mark describe it by using a Greek word that is the root of our word "metamorphosis." Jesus was *transformed*. Luke tells us that "the appearance of his face changed, and his clothes became dazzling white." Matthew says "his face shone like the sun."

The gospel writers seem to be suggesting that Jesus, who had been disguised as a Galilean peasant, threw off his human image and reverted to his heavenly, glorified appearance. Perhaps his clothes shone so brightly because his body, like his face, was shining through. If the event took place at night, as Luke's account of sleepy disciples implies (Luke 9:32), the effect would have been especially impressive.

Jesus was *transformed*. Somehow, some way, something miraculous happened. God's eternal world and time bloomed into our ordinary world and time, and the disciples were granted a brief vision of something beyond.

Matthew probably expected readers to recall that Moses' face had also shone so brightly after spending time with God that it frightened the Israelites, and he had to wear a veil (Exod. 34:29-35). As the disciples looked at Jesus, "his face shone like the sun."

Special guests
(vv. 3-4)

Suddenly, Jesus was not only transformed, but also standing in the company of Moses himself, along with the prophet Elijah (v. 3). Luke says that Moses and Elijah appeared "in glory," suggesting that their appearance may have been much like that of Jesus. The Old Testament claimed that Elijah did not die, but had been carried to heaven in a fiery chariot (2 Kgs. 2:11). Moses' death was shrouded in such mystery that a rabbinic tradition presumed that God had also taken him directly to heaven. **[Did Moses die?]**

The presence of Moses and Elijah carried significant symbolism. Judaism had strong traditions that Moses and Elijah would return to earth before the "Day of the Lord." Moses represented the Law, and Elijah the Prophets. The Law and the Prophets were the twin traditions upholding

---

Did Moses die? The book of Deuteronomy says that Moses went up Mount Nebo alone, where God allowed him to see the Promised Land, though he would not be allowed to enter it. "Then Moses, the servant of the LORD, died there in the land of Moab, at the LORD'S command. He was buried in a valley in the land of Moab, opposite Beth-peor, but no one knows his burial place to this day" (Deut. 34:5-6).

While the NRSV translates "he was buried" as passive, the Hebrew word, as preserved in the traditional Masoretic text, is in the active voice, and should be translated "he buried him." The implication is that, after Moses died at God's command, God buried him.

Some later manuscripts make the verb plural, so that it would read "they buried him," but it's hard to imagine that the Israelites would have buried their great leader Moses without leaving a clearly marked burial site. That Moses was alone with God and died "at the LORD's command," along with the observation that "no one knows his burial place to this day" led to a tradition that Moses didn't actually die, but was taken to heaven by God. Evidence of this is found in Jude 9, which says the archangel Michael and the devil disputed over Moses' body, and in the pseudepigraphal "Assumption of Moses."

Israel's faith. Yet now the Law and the Prophets, present in Moses and Elijah, were upholding Jesus and giving way to him.

Of the three dumbfounded disciples, Peter alone had the wherewithal to speak, though he wasn't sure what to say. He knew the moment was special. He didn't know how long Moses and Elijah would stay, but felt an obligation to show them proper hospitality. So, he spoke up in fumbling, embarrassed words and offered to cut down limbs from the trees to build temporary shelters for Jesus and Moses and Elijah (v. 4).

It's almost comical to think about it – the idea that Moses and Elijah, having "beamed down" from heaven in fiery, glorified bodies, would have any interest in taking up lodging in leafy lean-tos. At least Luke was kind enough to add that he didn't know what he said (Luke 9:33). The suggestion, however, was not entirely inappropriate, because faithful Jews built similar shelters every year when they observed the "Feast of Booths," which celebrated the Exodus.

Special words
(vv. 5-8)

If Jesus responded to Peter's request, Matthew does not record it, for as he was speaking, a bright cloud descended with surprising suddenness, enveloping them all (v. 5). The disciples, understandably, were terrified. In addition to the inherently spooky nature of the event, they would have remembered that in the Old Testament, when God appeared, it was often in a cloud, as in the accounts of Moses meeting God on Mount Sinai in Exodus 24.

Try to imagine the scene: when the cloud descended over Jesus, Moses, Elijah, and the three disciples – God was present. They could *feel* the divine nearness. They were shaking in their sandals.

From the cloud came a voice – obviously to be understood as the voice of God – and the three awestruck disciples fell to their faces. When God spoke, the voice repeated the same words that were spoken at Jesus' baptism, with the addition of an injunction to pay him heed: "This is my Son, the Beloved; with him I am well pleased; listen to him!" (v. 5).

As quickly as the voice had spoken, all was still and the cloud departed. When the bedazed and bedazzled disciples peeked out through their fingers, there was Jesus alone. Only Matthew says that Jesus came and offered a comforting touch and encouraging words: "Get up and do not be afraid" (v. 7).

"This is my Son …," God had said. "Listen to him!" Had they been awake, or sleeping? Was it real, or was it a dream? Matthew, alone of the gospels, called it a vision (v. 9). Whether visionary or real, the effect was the same. The disciples were overwhelmed with wonder.

That Jesus was left alone after the heavenly visitors departed underscored his supremacy to the Law and the Prophets, whose representatives had gone. Only Jesus remained (v. 8). Just as God's voice had spoken at Jesus' baptism, validating his call and his ministry, so now God's voice had spoken again to impress the disciples with the truth that Jesus knew who he was and what he was doing – and they had best give attention to his words.

One can imagine how excited the disciples were to have caught a heart-stopping glimpse of Jesus' true nature, with Moses, Elijah, and the voice of God from a cloud witnessing to his divinity. Surely they would have been buzzing with exhilaration, anxious to tell others what they had seen – and no doubt they would have been completely confused when Jesus instructed them to keep it to themselves: "Tell no one about the vision until after the Son of Man has been raised from the dead" (v. 9).

Why would Jesus want them to keep such amazing news a secret? Perhaps it is because neither the disciples nor the broader coterie of his followers could yet comprehend what Jesus was really about. Jesus knew that many people expected God to send a military messiah who would lead an uprising against Rome. He had trouble enough controlling that sentiment as it was, even among his own disciples. If word of Jesus' divine transformation and attestation became public knowledge, public clamor for Jesus to lead a political uprising could derail his mission.

Only after Jesus' death and resurrection would it be appropriate to reveal what the disciples had seen, reinforcing the divine intention behind those two events. In a sense, the Transfiguration foreshadowed Jesus' ascension to heaven, which would also take place on a mountain (Matt. 28:16-20). In the meantime, the three disciples would have to sit tight on an awesome secret.

The good news of this story is that Jesus' transformation carries with it the promise of our own inner and ultimate transformation. It may be hard for us to believe this. The real world we inhabit surrounds us with family demands, financial concerns, work to do, and people to please. Yet, we are also privy to what the disciples saw as a touch of heaven come to earth, and the witness "This is my Son … Listen to him!" When we listen to Jesus, he calls us to be born again, to be transformed, to become new creations by his power.

That may not happen immediately, but it does happen. We can experience God's saving grace in a moment, but our transformation is a life-long process. As Paul described it to the Corinthians: "And all of us, with unveiled faces, seeing the glory of the Lord as though reflected in a mirror, are being transformed into the same image from one degree of glory to another; for this comes from the Lord, the Spirit" (1 Cor. 3:18).

Amazing.

The Hardest Question
Why were the disciples so terrified by the cloud?

The disciples were Jewish, and they would have been familiar with stories from the Hebrew Bible, several of which contained references to God appearing within a cloud. The thick cloud terrified them because they believed God was in it.

Recall some of the many stories. Memorably, God was thought to be present within a "pillar of cloud" that led the people of Israel in the wilderness, with fire in its midst during the night. The cloud would rest on the tabernacle as long as God wanted them to stay in one place, and when it lifted, they would venture on (Exod. 13:21; cf. Exod. 16:10, 40:36-39; Num. 9:15-22, 10:11-12, 34).

God appeared to Moses in a "dense cloud" (Exod. 19:9-16) when the people arrived at Sinai, and again when Moses climbed up to meet Yahweh, when "the cloud covered the mountain, and the glory of the LORD settled on Mount Sinai, and the cloud covered it for six days; on the seventh day he called to Moses out of the cloud. Moses entered the cloud, and went up on the mountain" (Exod. 24:15-18).

When Moses entered the tent of meeting, "the pillar of cloud would descend and stand at the entrance of the tent, and the LORD would speak with Moses" (Exod. 33:9-10). When Moses returned to the mountain, "the LORD descended in the cloud and stood with him there, and proclaimed the name, 'The LORD'" (Exod. 34:5).

When the tabernacle was dedicated, "the cloud covered the tent of meeting, and the glory of the LORD filled the tabernacle," to the extent that even Moses was unable to enter (Exod. 40:34-35). God told Moses to instruct Aaron not to come into the holy of holies, lest he die, "for I appear in the cloud upon the mercy seat" (Lev. 16:2).

When Moses grew weary of leadership and uttered an agonized prayer, God told him to call out 70 elders to help share the load of settling disputes. "Then the LORD came down in the cloud and spoke to him, and took some of the spirit that was on him and put it on the seventy elders …" (Num. 11:25).

When Aaron and Miriam complained against Moses because his wife was a "Cushite" and because they believed God had spoken to them also, God summoned all three to the tent of meeting. "Then the LORD came down in a pillar of cloud, and stood at the entrance of the tent, and called to Aaron and Miriam; and they both came forward" (Num. 12:5). Yahweh strongly rebuked the pair for resisting Moses, leaving Miriam leprous for seven days (Num. 12:6-16).

These are a few of the many references to God's characteristic appearance in a cloud during the wilderness period, later recalled by Nehemiah (9:12, 19), in the Psalms (78:14, 97:2, 99:7, 105:39), and by Isaiah (4:5).

These were not the end of God's "cloudy" appearances, however. When Solomon's temple was dedicated, "a cloud filled the house of the LORD, so that the priests could not stand to minister because of the cloud; for the glory of the LORD filled the house of the LORD" (1 Kgs. 8:10-11; cf. 2 Chron. 5:13-14).

In Ezekiel's inaugural vision of God, he described "a great cloud with brightness around it and fire flashing forth continually, and in the middle of the fire, something like gleaming amber" (Ezek. 1:4). In a later vision of the temple, Ezekiel also spoke of a cloud as indicating God's presence (10:3).

The psalms could describe God as being surrounded by "clouds and thick darkness," and prophets used the image in a threatening manner. In describing judgment that would come on the "day of the LORD," they spoke of God's approach "in clouds and thick darkness" (Joel 2:2, Zeph. 1:5).

These traditions clearly associated God's fearful, awe-inspiring presence in association with clouds. It's no wonder the three disciples "were terrified." I suspect we would have been no less afraid.

Index of Lectionary Texts
Year A, Volume 1